AF249139

The Politics of Drink in England, from Gladstone to Lloyd George

The Politics of Drink in England, from Gladstone to Lloyd George

By

David M. Fahey

Cambridge
Scholars
Publishing

The Politics of Drink in England, from Gladstone to Lloyd George

By David M. Fahey

This book first published 2022

Cambridge Scholars Publishing

Lady Stephenson Library, Newcastle upon Tyne, NE6 2PA, UK

British Library Cataloguing in Publication Data
A catalogue record for this book is available from the British Library

ISBN (10): 1-5275-7818-6
ISBN (13): 978-1-5275-7818-0

For my family,

Mary, Juliana, and Sable

TABLE OF CONTENTS

LIST OF ILLUSTRATIONS

Alliance News, 1923
Leif Jones

Black & white parliamentary album, 1895
Sir Henry Campbell-Bannerman
Herbert Gladstone
Sir Wilfrid Lawson
Lord Salisbury

National Portrait Gallery (by permission)
Sir Thomas Palmer Whittaker

John Newton biography
WS Caine

Thomas Jones biography
David Lloyd George

Blanche Dugdale biography
Arthur Balfour

J.A. Spender and Cyril Asquith biography
Herbert Asquith

Alchetron encyclopedia
Arthur Sherwell

PREFACE

In 1971, the *Journal of British Studies* published my article, "Temperance and the Liberal Party—Lord Peel's Report, 1899." Shortly afterwards I began the present book. As it took me five decades to complete my manuscript, I lost the opportunity to be pioneering. Interest in other topics such as the Good Templars help explain repeated delays. I did not completely neglect the topic of the postponed book, as I published related articles and entries in reference works. The long gestation made for a better book, or so I hope. There remain rough spots, especially in the final chapter. In my mid-80s and in ill-health, I am sorry that I did not do more when I was young and enjoyed good eyesight.

Problems challenged me almost to the end. I was within about a week of completing my manuscript when my hard disk failed. I discovered that my backup did not work. A reminder to have backups of backups! Swallowing my frustration, I rewrote the book based on earlier drafts that I had emailed to myself six or seven weeks earlier. Sorry if I left out things that were part of the lost manuscript.

I have no reason to complain. Early in 2021, I was twice hospitalized after my family, terrified that I was unresponsive, called an ambulance. I am grateful to my wife Mary Fuller for her indispensable help in my recovery. Although still unsteady on my feet, I am comfortable at my computer.

This is a book about politics centered on Parliament, party leaders, and pressure groups. I have written elsewhere about the temperance movement and the licensed drink trade. They appear in the present book but are not prominent in it. For a more rounded view of the drink question, I offer my book *Temperance Societies in Late Victorian and Edwardian England* (2020), four recent articles in *Brewery History*, earlier articles (one as old as 1974), many entries in biographical collections and historical encyclopedias, and a few book reviews, most of them listed in the bibliography. The opening chapter of my new book borrows from "Worrying about Drink," *Brewery History* (2016).

I am grateful to my friend David W. Gutzke for source references that supplement my own research and for advice on chapter ten. I also am grateful to my nephew Michael Rinella for help with illustrations. Chuck Angel of Miami's IT made a Saturday morning house call to help me with a Microsoft Word problem. Adam Rummens and Amanda Millar of Cambridge Scholars Publishing were indispensable. The Miami University interlibrary loan service provided important books and articles that allowed me to complete my work in a small college town in southwestern Ohio. Most of all, I thank the many libraries in England and their manuscript and rare print collections for making my book possible. I also thank the many historians whose work improved my own. Although I cite recent scholarship, I have written principally based on primary sources. The exception is the last chapter on the war years which was not part of my original plan.

THE MAKING OF THIS BOOK

I began my work as a historian of the English temperance movement "in virtual isolation [while] a young assistant professor at one of Indiana University's 'parking lot' branch campuses."[1] My doctoral dissertation (1964) had nothing to do with temperance or drink or even the late Victorian and Edwardian years, so how did I stumble upon this fresh line of research? It was an accident. Reading an old volume (published, 1936) in the *Oxford History of England*, I was struck by R.C.K. Ensor's brief reference to the Licensing Act of 1904. Intrigued, I began research on it. I quickly realized that what happened in that year could not be understood without a larger context. After reviewing the skimpy secondary literature, I traveled to London for archival research in the late 1960s. A summer at the British Museum enabled me to write an article for the *Journal of British Studies*, "Temperance and the Liberal Party--Lord Peel's Report, 1899," published in May 1971 and reprinted in 2008.[2]

For years I spent nearly every summer in England doing archival and rare print research. I visited temperance and drink organizations, as well as reading extensively in temperance and drink trade periodicals. I quarried the papers of politicians and read major newspapers and other periodicals, as well as parliamentary debates, royal commission evidence and reports, and a small mountain of polemical literature. I then put my manuscript aside to pursue different research.

The sites where I consulted primary sources often have changed. I first read Good Templar annual proceedings at the Order's Birmingham headquarters where I squatted on the floor while a charwoman mopped around me. Afterwards the records moved to the United Kingdom Temperance Alliance library. The Institute of Alcohol Studies inherited this collection. I followed the London publicans as their headquarters moved from Bedford Square to smaller quarters on Kilburn High Road and finally to Farnham in Surrey when they merged with a provincial retail organization. The London Metropolitan Archives later acquired the licensed victuallers' records, as well as the papers of the Brewers' Company (Brewers' Hall) that I had consulted at the Guildhall library. The archives for the brewers' defense organizations at Portman Square were hard to enter. I first was told that during the Second World War enemy aircraft had destroyed the relevant manuscripts, a couple of years later that they existed but I would not be permitted to see them, and finally I got a warm welcome. The manuscripts are now at the Modern Records Centre, University of Warwick, while the books formerly at Portman Square are now at Oxford Brookes University as part of the National Brewing Library. The manuscripts include those of the Country Brewers' Society, the Brewers' Society, and the National Trade Defence Association. I read other Birmingham-based NTDA records at the Staffordshire Record Office. I consulted the papers of Sir William Harcourt when they were unsorted in trunks in a storage room at his ancestral home, then at the Bodleian when they were only partly catalogued, and finally when full citation information was available. My Harcourt references vary in format depending on when I took my notes. A few other manuscript collections have moved. For instance, the papers at the Beaverbrook Library are now at the House of Lords Record Office. The Hambleden papers that I consulted in London are now at the W.H. Smith Archive in Swindon. Rare print and manuscript material that I read in Sheffield at the Livesey-Clegg House is now at the University of Central Lancashire. The papers of Lord Salisbury that I saw at Christ Church, Oxford, are now at Hatfield House.

After retirement from teaching, I returned to the manuscript that I had begun with the naive expectation of a quick book. In fact, it has occupied most of my professional life. Revisiting my treasure trove of source materials after so many years, I wish that my penmanship had been better. Scribbles in smudged pencil are especially difficult. Sometimes photocopies have blurred. It does not help that, in my mid-80s, genetic cornea scarring makes my vision fuzzy. Citation details are not always consistent. I have page numbers for some newspaper articles and not others.

The focus of this book is England and not Britain or the United Kingdom. The political and religious situation in Ireland, Scotland, and Wales differed from that in England. Moreover, the licensed drink trade was more powerful in England than elsewhere. By the late nineteenth century full-day Sunday closing affected retail drink sales (other than for hotel guests) in Scotland, Wales, and most of Ireland. Parliament had no stomach for complete Sunday closing in England. In the early twentieth century Scotland uniquely acquired the right of prohibition by local option, a right rarely exercised.

My book outlines the politics of drink from the early 1870s when William Gladstone was Prime Minister until the early 1920s when David Lloyd George resided at 10 Downing Street. Concern over drinking by workingmen was widespread, but there was no consensus on how to address the problem. My book may be regarded as a sequel to Brian Harrison's

Drink and the Victorians: The Temperance Question in England, 1815-1872.

A central theme for my book is the repeated disappointment of frustrated pressure groups.[3] Beginning in the early 1880s, party discipline grew, as did the government's control over legislative time. This meant that the pledges that pressure groups obtained from parliamentary candidates mattered less. Leaders retained discretion about priorities. I argue that the drink controversy peaked near the turn of the century when moderate drinkers and some abstainers promoted alternatives to prohibition. It revived briefly during the First World War.

This book combines thematic and chronological chapters at the price of some duplication. Crucial decades demand the most detail. From 1888 to 1908 the debate over the sale of alcoholic beverages mattered more in national politics than during any earlier or later time. The First World War provides a kind of epilogue when wartime patriotism and a coalition Cabinet kept pressure group politics largely out of view and allowed Government flexibility.

Writing is a collaborative process, and I have reason to be grateful to the many historians cited in footnotes. Without them I could not have written this book. I am especially indebted to David W. Gutzke. We have exchanged ideas since the 1970s when we discovered our overlapping research plans recorded in register entries at the Guildhall library.

I thank the archives and libraries to which I owe so much. I also am grateful for research grants from Indiana University, Miami University, and the National Endowment for the Humanities.

I have borrowed from my articles in the *Journal of British Studies*, *Histoire sociale*, and *Brewery History*, and to a lesser extent from some of my other publications that I cite when relevant.[4] This book was written while I was mostly confined at home during the Covid 19 pandemic as also had been the case when I was writing my related book, *Temperance Societies in Late Victorian and Edwardian England* (2020). Further complicating my work, my original manuscript when near completion was lost when my hard drive failed as did my backup. Moreover, in 2021 I was seriously ill.

Notes

---

[1] David M. Fahey, "Chance and Change," *Social History of Alcohol Review* 34/35 (1997): 8.
[2] Reprinted in Moria L. Plant and Martin A. Plant, eds., *Addiction* (4 vols.; Routledge, 2008).

[3] I outlined my interpretation in an early article, "Drink and the Meaning of Reform in Late Victorian and Edwardian England" *Cithara* (May 1974), and further developed it in "The Politics of Drink: Pressure Groups and the British Liberal Party, 1883-1908," *Social Science* (Spring 1979). I summarized my interpretation in entries for the Conservative and Liberal parties in Jack S. Blocker, Jr., David M. Fahey, and Ian R. Tyrrell, eds., *Alcohol and Temperance in Modern History* (ABC-CLIO, 2003) and occasionally referred to it in entries in the *Oxford Dictionary of National Biography* and the *Biographical Dictionary of Modern British Radicals*.

[4] "Temperance and the Liberal Party–Lord Peel's Report, 1899," *Journal of British Studies* (May 1971). "Brewers, Publicans, and Working-Class Drinkers: Pressure Group Politics in Late Victorian and Edwardian England," *Histoire sociale* (May 1980); "Worrying about Drink," *Brewery History* (Summer 2016); "E.N Buxton (1840-1924): Liberal Brewer, Big Game Hunter and Conservationist," *Brewery History* (Spring 2019); "Brewers, Publicans, and Staff in Late Victorian and Edwardian Licensed Trade Societies," Part I *Brewery History* (Summer 2019); Part II (Winter 2019).

CHAPTER ONE

DRINK AND SOBRIETY

My book describes the politics of drink in England from the early 1870s, when Gladstone was Prime Minister, until the early 1920s, when Lloyd George occupied 10 Downing Street. These were years when most everybody who was anybody regarded drink as a problem, although without agreement on what the problem was and even less on how to address it. Total abstainers were few. Those who worried about the excessive drinking by urban workingmen almost always drank themselves.

The place to begin our story is with Brian Harrison's *Drink and the Victorians* (1971). After its publication, other British historians accepted Harrison's argument that alcoholic drink and the temperance movement mattered, although they seldom chose to write about it.[1] Despite the acclaim that Harrison's book and accompanying articles received, the drink question in Britain remained a marginal topic.[2] Harrison himself moved on to other things.[3] Although an epilogue to *Drink and the Victorians* explored the socialist critique of drink, it concluded its detailed narrative in 1872. A revised edition (1994) made no important changes. Harrison's pioneering work left much undone. Other books on drink and sobriety only slowly appeared.

The story that confronted Harrison and his successors was not a simple one. Although teetotalers always were a minority, many drinkers supported new restrictions on the sale of drink. Unfortunately, they did not always agree with one another about what should be done. The temperance movement too was not united about what it wanted. Those who made or sold drink also were divided.

Drink and the Victorians ambitiously researched drink, temperance, the role of Parliament and of pressure groups. The first approach to drink that Harrison discussed was free licensing. For a fee of two guineas the Beer Act of 1830 offered beer house licenses.[4] Unlike public houses, beer houses sold only beer and cider and had shorter hours.[5] Allegedly, competition created by the new drink sellers would cleanse the trade in beer.[6] In 1869, at the height of laissez faire, free licensing of beer houses was abandoned nationally. Almost nobody (except William Gladstone [1809-98]) proposed that it be revived. Free licensing did not appeal to brewers, as more licenses would reduce the value of existing licensed property. Nor did temperance reformers want to provide extra opportunities to buy drink.[7]

Harrison devoted the core of his book to the temperance movement. Respectability was its key theme. Harrison divided the temperance movement's formative period, from the late 1820s to the early 1870s, into three overlapping stages. Each was more radical in objectives than its predecessor. The middle and upper classes dominated the anti-spirits agitation in the early days of the English temperance movement. Drunkenness, not drinking, was condemned. Later respectable workers demanded teetotalism. They were utopian radicals who rejected theological pessimism about sinful human nature. They sought to educate others through what was called moral suasion. They combined communal self-help with individual self-improvement. Next came a prohibition movement, partly inspired by the experiment in the American state of Maine, which supplemented the voluntarism of personal abstinence with legal coercion.[8] After Harrison's time-periods, disinterested or non-commercial management of the retail drink trade (the Gothenburg scheme) offered another solution to the drink question.[9]

Harrison argued that the reformation in drinking habits was only loosely related to the organized temperance movement. The speed of the railroad, by curtailing the drink seller's role in providing the traveller with refreshment, did more for practical temperance than did temperance agitation.

Harrison minimized class conflict. Middle class advocacy for the reduction or the prohibition of drink could not be reduced to economic motives alone. Not all workingmen rejected temperance reform as class oppression.[10] Instead of social control exercised by elites, moral reform joined together different social classes or at least some of their members in class collaboration. Temperance had its strongest roots in Nonconformist culture.

Harrison characterized the licensing crisis that erupted in the early 1870s as "a turning point in temperance history." By then the organized temperance movement had proved itself to be a political force, the prohibitionists within it had shown a destructive half-heartedness toward any licensing reform which allowed the drink trade to survive, and the Liberal Party had begun to be identified with aggressive temperance legislation. The Liberals were friendly to local control, the strategy proposed by prohibitionists and by advocates of other local options.[11] The Liberals disliked monopolies, and in the absence of free licensing the drink trade had taken on the appearance of a privileged monopoly.

Harrison was a historian of the drink trade as well as of the agitation on behalf of sobriety, but he did not investigate normal or moderate drinking in depth.[12] For the "wet" side of his story, Harrison described how the licensed trade began to awake as a political force, eventually allied with the Conservative Party. A study of Oldham in South Lancashire by another historian contrasts the 1830s, when the drink trade was "the mainstay of the radical vote," with 1865, when nearly eighty per cent of drink sellers voted Tory.[13] The drink trade could count on the Conservatives to defend property rights, even rights as legally ambiguous as those of license holders, and the freeborn Englishman's liberty to choose to buy drink. The licensed trade accommodated itself to changing attitudes. It insisted that drinking did not mean drunkenness. It could be moderate, responsible, and respectable.

Recently Thora Hands complained that historians say little about normal or moderate drinkers. Instead, they focus on drunkards and other pathological drinkers. She sees this as a limitation in Harrison's work. She argues that his *Drink and the Victorians* "fails to deliver an analysis of Victorian drinking."[14] Her own book removes the spectre of the drunkard from a central position in the story of drink.

With a short overlap, the present book succeeds Harrison's chronologically.[15]

The upper and middle classes construed the drink problem in class and gendered terms They took for granted that the urban workingman constituted the problem, together with the public houses and beer houses where he drank his beer.[16] What alarmed the upper classes was in fact not new, that workingmen drank a great deal of beer and some of them got drunk.[17] Few teetotallers belonged to the elite classes. Instead, they were working class or lower middle class, for example, Good Templars and Rechabites, members of large fraternal temperance societies. They agreed with the elite analysis that situated the problem in the pub.[18]

Those who drank at pubs rarely ate there. Explaining his focus on closing public houses, Sir William Harcourt (1827-1904) explained that he was against "tippling," drinking apart from meals, and was not against drinking at meals.[19]

The upper and middle classes regarded their mealtime wine drinking as respectable.[20] Even the lower middle class could afford cheap wines. Since the 1850s the upper and middle classes had drunk in privacy at homes or in semi-privacy at clubs and restaurants. Rarely did they drink beer. The propertied classes regarded drinking beer at public houses as vulgar, lacking in respectability and manly discipline. In a House of Lords debate over Sunday closing legislation, on 8 May 1880, Lord Salisbury defended the rights of beer-drinkers but acknowledged: "I do not drink beer myself."[21]

Reformers focused their attacks on the pub and only indirectly on its beer and the drinker.[22] Temperance people and their Liberal allies directed their fire not at the publicans but at the wealthy brewers who in the late nineteenth and early twentieth centuries owned or controlled almost all the pubs.[23] Reformers did not emphasize licenses for off-premises consumption other than those of grocers who allegedly tempted middle-class women who could hide drink purchases amid ordinary groceries.

Worrying about drink meant worrying about an urban society undergoing complex socio-economic, cultural, and political change. It meant worrying about the future.

Despite broad support for some kind of reform, legislation about drink was almost always bitterly divisive. Drink reform became a partisan issue. Although most reformers and brewers were willing to compromise, they disagreed on what for them would be an acceptable compromise.

Did contemporaries exaggerate the extent that the drinking problem was a workingman's problem, a public house problem, a beer problem? Expensive wine intoxicated too. Part of the reason why the philosopher T.H. Green (1836-82) became an ardent temperance reformer was that his older brother was a binge drinker who had been expelled as a drunkard from colleges at both Oxford and Cambridge.[24] University students, born to privilege, often were hard drinkers, for instance, the members of the Bullingdon club at Oxford who included Lord Randolph Churchill (1849-95) and the future Lord Rosebery (1847-1929).[25] During parts of their lives politicians such as H.H. Asquith (1852-1928), a Liberal, and F.E. Smith (1872-1930), a Tory, were famously drinkers.[26] So was Winston Churchill (1874-1965) who loved Pol Roger champagne.[27] Sir William Harcourt, the main exponent of prohibition in the Liberal leadership, was no teetotaler. His son's journal for 13 November 1885, reports that he and his father "had drunk about [three and a half] bottles of claret during the evening" and added: "that is what comes of talking local option and temperance."[28] A.J. Balfour's brother Eustace died an alcoholic. Albert Victor, Prince of Wales, was another heavy drinker.

David Lloyd George (1863-1945) rarely is seen as a tippler, but as a young temperance reformer he enjoyed a drink. His diary entry for Saturday, 12 August 1882, reports that over the course of this single day he had drunk a glass of port, two glasses of beer, and a glass of porter, "so that's keeping the Blue Ribbon Pledge grandly," he joked.[29] Teetotalers showed their commitment to total abstinence by wearing a blue ribbon.

Respectable households sometimes contained what a recent historian has called a "perfumed alcoholic."[30] Bored women of the comfortable classes consumed alcohol covertly and excessively. Tonic wines were popular.

Was William Gladstone (1809-98) alone in regarding drunkenness among the higher classes as "outrageous," while over-indulgence among the poor was "excusable [and] not unnatural"?[31] He spoke for an earlier age when heavy drinking was considered a nuisance instead of a threat to national survival. The revolution in attitudes can be seen in the contrast between two other prime ministers, William Pitt the Younger (died in office, 1806), who allegedly drank several bottles of port a day, and Andrew Bonar Law (resigned and died, 1923), who was a teetotaler.[32]

Despite colorful exceptions, drinking moderated among the upper classes during Gladstone's lifetime. Reporting on a famous London club, one of its members reported that in 1838 Athenaeum members typically drank a pint of sherry at dinner and afterwards a pint of port, but by 1889, only a quarter pint of claret or other light wine. The club had to sell a quantity of port because of a lack of demand for it.[33] Algernon Bourke took over management of White's in 1888.[34] On 1 July 1896, he testified to the Royal Commission on Liquor Licensing Laws that alcohol consumption had fallen among the upper-class men who belonged to his and other West End clubs. During the hot summer months, many members of White's preferred non-alcoholic barley water to a whiskey and soda.

Ironically, concern about drink grew in the late nineteenth and early twentieth centuries, despite a decline in per capita drinking. The upper and middle classes worried more about the drink problem as it became less acute. During the years 1875-79 England and Wales averaged 40.5 gallons of beer per capita. Per capita consumption then declined unevenly with downward zigs and upward zags. For instance, after falling earlier, it rose for several years late in the century. Average consumption in 1895-99 reached 34.5 gallons. After this period of greater consumption, "consumption of beer fell in every year from 1899 to 1909: in England, by some [cumulative] 14 per cent." During the years 1910-13 England and Wales averaged 29.4 gallons of beer per capita. Wartime saw a sharp decline in the alcoholic strength of beer. Per capita United Kingdom consumption of beer fell in 1918 to 10 gallons.[35]

By 1901 the number of pubs declined by almost 16,000 from an 1869 high of 118,499.[36] Many of those that lost their licenses were seedy beer houses and not fully licensed public houses.[37]

In the United Kingdom the percentage of working-class income spent on alcohol declined from over fifteen per cent in 1876 to under nine per cent in 1910. Food, clothing, shoes, furniture, and other consumer goods became cheaper, so real wages grew sharply from the mid-1870s until the mid-1890s. Beer prices remained steady, making beer relatively expensive.[38]

Three kinds of official statistics shed light on Victorian and Edwardian drinking. First of all, tax records show how much was produced or imported and presumably consumed. These statistics are organized into broad categories of alcoholic beverages: beer, spirits (whiskies, gin, rum), and wine. These statistics do not tell who did the drinking or under what circumstances.[39] Second, license records show how many public houses, beer houses, and other retailers had the right to sell alcohol for on-premises or off-premises consumption. They show the high density of drink shops in poor urban districts. In 1892 the port town of King's Lynn in Norfolk could boast one out of every twenty-three of its houses as being licensed to sell drink.[40] In the mid-1890s the smallest London police district (the "C" or St. James in Soho) had 545 licensed houses of all kinds in an area of only 0.70 square miles.[41] In Manchester there was a licensed house for every 180 inhabitants in 1898.[42] In 1904 the seven thousand residents of Birmingham's Floodgate Street district could drink at forty-three public houses "or about one to every 88 adults."[43] Third, police records for public intoxication reveal broad trends. These figures are less reliable than the other statistics as they stumble over inconsistent police standards for determining public drunkenness. Arrests for public intoxication were almost always arrests of workingmen. These statistics ignore middle- and upper-class drunkenness that rarely happened in a public place.

Liverpool, a port city with a large Irish population, often was stigmatized as the most drunken city in England.[44] Prosecutions for public drunkenness exceeded 21,000 in both 1870 and 1875 but fell to less than 10,000 in the 1890s.[45] Nationally arrests for public intoxication fell drastically after 1901.

Despite the problems with police arrests as evidence of drinking, these statistics bring into doubt the existence of a new national drinking problem. As Paul Jennings has argued, there was "a real decline in the incidence of drunkenness."[46]

Generalizations about drink consumption are guesses. In 1882 a special committee of the British Association (consisting of Leone Levi and others) estimated that the working classes drank 75% of the beer and spirits and 10% of the wine, with the remainder being consumed by the middle and higher classes.[47] Joseph Rowntree (1836-1925) and Arthur Sherwell (1863-1942) estimated that that each year men of all classes averaged 73 gallons of beer, 2.4 gallons of spirits, and slightly less than a gallon of wine. Supposedly, women drank only half as much as men, while children under the age of fifteen did not drink. Rowntree and Sherwell may have underestimated consumption by regular drinkers. Receipts for a York workingmen's club reported that "the typical member consumed nearly two pints daily."[48]

Statistics blur the fact that the beers consumed varied greatly in taste, color, price and alcoholic content. "Pale, bitter ales made great headway in the 1840-1900 period, the golden age of British beer drinking."[49] Englishmen also drank Guinness, a dry stout brewed in Ireland. They rarely drank lagers. Advertising by brewers, although limited, became more common in the late nineteenth and early twentieth centuries.[50]

In the early 1860s the Government encouraged wine drinking. Import duties were lowered, and licenses to sell wine were made easy to obtain. Thousands of so-called "grocers' licenses" made inexpensive wines readily available. Despite these reforms, wine consumption remained low. Working-class women sometimes drank wine, but wine was nearly always an upper class and upper middle-class drink. The lower middle class could afford cheap wines. In *The Diary of a Nobody* (1892) by the Grossmith brothers, the clerk Charles Pooter entertains with champagne.

Although in the nineteenth century tastes shifted away from fortified wines, port and sherry made up half the wine consumed as late as 1914 and were consumed with food as table wines. The new trend by the 1880s saw champagne drunk with the first courses, claret (a red from Bordeaux) with the roasts, and brandy or port at the end of the meal.[51] When dining in mixed company, males of elite classes extended mealtime drinking after the women withdrew. The gentlemen then smoked cigars and drank brandy or port.

Both elites and the poor drank spirits. Rum was almost exclusively a workingmen's and sailors' drink, but gin and whiskey crossed class lines. By the 1860s workingmen drank less gin than whiskey. The fashion of things Scottish promoted by Victoria encouraged whiskey drinking. Lighter "blended whiskies" from Scotland were heavily advertised. By the end of the nineteenth century, whiskey had largely replaced gin among the elites, although many gin cocktails remained popular, as were other mixed drinks. The Prince of Wales cocktail, supposedly created by or for the Queen's son, included rye whiskey, Angostura bitters, Maraschino, and champagne.

The popularity of gin and quinine in the tropical empire helped gin and tonic become a summer drink in England.[52] Sometimes ladies at teatime served gin, calling it "white wine." Gin was made in England, particularly London. "London dry gin" was popular, with its rival being the sweeter "Old Tom gin." Sloe gin, flavored with sloe berries, was a female favorite.

Cheap gin was associated with drunken working-class women. Sometimes flavored with turpentine, "blue ruin" was a notorious drink. In 1907 George Robert Sims described working-class women as quieting their babies by repeatedly putting a dirty finger in a glass of gin and then into the infant's mouth. Charles Booth quotes a policeman as describing many older women as "regular soakers."[53]

By the turn of the century the pub had become less central to working-class leisure. New technology for bottling beer meant that working-class drinking often took place at home. As early as the 1840s, off-sales accounted on average for a third of the takings of some houses also licensed for on-sales.[54] By the 1890s sealed bottles superseded the old jug trade. In 1872 an Englishman invented the internal screw stopper, while twenty years later an American invented the cork crown cap. Four-quart crates became popular. In 1911 Cosmo Bonsor (1848-1929) complained that Watney, Combe, Reid had sold more beer but for less profit because of the cost of bottling.[55] In 1914 bottled beer made of 58% of the gross sales of Whitbread's London brewery.[56]

Clubs also became a popular drinking place. Clubs that served drink numbered 1,982 in 1887, 3,655 in 1896, and about 8,700 in 1914.[57] Most workingmen's clubs were orderly and respectable. Unlike public houses, clubs did not admit strangers who were more likely to cause trouble than regulars.[58]

"It was ironic that just as the brewers had virtually completed their ownership of tied houses, the popularity of the public house, that old citadel of working-class leisure, declined."[59] Tied houses were public houses controlled by brewers to secure an outlet for their beer, sometimes by owning freeholds or leaseholds and sometimes through mortgages.

Elites were conflicted over stigmatizing the public house. Although they agreed that there was a drink problem, they were divided about their support for specific reforms in part because they themselves intended to keep on drinking, in part because they were concerned about the property rights of the drink trade and the personal rights of drinkers, and in part because they disagreed about the role of law in changing behaviour. Life without the pub and the beer drunk there was unthinkable. The public house and its beer were part of the kingdom's historic identity, older than afternoon tea.[60]

In Victorian and Edwardian England drink was both a deeply rooted popular culture and a powerful economic interest.[61] Public houses and beer houses outnumbered places of worship. Property rights and the Englishman's traditional liberties made attacks on problematic drinking difficult.[62] Seventy-five per cent of the population was working class, so workingmen did most of the country's drinking.

The British government would have struggled without money from drink. In 1879-80 liquor taxes provided the Exchequer with 43.4 per cent of the national revenue, a proportion that fell to 38.4 by 1899-1900 as a result of the growth of other taxes.[63] This reliance on drink taxes prompted a facetious reformer to describe the habitual drunkard as "the sheet anchor of the British Constitution."[64]

Brewers sometimes were very wealthy. For instance, in 1893 the largest estate upon which probate was paid was that belonging to a Liverpool brewer, Sir Andrew Barclay Walker, Bt., whose personal property was valued at £2,874,000 and who additionally left considerable freehold property.[65] In 1905 the brewery firm of Watney, Combe, and Reid reported the second highest valuation of any industrial company, nearly £15 million. Seventeen of the forty-seven largest industrial companies in the United Kingdom were breweries and another was a distillery.[66] Many brewers served in the House of Commons, while enough of them were elevated to the House of Lords to inspire jokes about a "beerage."[67]

The governing elite did not want to provoke pub drinkers, as the Salvation Army had done with violent consequences in the 1880s. When aroused and threatened, the "masculine republic" of public house drinkers could respond vigorously.[68] Workingmen increasingly outnumbered property holders in the electorate. In the United Kingdom the parliamentary electorate grew after the Second Reform Act from 1.3 million in 1866 to 2.4 million in 1869. It then climbed to 3.1 million in 1883 and, after the Third Reform Act, to 5.7 million by 1885. By 1912, it was 7.7 million.[69]

Workingmen who drank at pubs resented patronizing interference. More than a place to drink, the public house was a home away from home, a cheerful place for chat and relaxation after a day of hard work, socializing with neighbors and workmates. Workingmen drank as part of a community with implicit rules and not as solitary boozers. Male bonding initiated newcomers into the rituals of pub drinking. Tory populists sometimes benefitted from working class resentment against Liberal moral reform. For instance, in 1891 two Tory publicans ousted two Liberal temperance reformers from the local council in London's East End.[70]

Workingmen who drank at a public house could be respectable. In the mid-1870s a temperance reformer who expected to find only "rough" drinkers at a Bradford public house instead found respectable customers who included Sunday-school teachers.[71]

A few abstainers recognized that the pub was more than a drinking place. A Congregational minister pointed out to another teetotal divine:

"very much of our temperance effort is not only handicapped, but to a large extent ineffective and abortive, because all the time the publican is catering for and exploiting what is a true and most vital human need—the need of sound fellowship and pleasant recreation, after the weariness and monotony of the daily work."[72]

Perhaps unfairly, heavy drinking was seen as the vice of the lowest class of workingmen, or at least they were the most likely to be arrested. "Of those charged with drunkenness in Manchester, Liverpool and Leeds in 1872, for instance, ninety-five per cent or more were semi- or fully illiterate."[73] In fact, it was not just the very poor who drank too much. Highly paid workers who had not developed expectations about better housing, food, and clothing might spend their extra wages at the pub. As late as the 1870s, skilled artisans dominated the ranks of heavy drinkers.[74] Later in the century they drank less. In 1889-1890 a study of the budgets of over a thousand English working-class families found that about half the workers drank virtually not at all, while the others spent considerably less than five per cent of their incomes on alcohol.[75] Hard drinkers remained. Robert Roberts, in a memoir of Edwardian Salford, wrote about his father, a journeyman engineer. He "seldom drank less than four quarts a day."[76]

The ideal of the moderate pub drinker was not a reality everywhere. In Edwardian times, a publican at a "rough" public house described his customers as "60 per cent. Sober; 30 per cent. Occasionally drunk; 7 ½ per cent. Continual drunkards; 2 ½ per cent. Habitual drunkards."[77] Probably the distinction was that, in contrast with a continual drunkard, a habitual drunkard could not control his drinking. Legislation in 1879 and 1898 provided for institutionalizing habitual drunkards in a retreat for inebriates.

Probably twenty-five to thirty per cent of pub drinkers were female, and they were moderate drinkers.[78] Seebohm Rowntree (1871-1954) studied two public houses in York in 1900. A pub in a slum district was visited on a Saturday in July by 258 men, 179 women, and 113 children, while one in a better neighborhood was visited by 508 men, 114 women, and 61 children.[79] A relieving officer in Hackney complained about a London pub called the George "always full of women."[80] Charles Booth's notebooks report: "Monday is recognized as ladies day; in Carr Street it is known as 'çowshed' day …. Poor women being known by their husband and male neighbours as 'cows.' Monday is their drinking day because they still have a little pocket money left; they drink in public houses which become in consequence 'cowsheds.'"[81]

Although typically women drank much less than men, there were females who abused alcohol. Only among the very poor did women drink at pubs unaccompanied by their husbands, but drinking at home could intoxicate.[82] On 21 September 1891 a Baptist missionary in Bristol described such a woman: "Mrs Deveral, so addicted to drink that she sold the pail, teapot, lamp and her husband's trousers to satisfy her craving."[83] In 1895 Ellen Sweeney of Swansea was convicted of public drunkenness for the 279th time.[84]

Who was a moderate drinker? Was a moderate drinker simply an upper- or middle-class drinker who managed not to embarrass friends and family? Some people regarded as moderate drinkers drank a good deal. Most people saw a dichotomy, drunkards and respectable moderate drinkers (like themselves) rather than all drinkers situated on a blurry and shifting continuum. In the 1860s a British physician, Francis E. Anstie (1833-74), developed what was called "Anstie's Limit": one and a half ounces of pure alcohol daily would not affect a normal person's health adversely.[85] In 1883 Matthew Arnold provided an anecdotal description of a moderate drinker, himself. "As a general rule, I drink water in the middle of the day; and a glass or two of sherry, and some light claret, mixed with water, at a late dinner; and this seems to suit me very well."[86] No doubt W.E. Gladstone also regarded himself as a moderate drinker: "a glass or two of claret at luncheon, the same at dinner, with the addition of a glass of light wine." [87]

A few moderate drinkers stood at the fringe of the organized temperance movement. A semi-teetotal pledge society was organized in 1903 with a retired field marshal as its figurehead. Members promised not to drink other than at the midday and evening meals (and, according to an American religious magazine, no more than an ounce and a half of alcohol in any day). In 1904 it affiliated with the Church of England Temperance Society, a denominational organization that admitted into membership moderate drinkers as well as total abstainers.

Coping with the workingman's drink problem seemed to be a key to social reform. At the turn of the century, intense international economic competition aroused fear of national degeneration and calls for national efficiency.[88] The large number of volunteers for the Boer war (1899-1902) rejected because of ill health startled and dismayed the country. Appalling infant mortality threatened the future of the country. At the turn of the century what can be described as a moral panic identified women's drinking as a danger to their children.[89]

Sir George White (1840-1912) was representative of the provincial upper middle class. He was a wealthy Norfolk boot and shoe manufacturer, a prominent Baptist layman, and a Liberal MP from 1900 to 1912. Although he was a teetotaler and a prohibitionist, his concern over drink resonated widely among the middle and upper classes. The historian Barry M. Doyle summarizes White's condemnation of drink. "[He] saw a moral and social dimension to the drink question, believing it to be the chief cause of divorce and absence from church, [but] at root his interpretation was economic." According to White,

> [Drink was] more damaging to the country's resources than war, greater in cost than all local and national taxation or the rental value of all the country's houses, shops and hotels, and . . . responsible for reducing the consumption of useful goods by £70,000,000, [while in addition] drink undermined the efficiency and consumption of the individual worker and led to the loss of fifteen per cent of his work time--a figure more serious in its effects on the economy than "the worst strike which ever happened."[90]

The English temperance movement peaked in the late nineteenth and early twentieth centuries.[91] At the turn of the century by a contemporary estimate, teetotalers were fewer than nine percent of the adult population. Most of them were working class, although their leaders typically were middle-class Nonconformists.

Total abstainers were not content to refrain from drink themselves. They sought to convert others, and by the late nineteenth century, almost all of them sought legislation to help create a society free of drink. There were a few exceptions who rejected making people sober by acts of Parliament. Throughout his long life the founder of teetotalism in England, Joseph Livesey, remained committed to moral suasion exclusively. He argued that focus on the traffic in drink was a mistake. Without rejecting moral suasion, most teetotalers thought it was not enough.

As total abstainers were a minority in England, they needed allies. The two most prominent anti-drink organizations, the prohibitionist United Kingdom Alliance and the Church of England Temperance Society, did not require total abstinence as a condition for membership, and the latter had a sizeable minority of moderate drinkers.

Drink trade general election posters caricatured total abstainers as narrow-minded faddists, killjoy enemies of working-class conviviality. In contrast, English temperance reformers saw themselves as part of an international reform movement, embracing progressive values that others would belatedly follow. A generous estimate of the number of teetotalers, made in 1898 by the general secretary of a prohibition organization, claimed that there were eight million total abstainers in the United Kingdom, a figure padded with children of abstainers and members of the huge Bands of Hope juvenile temperance society.[92] The social reformers Rowntree and Sherwell more modestly estimated three million teetotalers. A modern estimate described ten percent of the adult population as teetotalers in 1900.[93]

Many total abstainers were women. There even was a United Working Women's Teetotal League whose stronghold seems to have been London's laundry trade.[44] In the late nineteenth century the largest total abstinence society was the mostly middle-class British Women's Temperance Society and its successor organizations.[45] Women's temperance societies and women in mixed-sex societies played only a marginal role in the leadership of the national temperance movement.

Teetotalers were marginalized. Until the end of 1905 no total abstainer sat in the Cabinet.[46] Temperance strength in Britain was concentrated far from London, in the north of England, in Cornwall, and in Wales, as well as on Scotland. By 1890 there were 45 teetotal mayors in England and Wales.[47]

It is safe to say that in England the majority of those who abstained from drink were humble men and women, content with membership in obscure local organizations. Despite the prominence of the middle class in national and regional temperance societies, most total abstainers were working class.[94] A prohibitionist leader described "the flower of the working classes in all the large towns of England" as his supporters.[95] The standard history of the Welsh temperance movement emphasizes the working-class membership of early temperance societies with self-employed shoemakers and tailors as typical members.[96]

Many pioneers of what became the Labour Party such as the coal miner Thomas Burt (1837-1922) did not drink. Philip Snowden (1864-1937) claimed that a majority of Labour MPs in the Edwardian parliaments were teetotal.[97] In a contrast with other workingmen's clubs, only three percent of those affiliated with the Independent Labour Party sold alcoholic drink in 1909.[98]

The late Victorian temperance movement is often identified with Nonconformity.[99] In political campaigns Nonconformist abstainers provided much of the energy for the temperance cause. In fact, temperance politics diverted them from religious activities. "Prayer Meetings were cancelled in favour of electioneering during the 1906 general election."[100]

The elected officers and salaried officials of most national and regional temperance societies, as well as most teetotal M.P.s, were middle-class Nonconformists. This explains the reputation of the temperance agitation as middle class and Nonconformist. Yet in the late nineteenth and early twentieth century many middle-class Nonconformists drank. None of the three most prominent middle class Nonconformist politicians--John Bright (1811-89), Joseph Chamberlain (1836-1914), David Lloyd George--

was a lifelong total abstainer. (Bright only gave up drink when in his sixties.) The United Kingdom Alliance did not have a Nonconformist as its president until 1932.[101]

Further complicating the image of the English temperance movement, a powerful temperance movement within the Church of England lived uneasily beside that of dry Dissenters. Churches competed with chapels in the temperance movement. Finally, although English teetotallers typically were devout Christians, a few prominent reformers rejected any kind of a religion.

Generalizations about the relationship between Nonconformity and temperance need caution. In late Victorian and Edwardian England, prominent total abstainers included a Roman Catholic cardinal, Henry Manning (1808-92). In 1873, he founded a teetotal society for Catholics, the League of the Cross.[102] Within a few years in London alone it had thirty-one branches with 35,000 active members.[103]

Reform could be a substitute for religion. Rosalind Howard, Countess of Carlisle (1845-1921), led the National British Women's Temperance Association from 1903 until her death. She took the pledge in 1881.She was an agnostic or atheist. A bemused friend pointed out: "She believes in no form of religion, but goes to church, I hardly know why, if it is not to distribute teetotal leaflets at the door."[104] Her former secretary, Leif Jones (1862-1939), became president of the United Kingdom Alliance in 1906 and served until 1932. Although a minister's son, he too was an agnostic or atheist.

In 1881 an essay about the temperance work in the churches began with an apology. T.E. Williams acknowledged that "the Christian Church in this country has been slow to identify itself with the Temperance Movement."[105] Denominational temperance societies among the Nonconformists had few members and little money. The Bible Christians, regarded as a teetotal denomination, did not have a temperance society until 1882. The Baptists had organized one earlier (1874), but its income was only £56. In 1892 its income had grown to £567.[106] To a large extent, it was a society of ministers. In 1881 its membership of less than 1,100 included between five hundred and six hundred ministers.[107] The Primitive Methodists organized a temperance league belatedly in 1883. The New Connexon Methodists never organized a denominational temperance society.[108] Did this matter? Writing in 1893, Dawson Burns (1828-1909) said: "during the last seven years the Methodist New Connexion Conference has not received a minister or college student who has not been an abstainer."[109]

Although individual Quakers were prominent in the temperance movement, the Society of Friends were slow to organize a temperance society of their own. A Friends' Temperance Union was organized in 1852. No records were kept and "little was done." It was reconstructed in 1877, but experienced "ups and downs." By 1891, "it had got into low water."[110]

The peak for teetotalism among Nonconformist ministers did not occur until the early years of the twentieth century. When the Congregational Total Abstinence Association was formed in 1874, about a quarter of Congregational ministers in England were teetotallers.[111] The number of abstaining ministers quickly grew. The number of total abstainers among Congregational ministers rose from 760 out of about 2,000 in 1879 to about 2,500 out of 3,000 in 1904, while 2,650 out of 2,950 were abstainers in 1908. The statistics refer to membership in Congregational Total Abstinence Association, and not all teetotalers were members.[112] Its income for 1891 was £265.[113] Among Baptist ministers, a sixth were teetotalers in 1860, a cohort that grew to 1,100 out of 1,900 in 1886. By 1908, the number of abstainers had grown to 2,321 out of 2,647 Baptist ministers. Confirming the upward trend, 211 out of 214 Baptist seminary students were total abstainers in 1907. In 1898, out of 370 ministers on Free Methodist home circuits, 357 were total abstainers. As older Free Methodist ministers retired, the teetotal proportion grew: "almost without exception year by year the ministers on probation, all the students in the Theological Institute in Manchester, and the boys in Ashville College at Harrogate are abstainers." According to the *Alliance News*, in 1896, the Primitive Methodists numbered 1,113 ministers and 30 students in training for the ministry, nearly all total abstainers, as were "a very large proportion of the 10,742 local preachers." According to the same source, among Bible Christians, all 293 ministers and all students were abstainers, as were nearly all 1,937 local preachers.[114] In the Presbyterian Church of England, its 307 ministers included 206 abstainers and of its sixteen students, all but one were abstainers. In 1892 the English Presbyterians organized a total abstinence society. Unlike most Nonconformist ministers, a majority of Unitarian ministers drank, with only 146 abstainers out of 369 ministers in 1907.[115]

Whatever the ministers did, many members of the Nonconformist laity drank. In 1897 the Baptist Union rejected a proposal that total abstinence be a requirement for holding church office. Resolutions in the Wesleyan Methodist church to exclude people in the drink trade from office failed every year from 1898 to 1901.[116] In 1896 E. Tennyson Smith (1850-1925), a Good Templar, organized the Temperance Ironsides to urge the expulsion of drink sellers from church memberships.[117]

There are no statistics for office holders who drank or other Nonconformist drinkers, but such drinkers existed. Thomas Clowes was the chairman of the Manchester Brewers' Central Association. In his will, he left £500 to his Congregational chapel.[118] When John Massey, an agent for the National Trade Defence Association, died in 1906, he was a lay preacher at the Ebenezer Methodist New Connexion Church in Newcastle.[119]

An additional caveat needs mention in assessing the role of the Nonconformists in the English temperance movement. The Church of England played at least as large a role. In 1869, the Convocation of Canterbury called drunkenness a "terrible vice." Organized in 1873, the Church of England Temperance Society became the largest denominational temperance organization. Supposedly 6,000 Anglican priests were total abstainers in 1897.[120] The CETS included all the Anglican parties: evangelicals, broad churchmen, and Anglo-Catholics. A large minority of CETS members were moderate drinkers.[121] Predominantly upper middle class, they included the CETS representatives in the House of Commons. Working-class and clerical abstainers made up a majority of the membership. By the end of the nineteenth century most Anglican diocesan bishops were total abstainers.[122] The drink trade increasingly regarded Church of England clerics as enemies.[123]

Although as compared with the UKA and the CETS, the London-based National Temperance League had few members, it was influential within the temperance movement. It helped organize other anti-drink societies, for instance, for the Royal Navy and the army. It was a major publisher of temperance books, magazines, and pamphlets. Between 1880 and 1896 its publishing depot sold publications valued at £130,000.

In the late nineteenth and early twentieth century the English temperance movement enlisted a large minority of the general population, but teetotalers and their allies were never united about drink.

In late Victorian and Edwardian England, the four leading temperance politicians were Sir Wilfrid Lawson (1829-1906), W.S. Caine (1832-1903), T.P. Whittaker (later Sir Thomas Palmer Whittaker) (1850-1919), and Leif Jones (later Lord Rhayader) (1862-1939). These four parliamentarians illustrate the rise and decline of prohibition and, as a result, the rise and decline of the United Kingdom Alliance.

The relative obscurity of these four MPs today is partly the result of the thinness of source material. There is no collection of correspondence for any of them. Lawson's personal archive was destroyed in a house fire. The other MPs appear not to have kept their letters or at least did not ensure their survival. Lawson, Caine, and Leif Jones have *Oxford Dictionary of National Biography* entries, while Whittaker has only an entry in the obscure *Biographical Dictionary of Modern British Radicals*. Lawson and, to a lesser extent, Caine figure prominently in histories of the United Kingdom Alliance. They also have books devoted specifically to them. A prominent journalist edited Lawson's memoir.[124] An Alliance official wrote a stout biography of Caine.[125] Another Alliance official produced a book about Leif Jones that at first glance looks like a biography but in fact is mostly a collection of his speeches.[126] Despite his importance in drink politics, Whittaker has been ignored. In search of his papers, I tracked a daughter to Argentina where she had emigrated. Unfortunately, by the time of my query, she was very old, and all that her family could get her to remember was that her father sometimes was called Lord Drinkwater.[127]

Although Caine and Whittaker remained prohibitionists in principle, by the end of the nineteenth century they had dropped prohibition by Local Veto from their program as politically impractical. Whittaker eventually left the United Kingdom Alliance and became a champion of disinterested management. Lawson and Leif Jones remained loyal to the lost cause of Local Veto.

In 2017 the Office of National Statistics reported that more than a fifth of British adults, 16 or older, self-identified as teetotalers, 20.4%. They included 22.6% of women and 18.1% of men. Once stony ground for the temperance movement, London had the highest proportion of total abstainers, probably because of its large Muslim population. Today some drinkers pay respect to total abstinence by observing Dry January. Whatever their disagreements, our four teetotal politicians would be gratified and probably surprised.

Notes

[1] Among contemporary reviews of *Drink and the Victorians*, the most detailed is Clyde Binfield, "Temperance and the Cause of God," *History* 57 (Oct. 1972): 403-10. Before Harrison, the best book about temperance in England had been written for a popular audience. Norman Longmate, *The Waterdrinkers: A History of Temperance* (Hamish Hamilton, 1968), is now virtually forgotten. The revival of historical studies of temperance began a bit earlier in the United States with Joseph R. Gusfield's *Symbolic Crusade: Status Politics and the American Temperance Movement* (University of Illinois Press, 1963), James H. Timberlake, *Prohibition and the Progressive Movement, 1900-1920* (Harvard University Press, 1963), and Norman H. Clark's *The Dry Years: Prohibition and Social Change in Washington* (University of Washington Press, 1965). State and national prohibition help explain America's rich historical scholarship about temperance that far exceeds England's.

[2] In the early and mid 1970s several relevant doctoral dissertations were completed at American, Australian, British, and Canadian universities. Most of them had

difficulty finding a publisher. For instance, Lilian Lewis Shiman completed her dissertation at the University of Wisconsin a year before Harrison published his great book. Her *Crusade against Drink in Victorian England* had to wait until 1988 to be published. She was told that Harrison had "covered" temperance. Shiman, "Reflections: 'Lilian Turns to Booze'," *Social History of Alcohol Review* 36/37 (Spring/Fall 1998): 14. Until recently the coolness of publishers toward British temperance and drink history was unmistakable. Harrison did not publish his book with a major academic press, although Faber and Faber is a prestigious commercial press. For an American publisher, he got the University of Pittsburgh Press. The little known Keele University Press published his slightly revised second edition.

[3] In addition to the second edition of *Drink and the Victorians*, published in 1994, Harrison discussed temperance reform in occasional detail in *Peaceable Kingdom*, published in 1982.

[4] James Nicholls argues: "One impact of the 1830 Beer Act would be to transform an anti-spirits movement which stretched back to the days of the gin craze into a radical and well-organised teetotal campaign." *The Politics of Alcohol: A History of the Drink Question in England* (Manchester University Press, 2009), pp. 80-81.

[5] There were a few cider houses, only 25 in 1906-07. Samuel Evans, House of Commons, 2 Nov. 1908. Cider houses were found mostly in the West Country.

[6] In an experiment, from 1861 to 1865, Liverpool justices offered public house licenses to applicants of good character and with suitable premises without regard to the need for additional pubs. As a solution to the drink problem, "it was a dismal failure." Dan Malleck, ed., *Drugs, Alcohol and Addiction in the Long Nineteenth Century* (Routledge, 2020), p. 10.

[7] Pre-1869 beerhouses retained a right to license renewal unless they had violated specified rules. For beerhouses, see Paul Jennings, in Scott C. Martin, ed., *The Sage Encyclopedia of Alcohol* (Sage, 2015); Ron Pattinson, "The Rise and Fall of Beer Houses" [History by the Glass], *Beer Advocate* (Oct. 2016). Pattinson points out that a fully licensed pub was worth four or five times that of a beer house. He adds that as late as 1910 about a third of all pubs were beer houses.

[8] Lilian Lewis Shiman emphasizes that the arrival of the prohibition movement did not mean the end of moral suasion. "Gospel temperance appeared on the scene in the mid-1870s [shortly after Harrison's time-period]. Linking the anti-drink reform with religion, it again stressed personal abstention." *Crusade against Drink in Victorian England* (Martin's Press, 1988), p. 4.

[9] David W. Gutzke provides an excellent account of disinterested management in England hidden, unfortunately, under a misleading title. "Gentrifying the British Public House, 1896-1914," *International Labor and Working-Class History* 45 (Spring, 1994): 29-43. Gutzke also wrote the entry "Gothenburg Schemes/Disinterested Management" in Jack S. Blocker, David M. Fahey, and Ian R. Tyrrell, eds. *Alcohol and Temperance in Modern History* (ABC-CLIO, 2003).

[10] M.J.D. Roberts, *Making English Morals: Voluntary Association and Moral Reform in England, 1787-1886* (Cambridge University Press, 2009), pp. 8-9.

[11] In the early twentieth century proposals for reform took on a centralized approach.

[12] Thora T. Hands wrote a Ph.D. dissertation at Strathclyde University about moderate drinkers, "Reframing Drink and the Victorians: The Consumption of

Alcohol in Britain, 1869-1914" (2016), published in 2018 by Palgrave Macmillan as *Drinking in Victorian and Edwardian Britain: The Spectre of the Drunkard*. See also about moderation Joanne Woiak, "'A Medical Cromwell to Depose King Alcohol": Medical Scientists, Temperance Reformers, and the Alcohol Problem in Britain," *Historie Sociale* 27 (1994); James Kneale, "'These Are the Cases Who Call Themselves 'Moderate Drinkers,' Because They Are Never Seen Embracing a Lamp-Post: The Problem of Moderate Drinking in Nineteenth- and Early Twentieth-Century Britain." In Matthew Ingleby and Samuel Randalls, eds., *Just Enough. The History, Culture and Politics of Sufficiency* (Palgrave Macmillan, 2018).

[13] John Foster, *Class Struggle and the Industrial Revolution* (Routledge, 1974), p. 218. See also J.R. Vincent, *Pollbooks: How Victorians Voted* (Cambridge University Press, 1967), particularly pp. 65-66, Table 8, "The Voting of Publicans and Beersellers, 1852-72," and analysis of individual constituencies.

[14] Thora T. Hands, "Re-Framing Drink and the Victorians: New Theoretical Approaches to the Study of Alcohol History" (conference abstract, 2013, available on the Internet). Virginia Berridge suprisingly described Harrison's *Drink and the Victorians* as "really concerned with the role of temperance as part of the reformist post-Chartist labour movement." "History and Addiction Control: The Case of Alcohol," in John Maynard and others, ed., *Controlling Legal Addictions* (St. Martin's Press, 1989).

[15] I also borrow from Shiman's *Crusade against Drink in Victorian England* which extended the story chronologically beyond Harrison to 1895. Shiman made a major contribution to social history, particularly for the North of England. Her book incorporated material from many of her articles, including those for Birstall and Bradford that had appeared in the *Yorkshire Archaeological Journal.*

[16] Much of the remainder of this chapter borrows from David M. Fahey, "Worrying about Drink," *Brewery History* 166 (Summer 2016).

[17] Hands, *Drinking in Victorian and Edwardian Britain: Beyond the Spectre of the Drunkard* (Palgrave Macmillan, 2028), ch. 3, "The Great Army of Drinkers: and ch. 11, "Neither Carnival nor Lent: Everyday Working Class Drinking." Recent research suggests that the general public did not condemn occasional drunkenness. Richard Robinson, "Off Beat and in Drink: Impropriety and Insobriety in Brighton's Police, 1880-1921," *Social History of Alcohol and Drugs* 30 (2016): 4-30.

[18] Annemarie McAllister, *Demon Drink? Temperance and the Working Class* (self-published, 2014). For drinking places in Britain and elsewhere, see James Kneale, "Good, Homely, Troublesome or Improving? Historical Geographies of Drinking Places, c. 1850–1950," *Geography Compass* (2021).

[19] *Parliamentary Debates*, 4th ser., IX (27 Feb. 1893), col. 488.

[19] Hands, *Beyond the Spectre of the Drunkard*, ch, 12, "The Drinking Culture of the Higher Classes."

[21] Middle- and upper-class distaste for beer should not be exaggerated. An inquiry in the early 1880s into the smoking and drinking habits of men of letters and of science showed that a minority drank beer. For instance, the historian Samuel Rawson Gardiner wrote: "I take beer at luncheon and dinner, and occasionally a glass or two of wine, but very often I am four or five days without doing that." Alfred Arthur Reade, *Study and Stimulants: or The Use of Intoxicants and Narcotics in*

Relation to Intellectual Life, as Illustrated by Personal Communications on the Subject, from Men of Letters and of Science (A. Heywood, 1883), p. 53.

[22] The United Kingdom Alliance wanted to close all the pubs, but it was an open secret that its honorary secretary Samuel Pope drank. See also James Kneale, "The Place of Drink: Temperance and the Public, 1856-1914," *Social & Cultural Geography* 2 no. 1 (January 2001): 43-59.

[23] Despite his dislike of the drink trade, the eccentric Sir Wilfrid Lawson declined to join attacks upon it that he regarded as unfair. He could not support complaints about the adulteration of beer (which he said were unfounded), and he did not see tied houses, controlled by brewers, as any worse than other public houses. Pointing out that the licensing law required that publicans be persons of good character, a requirement that other retailers did not have to meet, he did not waste his time deriding the publicans. It was the product that they sold which was evil. A hater of drink and not of drink traders, Lawson counted a Liberal brewer among his parliamentary friends. According to Lawson's memoir, M.T. Bass told him: "'I'll settle a beer a day on you for life, if you'll give up the Permissive Bill [for local prohibition].' To which I replied that 'I couldn't do it under a barrel'." *Sir Wilfrid Lawson: A Memoir*, ed. George W.E. Russell (Smith, Elder, 1909), p. 62.

[24] Denys P. Leighton, *The Greenian Moment: T.H. Green, Religion and Political Argument in Victorian Britain* (Imprint Academic, 2004), p. 51.

[25] Set in the early 1920s, Evelyn Waugh's *Brideshead Revisited* (1945) deserves a mention for Lord Sebastian Flyte and his inebriated friends.

[26] Marvin Rintala, "Taking the Pledge: H. H. Asquith and Drink," *Biography* 16 no. 2 (Spring 1993): 103-35.

[27] Marvin Rintala, "Family Portrait: Churchills at Drink," *Biography* 21 no. 1 (Winter 1998): 1-23; David Lough, *No More Champagne: Churchill and His Money* (Picador, 2015).

[28] Patrick Jackson, ed. *Loulou: Selected Extracts from the Journals of Lewis Harcourt (1880-1895)* (Fairleigh Dickinson University Press, 2006), pp. 110-11.

[29] W.R.P. George, *The Making of Lloyd George* (Faber and Faber, 1976), pp. 104, 112.

[30] Hands, *Beyond the Spectre of the Drunkard*, ch. 4, "The Secret Army of Drinkers"; Julia Skelly, "When Seeing is Believing: Women, Alcohol and Photography in Victorian England," *Shift: Queen's Journal of Visual & Material Culture* 1 (2008): 2. See also David E. Wright and Cathy Chorniawry, "Women and Drink in Edwardian England," *Historical Papers* 20, no. 1 (1985): 117-131; and the doctoral thesis by Bronwyn Louise Morrison, "Ordering Disorderly Women: Female Drunkenness in England c.1870-1920" (Keele University, 2005). Most recently, see David Beckingham, "Private Spirits, Public Lives: Sober Citizenship, Shame and Secret Drinking in Victorian Britain," *Journal of Victorian Culture* 22 April 2021.

[31] *Times,* 27 June 1892, quoted in Michael K. Barker, *Gladstone and Radicalism: The Reconstruction of Liberal Policy, 1885-94* (Harvester, 1975), p. 210.

[32] Charles Luddington, *The Politics of Wine in Britain* (Palgrave Macmillan, 2013), pp. 194-96, and more generally, ch. 10, "By G-d, He Drinks Like a Man!': Manliness, Britishness, and the Politics of Drunkenness, c. 1780-1820s"; Joshua

Scarlett, "Pitt and Port: A Study of a Prime Minister's Drinking" (Internet, 14 April 2015). http://standrewshistorysociety.co.uk/2015/04/pitt-and-port-a-study-of-a-prime-ministers-drinking/. Bonar Law was born in New Brunswick, the son of a Presbyterian minister.

[33] Edwin Chernud to E.W. Benson, Archbishop of Canterbury, 29 Nov. 1889. Lambeth Palace Library, Benson papers. Quoted in Gerald Wayne Olsen, "Drink and the British Establishment--The Church of England Temperance Society, 1873-1919" (typescript, 2003), p. 42.

[34] The Hon. Algernon Bourke, third son of the sixth Earl of Mayo, and his wife Guendolen were caricatured as two of the main characters in Oscar Wilde's *The Importance of Being Earnest* (1895).

[35] T.R. Gourvish and R.G. Wilson, *The British Brewing Industry, 1830-1980* (Cambridge University Press, 1994), pp. 30, 285 (quotation); George B. Wilson, *Alcohol and the Nation: A Contribution to the Study of the Liquor Problem in the United Kingdom from 1800 to 1935* (Nicholson and Watson, 1940), pp. 58, 308, Table 1, pp. 332- 33.

[36] Paul Jennings, "Policing Drunkenness in England and Wales from the Late Eighteenth Century to the First World War," *Social History of Alcohol and Drugs* 26 no. 1 (Winter 2012): 69.

[37] Public houses could be respectable. For instance, the Radcliffe Arms established a library in 1833. "The Radcliffe Arms Library survived the creation of the Nottingham Free Library, possessing 4,000 books in 1869 and 8,000 by 1893." Michael A. Smith, "Social Usages of the Public Drinking House: Changing Aspects of Class and Leisure," *British Journal of Sociology* 34 no. 3 (1983). 377.

[38] A.E. Dingle, "Drink and Working-Class Living Standards in Britain, 1870-1914," *Economic History Review* 25 no. 4 (Nov. 1972): 611-12.

[39] John Burnett, *Liquid Pleasures: A Social History of Drinks in Modern Britain* (Routledge, 1999), chs. 6, 7, 8; and, more briefly, David M. Fahey, "Alcohol, Consumption of (United Kingdom)," in Blocker, *Alcohol and Temperance in Modern History* 1: 16-18. For statistics, see Wilson, *Alcohol and the Nation*. There is a useful analysis of drink statistics by Arthur Shadwell, *Drink, Temperance and Legislation* (Longmans, Green, 1903; revised in 1915).

[40] http://www.norfolkpubs.co.uk/kingslynn/kingind.htm

[41] Arthur Sherwell, *Life in West London: A Study and a Contrast* (1897; 3rd ed., Methuen: 1903), p. 128.

[42] Rowntree and Sherwell, *The Temperance Problem and Social Reform* (1899; Hodder and Stoughton, 7th ed., 1900), p. 672.

[43] George B. Wilson, "Looking Back," *Alliance Year Book and Temperance Reformers' Handbook for 1947*, p. 47.

[44] David Beckingham, "Geographies of Drink Culture in Liverpool: Lessons from the Drink Capital of Nineteenth-Century England," *Drugs, Education, Prevention and Policy* 15 no. 3 (2008). 305-31. See also Beckingham's book, *The Licensed City: Regulating Drink in Liverpool, 1830-1920* (Liverpool University Press, 2017).

[45] John E. Archer, *The Monster Evil: Policing and Violence in Victorian Liverpool* (Liverpool University Press, 2011), p. 23. In contrast, per capita arrests for public

intoxication grew in the Metropolitan Police District during 1870-1914. Stefan Petrow, *Policing Morals: The Metropolitan Police and the Home Office, 1870-1914* (Clarendon Press, 1994), p. 215.

[46] Paul Jennings, "Policing Public Houses in Victorian England," *Law, Crime and History* 3 no. 1 (2013): 87.

[47] Rowntree and Sherwell, *The Temperance Problem and Social Reform*, p. 10. See also James Kneale, "Consumption." In Deborah Toner, ed., *Alcohol in the Age of Industry, Empire, and War* (Bloomsbury Academic, 2021).

[48] David W. Gutzke, *Protecting the Pub: Brewers and Publicans against Temperance* (Royal Historical Society, published by Boydell, 1989), p. 40.

[49] R.G. Wilson, "The Changing Taste for Beer in Victorian England," in T.R. Gourvish and R. G. Wilson, eds., *The Dynamics of the International Brewing Industry* (Routledge, 1998), p. 99. Lager sales lagged in contrast with continental Europe, the United States, and Australia.

[50] Jonathan Reinarz, "Promoting the Pint: Ale and Advertising in Late Victorian and Edwardian England," *Social History of Alcohol and Drugs* 22 no. 1 (Fall 2007): 26-44.

[51] John Burnett, *Liquid Pleasures*, p. 151. Balfour preferred port, Gladstone claret and port. "Drinks of Great Men," *Victualing Trades Review* (1900), cited in Hands, *Beyond the Spectre of the Drunkard* p. 21. See also Graham Harding, *Champagne in Britain, 1800-1914: How the British Transformed a French Luxury* (Bloomsbury Academic, 2021).

[52] Today the country that drinks the most gin is the Philippines, the popular local brand being Ginebra San Miguel.

[53] Richard Barnett, *The Book of Gin* (Grove Press, 2012).

[54] Mark Girouard, *Victorian Pubs* (Yale University Press, 1984), p. 29. Girouard's source is the booklet by Henry Bradshaw Fearon, *Suggestions and Correspondence Relating to Magistrates Licenses* (1830), p. 33. Fearon was a London wine and spirit merchant.

[55] *Cheltenham Chronicle*, 5 August 1911, p. 7, quoted in http://barclayperkins.blogspot.com/2013/09/change-in-public-taste.html/. For leading Victorian and Edwardian brewers, see Ray Anderson, "The Brewing Connection in the Oxford Dictionary of National Biography," *Brewery History* 119 (Summer 2005).

[56] Gutzke, *Protecting the Pub*, p. 205.

[57] Gutzke, *Protecting the Pub*, p. 195.

[58] Laurence Marlow, "A Menace to Sobriety? The Drinking Question and the Working Men's Club, c. 1862-1906," in Lex Heerma van Voss and F.L. van Holthoon, eds., *Working Class and Popular Culture* (Stichting Beheer, 1988), p. 112.

[59] Gourvish and Wilson, *The British Brewing Industry*, p. 285. See also Gutzke, *Protecting the Pub*, pp. 203-05.

[60] For the public house and its patrons, see Paul Jennings, *The Local: The History of the English Pub* (Tempus, 2007). Nostalgia about the Victorian public house has produced an enormous number of local histories such as Wendy Bell Scott, *A Pub*

on Every Corner? Drink and the Licensed Trade in Nineteenth-Century Berwick upon Tweed (Blue Ribbon Publications, 2009).

[61] See James Kneale, "Victorian England," in Martin, ed., *The Sage Encyclopedia of Alcohol* 3: 1317-21.

[62] Libertarian and anti-socialist sentiment took an institutional form in the Liberty and Property Defence League founded in 1882, a staunch defender of the drink trade.

[63] Wilson, *Alcohol and the Nation*, p. 197. By 1919-20 liquor taxes had fallen to 13.4 per cent.

[64] Sir Wilfrid Lawson in *Parliamentary Debates*, 3rd ser., CCXV (April 7, 1873). col. 676. Since the eighteenth century the Royal Navy distributed a daily grog ration of diluted rum.

[65] *Temperance Chronicle*, May 4, 1895. See also W.D. Rubinstein, "British Millionaires, 1809-1947," *Bulletin of the Institute of Historical Research* 47 (1974): 210-11; for the brewery, Alistair Mutch, "Public Houses as Multiple Retailing: Peter Walker & Son, 1846-1914," *Business History* 48 no. 1 (2006): 1-17.

[66] P.L. Payne, "The Emergence of the Large-Scale Company in Great Britain, 1870-1914," *Economic History Review*, 2nd ser., 20 (1967): 530-32, 539-40.

[67] For the brewers, see David W. Gutzke, "Rhetoric and Reality: The Political Influence of British Brewers, 1832-1914," *Parliamentary History* 9 (May 1990): 78-115

[68] Victor Bailey, "Salvation Army Riots, the 'Skeleton Army' and Legal Authority in the Provincial Town," in *Social Control in Nineteenth Century Britain,* ed. A.P. Donajgrodski (Croom Helm, 1977), pp. 231-53; Chris Hare, "The Skeleton Army and the Bonfire Boys, Worthing, 1884," *Folklore* 99 no. 2 (1988): 221-31; Bethany Bell, "Menace to Sobriety: When Salvationists fought Skeletons," BBC News, 17 Oct. 2020. See also Brian Harrison, "Sunday Closing Riots of 1855," *Historical Journal* 8 no. 2 (1965).

[69] Martin Pugh, *State and Society: A Social and Political History of Britain since 1870* (4th ed,, Bloomsbury Academic, 2012), Table 2.1.

[70] Jon Lawrence, *Speaking for the People: Party, Language and Popular Politics in England, 1867-1914* (Cambridge University Press, 1998), p. 107.

[71] Paul Jennings, *A History of Drink and the English, 1500-2000* (Routledge, 2016), pp. 21-22. For drinkers who avoided excess, see also Jennings, "Policing Public Houses in Victorian England," p. 74.

[72] J.L. Paton, *John Brown Paton: A Biography* (1914), p. 214, quoted in Clyde Binfield, "Temperance and the Cause of God," *History* 57 (October 1972): 409. Paton was president of the Licensing Laws Information Bureau, 1898-1902.

[73] Gutzke, *Protecting the Pub*, p. 33. In addition, brewery workers took advantage of their jobs to drink heavily. Martyn Cornell, review of Ian Webster, *Ind Coope & Samuel Allsopp Breweries,* in *Brewery History* 164 (Winter 2015): 79.

[74] Dingle, "Drink and Working-Class Living Standards," pp. 615-17. In 1873 a Welsh employer complained that better pay meant more drunkenness and more absenteeism. W.R. Lambert, *Drink and Sobriety in Victorian Wales* (University of Wales Press, 1983), p. 44.

[75] Lynn Hollen Lees, "Getting and Spending: The Family Budgets of English Industrial Workers in 1890," in John M. Merriman, ed., *Consciousness and Class*

Experience in Nineteenth-Century Europe (Holmes and Meier, 1979), pp. 169-86, cited in Gutzke, *Protecting the Pub*, p. 39. Most of the men worked in skilled jobs.
[76] Robert Roberts, *The Classic Slum: Salford Life in the First Quarter of the Century* (Penguin, 1971), p. 93.
[77] Noel Buxton and Walter Hoare, "Temperance Reform," in C.F. G. Masterman, ed., *The Heart of the Empire: Discussions of Problems of Modern City Life in England* (1901), edited and introduced by Bentley B. Gilbert (Harvester Press, 1973), pp. 175, 191. For a modern distinction between the almost alcoholic and the true alcoholic, see Robert L. Doyle and Joseph Nowinski, *Almost Alcoholic* (Hazelden Books, 2012).
[78] Gutzke, *Protecting the Pub*, p. 34.
[79] David Wright and Cathy Chorniawry, "Women and Drink in Edwardian England," *Historical Papers* (1985): 121.
[80] Thomas R. C. Gibson-Brydon, *Moral Mapping of Victorian and Edwardian London: Charles Booth, Christian Charity, and the Poor-but-Respectable* (McGill-Queen's, 2016), pp. 160-61.
[81] http://booth.lse.ac.uk/notebooks/b346/jgp/41.html.
[82] David W. Gutzke, *Women Drinking Out in Britain since the Early Twentieth Century* (Manchester University Press, 2014), pp. 17-22.
[83] David Roberts, "Thomas Howe, Bristol Missioner, by Love Serving One Another," *Baptist Quarterly* 38 no. 4 (October 1999): 170.
[84] Roy M. MacLeod, "The Edge of Hope: Social Policy and Chronic Alcoholism, 1870-1900," *Journal of the History of Medicine* 22 no. 3 (July 1967): 235 n. 92.
[85] James Kneale and Shaun French, "Moderate Drinking before the Unit: Medicine and Life Assurance in Britain and the US, c.1860–1930," *Drugs: Education, Prevention, and Policy* 22 no. 3 (2015): 111-17.
[86] Reade, *Study and Stimulants*, p. 13.
[87] Reported by his son Herbert Gladstone, in Reade, *Study and Stimulants*, p. 54. John Burnett, in contrast, said that Gladstone enjoyed a quart of champagne at dinner. Burnett, *Liquid Pleasures*, p. 149.
[88] G.R. Searle, *The Quest for National Efficiency: A Study in British Politics and Political Thought, 1899-1914* (1971). Fear of German competition did not always encourage temperance reform. Ernest Williams wrote the alarmist *Made in Germany* (1896). When the True Temperance Association was created in 1908 in support of the drink trade, Williams became its honorary treasurer.
[89] See David W. Gutzke, "'The Cry of the Children': The Edwardian Medical Campaign against Maternal Drinking," *British Journal of Addiction* 79 (1984): 71-84, Gutzke, *Women Drinking Out*, pp. 240-49.
[90] Barry M. Doyle, "'Through the Windows of a Baptist Meeting House': Religion, Politics and the Nonconformist Conscience in the Life of Sir George White, M.P.," *Baptist Quarterly* 36 no. 6 (1996): 302. See also Doyle, "Modernity or Morality? George White, Liberalism and the Nonconformist Conscience in Edwardian England," *Historical Research* 71 (October 1998): 330-31; and his "Temperance and Modernity: The Impact of Local Experience on Rank and File Liberal Attitudes to Alcohol," *Journal of Regional and Local Studies* 16 no. 2 (1996): 1-10.

[91] Much of this section is borrowed from David M. Fahey, *Temperance Societies in the Late Victorian and Edwardian England* (Cambridge Scholars Publishing, 2000).
[92] James Whyte, 14 June 1898, in Royal Commission on Liquor Licensing Laws, Minutes of Evidence, vol. 8. Parliamentary Papers 1899 (C. 9075), XXXIV, Q. 67,843 (p. 508); Susannah Mary Bailey, "'Teetotal and Proud': Preston and the Band of Hope Movement, 1847-1939" (M.A. thesis, University of Central Lancashire, 2019).
[93] John Simkin, "Temperance Society," *Spartacus Educational*. Earlier I mentioned a contemporary estimate, less than nine per cent of the adult population. The difference between the two figures is not great.
[94] McAllister, *Demon Drink? Temperance and the Working Class*.
[95] Sir Wilfrid Lawson, quoted in Dingle, *Campaign for Prohibition*, p. 206.
[96] Lambert, *Drink and Sobriety in Victorian Wales*, ch. 3, "The Temperance Society." As early as the 1850s, there were fourteen different Welsh-language temperance periodicals.
[97] Philip Snowden, *Socialism and Teetotalism* (1909), cited in Peter Catterell, *Labour and the Politics of Alcohol: The Decline of a Cause* (Institute of Alcohol Studies, 2014), p. 9.
[98] Catterell, *Labour and the Politics of Alcohol*, p. 10.
[99] It may be better to speak of evangelicalism. Many Anglicans and almost all Nonconformists were evangelicals. According to David W. Bebbington, evangelicalism was characterized by conversionism (being "born again"), activism (sharing the faith, notably in missionary work), biblicism (the Bible contains all important religious truths), and crucicentrism (the centrality of Christ's redeeming sacrifice on the Cross). *Evangelicalism in Modern Britain* (Unwin Hyman, 1989).
[100] David W. Bebbington, review of Dominic Erdozain, *The Problem of Pleasure: Sport, Recreation and the Crisis of Victorian Religion*, in *Reviews in History*, 23 Sept. 2010 (online).
[101] He was Robert Wilson Black. See the biography by Henry Townshend (1954).
[102] Other than Cardinal Manning, the best-known Catholic priest in the English temperance movement was James Nugent (1832-1905) who saw teetotalism as a way to improve the lot of Irish immigrants in Liverpool. Nugent's nephew Father Francis C. Hays (1870-1943) began a Catholic temperance revival in 1896. See the pamphlet by W.L. Bowditch, *Father Hays, the Apostle of Temperance* (Temperance Council of Churches, [c. 1923?]).
[103] National Temperance League's *Annual* (1881), pp. 76-77. In the 1880s the League of the Cross published four volumes of the *Catholic Temperance Magazine*.
[104] W.S. Blunt, manuscript "Secret Diaries," vol. 13 (1890), f. 250. Fitzwilliam Museum, Cambridge. I owe this reference to the late Norman Kelvin. Lady Carlisle's birth family was complicated religiously. For instance, one brother was a Muslim and another a Roman Catholic bishop.
[105] National Temperance League, *Annual* (1881), p. 101. T.E. Williams was a member of the executive committee of the National Temperance League.
[106] Burns, "Nonconformist Temperance Societies in England," in J.N. Stearns, ed., *Temperance in All Nations* (National Temperance Society and Publication House, 1893)) 1: 223.

[107] National Temperance League, *Annual* (1881), p. 175.

[108] *Ashgate Research Companion to World Methodism*, ed. William Gibson, Peter Forsaith, and Martin Wellings (Ashgate, 2013), pp. 373-74.

[109] Burns, "Nonconformist Temperance Societies in England," pp. 223-24.

[110] *United Temperance Gazette* (date missing), p. 142. Article was part of the Typical Organizations series.

[111] Sir R. Murray Hyslop, *The Centenary of the Temperance Movement, 1832-1932* (Independent Press, 1932), p. 49.

[112] In the early 1880s there were 105 abstainers out of the 527 Congregational ministers in Wales. National Temperance League's *Annual* (1881), p.74.

[113] Burns, "Nonconformist Temperance Societies in England," p. 222.

[114] The Bible Christian historian Thomas Shaw doubted that all the ministers were teetotal. Shaw, *The Bible Christians, 1815-1907* (Epworth Press, 1965), p. 53, cited in Shiman, *Crusade against Drink*, p. 57.

[115] Supplementing Bebbington, see National Temperance League, *Annual* (1908), p. 44; for the Free Methodists, *United Temperance Gazette*, Sept. 1898, p. 123; *Alliance News*, 16 Oct. 1896, p. 670. The New Church (Swedenborgian) organized a temperance society in 1880.

[116] David W. Bebbington, *The Nonconformist Conscience: Chapel and Politics, 1870-1914* (G. Allen & Unwin, 1982), p. 46. E.C. Urwin, *Methodism and Sobriety* (Epworth Press, 1945), pp. 50-51, reports the resolutions in 1897 (not 1898) and 1899. The 1897 resolution referred to "manufacturers of strong drink," That in 1899 was broader, "any person directly engaged in the Liquor Traffic."

[117] For Smith, see his memoirs, *From Memory's Storehouse* (S.W. Partridge, 1914). E. Tennyson Smith (1850-1925) illustrates how temperance united many parts of the English-speaking world. He worked for temperance in Australia, New Zealand and Canada as well as in Britain.

[118] *Brewers' Guardian*, 10 Dec. 1889, p. 392.

[119] *Licensed Trade News*, 22 June 1906, p.6.

[120] *Temperance Witness*, March 1897, p. 37. Harrison reported figures from two contemporary lists: in 1848 four percent of ministerial abstainers were Anglican priests, in 1866 this had grown to 22%. Harrison, *Drink and Victorians*, pp. 168. I was reminded of this by Frances Knight, "Recreation or Renunciation: Episcopal Interventions in the Drink Question in the 1890s," ch. 10 in Stewart J. Brown and others, eds., *Religion, Identity and Conflict in Britain* (Routledge, 2016), p. 161.

[121] Beginning in 1878, the Wesleyan Methodists created temperance societies that included both abstainers and non-abstainers, a structure similar to that of the CETS. Christopher Oldstone-Moore, *Hugh Price Hughes* (University of Wales Press, 1999), p. 76.

[122] G.W. Olsen, "Drink and the British Establishment--The Church of England Temperance Society, 1873-1919," p. 29 (typescript). I am grateful to Gerry Olsen for letting me see his unpublished book. The CETS succeeded a teetotal Anglican society founded in 1862. For the role of the Church other than that of the CETS, see John R. Greenaway, "Bishops, Brewers and the Liquor Question in England, 1890-1914," *Historical Magazine of the Protestant Episcopal Church* 53 no. 1 (1984): 61-

75; Knight, "Recreation or Renunciation: Episcopal Interventions in the Drink Question in the 1890s."

[123] Some in the drink trade threatened to reduce their contributions to the Church. The licensed trade estimated £250,000, either directly or indirectly coming from brewers and others in the drink business. *Licensed Trade News*, 6 May 1905, pp. 308-09.

[124] *Sir Wilfrid Lawson: A Memoir*, ed. George W.E. Russell (Smith Elder, 1909).

[125] John Newton, *W.S. Caine, M.P., A Biography* (James Nisbet, 1907).

[126] George B. Wilson. *Leif Jones, Lord Rhayader, Temperance Reformer and Statesman, 1862-1939, President of the United Kingdom Alliance, 1906-1932* (United Kingdom Alliance, [1948]. WorldCat reports only one American library and one British library as claiming to have a copy of this book.

[127] Hester (Whittaker) Reynolds (1882-1971).

CHAPTER TWO

STRATEGIES OF REFORM

There have been few new ideas in the history of temperance reform. Most of the reforms that dominated public debate in the late nineteenth and early twentieth centuries had reached Parliament in the 1860s and 1870s. When first proposed they nearly always aroused more opposition than support. Asquith once declared: "The history of the temperance question is the history of lost opportunities."[1]

In the earlier period a consensus developed in favor of one fundamental change in policy that in turn impacted the larger debate over drink licensing. At the zenith of free enterprise ideology almost everybody agreed that unlimited competition was undesirable in the retail sale of drink. By enacting a Tory backbencher's bill to end forty years of the free licensing of beer shops, Parliament in 1869 repudiated the principle of laissez-faire for alcohol.

Afterwards new beer house on-licenses were issued only at the discretion of the local licensing justices, as had already been true for licenses for public houses that sold both beer and spirits.[2] Pre-1869 beer houses had a legal right to renewal. Licenses for public houses and post-1869 beer houses were nominally for one year only, but in practice renewal was nearly automatic. As a part of the consensus against the proliferation of drink sellers, the magistrates refused most applications for new licenses. Often beer houses were marginally profitable hole-in-the-wall bars. It was the public houses that mattered, so the restrictive policy of the JP's created substantial monopoly values in public house property.[3]

In 1871 the Liberal Home Secretary, H.A. Bruce (1815-95), proposed a comprehensive licensing bill for England. Some might call his bill miscellaneous or even incoherent. It combined many of the approaches toward reform that would reappear over the next fifty years. Bruce wanted to reduce the number of licensed premises and their hours of sale, minimize the danger of the creation of large monopoly values, introduce popular control over licensing, impose penalties for the adulteration of beer, and guarantee good conduct in licensed houses, while appeasing existing license holders with a secure status during a transitional period. Under his bill a three-fifths' majority in a referendum of ratepayers could prevent justices from issuing new licenses in excess of a proportion of one per thousand inhabitants in urban areas and one per six hundred in rural areas.[4] The bill reduced the hours of sale statutorily and authorized a referendum that could reduce weekday hours further and impose Sunday closing. The bill attacked private profit in monopoly values by auctioning the available licenses to the highest bidder. As a concession to existing license holders the bill allowed them an initial license that carried a life of ten years and fixed license fees. The bill also proposed a force of special licensing inspectors.

The drink trade denounced the bill, the publicans and provincial brewers with characteristic vehemence. Conservative members of the House of Commons generally opposed it. Remembering the Hyde Park riots of 1855, the *Daily Telegraph* worried that restrictions on opening hours in London might mean: "we shall have street riots of the most formidable kind."[5] Prohibitionists lent only halfhearted support because Bruce had omitted any provision for a local option of prohibition.

When the Government withdrew the bill with the lame excuse that the parliamentary schedule was too crowded, moderate reformers blamed the prohibitionists. They mourned the abandonment of the licensing bill of 1871 as the loss of a great opportunity for drink reform and evidence that the prohibitionists made reform difficult because they would not compromise. Prohibitionists argued that they had not opposed the bill. Although they had asked for elimination from the bill of ten-year licenses, they had made it clear that it was not indispensable for their support. The prohibitionist W.S. Caine pointed out that he had convened the only public meeting in Liverpool in support of the bill.[6]

Bruce was to blame for inept management of a very complex bill. It did not help that Gladstone invested little political capital in it. "Unfortunately Gladstone cares for nothing but 'Free Trade,' [in licensing] which the House won't have, and I cannot get him really to interest himself in the subject [of licensing]."[7]

In the following year the Liberal Government introduced a much less ambitious bill that owed more to Lord Kimberley, the Colonial Secretary, than to Bruce.[8] Introduced in the House of Lords, it was enacted after amendments left it even more modest. One amendment killed the proposed special licensing inspectors, an idea that thereafter disappeared from Government bills.[9] Working-class drinkers regarded such inspectors as spies. In its final form the Licensing Act of 1872 reduced the hours of sales slightly, strengthened police powers over licensed premises, and altered administrative procedures. It made public intoxication a crime. Although the bill contained nothing drastic, it angered the drink trade as it resented any new restrictions. The organization of London publicans spent £1,700 in fighting the proposal.[10] In retrospect, the 1872 bill, coupled with the 1869 legislation that ended free licensing of beer shops, began a long period of increasing restrictions on the sale of beer.

The sociologist Henry Yeomans argues that "the Licensing Act 1872 markedly increased both the scale and scope of alcohol legislation." For instance, it included the first statutory age regulation. Pubs could not sell spirits to those under sixteen. Perhaps more important, it defined various forms of drunkenness that violated the law. Yeomans went on to argue that "the Licensing Act 1872 is better understood as a statutory framework allowing for a series of behavioural choices that are constructed in moral terms as either approved or condemned, right or wrong, or good or evil."[11]

Following the passage of the Licensing Act of 1872, the Liberal Party was defeated in the next general election. William Gladstone complained that his party had been "borne down in a torrent of gin and beer."[12] This was an exaggeration. At the time of the general election of 1874 the drink trade was ill organized and divided.[13] People engaged in the drink trade still could be elected to office as Liberals.[14] Owned by a licensed victuallers' benevolent society, the *Morning Advertiser* only slowly "drifted into the Tory camp" after many decades as a Liberal newspaper.[15]

The Tories respected the influence of the drink sellers at the polls, and when the Conservative Party took office, it sought to appease them. Benjamin Disraeli's ministry enacted the Licensing Act of 1875 that reduced the right of police entry, extended opening hours slightly, and withdrew from the provincial magistrates their discretionary power over hours.[16]

It would be a mistake to place a close alignment between the Conservative Party and the drink trade in the 1870s or even the 1880s.[17] A future leader of the party in the House of Commons was willing in 1884 to offer cautious support for temperance legislation at least in a private letter. "The majority of our men would be very glad to go as far as it is really practicable in the way of temperance legislation,--and individually I am quite prepared to support anything which experience shows will really forward the object we have in view."[18]

Moderate drinkers increasingly worried about excessive drinking by urban workingmen, but the controversy aroused by Bruce's licensing bills discouraged subsequent Governments from sponsoring major licensing reforms.[19] Moreover, beginning in 1877 and intensifying in the early 1880s, the Gospel Temperance or Blue Ribbon movement revived focus on moral suasion instead of legislation.[20] In the late 1870s and the early 1880s Parliament debated temperance reform only as private member's bills and resolutions deemed fortunate to get a symbolic second reading division.

Parliament enacted a beer duty in 1880 to replace the malt tax which farmers had disliked and Sabbatarian reforms for parts of the Celtic fringe: Sunday closing for Ireland other than its largest cities in 1878 and for all of Wales in 1881.[21] (Scotland had obtained statutory Sunday closing as early as 1853.) Until the late 1880s no Government dared to propose a major licensing bill, and until the first years of the twentieth century no Parliament enacted major licensing legislation affecting the consumption of drink in England.

Private members, mostly Liberals, kept the drink question before Parliament and the public. Some proposals embodied the views of only a handful of sympathizers other than the sponsoring M.P., others represented the program of an organized pressure group. In the first category Joseph Chamberlain's resolution in favor of what became called a Gothenburg scheme stands out.

In the 1860s the Swedish port of Gothenburg had pioneered the public management of the sale of liquor consumed on premises.[22] Bars that sold spirits and wine became the monopoly of semi-official philanthropic companies. Other Scandinavian towns adopted similar and sometimes more draconian schemes. For instance, Bergen in Norway discouraged prolonged drinking by forbidding chairs in barrooms. In Britain reformers called any plan a Gothenburg scheme if it provided non-commercial management of the retail sale of drink. Specifics could vary a great deal, but all British Gothenburg Schemes included beer unlike those in Scandinavia where the urban working class typically drank spirits. A number of British politicians and reformers hoped that public management companies, largely free of the temptation of profit, would stop pushing drinks on hesitant customers and would accept reforms that diminished sales such as reduced hours. Bruce had considered incorporating a Gothenburg scheme in his first licensing bill, but it was Chamberlain who brought the Gothenburg scheme before Parliament. The young Radical was one of Birmingham's Liberal MP's.

Earlier Chamberlain had supported a local option of prohibition out of a desire to replace the oligarchic authority of the justices of the peace with the principle of popular control. After losing a parliamentary election in which the drink trade had strongly opposed him, he dropped his advocacy of prohibition and took up the policy of public management.[23] Chamberlain believed that Gothenburg offered a practicable solution to the drink problem in large industrial cities such as his own Birmingham where the people were unlikely to vote for prohibition. It had the additional advantage of driving the drink trade out of politics. In the 1870s progressive towns supplied gas and water to the public. Why could they not also sell beer?

Chamberlain proposed public management in an article in the *Fortnightly Review* published in May 1876. After having visited Sweden to inspect Gothenburg's drink scheme, he organized local support in Birmingham from the Liberal caucus, the board of poor law guardians, the town council, clergymen and ministers, and temperance reformers. In March 1877, he introduced a resolution in the House of Commons to allow municipalities to purchase licensed houses compulsorily and manage them. He hoped to experiment with the scheme in Birmingham.

Outside of his home city of Birmingham, Chamberlain found few allies. Many temperance reformers feared that the profits derived from municipalization might give local government a vested interest in continuing the sale of drink. Sir Wilfrid Lawson (1829-1906), a prohibitionist who voted for Chamberlain's resolution, on the ground that it constituted a sincere attack on the drink trade, criticized the proposal in and out of Parliament as a dangerous irrelevancy. Drink was the problem, not who sold it.

Unsurprisingly the House of Commons rejected Chamberlain's proposal, and when a Select Committee of the House of Lords later offered cautious support, the Government ignored the recommendation. As a practical man, Chamberlain never again made the Gothenburg scheme a matter of priority, although he consented to attend a few conferences on its behalf when the Bishop of Chester revived the idea in the 1890s.[24] By then Chamberlain's relations with the licensed trade had warmed.[25]

On 1 October 1885, prior to the Home Rule schism, Chamberlain told an audience at Bradford that he voted for Lawson's Permissive Bill "not because I always agreed with his methods, but because I am anxious to sink differences in order to secure one common object and to attain popular control of a Traffic that is the cause of so much misery and crime."[26]

During his subsequent Liberal Unionist years Chamberlain cultivated good relations with the drink trade, although he nominally remained a temperance reformer. As a young Radical, he had ridiculed "beer and bible Tories," but in the last decades of his career he became a close ally of the Conservatives.

Unlike Chamberlain's bill most private members' proposals represented the sustained agitation of a pressure group outside Parliament. Preeminently this was the case for prohibition by Direct Local Veto, the most controversial issue in the politics of temperance reform. The principal prohibition lobby was founded in 1853 with the expressive name of the United Kingdom Alliance to Procure the Total and Immediate Legislative Suppression of the Traffic in All Intoxicating Liquors as Beverages.[27] The Alliance rejected licensing reform as inadequate. Since drink was innately evil its licensed sale must be ended. The business of selling drink did not deserve the respectable name of a trade. It should be called a traffic, the same as any vice operating outside the law. The prohibitionists called themselves the advanced temperance party in contrast with licensing reformers whose proposals sought to restrict, but not end, the sale of drink.[28] The temperance movement had its strongholds in England's industrial society, so it was appropriate that the Alliance made Manchester the location of its headquarters.[29]

The UKA agitated for national statutory prohibition for only a few years. It then put aside as politically impracticable its dream of a Maine law, the legislative prohibition of the sale of drink, named after the American state that had pioneered it in 1851. Four years after the founding of the Alliance it offered a compromise, prohibition by local option referendum.[30] Virtually all British prohibitionists adopted this new policy which sought to confer on electors the power to stop the licensed sale of drink in their localities. Prohibitionists realized that they were a minority, but they argued that advanced reformers constituted a majority in some districts, particularly in the north and west of England and in Scotland and Wales, and that many electors who drank would vote to close public houses in their own neighborhood. Non-abstainers could import drink for home consumption from other districts. Furthermore, prohibitionists argued that even localities that did not have a majority against licensing would benefit, since fear of the consequences of a bad reputation would force drink sellers to stop the most flagrant abuses such as the serving of intoxicated customers. Direct Local Veto became a symbol of the recognition of the legitimacy of teetotal values, an end in itself as well as a means to piecemeal prohibition.

A few members of the Alliance protested that the leaders of the UKA had "lowered the flag," sacrificed the principle for which the organization had been created out of shortsighted opportunism. In 1879, a youthful reformer reminded the annual meeting of the Alliance that it had been founded to promote the cause of prohibition, not that of local autonomy. T.P. Whittaker (1850-1919), the son of a pioneer teetotal evangelist, rejected the relevancy of local majorities on questions of morality.[31] Although always in principle a prohibitionist, the younger Whittaker later accepted a series of compromises.

A handful of militants continued to agitate in favor of a revival of the policy of statutory prohibition and of independence from ordinary political parties. In 1887, a dissident member of the Alliance, a Swedish-born American Axel Gustafson, proclaimed the existence of the National Prohibition Party for immediate and total national prohibition. It got virtually no support. At the turn of the century several similar prohibitionist political parties were organized in England and Scotland.[32] Such militants lived on the margin of the prohibition movement. In contrast, more typical prohibitionists in England and throughout the United Kingdom supported local option referendums as the best legislation obtainable and, as a result of years of rhetoric about the virtues of letting the people decide as a right of local self-government, virtually forgot about statutory prohibition. They regarded the Liberal Party as their natural home.

A local prohibition bill was introduced in the House of Commons for the first time in 1864.[33] For all practical purposes, it was an Alliance bill, although the MP who introduced it (Sir Wilfrid Lawson) drafted its provisions on his own.[34] The bill confined the plebiscite to the prohibition of retail sales in contrast with the kind of local option that the Alliance had contemplated in 1857 that would have prohibited the manufacture of alcohol too. Lawson's proposal was called the Permissive Prohibitory Bill or simply the Permissive Bill to emphasize that Parliament was only asked to authorize local voters to say yes or no to the licensing of the sale of drink. "The Bill was as free from detail as possible."[35] The bill justified the right of the electorate to suppress the drink trade on the ground that "the common sale of intoxicating liquors is a fruitful source of crime, immorality, pauperism, disease, insanity, and premature death, whereby not only the individuals who give way to drinking habits are plunged into misery but grievous wrong is done to the persons and property of Her Majesty's subjects at large, and the public rates and taxes are greatly augmented." Lawson made no promises that the Veto would extinguish the drink trade. "I 'expect' nothing and I hope for everything. I have always carefully guarded myself from prophesying what the people will do when they obtain the power of self-protection. But I know one thing--that they are entitled to have it."[36] A large nonpartisan majority in the House of Commons rejected Lawson's Permissive Bill in 1864 and again in every year from 1869 through 1876 (except in 1872 when there was a debate but no division) and finally in 1878.

In 1879, the year that Lawson became its president, the Alliance changed its parliamentary strategy. Lawson dropped his Permissive Bill in favor of a resolution, so that members of the House of Commons could vote on the principle underlying prohibition by local option referendum without committing themselves to details. In a letter to Gladstone, Lawson said that the use of a resolution would unite the Liberals behind a common temperance policy.[37] He borrowed most of the language of his resolution from a report that the Convocation of Canterbury had adopted in 1869. With studied ambiguity, Lawson's resolution urged: "That, inasmuch as the ancient and avowed object of Licensing the Sale of Intoxicating Liquors is to supply a public want, without detriment to the public welfare, this House is of opinion that a legal power of restraining the issue or removal of Licenses should be placed in the hands of the persons most deeply interested and affected, namely, the inhabitants themselves, who are entitled to protection from the injurious consequences of the present system, by some efficient measure of local option."

A Quaker politician, John Bright, who had criticized the Permissive Bill, claimed that it was he who had persuaded Lawson to adopt the new strategy of a resolution. Although Lawson denied this in his memoir, his letters to Bright late in 1878 and early in 1879 make the resolution look at least in part like a device to win over a prestigious critic. A few weeks after an off-the-record meeting between Bright and a UKA deputation on 9 October 1878, Lawson asked Bright for "a Holy Alliance" on behalf of a local option resolution.[38] The historian A.E. Dingle sees the Alliance shift to from a bill to a resolution as "largely determined by outside influences" and recognition that a private member's bill had little prospect of success.[39]

A concentration on general principles suited the Alliance. It had never officially drafted a bill of its own. It supported Local Veto bills without too much concern about legislative details. Many Alliance supporters had regretted provisions in Lawson's Permissive Bill, including a requirement for a two-thirds majority, understandable in the mid-1860s when prohibition was an American novelty but considered an excessively large majority by most prohibitionists in the late 1870s.

After the abandonment of the Permissive Bill, the UKA policy was called Direct Local Veto, Local Veto, or simply the Veto. The Alliance wanted a referendum limited to a simple choice between allowing licensing or not. For the Alliance, it was a distinctive application of the broader principles of local control or local option, although politicians often used all three terms interchangeably. An example of local option other than the Veto would be a licensing authority elected by the people or chosen by an elected local government council in place of one chosen by the appointed justices of the peace.[40] Local option often involved referendums, whether for prohibition or a reduction in the number of licensed houses or Sunday closing. Although Lawson's resolution did not explicitly provide for a Veto referendum, the UKA interpreted it as a call for the Alliance nostrum.

The House of Commons rejected Lawson's referendum when he first proposed it in 1879 and again in March 1880, but it got many more votes than the Permissive Bill ever had received. Although advanced Radicals generally had voted for the Permissive Bill, few others had, whereas about half of all Liberal MPs supported the resolution in the first two divisions. Only a single Conservative MP voted for the March 1880 resolution. After the Liberal Party won a general election, the House passed the resolution on 18 June 1880. Reinforced by many newly elected Radicals and Nonconformists, a large majority of the Liberals voted for the resolution, among them nineteen members of the Government. This Liberal consensus showed a concern over the effects of drink, a sympathy with the notion that local people should have more of a say over the licensing of its sale, resentment over the influence which the drink trade wielded in political life as a privileged monopoly, and a recognition that the drink question mattered for many voters. It did not mean an unequivocal and enthusiastic commitment to the UKA program of the Veto.

The next year, on 14 June 1881, Lawson introduced a new resolution that urged that the principle of the previous one be embodied into law. A majority in the House of Commons voted for it. On 27 April 1883, Lawson introduced a third resolution asserting that there was an urgent need for such a bill. It passed with an improved majority and unlike the earlier resolutions received the official endorsement of the Liberal Government.[41] A Liberal Government bill on the lines of Direct Local Veto had become imaginable, although Gladstone probably thought only of an elected licensing authority making the decision and not of a plebiscite.

By then Lawson had completed the most successful years of his leadership. Whether out of tactics or temperament or ill health, he played a smaller role thereafter.[42] For instance, he was not chosen president when a committee of temperance MPs was organized in 1884. Nor did he play a major role in the umbrella organization of advanced temperance societies, the National Temperance Federation, set up in the same year. He was seriously ill in 1885. His political influence declined after he opposed a parliamentary memorial honoring General Gordon who had died fighting the Mahdi in the Sudan.

In 1891, in a final achievement Lawson helped squeeze a public commitment to Local Veto out of a reluctant Gladstone and to persuade him to be silent about compensation of dispossessed license holders despite Gladstone's sympathy for such a compromise.

Lawson's absolute commitment to the Veto, combined with his holding a parliamentary seat and a baronet's aristocratic prestige, had earned him the presidency of the UKA in 1879, an office that he held until his death in 1906.[43] Originally the Alliance saw Lawson as a stopgap as president, but he became enormously popular. Sir Wilfrid Lawson became the parliamentary symbol of the United Kingdom Alliance and Direct Local Veto.

As president Lawson strengthened the identification of the UKA with the Radical section of the Liberal Party. Perhaps this was his major contribution. In his unpublished autobiography, Herbert Gladstone (who quarreled with Lawson over the Veto) complimented him: "He was one of the few men who combined uncompromising adhesion to his own views with consistent loyalty to the [Liberal] party."[44]

Although president for over a quarter century, he never controlled the Alliance machinery. Nor did the middle-class officials and executive council in Manchester control him. "His miraculous political insensitivity" was joined with an "exasperatingly attractive" personality.[45] By the time of his death, he clearly was a failure.

Lawson was more than a prohibitionist. A journalist who later edited Lawson's memoir, described him in 1900 as "chiefly known as a pro-Boer" while "anti-everything else."[46] Lawson was an all-around Radical gadfly: pro-Home Rule before Gladstone endorsed Irish self-government, anti-militarist and anti-imperialist, friendly to women's and universal suffrage, advocate of the abolition of the House of Lords, opposed to the privileges of his own Church of England, and against all sorts of other things that a Radical should be against and in favor of the things that a Radical should favor.[47] Ending the parliamentary adjournment for Derby day, that enabled M.P.s to attend the races, became one of his symbolic crusades. An enemy of all privilege, he loved "to fight publicans, parsons, and peers."[48] Lawson was a zealous Liberal partisan, although for him prohibition came first.[49] In 1881 Queen Victoria described him in her journal as "one of *the* worst Radicals."

His were the politics of moral principle. Lawson had been reared in an evangelical Nonconformist household but as an adult returned to the Church of England in which he had been baptized. Totally without ambition, he never held Government office despite his long years in the House of Commons. In the year of his death, he turned down a privy councillorship. The only honor that he valued was his seat in the House of Commons. As he left an estate of about a quarter million pounds, he could afford independence. Surprisingly, in a memorial notice a fellow militant spoke of Lawson's "heroic self-conquest of a nervous temperament."[50] No puritan, in a predominantly middle class and sometimes stuffy temperance movement, he stood out as a wealthy Cumberland landlord who had inherited a baronetcy in 1867, owned about 8,000 acres, and was known in his county for his pack of fox-hounds and splendid horses, one of them named Radical. Lawson loved playing billiards, a game that provoked the suspicion of many Nonconformists. For many years, the teetotal baronet served strong drink to his guests.

He had a reputation as a wit. For instance, when he doubted that James Bryce would agree to preside over the Alliance's annual meeting, he pointed out: "he is a highly educated man and such are generally keen supporters of drink!"[51] When he asked for an anti-drink resolution to be drafted he asked "that it should be (like good Ale!) *strong* and *clear*."[52] No killjoy, he composed comic verse at his seat in the House of Commons. For instance, when a Unionist Government proposed instituting prohibition in the African colony of Bechuanaland, Lawson wrote: "The Bechuana men are black/So Prohibition's right;/But who dare England's creed attack. That white men *may* get Tight?"[53] Lawson's comic verse falls a bit flat today. A better way of seeing his amiable and witty personality is to read his anecdote-rich memoir edited by George W.E. Russell. Written in 1901-1904, it ended with Lawson's defeat in the Khaki general election of 1900. It contains generous excerpts from Lawson's otherwise lost journal that often includes jibes of the time. Here is an example: "We got through the Session without going to war with anyone in order to promote Christianity and civilization."

Contemporaries (and the historian A.E. Dingle) have criticized Lawson for his mixture of doctrinal rigidity and lack of tactical initiative. In a book review Paul McHugh derided Lawson's "silliness."[54] He refused to organize a coalition between the Alliance and the moderate reformers on behalf of a compromise program combining licensing reform with local option prohibition. His attitude reflected a kind of realism. In a favorite analogy, he explained what to others seemed like impractical rigidity: a man who stays on the straight road doesn't get lost. He disliked action for the sake of action. "I never see *much* good in Deputations to ministers."[55] Dingle regards Lawson as one of the Alliance's moderates in the 1880s.[56]

Lawson knew that compromises divided as well as united, and he questioned their utility unless they came from a Government capable of action. The only principle holding together the United Kingdom Alliance was prohibition by Direct Local Veto. Lawson argued that the UKA had to work solely as "an anti-licensing organization." Fending off the idea of the Alliance joining with other temperance reformers in a broad reform program, he pointed out: "directly as discussion arises as to the how, when and where Licensing should be carried on, we find that there are about as many differences of opinion amongst us as there are members of our association."[57] As individuals most members of the Alliance supported some kind of licensing reform.

Near the end of his long career, Lawson told the Alliance general secretary: "the Alliance is much better employed in forming Prohibition public opinion than in suggesting and proposing the details of a measure." He added: "leave legislation to the legislators, who, if we are wise, we can make to do our bidding, *i.e.* make them advance on the right lines of policy without making ourselves responsible for their legislative details."

"Whenever there has been a decent bill (and a perfect Bill is impossible) we have rallied well in its support."[58]

Lawson was the independent-minded and sometimes undisciplined conscience of the advanced temperance party. His was a prophetic style of leadership, passionately committed to a few general principles, uncomfortable with negotiation over technical details, sanguine about a moral awakening which would transform the apathetic into activists, and intermixing intervals of comparative inactivity with vehement declarations of anathema (or, more rarely, an imprimatur) for legislative proposals regarding drink. He was a success on the speakers' platform of a great temperance meeting more than at the House of Commons or in organizational politics. Yet it is not easy to imagine that there was anyone else (before the rise of T.P. Whittaker in the late 1890s) who could have headed the Alliance with greater success. Other possible leaders had their own weaknesses, whether of policy or of personality, of social-economic status or of political circumstance. Whatever his limitations, Lawson was the necessary man.

Lawson thought that ending the sale of drink was the only true temperance reform. He voted for Sunday closing when it came before Parliament, but, having little use for half measures (and not being a Sabbatarian), he irreverently said that if he had the opportunity to prevent the sale of drink on only one day he would choose Saturday. More drink was sold that day than on the Sabbath.[59] Similarly, when a friend asked him what he thought about making it illegal for women to work as barmaids, Lawson replied: "the way to get rid of barmaids is to abolish the bars."[60]

Despite his dislike of the drink trade Lawson declined to join attacks upon it that he regarded as unfair. He could not support complaints about the adulteration of beer (which he said were unfounded), and he did not see tied houses as any worse than other public houses. Pointing out that the licensing law required that publicans be persons of good character, "a requirement that other retailers did not have to meet," he did not waste his time deriding the drink sellers. It was the product that they sold which was evil. A hater of drink and not of drink traders, Lawson counted a Liberal brewer among his parliamentary friends. According to Lawson's memoir, M.T. Bass told him: "'I'll settle a beer a day on you for life, if you'll give up the Permissive Bill.' To which I replied that 'I couldn't do it under a barrel'."[61] When Gladstone said that the drink trade had its high-priests and hierarchy, Lawson dubbed his friend as "Archbishop Bass."

The great symbolic victory that the prohibitionists had achieved in 1883 in their campaign to win the Liberal Party for Direct Local Veto had not been inevitable. Virtually no teetotalers and few enthusiastic Vetoists sat on the Liberal front bench then or later. Left to themselves the Liberal leaders would have offered a temperance program little more drastic than what their Conservative rivals accepted. For instance, in 1886, prior to the Home Rule split, Joseph Chamberlain as President of the Local Government Board drafted a bill which would have transferred the licensing powers of the magistrates to elected parish, district, and county councils, and would have allowed license holders compensation for renewal in cases when a reduction in numbers, rather than wrongdoing, was the cause of the loss of the license.[62] The bill was not presented to Parliament.

Bit-by-bit, the Veto became Liberal policy. It did so because it was supported by a well-organized pressure group (the advanced temperance party dominated by the UKA) and the one that those party activists who cared the most wanted. Soon the Veto acquired another advantage: it was the only kind of temperance reform with an ardent champion within the party leadership, Sir William Harcourt.

According to Harcourt, Direct Local Veto was supposed to help the Liberal Party by arousing the enthusiasm of its Nonconformist provincial cadres. He told Gladstone that the "Temperance Party form an important, perhaps the most important, section of the Liberal Party."[63] A veteran prohibitionist claimed that in every constituency teetotalers (whom he equated with Veto advocates) comprised at least thirty per cent of the active Liberal workers.[64] Following the redress of their religious grievances, Nonconformists expressed continued resentment of the Anglican-dominated social order through the politics of moral reform. At the end of the nineteenth century the Liberals flew the banner of advanced temperance reform to attract Nonconformist support. As Harcourt bluntly explained, "Temperance is the backbone of the Liberal Party *vice* [the religious disabilities of] Nonconformity retired."[65] After the Home Rule schism, the Gladstonian Liberals needed policies that appealed to electors who might otherwise support the Liberal Unionists.

Sir William Harcourt acted as Lawson's chief ally in the party leadership. This was a surprise. Previously Harcourt had favored education and not compulsion in dealing with heavy drinking. He regarded it a mistake to enact laws that were ahead of public opinion. He liked a glass of wine and declared in 1869: "I should not think of imposing on others what I should deem a hardship to myself."[66] Harcourt had been a libertarian critic of the mild Licensing Act of 1872 who sneered, in his annual Oxford constituency speech, 30 December 1872, about the kind of "grand-maternal Government which ties nightcaps on a grown-up nation by Act of Parliament."[67] Speaking at the Oxford Town Hall in 1872, he opposed "petty molestation and irritating dictation, whether by a class or by a majority. I am against forbidding a man to have a glass of beer if he wants a glass of beer."[68] One of Harcourt's biographers sees the beginning of his conversion to Local Veto happening about the time that he visited Lawson in October 1881.[69]

Sir Charles Dilke marveled at Harcourt's conversion to Local Veto, "a curious intellectual phenomenon, this development of a belated conviction in a mind hitherto essentially opportunistic."[70] Harcourt attributed his change of mind to his practical experience with the consequences of drink while Home Secretary. He voted for the first of Lawson's successful local option resolutions soon after he had taken charge of the Home Office.[71] His enemies sometimes belittled his support for the Veto as an act of revenge after a Tory brewer had defeated him for re-election for his old seat at Oxford.

Although Harcourt's ability in debate in the House of Commons was real, he was not a popular man among his colleagues in the Liberal leadership who found his temper grating and rude.[72] His style was often "hectoring & bullying," mixed with threats of resignation if he did not get his own way.[73] In 1886 Balfour described Harcourt "as dogmatic, as blustering, and (to do him justice) as amusing as ever."[74] His Liberal colleague, Lord Kimberley, later described Harcourt as "utterly without principle, an *arrant* coward and a blustering bully."[75] A biographer more sympathetically characterized him as "a boisterous larger than life Falstaffian figure."[76] In a colorful review another historian (Martin Pugh) described Harcourt as "intelligent, cultured and well-read but also robust and aggressive, and in fact a … bully towards colleagues and opponents alike … impulsive, condescending, larger-than-life … a brilliant public speaker who enjoyed attacking his own party as much as his opponents … unable to resist the temptation to be funny and flippant … gave the impression of enjoying the game too much, hence the accusations of lawyerly opportunism."[77]

In private arguments both Harcourt and Lawson put political expediency to the fore. In April 1883 Harcourt warned Gladstone that there would be dissatisfaction in the party, "if we do not give [the resolution] of Lawson a substantial support."[78] In the following January he characterized the need for Government action on local option as "very urgent."[79] At the annual meeting of the Alliance in 1883 Lawson and the other UKA leaders faced a revolt led by the Birmingham auxiliary that had lost patience with the Liberal Party. In April 1884 Lawson told Harcourt that the Government should introduce a Local Veto bill even if it did not know whether it could proceed with it. He offered to cooperate with whatever supplementary licensing reforms the Government considered desirable. His people would accept whatever kind of licensing authority the Government might propose to replace the justices of the peace.[80] When the Government did nothing,

Lawson complained to Harcourt in December, adding that "no one can say that I or my friends have been unduly pressing." He coupled his disclaimer with a warning. Unless Harcourt assured Lawson that there would be a Government bill, he would move a new resolution condemning any further delay. Lawson insisted that a Veto bill was politically expedient: the Reform Act of 1884 had enfranchised few additional publicans as they already had been electors, but had conferred the vote on "thousands and thousands of the publicans' enemies."[81] In January 1885 Harcourt appealed to Gladstone to reward the "very patient" support of the temperance reformers, "an important perhaps the most important section of the Liberal Party." "We have given them good words but nothing else and it is not unreasonable that they should expect some better butter for their parsnips."[82]

Unfortunately for Lawson and Harcourt, the Grand Old Man of Liberal politics did not favor drastic temperance legislation. In the 1860s he had sponsored the creation of grocers' licenses that temperance reformers regarded as an enticement of women to drink. He was one of the last of the Liberal free traders who had favored the issue of unlimited numbers of licenses: competition would solve the drink problem. He appears to have regarded occasional drunkenness among the laboring classes as inevitable and relatively harmless.[83] During his Midlothian campaign he had refused to give a specific pledge to the advanced temperance party and had suggested that license holders who lost their licenses because of a change in public policy should be compensated, "if they can make good their case."

Gladstone said (in tortuously ambiguous language): "in that principle [of local option] I do not see myself anything that is justly to be condemned." The timing for practical legislation depended on public opinion.[84] In 1881 Gladstone voted for Lawson's resolution and spoke for it. He claimed then to have been a consistent supporter of the principle of local control who had voted against the earlier resolutions out of a dislike of a Government supporting a general proposition without having a plan to give it statutory effect. Other business and parliamentary obstruction continued to make it impossible for the Government to do anything and he interpreted anything as meaning the creation of elected licensing authorities.[85]

Gladstone resisted the agitation for Local Veto. When Harcourt presented the case for a Veto bill in 1885, Gladstone expressed surprise that the Government had ever committed itself to Lawson's resolution. "I do not recollect that [the] Government had *supported* the Resolution for Local Option;" "did not Hartington and I hold off?"[86] After Gladstone had retired from the party leadership in the mid-1890s and so had regained his freedom, he publicly questioned the practicability of prohibition by Local Veto, criticized the reform favored by most moderate reformers (the reduction in the number of public houses) as unlikely to diminish intemperance, and declared his sympathy for a Scandinavian scheme of eliminating the profit motive from the retail sale of drink.[87] In reaction, Harcourt angrily reminded a fellow Cabinet Minister that in 1883 the G.O.M. had pulled at his coat tails to tell him to say that in supporting Lawson's resolution he spoke for the Government. Glumly he concluded that "at heart [Gladstone] has always abhorred temperance."[88] More accurately, temperance reform for Gladstone did not mean Local Veto or any of the schemes dear to the hearts of most reformers. As happened so often on social questions which they did not regard as of first-class importance, Gladstone and most of his colleagues in the Liberal leadership had reluctantly followed the initiative of those with strong opinions and which provincial party activists wanted.

Notes

[1] Arthur Sherwell, *Drink Peril in Scotland* (Oliphant, Anderson, and Ferrier, 1903), p. 23. Quoting Asquith at Edinburgh in 1901.

[2] In 1882 the magistrates acquired the power to reject applications for new beerhouse off-licenses, that is, for beer to consumed off premises.

[3] For a revisionist explanation of the growth of tied houses (owned or controlled by brewers), see Gutzke, *Protecting the Pub*. pp. 19-20.

[4] Subsequent reduction schemes provided a ratio between licensed premises and population as the maximum allowed. For Bruce, the ratio was a minimum before local electors would be asked if they wanted to veto additional licenses. Bruce believed that if there was a large reduction in numbers, raising the value of surviving licenses, licenses should be allocated by bidding. Aberdare [Bruce] to his son-in-law Champion Russell, 16 May 1890, in *Letters of the Rt. Hon. Henry Austen Bruce, G.C.B., Lord Aberdare of Duffyrn* (2 vols., printed for private circulation, 1902) 2: 275. For a brief account, see John Greenaway, *Drink and British Politics since 1830* (Palgrave Macmillan, 2003), pp. 31-33.

[5] 10 May 1871, p. 4, quoted in Harrison, *Peaceable Kingdom* (Oxford University Press, 1985). p. 142.

[6] W.S. Caine, "The Attitude of the Advanced Temperance Party," *Contemporary Review* 69 (January 1893): 51.

[7] Bruce to his wife, 14 Dec. 1871, *Letters*, 1: 318-19. Bruce's colleague, Lord Kimberley, believed that Bruce's bill was disastrous for the Liberal Party. "Licensing Bill wh. I was always opposed is enough to destroy us utterly. Dizzy [Disraeli] knows what a prodigious advantage the rage of the publicans gives the Tory Party." *Journal of John Wodehouse First Earl of Kimberley, 1862-1902* (Camden Fifth Series), ed. Angus Hawkins and John Powell (Cambridge University Press, for the Royal Historical Society, 1998), p. 259.

[8] Greenaway, *Drink and British Politics since 1830,* p 34. See Ethel Drus, ed., *A Journal of Events during the Gladstone Ministry, 1868-74,"* by John, first Earl of Kimberley (Camden Miscellaney, 21 (1958): 29-30.

---

[9] In the 1890s the Westminster bill and a bill sponsored by the CETS included licensing inspectors.

[10] *Licensed Victuallers' Year Book* (1874), p. 141.

[11] Yeomans, *Alcohol and Moral Regulation Public Attitudes, Spirited Measures and Victorian Hangovers* (Policy Press, 2014), pp. 74-75, 86.

[12] Gladstone to his brother Robertson, 6 February 1874. Quoted in John Morley, *Life of William Ewart Gladstone* (Macmillan, 1903) 2: 495.

[11] David W. Gutzke, "Rhetoric and Reality: The Political Influence of British Brewers, 1832-1914," *Parliamentary History* 9 (May 1990).

[14] For instance, in Leeds a Liberal licensed victualler was elected to the town council for East ward in 1877. He declined to stand for re-election in 1883. A wine and spirit merchant who owned many public houses had been a Liberal member of the Leeds council since 1871. He was defeated in 1883. "They were the last members of the trade among the [Leeds] Liberal councillors." E.P. Hennock, *Fit and Proper Persons: Ideal and Reality in Nineteenth-Century Urban Government* (Edward Arnold, 1973), p. 217. A dwindling number of English brewers were elected to the House of Commons as Liberals as late as 1906.

[15] Stephen Koss, *The Rise and Fall of the Political Press in Britain: The Nineteenth Century* (University of North Carolina Press, 1981), p. 199.

[16] Brian Harrison, *Drink and the Victorians*, ch. 12; Paul Smith, *Disraelian Conservatism and Social Reform* (Routledge and Kegan Paul, 1967), pp. 145-48, 166-71, 189-90, 208-13; H.J. Hanham, *Elections and Party Management: Politics in the Time of Disraeli and Gladstone* (Longmans,1959), pp. 22-25.

[17] After a treaty lowered tariffs on French wine, Gladstone sponsored legislation that opened the wine trade in England by offering wine merchants excise licenses over which the licensing justices had only limited authority. Harrison, *Drink and the Victorians*, pp. 228-31. Licensed grocers became identified with the Liberal Party.

[18] W.H. Smith to Lord Cairns, 13 March 1884, quoted in Greenaway, *Drink in British Politics since 1830*, p. 43.

[19] David M. Fahey, "Worrying about Drink," *Brewery History* 166 (Summer 2016).

[20] Lilian Lewis Shiman, "The Blue Ribbon Army: Gospel Temperance in England," *Historical Magazine of the Protestant Episcopal Church* 50 (1981).

[21] In 1906 the Sunday opening hours at the exempted Irish cities were reduced from five to three. For Wales, see W.R. Lambert, "The Welsh Sunday Closing Act, 1881," *Welsh History Review* 6 (1972): 161-89.

[22] Gutzke, *Protecting the Pub*, pp. 50-51.

[23] When John Morley reproached Chamberlain for voting for Lawson's Permissive Bill, Chamberlain defended his vote in a letter dated 20 November 1876. "There is much in what you say about [the weaknesses of] the Permissive Bill, yet as a matter of *policy* I am convinced that I am right. Nothing can be done *without* the Alliance— if they were actively hostile as they have hitherto been to all similar proposals, I could not hope to succeed." Quoted in D.A. Hamer, *The Politics of Electoral Pressure: A Study in the History of Victorian Reform Agitations* (Harvester Press, 1977), p. 338 n. 68.

[24] James B. Brown, "The Temperance Career of Joseph Chamberlain, 1870-1877: A Study in Political Frustration," *Albion* 4 (1972): 29-44. Brown claimed to have

completed a UCLA doctoral dissertation on the Liberal Party and temperance, 1880-1895, which he hoped to extend to 1914 before publication. He gave me his book's TOC, mostly topical such as a chapter on drink and the Exchequer. The dissertation was never completed. Nor was the book. Brown's articles remain useful.

[25] After Chamberlain broke with Gladstone over Irish Home Rule, he became friendly with the drink trade. On the eve of Liberal Unionist secession, he was not. For instance, he refused to answer trade test questions. Replying to Henry C. Edwards, general secretary of the Birmingham and District Licensed Victuallers Friendly and Protection Society, 12 Sept. 1885, Chamberlain said: "I am not prepared to admit the right of any external organization to interfere between myself and those whom I hope to represent in the next Parliament." *Brewers' Guardian*, 22 Sept. 1885, p. 304.

[26] "The Chamberlain Brew: A Study in Sops," *Daily Argus*, 6 April 1893, p. 2 (second pink edition). Bodleian, Harcourt MS 159.

[27] Since it sought to suppress "Intoxicating Liquors as Beverages," it accepted sacramental and medical use of alcohol, although some reformers rejected that too. Despite calling itself the United Kingdom Alliance, it was in fact an organization for England and Wales. In addition to discussion of the Alliance by Brian Harrison, see A.E. Dingle, *The Campaign for Prohibition in Victorian England: The United Kingdom Alliance, 1872-1895* (Rutgers University Press, 1980); and Hamer, *Politics of Electoral Pressure*, which includes five chapters on the Alliance.

[28] In this context, party did not mean a political party. The temperance party had the same meaning as the temperance movement and the advanced temperance party the same as the prohibitionist movement.

[29] Manchester was more than the Alliance headquarters. It was where the organization raised much of its funds, three times as much as in London in 1873-74. Harrison, *Peaceable Kingdom*, p. 130.

[30] For late nineteenth-century justifications of the referendum, see R.J. Williams and J.R. Greenaway, "The Referendum in British Politics: A Dissenting View," *Parliamentary Affairs* 28 no. 3 (1974), especially pp. 251-54. See also Greenaway's doctoral dissertation, "The Local Option Question in British Politics, 1864-1914" (University of Leeds, 1974). Effective in 1920, legislation enacted in 1913 authorized localities in Scotland to hold votes for a reduction in the number of licensed premises or their complete elimination. These polls were abolished in 1976. In 1961 Sunday closing in Wales, mandatory since 1881, became subject to local votes. In 2003 the right to vote for Sunday closing in Wales was repealed.

[31]. T. O. Whittaker, Annual Meeting, in *Alliance News*, 25 Oct. 1879, p. 676. When Whittaker spoke, there were "signs of impatience" in the audience.

[32] The second National Prohibition Party was organized in 1899, while the National Independent Tempernce Party was formed in 1905. The Scottish Prohibition Party, organized in 1901, was more successful than the parallel English parties. Edwin Scrymgeour defeated Winston Churchill in 1922 for the parliamentary seat at Dundee. He was the only prohibition party candidate ever elected to the House of Commons, as distinguished from prohibition supporters who were elected as Liberals or Labour.

[33] In 1863 Lawson had moved a resolution in favor of changing the licensing law.

---

[34] There is no modern biography of Lawson, perhaps because his papers were destroyed in a fire in 1918. G.W.E. Russell published a memoir that drew on Lawson's manuscript journal destroyed in the house fire. Russell also contributed a chapter on Lawson in his *Portraits of the Seventies* (T.F. Unwin, 1909) and the original entry for Lawson in the *Oxford Dictionary of National Biography* that David M. Fahey revised. Russell, ed., *Sir Wilfrid Lawson: A Memoir* (Smith Elder, 1909). See also the entry in Harrison, *Dictionary of British Temperance Biography* (Society for the Study of Labour History, 1973).

[35] Henry Carter, *The English Temperance Movement: A Study in Objectives* (Epworth Press, 1933), vol. 1, *The Formative Period, 1830-99*, p. 170. Militant prohibitionists complained that Carter's book had weakened the temperance movement by drawing attention to its old divisions. Yielding to these complaints (and the merger of his Methodist denomination with another that favored prohibition), Carter never published his second volume.

[36] Lawson to editor, 5 Sept. 1892, in *Speaker*, 10 Sept. 1892, p. 322.

[37] Lawson to Gladstone, 11 Jan. 1879. BL, Add. Ms. 44465, ff. 39-41.

[38] *Sir Wilfrid Lawson: A Memoir*, p. 145. See Lawson to Bright, 15 Sept., 1 Nov. 1878, 2 Jan. 1879. British Library, Bright papers, Add. Ms. 43389 ff. 289-94, 299-304, 312-15. Also see *Diaries of John Bright*, ed. R.A.J. Walling (Cassell, 1930), p. 413.

[39] Dingle, *Campaign for Prohibition*, p. 70.

[40] *Alliance News,* 24 June 1892, pp. 408-09; *Sir Wilfrid Lawson: A Memoir*, p. 76.

[41] Harcourt argued that Lawson's resolution was primarily a local government matter. He added that "if we do not give Lawson a substantial support there will be great dissatisfaction in the Party". Harcourt to Gladstone, 26 April 1883. British Library, W.E. Gladstone papers, Add. Ms. 44,198 ff. 48-51.

[42] On Lawson's chronic ill-health, see, for instance, John Slack to James Whyte, 29 Oct. 1889, in Alliance minutes, 6 Nov. 1889.

[43] Russell, *Sir Wilfrid Lawson: A Memoir* (1909).

[44] British Library, Herbert Gladstone papers. Add. Ms. 46118.

[45] Clyde Binfield, "Temperance and the Cause of God," *History* 57 (October 1972): 406.

[46] Russell, ed., *Sir Wilfrid Lawson: A Memoir*, p. 256, quoting his own article in the *Pilot*, 13 Oct. 1900. See also Graham Neville, *Radical Churchman: Edward Lee Hicks and the New Liberalism* (Clarendon Press, 1998), p. 133. For Lawson and foreign affairs, see Terry Carrick, "Wilfrid Lawson: Attitudes and Opinions on Britain's Imperial and Foreign Policy (1868-1892)" (Ph.D. dissertation, Sheffield Hallam University, 2007); Thomas William Heyck, "Studies in Late-Victorian Anti-Imperialism" (M.A. thesis, Rice University, 1962). Heyck saw hatred of war as the key to Lawson's dislike of imperialism.

[47] As a young man, Lawson like his father had been a Nonconformist. For Lawson as one of the most militant pro-Boers, see John W. Auld, "The Liberal Pro-Boers," *Journal of British Studies* 14 no. 2 (May 1975). For Lawson's radical views on imperial and foreign policy, see Carrick, "Wilfrid Lawson's Attitudes and Opinions on Britain's Imperial and Foreign Policy (1868-1892)."

[48] Lawson to Harcourt, 20 July 1886. Bodleian, Harcourt MS 215 f. 116. I am

grateful to Viscount Harcourt for allowing me to consult the papers of Sir William Vernon Harcourt. I began with the trunks at the family home.

[49] His son, the third baronet also named Sir Wilfrid, served in Parliament from 1910 to his resignation in 1916. He political views were similar to those of his father.

[50] Joseph Malins, in *Good Templars' Watchword*, 7 July 1906, p. 315.

[51] Lawson to McDougall, 29 May 1894. Alliance minutes, 30 May 1894.

[52] Lawson to McDougall, 29 January 1889, Alliance minutes, 30 January 1889.

[53] Sir Wilfrid Lawson and F. Carruthers Gould, *Cartoons in Rhyme and Line* (T. Fisher Unwin, 1905), p. 108.

[54] Paul McHugh, reviewing Dingle, *The Campaign for Prohibition in Victorian England*, in *Social History* 7 no. 2 (May 1982): 245.

[55] Lawson to Whyte, 13 Nov. 1892. Alliance minutes, 16 Nov. 1892.

[56] Dingle, *Campaign for Prohibition*, p. 93. The Alliance militants were led by people such as the newspaper publisher and Liberal politician William Saunders (1823-95).

[57] Lawson to Harcourt, 30 Sept. 1888. Bodleian, Harcourt MS 216, fol. 107.

[58] Lawson to James Whyte, 3 Jan. 1901. Alliance minutes, 9 Jan. 1901.

[59] When it seemed likely that there would be complaints about not making Sunday closing a question for local votes, Lawson said that he: "will do my very best to get the ardent Sunday people to be reasonable. It is a *great* pity that they are not already." Lawson to Wright, 25 Feb. 1893. Bodleian, Harcourt papers, MS145.

[60] Lawson to Hicks, 10 May 1896. Quoted in J.H. Fowler, *The Life and Letters of Edward Lee Hicks (Bishop of Lincoln, 1910-1919)* (Christophers, 1922), p.198.

[61] Russell, *Sir Wilfrid Lawson: A Memoir*, p. 62. For many years he provided drink to his guests. His wines were excellent. 3 Hansard 232 c. 1926 (14 March 1877). He later risked losing important visitors by denying them wine. Inviting Harcourt to visit him on his way to Scotland, Lawson warned him: "The establishment conducted *now* on strictly Temperance lines." Lawson to Harcourt, 24 Nov. 1897. Stanton Harcourt, Harcourt papers, uncatalogued when consulted.

[62] Joseph Chamberlain, *Political Memoir, 1880-92*, ed. C.H.D. Howard (Greenwood Press, 1975), p. 193. For Chamberlain's support for compensation while he was a member of Gladstone's government, see Chamberlain to Dawson Burns, 18 March 1886, University of Birmingham, Joseph Chamberlain papers JC 6/5/3/5.

[63] Harcourt to Gladstone, 18 January 1885. BL, W.E. Gladstone papers, Add. Ms. 44199, f. 174. Earlier he called local option "a very urgent business." Harcourt to Gladstone, 21 Jan. 1884. BL, W.E. Gladstone papers, Add, Ms. 44199, f. 3.

[64] Caine to Harcourt, 2 Aug. 1892. Bodleian, Harcourt MS 220, f. 124. See also Caine in *Westminster Gazette*, 28 May 1895, reprinted in *Alliance News*, 14 June 1895, p. 379.

[65] Harcourt to John Morley, 10 June 1888. Bodleian, Harcourt MS 17, f. 35. Quoted with minor changes in A.G. Gardiner, *The Life of Sir William Harcourt* (Constable, 1923), 2: 105. For a recent biography, see Patrick Jackson, *Harcourt and Son: A Political Biography of Sir William Harcourt, 1827 1904* (Fairleigh Dickinson University Press, 2004); and for his son and personal secretary, *Loulou: Selected Extracts from the Journals of Lewis Harcourt (1880-1895),* ed. Patrick Jackson (Fairleigh Dickinson University Press, 2006). Arnold Morley told Gladstone that

Harcourt believed that the drink question attracted voters without interest in other parliamentary questions. BL, W.E. Gladstone papers, Add. Ms. 44254, ff. 67-68. Morley to Gladstone 1 Jan. 1890 [actually 1891]. Morley believed that a proposal for Direct Local Veto would appeal to urban voters. Morley to Gladstone, 20 Dec. 1890.

[66] Gardiner, *Life of Harcourt* 1: 210.

[67] Quoted in Gardiner, *Life of Harcourt*, 1: 240; and Jackson, *Harcourt and Son*, p. 45. Despite this 1872 remark, Harcourt previously had been critical of an alliance between the Conservatives and the drink trade. In a speech at the Corn Hall, Oxford, on 31 Aug. 1868, he told his audience: "I have said that the Tory Party have made no declaration of public principle. But if they have no particular public principle, they have in its place great faith in the public house (laughter). One of the great difficulties in these days, when the Tories have thrown over their old principles and displayed a great affection for democracy, is to find out what they believe in, but, as far as I can ascertain, the only thing which the Constitutionalists really believe in is Beer! (loud laughter) If the Constitution is to be saved, it must be saved by beer! If the Church is to be defended, it must be defended by beer! (applause) ...they thought they were going to save the Crown and the Church by the miraculous conversion of a Radical Publican (much laughter and applause)." Transcript of speech by W.V. Harcourt from "verbatim shorthand notes," Ernest Elton Grey to Lewis Harcourt, 8 April 1907. I owe this material to my friend the late Frank J. Merli, who copied it at Stanton Harcourt.

[68] Quoted in *Brewing Trade Review*, 1 Nov. 1888, p. 415.

[69] Gardiner, *Life of Harcourt* 1: 417.

[70] Dilke to William Tuckwell, undated conversation. Quoted in Stephen Gwyn and Gertrude W. Tuckwell, *Life of Sir Charles W. Dilke* (John Murray, 1918), 2: 566.

[71] *Parl. Deb.*, 3rd ser., CCCXXV, 20 April 1888, col. 120. Harcourt repeated this at the annual meeting of the United Kingdom Alliance on 9 October 1888. Gardiner, *Life of Harcourt*, 2: 107.

[72] See, for instance, Hamilton diary, 3 Sept. 1894. *The Destruction of Lord Rosebery: From the Diary of Sir Edward Hamilton, 1894-1895*, ed. David Brooks (Historians' Press, 1986), pp. 167-68.

[73] Hamilton diary, 21 April 1895, p. 242.

[74] Balfour to Salisbury, 19 Oct, 1886, *Salisbury-Balfour Correspondence ... 1869-1892*, ed. Robin Harcourt Williams (Hertfordshire Record Society, 1988), p. 162.

[75] *Journal of John Wodehouse, First Earl of Kimberley for 1862-1902*, p. 438 (entry for 21 July 1895).

[76] Jackson, *Loulou*, p. 10.

[77] Martin Pugh, reviewing *Loulou* in *Journal of Liberal History* (Autumn 2005).

[78] Harcourt to Gladstone, 26 April 1884. BL, W.E. Gladstone papers, Add. Ms. 44198, f. 51.

[79] Harcourt to Gladstone, 21 January 1884. BL, W.E. Gladstone papers, Add. Ms. 44199, f. 3. Harcourt at this time favored local control but not necessarily a referendum. Gardiner, *Life of Harcourt* 1: 481.

[80] Lawson to Harcourt, 10 April 1884. Bodleian, Harcourt Ms. 313, ff. 27-28.

[81] Lawson to Harcourt, 17 Dec. 1884. Bodleian, Harcourt Ms 213, ff. 171-76.

[82] Harcourt to Gladstone, 18 Jan. 1885. Bodleian, Harcourt MS 9, ff. 118-19. Quoted in part in D.A. Hamer, *Liberal Politics in the Age of Gladstone and Rosebery* (Clarendon Pres, 1972), p. 98.

[83] Lord Rendel's diary, 26 Dec. 1888, in *Personal Papers of Lord Rendel*, ed. F.E. Hamer (E. Benn, 1931), p. 54.

[84] Gladstone, *Midlothian Speeches, 1879*, ed. M.R.D. Foot (reprint; Leicester University Press, 1971), p. 75.

[85] *Parl. Deb.*, 3rd ser., CCLXXVIII, 27 April 1883, especially, col. 1365.

[86] Gladstone to Harcourt, 19 Jan. 1885. Bodleian, Harcourt Ms 9, ff. 120-21.

[87] Gladstone to Lord Thring, [no day] Sept. 1894, *Times*, 19 Sept. 1895, p. 4. See also Gladstone to Thomas Snape, 11 Sept. 1895. *Times*, 5 Oct. 1895, p. 8.

[88] Harcourt to John Morley, 24 Sept. 1894. Bodleian, Harcourt Ms 26, f. 164. Also quoted in Gardiner, *Life of Harcourt* 2: 307.

CHAPTER THREE

COMPENSATION AND THE ROAD
TO NEWCASTLE

The drink trade demanded compensation in case of the non-renewal of public house licenses. Why? an interpretation of the law, a sense of fairness, and confidence in its political friends. Until drastic temperance reform seemed imminent, compensation had remained a dormant issue. It later sharply divided the political parties. Eventually, it encouraged the Liberal Party to embrace Direct Local Veto. The compensation controversy led to Gladstone's reluctant commitment to a prohibition Veto as part of the Liberal program announced at Newcastle.

At first, compensation had not seemed to be a necessarily partisan issue. Although Sir Wilfrid Lawson made no secret of his personal objection to compensation, he had left it an open question during the debates over his local option resolutions.[1] Gladstone was willing to consider the trade demand for compensation, particularly if it meant compensation paid to publicans. In 1888, when a Conservative government's bill providing compensation was debated, several militant temperance reformers privately offered to accept a version of it.

The alignment of the advanced temperance party with the Liberal Party owed much to the Conservatives tying their proposals for licensing reform to compensation paid to owners of licensed property. Increasingly they were the brewers. The Conservative Party leader, Lord Salisbury (1830-1903), was not a temperance enthusiast. In a speech at Kingston-on Thames in 1883, he declared: "Sobriety is a very good thing and philanthropy is a very good thing, but freedom better than either."[2] Salisbury's biographer added: "The right to drink went to the heart of his libertarian beliefs." He did not believe that the number of public houses significantly affected the amount of alcoholic drink consumed. "Salisbury did not want to see local authorities in nonconformist and Temperance areas … penalising publicans and brewers."

At first the commitment to compensation was theoretical. Salisbury sketched the Conservative licensing program in a speech at

Newport prior to the general election of 1885. He conceded to reformers that elected councils should obtain the existing licensing powers of the justices as a part of local government reform. He accepted Sunday closing for districts in England at the discretion of local licensing authorities but thought it should be imposed only for two or three years, so the licensing authorities could quickly recognize that Sunday closing was a mistake.

Despite the consensus among the political parties that the elected councils should take over the regulation of licenses, the JP's retained their power over licensing after they had lost virtually all their other administrative powers. Despite partial agreement among the parties over the principle of Sunday closing, it never was introduced in England (except in the Carlisle experiment).

Salisbury's licensing proposals controversially endorsed compensation. He hoped that the burden of paying compensation would discourage the proposed elected licensing authorities from doing away with large numbers of licensed houses.[3]

This was only a theory until the legislative proposals of a Conservative government in 1888 and 1890. Why did the Salisbury government introduce these bills? In part, it was the result of the influence of middle-class MPs in Salisbury's Cabinet, who wanted to reduce the number of licensed houses, notably C.T. Ritchie (1838-1906) and a Liberal Unionist, George Goschen (1831-1907). We can speculate about other motives. In part, it might head off a reform agitation for the reduction in the number of pubs that benefited the Liberals and which Salisbury's Conservative rival Lord Randolph Churchill (1849-95) hoped to use as a vehicle to return to office after his ill-considered resignation at the end of 1886.[4] In part, the Salisbury government might have hoped that licensing reform would strengthen the uneasy alignment of the Conservative Party with the Liberal Unionists. In fact, it strained it. Salisbury's ministry rested awkwardly on a Liberal division that might be temporary. As a Radical, Joseph Chamberlain was uncomfortable with his partnership with the Conservatives. He hoped to return to the Liberals as their leader when Gladstone (who was in his mid-70s) retired. Lord Hartington (1833-1908) and the Whigs, although political moderates, were not eager to lose their ancestral Liberal identity.[5]

The licensed trade had its own reasons for hoping to make its claim for compensation enshrined in statute law, although not in the form that Ritchie and Goschen proposed. Licensed to sell all kinds of liquor for consumption on and off premises, the public house provided the principal retail outlet for alcoholic drink, particularly beer. Any major temperance legislation would attempt to curtail the number of public houses or eliminate them.[6]

Nominally a public house license was for one year only, but in practice renewal almost always took place except in case of misconduct. The trade argued that the procedural differences between an application for a new public house and a renewal of an existing one showed that the licensing justices lacked the same discretionary authority over a renewal that they enjoyed over a new application. The courts discouraged the contention that the expectation of renewal had a legal basis. Only beer houses licensed before 1869 for on-premises consumption had a clear statutory right to renewal that the magistrates had to respect. Beer houses could sell only beer and cider. As they often were small and unprofitable, they declined in numbers despite the privileged legal status that they enjoyed. In the Over-Darwen case in 1882 the Court of Queen's Bench ruled that those beer houses licensed to sell only for off-premises consumption lacked a right to renewal. It had been publicans who asked justices whether the off-licenses had a right to renewal. Ironically, this led to a denial of the right to renewal of on-licenses too.[7]

The case of *Sharp v. Wakefield* struck the decisive blow against the trade's interpretation of the legal status of public houses.[8] On 10 September 1887 the licensing bench in the Kendal division of Westmoreland refused to renew the license of the Low Bridge Inn in the Lake District on the ground that it was not needed and too remote for police supervision. An isolated hamlet, Kentmere had a population of only 174, Including 77 children. A petition opposing renewal of the license was signed by all the adult inhabitants except fifteen. On 21 October 1887 the Westmoreland Quarter Sessions, whose chairman was William Henry Wakefield, sustained the refusal by the narrow vote of fourteen to thirteen.[9] The Quarter Sessions included only one teetotaler and one Liberal (not the same person) which makes it difficult to say that the membership was prejudiced.

The owner, Susannah Sharp or Sharpe, stubbornly and disastrously pursued an appeal through the high courts, the Court of Queen's Bench (30 April 1888), the Court of Appeals (15 December 1888), and finally the House of Lords.[10] The Lords ruled against her definitively on 20 March 1891. Sharp received financial assistance from organizations of licensed victuallers and northern brewers, but major brewers' societies stood aloof. They tried to end the appeal by purchasing the property from Sharp.[11] When Sharp refused to sell, the London and country brewers reluctantly decided to take over the conduct of the case and pay the legal expenses. After acquiring information that "the house had been very badly conducted and had become a nuisance," the London brewers decided to withdraw, as it was a poor test case.[12] Organizations of Manchester brewers and licensed victuallers continued to support Sharp.[13] Irritated when the London publicans contributed to the appeal to the House of Lords, the London brewers refused to renew their annual subscription to the London licensed victuallers' organization.[14] In turn, publicans were angry at the "large brewers and distillers" for standing aside during the appeal.[15]

At the time there was little danger that the justices would exercise their discretionary powers to refuse the renewal of public house licenses on a large scale. Yet *Sharp v. Wakefield* encouraged the formation of the License Insurance Corporation and Guarantee Fund, Ltd. Provided that non-renewal by licensing justices remained rare, it could charge affordable insurance payments and still guarantee compensation. The real problem for the trade was that *Sharp v. Wakefield* destroyed the legal basis of the trade's claim to compensation as a part of any new licensing legislation.

During this period, the 1880s and the early 1890s, changes in the commercial structure of the trade, together with the growth in its political activity, reduced popular sympathy for license holders in danger of being denied renewal of their licenses. Compensation no longer meant paying a modest sum to a lower middle-class publican whose livelihood was bound up in a single public house. Large brewery firms acquired control over most public houses. As a result of the competition of the brewers for the limited number of licensed premises, the price of licensed property soared. The payment of market value compensation became alarmingly expensive. Most would be paid to the brewers who had bought up the freeholds and leaseholds, little to the publicans who served as tenants or as managers. Practically everyone in the trade insisted that the compensation be funded out of general taxation or local rates.[16] Virtually everyone outside the trade insisted that if there was to be any compensation that it should be funded out of taxes and fees paid by the trade and its customers.

Nearly all the value of licensed property resulted from its license for which the license holder had paid only a nominal fee. To many people the drink trade looked like an arrogant privileged monopoly, defending its privileges as rights and demanding payment when the State dared to withdraw what it had bestowed. The attacks on the sale of drink had provoked the trade into conspicuous political activity that irritated much of middle-class public opinion. What the trade considered self-defense many outsiders viewed as a selfish and corrupt influence with no legitimate place in public life.

In 1888 and 1890 the Conservative Government of Lord Salisbury attempted to enact legislation that would have encouraged compensation. The men behind the proposals, C.T. Ritchie, the President of the Local

Government Board, and George Goschen, the Chancellor of the Exchequer, a Liberal Unionist who had voted for Lawson's local option resolution in 1881, wanted to reduce the number of licensed premises. They considered compensation necessary as a prerequisite. The cautious Goschen was a weightier figure than Ritchie. Goschen was respected for his honesty and good nature but sometimes irritated his colleagues by his fussiness and fidgetiness.[17]

In 1888 Ritchie introduced a much overdue reform of local government that created County Councils and, for large towns, County Borough Councils, to assume most of the administrative powers formerly exercised by the justices of the peace. Among other things, this meant, as Lord Salisbury had promised at Newport, that the Council members would act as the local licensing authorities with the old powers of the justices, supplemented by the new permissive power to require Sunday closing. The Liberal Party, as a whole, strongly supported these proposals, although advanced temperance reformers disliked elected licensing authorities on the grounds that they would increase the complicity of the people in the drink traffic and motivate the drink sellers to corrupt local elections. An elected licensing authority made the trade nervous unless a statutory right to license renewal accompanied its establishment.[18]

The controversy concerned compensation.[19] Ritchie proposed that the Councils be authorized to pay compensation when they refused to renew licenses for the purpose of reducing the number of licensed premises. No compensation would be paid if the license holder had been guilty of misbehavior. A major source of income for the Councils would be licensing fees that the bill assigned them. To facilitate compensation Ritchie allowed the Councils to increase licensing fees by twenty per cent and also assigned the Councils the proceeds of a new tax on whiskey. Technically the duties and taxes on drink were not designated for compensation but their creation would allow the Councils to pay for compensation out of trade revenues.

Ritchie knew that his bill might be controversial among the trade. He wrote Joseph Chamberlain on 11 May 1888:

> Don't make too much in public, at present, of the provision in the Bill about which I spoke to you this afternoon. I don't want to disguise its operations from the publicans. Neither I want the matter put in such a way as would alarm them. I am breaking it to them quietly and I hope by the time the clauses come on they will realise and accept the position so that we may then make the most of the [temperance] argument without fearing the effect on the publicans.[20]

The drink trade did not unite solidly behind the licensing clauses.[21] As a result of pressure from the London brewers, the County Brewers' Society decided that in order to obtain parliamentary recognition of the principle of compensation it would not oppose the licensing clauses on the second reading.[22] At the court of the Brewer's Company), Edward North Buxton (1840-1924), who chaired the meeting, pointed out on 6 April 1888 that "the main object was to get the principle of compensation admitted." Buxton was a former Liberal M.P. Another brewer, who was a Conservative M.P., Cosmo Bonsor (1848-1929), argued: "they would never get such another chance of obtaining a vested Interest in the Licenses." He did not want a large compensation fund that might encourage a policy of reduction in the number of public houses and hoped for changes in the details of the compensation clauses to discourage the closing of licensed premises. Samuel Whitbread (1830-1915) was afraid that the final version of the bill would encourage licensing magistrates to pursue a reduction in numbers policy.[23] The Northumberland and Durham Brewers Association disliked the proposed increase in the license duty and Sunday closing, but if it could not get the government to change these clauses, it would support the bill. It feared that if a future Liberal government legislated on the topic "the claims of the trade would probably not be so fairly considered."[24] In contrast, the militant Manchester brewers rejected the clauses entirely.[25] As most provincial publicans were tenants who would receive nothing, they understandably were unenthusiastic.[26]

Ritchie privately told a trade deputation that public opinion would not support a bill that offered the trade better terms.[27] By the end of May, the Country Brewers Society "were willing, though reluctantly," to accept Whitbread's proposal that licensing fees pay for compensation.[28] Frustrated that compensation would come from taxes on the trade and that the Sharp v. Wakefield decision would not be altered, the Country Brewers' Society sadly declared: "we are driven back to the cold comfort that even this may be better than leaving us alone to face a grim and unpromising future."[29] The Country Brewers' Society had yielded on "the strong representations of the London Brewers."[30] The trade drew the lesson that it could not simply rely on the good will of the government. It needed to organize public demonstrations to exert pressure.[31]

The temperance movement considered the bill unacceptable. The main problem from the standpoint of the reformers was compensation. Even the moderate Church of England Temperance Society that accepted compensation in principle wanted a time limit to any statutory right of compensation. At least this was the position of its leaders. A few weeks after Ritchie had introduced the Local Government bill with its controversial compensation clauses the Court of Queen's Bench issued its ruling in the appeal of the *Sharp v. Wakefield* case. It ruled in favor of the power of the licensing justices to deny license renewals and so undercut the argument that license holders had a right to renewal or compensation. Buoyed by this ruling, the Alliance and other advanced temperance reformers mounted an agitation that impressed observers more than anything that they had done before on behalf of Local Veto. For instance, an unfriendly witness, the *Times*, described an anti-compensation demonstration at Hyde Park as an "imposing display."[32] On the other hand, the newspaper ridiculed a second anti-compensation rally held there as "a very sorry affair." Supposedly "a very large part of the procession consisted of women and children of tender age."[33]

From 1888, compensation became an increasingly partisan issue. Despite Gladstone's resistance, Harcourt persuaded the Liberal leadership to adopt an intransigent policy of no compromise in fighting the Government proposals for a permanent right of compensation. Subsequently he told John Morley (1838-1923), "You don't know what trouble I had in screwing up the G.O.M. ... and (low be it spoken) even Wilfrid Lawson to the sticking point of no surrender."[34] If Lawson had ever been willing to compromise, that moment soon passed.

Most Liberal Unionists supported the Government. Joseph Chamberlain pointed out that in 1886 when he had served in a Liberal government as President of the Local Government Board, he had drafted a local government bill that like Ritchie's included compensation for license holders.[35] Privately, Chamberlain hinted to a Birmingham reformer that, if the prohibitionists accepted compensation, they might be able to persuade the Government to consent to legislation for Direct Local Veto. Compensation was inevitable, argued Chamberlain, and the Government's version the "very cheapest which could be secured." Hartington also accepted the Ritchie bill "though it is not free from objection, because it is I think on the whole the best compromise which they can make on a rather difficult question."[36]

In contrast with Chamberlain and Hartington, a section of Liberal Unionist MPs alarmed the Government by its determined opposition to the compensation clauses.[37] The leader of the rebels was W.S. Caine (1842-1903), the Liberal Unionist chief whip.[38] Sometimes impetuous, he was a natural politician, extroverted and a congenial figure, in Henry Labouchere's phrase, the "hearty ruffian." In many ways Caine was the stereotype of the Christian businessman turned Radical politician. He was a large man, over six feet tall, full-bodied, with thick curly hair and beard. His speeches were "plain, matter-of-fact."[39] Two of his sons-in-law served in Parliament, while a daughter not married to them became a physician.[40]

Caine devoted much of his life to religious and temperance reform. As a young man he was active in the Society for the Suppression of Vicious Practices. Converted by reading (while drinking a pint of sherry) Mrs. Julia Bainbrigge Wightman's *Haste to the Rescue*, he was a total abstainer since 1862. His wife was a daughter of the celebrated Baptist preacher, Hugh Stowell Brown. In 1873 he became a vice president of the National Temperance League. Out of his own pocket he maintained the Wheatsheaf mission in South Lambeth that he served as a lay preacher, beginning in 1884.[41] Eventually it was affiliated with the London Congregational Union. Anxious to provide workmen with an alternative to the public house, he helped organized the Hand-in-Hand Clubs or cocoa-rooms.[42]

Sometimes called "the member for India," Caine visited India several times. He helped organize the Anglo-Indian Temperance Association which fought alcohol and opium. He was its honorary secretary and treasurer. Caine criticized Nonconformist missionaries for their comfortable standard of living that contrasted with Indian poverty.

Caine served as president of the National Temperance Federation (composed of Nonconformist and regional prohibitionist societies) from the time that it was organized in 1884 and would continue as president until his death in 1903. He also had served as president of the British Temperance League, the Baptist Total Abstinence Association, the Congregational Total Abstinence Association, the Commercial Travellers' Temperance League, and the Liverpool Temperance Union, as well as serving as vice-president of nearly every other major temperance organization including the Church of England Temperance Society and the United Kingdom Alliance.

Although he was the official Liberal candidate at an 1886 by-election at Barrow-in-Furness, a Home Rule Liberal also was nominated. Caine feared that Arnold Morley (1849-1916) was behind the attempt to defeat him. In the event, the Conservative chief agent "paid off the Conservative candidate," so Caine was elected without difficulty. He had been helped by Chamberlain's "known personal connection" with him."[43] Labouchere claimed that Lord Hartington made it possible for Caine to break with Gladstone without risking his seat.[44] Cavendish influence was strong in Barrow. Later Caine helped organize Radical and working-class Liberal Unionists in metropolitan London.

Caine struggled with the conflict between his two loyalties, Liberal Unionism and militant temperance reform. He resented the criticism that some Alliance activists directed at him for his support of Unionist parliamentary candidates over Liberal supporters of Local Veto.[45] When he attended a meeting of the United Kingdom Alliance auxiliary on 1 July 1887, he was greeted "with hisses and booing." One of those protesting Caine as "a traitor" said that fifty of the two hundred people present had joined in the hooting. The objection was not to Caine joining the Liberal Unionists but to his campaigning for anti-temperance candidates.[46]

Caine proved his loyalty to temperance in his fight against the compensation clauses. He spent over £600 of his own money to employ two firms of chartered accountants to calculate the market value for a sample of provincial and metropolitan public houses. The average valuation approached £3,000.[47] He donated £100 to support a London agitation against the 1888 bill.[48] In the debate in the House of Commons he argued that the compensation clauses sacrificed the important principle that a license was granted for twelve months and no longer in return for an insignificant reduction in the number of public houses ("the monstrous proposal to create … an entirely new vested interest").[49] The bill provided little money to fund compensation and required compensation at full market value that meant that few licenses could be denied. Caine emphasized the high prices that prevailed even for unpretentious-looking public houses, the result of the monopoly value which licensing bestowed gratuitously. Caine avoided unnecessary acrimony. He had no desire to break with his party, particularly its urban Radical wing that Chamberlain dominated.[50] He had once held minor office under Gladstone and may have aspired to office in a Government in which the Liberal Unionists would participate.

Privately, Caine and several other prominent members of the advanced temperance party, most of them Liberal Unionists, hoped for a compromise over compensation along the lines of the proposal of the Church of England Temperance Society, to allow money payments for a limited number of years only.[51] Apparently Joseph Malins (1844-1926), the Liberal Unionist leader of the militant Good Templars, had initiated negotiations between the advanced and moderate temperance reformers at the end of May. As a result, on 11 June the chairman of the CETS, Canon Henry John Ellison (1813-99), led a private deputation, representing both wings of the temperance movement, to consult Chamberlain. Chamberlain agreed to tell Ritchie about the proposal but warned the deputation that he suspected that it was too late. A meeting held the next day between representatives of the advanced temperance party and the CETS legislative subcommittee quickly dissolved since the reformers already knew that the Government had decided to withdraw the clauses rather than amend them. In lamentation Caine said that the Government ought to have known that he and the temperance party as a whole would have accepted a Government bill embodying the CETS amendments to limit compensation for a period of years. Several CETS leaders, angry that Caine had put off compromise too long, questioned that the Government could have made any such inference from his strongly negative speeches.[52]

Caine, Malins, and William Hussey, the secretary of the Birmingham auxiliary of the UKA, had represented the advanced temperance party at the CETS meeting.[53] Earlier, J.H. Raper (1820-97), the former parliamentary agent of the Alliance, had participated in the negotiations. Probably they could not have delivered the support of the advanced temperance reformers as a whole. The prohibitionists open to the compromise often were Liberal Unionists anxious to prevent the Gladstonians from gaining the permanent allegiance of the advanced temperance party. Like Hussey, Malins made his home in Birmingham, the citadel of Chamberlain's West Midlands fiefdom, and like Caine, Malins was a Liberal Unionist. Caine and Malins were close colleagues, respectively the president and the honorary secretary of the National Temperance Federation, which shared space with the Good Templars at the Birmingham headquarters of the English Grand Lodge.

In explaining the decision to withdraw the compensation and other licensing clauses Ritchie said that the Government lacked the time to fight the clauses through the House and did not want to complicate the first elections to the County Councils with the issues of licensing and compensation.[54] In fact, most ministers had little stomach for a scheme that both the temperance reformers and the drink trade criticized.[55] Salisbury complained: "the Teetotal world has fairly gone mad." Although he realized that the drink trade was also unhappy, "the inebriate world is the least insane of the two."[56] Late in May the Government lost a bye-election in Southampton, with some observers blaming the compensation clauses.

The Liberal leadership was relieved. Harcourt had feared that if the Liberals had defeated the compensation clauses, they "might have accused of being enemies to Local Option," since that principle was embodied in the Government scheme.[57]

Despite the opposition of the advanced temperance party, a form of compensation could have been enacted in 1888, if the Government had been determined to settle the question, and if all sections of the drink trade had realized the importance of obtaining a legal acknowledgment of the principle of compensation. The trade was unwilling to accept a time limit to compensation. Few MPs were irrevocably hostile to all forms of compensation. In 1880 Gladstone had endorsed the principle of compensation at least for publicans.[58] Some prohibitionists such as Caine and Malins had hoped for a settlement. It was the success of the fight against the compensation clauses that helped turn the Liberals and the compromisers among the prohibitionists against compensation in any form that the drink trade could accept. Later in 1888 the Court of Appeals decided against the right of renewal in *Sharp v. Wakefield*. Only the House of Lords had yet to speak in this most influential case. This would happen in 1891.

Leaders of the trade were anxious for an early settlement of the licensing question. Late in 1889 Cosmo Bonsor brought before the new National Trade Defence Fund the possibility of the trade proposing a bill. The manager of the Fund was directed to draft a bill that included no new licenses. Where a fresh license was required, a license would be transferred from another district. The committee directed that no details of the bill would appear in the minutes.[59] It never reached the light of day.

In a rancorous epilogue to the struggle about compensation the Liberal Party and most temperance reformers protested the decision of the Government to abandon its plans to transfer licensing administration to the County Councils and create a local option for Sunday closing. Ritchie privately had promised the trade that the Government would withdraw all the licensing clauses if circumstances forced the withdrawal of compensation. The Government did allow a free vote on a bill for Sunday closing. It was defeated on 14 December 1888.[60] The London licensed victuallers spent more money to fight Sunday closing (£2,654) than to support compensation (£1,024) suggesting their priorities.[61]

Supporting the Sunday closing option, Harcourt insisted that the Liberals "must smite [the Government] hip and thigh in their retreat."[62] In contrast, Caine argued that temperance reformers should wait for statutory Sunday closing and not accept the compromise of local option. Harcourt accused Caine of desertion after having urged support for the Sunday closing local option proposal.[63] Caine denied having spoken to Harcourt; he conceded only that he had agreed to support the Sunday closing option if the committee of House of Commons temperance reformers endorsed it. In a rejoinder to Harcourt's attack, he denounced the Liberal politician as a "political lurcher" who previously had attacked Sunday closing and other temperance reforms.[64]

Sir Wilfrid Lawson had been criticized within the UKA for inactivity in the 1888 struggle, but as a staunch Liberal he now came out in support of Harcourt.[65] He defended the local option of Sunday closing as what the temperance party could get immediately. He supported Sunday closing not out of Sabbatarian motives but because he always supported any proposals which reduced the sale of drink. Lawson accused the Government of having surrendered to trade pressures and, remembering the Latin saying of <u>cave canem</u> (beware the dog), he stung his comrade Caine with the jibe, "<u>Cave Canem</u>--beware of him indeed."[66] In horror, Joseph Malins, the chief of the militant Good Templar grand lodge, asked: are temperance reformers "to imbibe the venom of political papers and partisans, and denounce each other as traitors?"[67]

The indecisive compensation struggle in 1888 helped bring the Liberal and the advanced temperance party another step closer together. As a symbol of this emerging alignment Harcourt became the first ex-Cabinet member to preside over the public session of the UKA's annual meeting later that same year. He described himself as a worker who entered the vineyard at the eleventh hour. Other prominent Liberals increasingly emphasized the importance of temperance reform in their speeches. For instance, John Morley characterized temperance reform as the greatest, deepest moral movement since the campaign against slavery.[68] In 1892 Morley followed Harcourt in presiding over the public session of the Alliance's annual meeting.

The Liberal Party had made no commitment to Direct Local Veto. In 1883 the parliamentary leadership had endorsed only the principle of local option and that could mean almost anything. In 1884, the National Liberal Federation, an organization of constituency associations, added its endorsement of local option. Late in 1886, after the Home Ruler disruption, the Federation adopted a slightly stronger resolution, for "the right of popular control over the granting and transfer of licenses," which still did not specify a referendum. In his presidential address at the Alliance meeting, on 9 October 1888, Harcourt affirmed his personal support of the Veto principle as a right of the people. He bluntly added that he would not vote for prohibition if a referendum were held in the licensing district in which he lived but wanted the right to do so.

Many prohibitionists hoped to obtain a clear endorsement from the National Liberal Federation at its annual meeting held in Manchester, in December 1889. At first Lawson advised caution since an amendment introduced from the floor might reveal that the Federation was seriously divided.[69] He argued for discretion:

> In point of fact the speed of actual legislation will not be *materially* affected by what we do next week at the Liberal Caucus,--though of course good resolutions--like good intentions--pave the way. But you see the Liberal Party is like a big salmon. We, the Prohibitionists, have hooked him, and are now "playing" with the object of landing him as soon as possible. If we make a clumsy attempt to "gaff" him before the right moment he may get off the line altogether.[70]

"Fisherman" Lawson worried too much. As a result of negotiations with the young David Lloyd George, the leaders of the Federation accepted the demand for a commitment to the Veto, so a UKA amendment to the official program proved unnecessary. Lawson himself was designated to propose "the direct popular veto of the liquor traffic," as part of an omnibus resolution.[71] In the mid-1880s Lloyd George had been an officer in a Good Templar lodge. Although he was not a teetotaler except for brief periods, he strongly disliked drunkenness.

The executive committee of the Alliance had provided each delegate to the Federation's meeting with a statement of the policies of the advanced temperance party which included that assertion that no liquor reform would be "efficient" without the direct popular Local Veto, that the advanced temperance party did not ask for a change in the composition of the licensing authority, and that it "will not for one moment accept a change in the Licensing Authority, either as equivalent to, or in substitution for, or in postponement of, the enactment of the Direct Popular Veto." It opposed a municipal or other elected council as a licensing authority, something which had not been successful in Scotland, and "whose hostility to the liquor traffic is to be lessened" by the assignment of parliamentary liquor taxes.[72]

A new round in the compensation struggle was fought in 1890. Goschen and Ritchie, the proponents of the licensing clauses in the local government bill, again proposed a scheme to encourage a reduction in the number of licensed premises.[73] The national Exchequer would give the County Councils £350,000 a year to purchase and suppress licenses. By doing so, the bill created a form of compensation that implied that compensation was a right, without explicitly declaring that it was. Other members of the Government and much of the drink trade lacked enthusiasm. Earlier Goschen had failed to get the brewers to support the continuation of a temporary beer duty enacted in 1889 that he had hoped to apply to compensation.[74] W.H. Smith (1825-91), the Conservative leader in the Commons, argued that the brewers only wanted "to be left alone" and resented any new taxes created to fund compensation. Goschen contended, to the contrary, that the reduction in the number of licensed premises, reducing competition, acted as "the great sop" for the trade.[75] The 1890 scheme also forbade the creation of new licenses except in districts of growing population that had further added to the value of existing licenses.[76] Lord Salisbury imposed a compromise on his colleagues: Goschen and Ritchie could introduce their drink proposals in Parliament but not as part of the Budget. They would be part of the Local Taxation (Customs and Excise) Bill that could be abandoned if the proposals turned out to be too controversial.[77]

Although Goschen outlined the intentions of the Government in his budget speech, it was Ritchie who introduced the bill that authorized the

County Councils in England, Wales, and Scotland to purchase licensed houses for the purpose of reducing their numbers. Unlike the 1888 proposal, the bill did not affect the authority of the licensing justices. It funded compensation from existing beer taxes and new spirits taxes. It included "the novel idea of virtually banning new licenses."[78] The Liberal diarist Sir Edward Walter Hamilton (1847-1908) admired the scheme, "an ingenious scheme of dealing with the vexed licensing question by a side-door."[79]

The Government claimed that Ritchie's bill did not create any new right of compensation. It neither forced the Councils to buy nor the license holders to sell. It simply empowered the Councils to buy houses in order to make a start on the task of reducing the number of licensed premises. It also assigned the Councils the proceeds of a new tax on spirits and the increase in the tax on beer which had been enacted in 1889 as a temporary measure. The Councils were authorized to apply a portion of this money to the purchase of licensed property. To permit a considerable initial reduction the bill also allowed the Councils to borrow for this purpose. To win the half-hearted support of the Church of England Temperance Society the Government declared that the bill did not affect the statutory powers of the justices who continued to act as the licensing authorities. It did not create any right to compensation for licensed houses that the justices refused to renew. Yet, despite the appellate decisions in the *Sharp v. Wakefield* case the Government declined to say that it recognized the claim of the justices to unlimited discretionary powers of non-renewal.

Compensation was difficult for many Liberal Unionist temperance reformers to accept. A constituent told a Scottish member: "most temperance reformers amongst the Unionists will rather risk the return to power of Mr. Gladstone than retain the authors of compensation to publicans."[80]

The appellate decisions in *Sharp v. Wakefield* put the Government on the defensive. In opening the second reading debate Ritchie argued that the purchase clauses simply recognized that in practice licenses had a market value whatever the strict legal rights of renewal might be.[81] Temperance reformers once again rallied to fight the prospect of the trade obtaining a left-handed recognition of its claim to compensation. W.H. Smith complained to Caine that "your friends are treating us badly."[82] Goschen described himself as engulfed in "a yellow fog of telegrams" critical of the purchase clauses.[83] Ritchie vigorously denied that the trade had had any role in drafting the bill.[84] The growth of temperance reform as a political issue and the unfavorable court decisions frightened most of the trade into support for the bill. On 19 and 20 May, the principal trade organizations agreed to support the Government's proposals without amendments.[85] Earlier a trade society official related to W.H. Smith's wife told him that the brewers would cooperate with the County Councils to make the purchase scheme work.[86]

When the Government proposed an excise duty on beers and spirits to compensate those publicans who had been refused licenses by temperance-dominated local authorities, a political row broke out which was fought out over twenty-five nights, the longest amount of time spent on a customs measure since the Corn Laws.

Gladstone, who had sat in silence in 1888, attacked the Government bill as "the endowment of public houses, or . . . a bill to buy out a certain very limited number of publicans upon the terms which are agreeable to themselves." He denied any inconsistency. He had supported the compensation principle in a context of proposals for legislation for the extinction of public houses and before court decisions had rejected the right of license holders to renewal. He still reserved his final judgment about compensation in the event of a bill providing for a general settlement. He hinted that if there was to be compensation, it should be paid to the publican to whom the license was issued and not to the brewer who owned the leasehold or freehold.[87]

Harcourt denied that compensation was a prerequisite for a reduction in numbers. The magistrates already had the power to refuse to renewal unwanted public houses. He characterized the bill "as a thoroughly Liberal Unionist scheme . . . [that is, one which] pretends to be one thing and actually is another." He excused Ritchie, the bill's sponsor, from responsibility and instead blamed Goschen, "an accidental Liberal, who had returned to his natural fold," assisted by Chamberlain and perhaps T.W. Russell (1841-1920), a Liberal Unionist from Ulster who once had been a prominent prohibitionist.[88]

Adding to the Government's problems Lord Randolph Churchill, a former Chancellor of the Exchequer, had emerged as a temperance reformer. In April he had proposed his own licensing amendment bill that combined a local option plebiscite on licensing with the principle of compensation but no financial details. He later told a Liberal politician that alcohol was responsible for half of the crime and two-thirds of the poverty in England.[89] Churchill urged the Government to strengthen the bill's assault upon drink particularly by restricting the right of compensation to a period of ten years. Another Tory MP privately argued that Churchill's amendments appealed to "respectable" MPs who "desire *substantially* to reduce the drink traffic while being fair to 'the trade'." The Liberal Unionist critics of the Government bill would be largely satisfied by the adoption of Churchill's proposals.[90] A trade meeting (chaired by one of his constituents, publican Charles Walker [1836-1903), approved Churchill's bill in principle on 7

May 1890, and brewers E.N. Buxton, a Gladstonian Liberal, and Cosmo Bonsor, a Conservative MP, tried to work out an arrangement with Churchill.[91] The Liberal Sir Algernon West (1832-1921) also was involved with the making of Churchill's bill.

As in 1888 the attitude of the Liberal Unionists was critical. Lord Hartington, the party leader, and Chamberlain, its most dynamic force, supported the Government. [92] Caine again rallied many backbenchers in rebellion. Once more he hoped for a compromise that would allow advanced temperance reformers to remain loyal to the Liberal Unionist Party and support the Conservative Government.[93] He laid down a carefully worded amendment, "That this House declines to assent to a Bill which provides by payment out of public moneys for the extinction of annual licenses in the manner provided by said Bill." Caine did not rule out compensation under all circumstances. On 2 May at a public meeting he said "supposing they were willing to discuss compensation, he should object to discuss it except in connection with a scheme for a final settlement of the whole liquor trade question."[94] In Parliament on 12 May 1890 Caine described as "utter absurdity ... attempting to settle the principle of compensation apart from a general and comprehensive settling of the whole licensing question."[95] This was very much what Gladstone had said.

On 12 May, in the most important speech of Caine's life, he called for those who favored some other kind of compensation to join with those who opposed any compensation in rejecting the Government's proposals. As in 1888 he pointed out that the bill would concede the principle of what amounted to a freehold interest in annual licenses while providing only enough money to extinguish a handful of them. He reviewed the build-up of huge artificial monopoly values, the control the brewers exercised over the retail trade through a system of tied houses, and the legal decisions hostile to the claim of vested interests in annual licenses. He insisted that the temperance party stood united against the purchase proposals. Although a subcommittee of the Church of England Temperance Society had endorsed the bill, the organization as a whole had not. The CETS had proposed accepting a more limited kind of trade blackmail as a final settlement of the compensation question, a ten years' license for existing licensed property. If the Government supported such a scheme, "neither I nor anyone could prevent it coming in the Statute Book" as a final settlement. Although he stopped short of endorsing the CETS compromise, he obviously would have welcomed it as a Government bill.[96]

Although Harcourt did his best to rally the Liberals against the compensation clauses, even after Caine's speech he was "not sure" about the determination of the temperance reformers. He told his son Lewis: "I can't find out yet how much *real grit* there is in the Teetotal Party." He also was unsure of his own leader: "I *hope* we have got the G.O.M. up to the mark."[97]

On 15 May, Caine's amendment failed by only 73 votes. He continued his fight with a memorial to Lord Hartington which complained that the "strong feeling of dissatisfaction" about the licensing clauses threatened "serious dissension."[98] The United Kingdom Alliance collected signatures for the memorial from Liberal Unionist supporters around the country.[99] A Scottish MP received a letter from a constituent who demanded: "the Government should remember that some of the strongest Unionists are Temperance reformers." He added that such Liberal Unionists "make it a condition [of their support] that the chance of temperance legislation in the future is not to be destroyed by the gratuitous concession of the principle of compensation."[100] The Nonconformist religious press vigorously seconded the agitation against the purchase clauses.

Some observers, connected with neither the drink trade nor the temperance movement, hoped for a compromise settlement. Sir Algernon West wrote to Lord Randolph Churchill that the temperance reformers "surely must be amenable to reason." They know that if the Government makes it bill a priority it can carry it "by force majeure." The brewers and publicans must know that this is their last chance for compensation. "No other Government, certainly no Radical Government will again propose compensation." The Liberal Party too should see the advantage of a compromise. "The Opposition surely should see that it is better even than putting the Government in a hole, to get this thorny subject out of their way."[101]

On 12 June. Lord Hartington believed that he had obtained a compromise. He told a Liberal Unionist meeting that the Government would agree to an amendment explicitly stating that the bill did not alter the laws governing renewal or confer any new rights on the license holder. The Government also would accept the appointment of a Select Committee on compensation.[102] Probably Caine could have supported such a compromise if the Councils awarded no money for licenses until the committee reported. The compromise quickly collapsed. Four days later W.H. Smith said that the Government did not want a Select Committee, although it would acquiesce in its creation. Moreover, the Government would not postpone the implementation of the purchase clauses pending the conclusion of the inquiry.[103] Ritchie denied that Hartington had any role in the agreement to have a Select Committee. It had been Lord Randolph Churchill who had persuaded the Government to offer the concession.[104] Apparently the drink trade was responsible for the collapse of Hartington's compromise. The trade opposed any limitation to the right of compensation that a Select

Committee might propose, such as the ten-year time limit suggested by the CETS.[105]

The purchase clauses did not long survive this embarrassment. On Ascot Day, 19 June, the Government carried a major licensing division by only four votes.[106] A couple of days later Caine told a Welsh Liberal that he would leave the Liberal Unionist Party unless the Government abandoned the purchase clauses.[107] Goschen and Ritchie threatened to resign if the Government did not fight to keep them.[108] In the end, on 23 June, W.H. Smith announced the withdrawal of the purchase scheme.

Many Conservative backbenchers blamed Smith for the fiasco. For instance, in his journal Sir Richard Temple complained:

> This Licensing Bill ... was sprung upon us without notice and without mention in the Queen's Speech.
>
> The party were justly angered at this, which they regarded as nothing short of blundering, and which they would have stopped had they got even an inkling beforehand. Now this Licensing Bill mistake was attributed not to W.H. Smith by his followers, but to one or more of his ambitious colleagues in the Cabinet. But our men asked each other, What is the use of him as leader if he cannot check these vagaries?[109]

The Government and the trade quickly suffered another humiliation. The new drink tax had already been enacted as part of the Budget. When the Government tried to put the proceeds of the whiskey tax in escrow for a future compensation scheme, an Irish Nationalist, Tim Healey (1855-1931), queried the Speaker about the constitutionality of the taxes remaining unappropriated. When the Speaker ruled against the Government, the so-called whiskey money was assigned to pay for technical education.[110]

When Hartington asked the rebellious Caine to resign as party whip, Caine resigned not only that office but from the House of Commons to stand for re-election as an independent.[111] A historian of Liberal Unionism described Caine as having previously been "the most active of all [Liberal Unionist] Party organisers" and Chamberlain's close ally.[112]

Putting Caine aside, 1890 was a difficult year for the Unionists. The party was divided over Tithe legislation. Smith, the leader in the Commons, had to deal at divisions with many absentees. The party did not recover despite Parnell's involvement in a divorce case that divided the Irish nationalists.

Caine did not expect to be opposed at the bye-election at Barrow and presumed that if he were, temperance men of all parties would rush to his support. "I don't expect to be fought."[113] In fact both a ministerialist and a Gladstonian opposed him. Since the Home Rule candidate supported the

Veto, Sir Wilfrid Lawson refused to endorse Caine. Despite Lawson's position, the Alliance ignored its ordinary rule of neutrality in contests involving more than one Vetoist in order to work for Caine. Caine was furious at Lawson and worried about the effect of his neutrality. Indignantly he telegraphed the Alliance to "put on immediate pressure." Lawson's "refusal would be fatal." "If he persists in his refusal I shall resign my [UKA] vice-presidency the day after the election." He also threatened to give up his candidacy and blame Lawson.[114] Caine rejected a suggestion of a deal with the local Liberals in which they would support him in the bye-election in return for his withdrawal at the general election.[115] Instead Caine stood for election and lost.[116] One of Caine's electoral workers, a member of the UKA staff, criticized Lawson at the next annual meeting of the Alliance.[117] Caine's own indignation seems to have quieted by then. The bye-election produced reconciliation with Harcourt who had tried to get the Barrow Liberals to adopt Caine as their own candidate.[118] Shortly after his defeat as an independent, Caine returned to the Home Rule ranks. He told Chamberlain that although temperance reform furnished his main motive, as a Radical he had become generally dissatisfied with the Conservatives. "The bondage of the Tory alliance had become unbearable and their attack on the whole Temperance Movement, which I could never subordinate to anything, gave me emancipation."[119] Caine became a leader in the reorganization of the London Liberal and Radical Union that helped the Gladstonians win the 1892 general election.[120]

The other temperance stalwarts who sat in the House of Commons as Liberal Unionists did not join Caine in his revolt, although some of them belatedly rejoined the Liberal Party in the early 1900s over other issues, notably land reform (T.W. Russell) and free trade (A. Cameron Corbett [1856-1933]). Among Radicals the licensing questions sometimes caused the Liberal Unionists problems. For instance, the secretary of the West of Scotland Liberal Unionist Association reported in 1890 that "the question of the licensing clauses caused a temporary but very deep disturbance throughout our Association" and that "the severe shock shook the loyalty of not a few."[121] Caine apparently expected Liberal Unionists who believed in Liberalism would rejoin the Gladstonian Liberals after a settlement of the Home Rule question. On June 24, 1891, he told Gladstone: "the great bulk of *Liberal* Unionists in the country feel that the [Salisbury] Government has had its chance and lost it. We can only hope that when you are able to pronounce on the question, we may all find an amicable settlement of this weary strife & controversy."[122]

Nonconformist chapels had been aroused to fight the compensation clauses. "Charles Garrett (1825-1900) agitated in the *Methodist Times* against the compensation clauses, stimulating opposition to the Government among Methodists who were not normally closely identified with the anti-drink movement."[123] The Good Templars also were active in local agitations against compensation.

After this second compensation fight the road to Newcastle neared completion. The House of Lords pronounced the final judgment in the *Sharp v. Wakefield* case in March 1891, virtually simultaneously with the second reading in which a majority in the House of Commons voted for a private member's bill in favor of Local Veto for Wales. The advanced temperance reformers exalted. The right to license renewal had been rejected, compensation by statute had been stopped twice, and the principle of empowering the electors to prohibit the sale of drink in their locality had acquired broad acceptance. The advanced temperance party had showed its power to mobilize public opinion and so had emerged as an attractive ally in the eyes of Liberal politicians.

Moderate Liberals liked the idea of John Morley that local authorities be authorized to reduce the number of licenses or refuse to grant them. Morley's insistence on ad hoc authorities displeased those who favored empowering existing county and municipal councils.[124] In any event, Morley's suggestion never became Liberal policy.

Gladstone's commitment to the twin policies of Local Veto and no compensation remained ambiguous. He had attached a reservation to his acceptance of the House of Commons resolution in 1883 and was unbound by the National Liberal Federation resolution of 1889 that it had renewed in 1890. In 1888 and 1890 he rejected specific compensation proposals, not the principle of compensation. He remained favorably disposed toward some form of money compensation at least for publicans. By 1890 Gladstone apparently accepted the principle of local option for a prohibition referendum with the expectation that it would prove a dead letter.

On 26 December 1890, Gladstone sketched his ideas for an electoral program in a letter to his chief whip Arnold Morley. Although the letter has disappeared, its contents can be reconstructed from a memorandum which another Morley, John Morley, sent to Harcourt on 30 December and, in the case of temperance policy, from the disgruntled comment which Harcourt returned on 2 January 1891. Under the heading of Direct Local Veto, Morley remarked about Gladstone's proposals:

> Good as far as it goes. It would undoubtedly put heart into the Temperance people. They are no doubt on our side as it is. But the Irish business will chill them [the recent disclosure of C.S. Parnell's adulterous liaison with Kitty O'Shea], and they need to be stirred up by warm and active interest in their own question. On the other hand, S[ydney] Buxton [a member of

a brewing family] and other London members assure me that Temperance is very ill-fitted to rouse or please *London*, and I quite believe it.[125]

Harcourt thought John Morley unnecessarily polite in describing Gladstone's temperance policy as "good as far as it goes." His mood was angry in large part because he wanted to drop or downgrade Home Rule in the wake of the O'Shea scandal, the acrimonious divisions in the Irish party, and Parnell's desperate attacks on the Liberals. He resented Gladstone's imperious refusal to budge. In this mood Harcourt fumed that:

> G[ladstone]'s views upon the Temperance Question are hopelessly impossible. He has never really sympathised with it and does not in the smallest degree appreciate its importance to the sentiments of the party. This is sufficiently proved by his notion that he can satisfy the requirements by "giving time" to [Sir Wilfrid] Lawson and by admitting the claim to compensation. If he can't mend his hand about this he had better leave it alone altogether.[126]

Gladstone had proposed simply to allow Lawson time on the parliamentary calendar for a private member's veto bill and to agree on a compromise compensation scheme. When Harcourt wrote to Gladstone, he had calmed down. He politely asked only for greater emphasis on temperance reform and on a few other issues.[127] In a characteristically ambiguous reply Gladstone said that a Liberal Government could "give temperance a forward shove."[128]

Sometime in the next nine months Gladstone accepted the necessity to pledge a Government bill for Direct Local Veto, but he remained reluctant to abandon compensation. He consulted Caine who in 1890 had implied a willingness to accept compensation as part of a larger settlement. Apparently, Gladstone asked Caine if he could support a time limit that would provide licensed property with security for a few transitional years before new licensing legislation was implemented. A few days prior to the Newcastle meetings of the National Liberal Federation Caine answered that while he could not himself propose such a time limit he would accept one particularly if it were proposed by a Liberal Government, as he could trust it. "It is possible to accept what it is impossible to propose." He even admitted that a time limit probably would be necessary politically.[129]

Gladstone seems to have intended to couple his affirmation of Direct Local Veto at Newcastle with a concession to the drink trade, perhaps a time limit, with neither compensation nor license non-renewal during a transitional period, and perhaps with money compensation confined to publicans. At the end of September, Lawson fought against such schemes.

He urged the Liberal leader to refrain from any allusion to compensation in his speech to the Federation, as it would be misunderstood by suspicious prohibitionists and by pro-trade mischief makers, *"anxious* to misunderstand."[130]

Lawson had his way at the celebrated fourteenth annual conference of the National Liberal Federation held at Newcastle-upon-Tyne. He personally introduced the omnibus resolution on 2 October 1891. It once again included the "direct and popular veto on the liquor traffic."[131] The next day, when Gladstone responded to the so-called Newcastle Programme of the Federation, he explicitly endorsed the Veto, and he omitted any hint of a Liberal version of compensation. Instead, Gladstone attacked the recent Conservative compensation bill, congratulated Harcourt for his leadership in the fight against it, and rejoiced that the failure of the Government measure had encouraged the licensing justices to become more active in the exercise of their discretionary powers. He expressed confidence that his hearers:

> may witness a thorough and effective reform of the laws connected with the traffic in alcoholic liquors. I trust that among the conditions of that improvement you may find a fair and just acknowledgment of the right of local populations to deal in a proper manner with the question whether there shall be or shall not be within their borders any acknowledgment of public-house traffic at all.

The same powers were already enjoyed by great landlords who could prohibit licensed houses on their properties.[132]

In 1891 the G.O.M. committed the party to the resolutions adopted by the Federation since 1889. The advanced temperance party still had to worry about Gladstone's sympathy for compensation. Early in November 1891, several weeks after Newcastle, Lawson considered it necessary to lecture him against compensation and a time limit. Gladstone replied that he had "never said a word of compensation for any extinction of licenses under any law or system of law now existing." Lawson did not find this statement altogether satisfactory, since "sensitively suspicious friends" might fear that Gladstone might authorize compensation under a new system of laws. Lawson also strongly rejected the principle of the time limit that Caine had indicated that he could accept. Lawson pointed out that even money compensation had the advantage of allowing the drink shops to be closed immediately whereas a time limit would delay reform.[133] When the Liberal Party entered the general election of 1892 Gladstone remained unpledged on compensation.

Nor had Gladstone promised any priority for a Veto bill in a crowded legislative program dominated by Ireland. In his Newcastle speech he had hinted that those of his hearers unfortunate to be as old as himself might not see the happy day of the enactment of the Veto.[134]

Although Gladstone had not made prohibition by local option a priority, he had at least mentioned it at Newcastle. As large and miscellaneous a program as Newcastle was, he had left out what he did not want at all. He ignored Nonconformist demands for reform of elementary education, feminist calls for female suffrage, and so-called "labour" questions. John Morley has worried unnecessarily that Gladstone's eagerness to promote Irish Home Rule would encourage "the *fads* which infest the air like midges."[135] Some Liberal regarded Local Veto as a nuisance that they wanted to swat away. Fortunately for the advanced temperance party, Gladstone at least found it tolerable.

Notes

[1] *Parl. Deb.,* 3rd ser., CCLXII, 14 June 1881, col. 534.

[2] *Times*, 14 June 1883, quoted in Peter Marsh, *The Discipline of Popular Government: Lord Salisbury's Domestic Statecraft, 1881-1902* (Harvester Press, 1978), p. 128.

[3] *Famous Speeches*, ed. Herbert Paul (Pittman and Sons, 1912), 2: 270-71. Paul misdates the speech as 8 Oct. 1885. It was delivered on 7 Oct. 1885.

[4] Marsh, *Discipline of Popular Government*, p. 150.

[5] See the biography of Hartington by Patrick Jackson, *The Last of the Whigs: A Political Biography of Lord Hartington Later Eighth Duke of Devonshire (1833-1908)* (Farleigh Dickinson Press, 1994).

[6] Although the trade denied that there was any necessary connection between the number of licenses and drunkenness, some brewers acknowledged that "excessive competition" tempted publicans to encourage drinking. *Brewing Trade Review*, 1 Dec. 1886, pp. 49-50.

[7] Nicholls. *The Politics of Alcohol*, pp. 133-34.

[8] David M. Fahey, "Brewers, Publicans, and Staff in Late Victorian and Edwardian Licensed Trade Societies, Part 1," *Brewery History* 179 (Summer 2019): 7-8.

[9] *Weekly Reporter* 36 (June 2, 1888): 634-39.

[10] On 23 January 1888 the Country Brewers' Society denied Sharp help when counsel advised that her case was "not a favourable one for getting the general question of magisterial discretion" decided as the trade wanted. It was not a "clean case" because the justices had given as one of their reasons for refusing to renew the license the remoteness of the inn from police supervision. Country Brewers' Society M.B. 4.; *Brewing Trade Review*, 1 Feb. 1888. *Brewing Trade Review*, May 1888, p. 198, pointed out: "the case was brought forward and urged on, not by the appellant, who had no money to go to law on the above scale, but by the local Licensed Victualers

Society." See also J. Danvers Power, *Sharpe [sic] v. Wakefield: A Full & Revised Report of the Judgments in the Queen's Bench Division, Court of Appeal, and the Arguments and Judgments in the House of Lords* (J.S. Phillips, 1891) pp. viii, 68. Susannah Sharp or Sharpe had a sister Jane who was a co-owner, but she is rarely mentioned.

[11] Guildhall, Meeting of firms of the Court of the Brewers Company, 11 May 1888. MS 5468, f. 189.

[12] Guildhall, Meetings of firms of the Court of the Brewers Company, 8 June and 2 Aug. 1888. MS 5468, ff. 193, 208. Sir Edward Clarke argued in Parliament (12 May 1890) that Sharp v. Wakefield was not a proper test case became the pub had been closed for four months and the applicant never was in occupation.

[13] Country Brewers Society, M.B. 5, 12 April 1889.

[14] Guildhall, Meetings of firms of the Court of the Brewers Company, 14 Dec. 1888 and 15 Feb. 1889. MS 5468, ff. 211, 212. This annual grant seems not to have been paid in the previous year, a further sign of the friction between the brewers and the retailers. In 1890 the Court of the Brewers Company agreed that member firms could subscribe up to ten guineas to the Licensed Victuallers' Protection Society. Meeting of the firms of the Court of the Brewers Company, 14 Feb. 1890. MS. 5468, f. 242.

[15] Alderman Hyslop, president of the provincial publicans organization, the License Victuallers National Defence League, at its annual meeting, 22 April 1891. *Northern Brewers' and Victuallers' Journal*, 25 April 1891. Reference courtesy of David W. Gutzke.

[16] For instance, at its 15-16 March 1888 annual conference the Licensed Victuallers National Defence League wanted compensation out of local rates. *Brewing Trade Review*, 1 April 1888.

[17] Balfour to Salisbury, 23 Nov. 1888, *Salisbury-Balfour Correspondence: Letters Exchanged between the Third Marquess of Salisbury and his Nephew Arthur James Balfour, 1869-1892*, ed. Robin Harcourt Williams (Hereford Record Society, 1988), p. 260.

[18] *Brewing Trade Review*, 1 Jan. 1887.

[19] On April 10, 1888, the Liberal Unionist whip, W.S. Caine, warned James Whyte, secretary of the United Kingdom Alliance, that the Government would press the compensation clauses of the local government bill. "Unless the temperance party throughout the country make such a stir as they have never made before, these clauses will certainly pass, and by large majorities." Newton, *W.S. Caine*, p. 192.

[20] University of Birmingham, Joseph Chamberlain papers, JC 6/5/3/8. As the drink trade was ill organized at this stage, Ritchie allegedly regarded E.W. Norfolk, the secretary of the London retail society, as the principal trade spokesman, although he also consulted a few leading brewery firms and the Country Brewers' Society. *Brewers' Journal*, 15 Nov. 1895, pp. 549-50. This is hard to believe. The London licensed victuallers' society itself was not very effective at this point in its history.

[21] *Brewers' Journal*, 15 July 1888, p. 337. See also David M. Fahey, "E.N. Buxton (1840-1924): Liberal Brewer, Big Game Hunter and Conservationist," *Brewery History* 178 (Spring 2019); Fahey, "Brewers, Publicans, and Staff in Late Victorian and Edwardian Licensed Trade Societies, Part 1."

---

[22] Guildhall Library, MS 5468, ff. 177-83, Brewers' Company, minutes, 6 April 1888. If the Liberals returned to power, the trade could expect harsher treatment, so "factious opposition" to the Local Government bill "would be mistaken policy." *Brewers' Guardian*, 3 April 1888.

[23] Brewers' Company, MS. 5468 ff. 177-80. Quotations courtesy of David W. Gutzke. According to a trade newspaper, "Lord Burton was evidently for a policy of action; Mr. Bonsor was in favour of holding a watching brief and doing nothing." *Brewers' Journal*, 15 June 1888, p. 337.

[24] Northumberland and Durham Brewers Association, 22 March 1888. Reference courtesy of David W. Gutzke.

[25] The Manchester brewers argued that the trade could have obtained security for licensed premises without the compensation clauses and blamed the Country Brewers' Society for weakness. *Licensing Struggles of a Generation: A History of the Brewers' Central Association (Manchester) from its Foundation in 1860 to the Present Day* (1897), p. 56. The anonymous author dedicated the book to David Irvine Flattely, one of the founders of the organization. Flattely had been an unsuccessful Conservative candidate for Parliament in 1885. He died in 1897. David W. Gutzke shared his copy of this rare book. The *Brewers' Journal*, 29 May 1888, pp. 161-62, was "inclined to support the action of the Manchester brewers rather than adopt the Fabian policy which apparently actuates other branches of our trade." See also the letters in the *Country Brewers' Gazette*, 17 May 1888, pp. 247-48.

[26] Many London publicans were either long-term leaseholders or freeholders who would do better from the compensation scheme than would their country counterparts. Basil L. Crapster, "Our Trade, Our Politics: A Study of the Political Activity of the British Liquor Industry, 1868-1910" (Ph.D. dissertation, Harvard University, 1949). pp. 327-29.

[27] Ritchie to Country Brewers' Society deputation, 11 May 1888. Country Brewers' Society minutes, annual general meeting, 22 Oct. 1888. A year earlier a majority of the brewers queried by the Society favored compensated reduction if it was confined to limited areas but disagreed on the methods. *Ibid.*, 25 Jan. 1887. W.H. Long opposed making concessions to the licensed victuallers. Long to Akers Douglas, 14 May 1888. U564 C346/2. References courtesy of David W. Gutzke.

[28] Whitbread made the proposal on May 9, 1888. Country Brewery Society, M.B. 4, May 29, 1888. Reference courtesy of David W. Gutzke

[29] *Brewing Trade Review*, 1 June 1888.

[30] Country Brewers Society, M.B. 4, 22 Oct. 1888. Reference courtesy of David W. Gutzke.

[31] *Brewing Trade Review*, 1 July 1888.

[32] *Times,* 4 June 1888, p. 8. The demonstration was organized and financed by Frederick Charrington, the teetotal member of a wealthy brewing family.

[33] *Times*, 9 June 1890, p. 10.

[34] Harcourt to Morley, 10 June 1888. Bodleian, Harcourt Ms 17, f. 36. Quoted with minor changes in A.G. Gardiner, *Life of Sir William Harcourt* (Constable, 1923) 2: 105. The biographer Gardiner had become a Radical in part because of the drink question, and in later life was a close friend of Leif Jones, then the president of the

United Kingdom Alliance. Stephen Koss, *Fleet Street Radical: A.G. Gardiner and the Daily News* (Archon Books, 1973), p. 23.

[35] *Parl. Deb.*, 3rd ser., CCCXXV, 10 April 1999, cols. 115, 116; J.L. Garvin, *Life of Joseph Chamberlain* (Macmillan, 1931-69) 2:181. (Garvin wrote the first three volumes, while Julian Amery wrote the final three volumes.) See also Gardiner, *Life of Harcourt* 2: 104-05.

[36] Hartington to Viscount Wolmer, 11 June 1888, Quoted in Peter George Davis, "The Role of the Liberal Unionist Party in British Politics, 1886-1895" (Ph.D. dissertation, University of London, 1974), p. 167.

[37] Many temperance minded Liberal Unionists, in and out of the House of Commons, drifted back to the Gladstonians in large part because of how the parties acted on the drink question. For instance, Alderman Alexander McDougall, JP (1836-1909), chairman of the United Kingdom Alliance executive committee for twenty years, was a Liberal Unionist candidate for Parliament in 1886 and a Gladstonian candidate in 1892. He was a Nonconformist who made his money as a manufacturing chemist and corn miller. See his obituary in *Alliance News,* 16 Dec. 1909, p. 812.

[38] Caine split with the Gladstonians over Irish Home Rule. See John Lea, "W.S. Caine and Irish Home Rule--A Study of the Radical Opposition of 1886," *Historical Studies* 1 no. 2 (Oct.1968): 55-66. Remaining a temperance militant, he demanded in 1887 that after the Irish question had been "settled," Parliament must address temperance. "We have been shunted a little too often, and we must take care that we are not shunted any more." Quoted in D.A. Hamer, *Liberal Politics in the Age of Gladstone and Rosebery* (Clarendon Press, 1973), p. 170.

[39] Marsh, *Discipline of Popular Government*, p. 12.

[40] Caine was the stereotype of the Christian businessman turned Radical politician, but he sometimes did the unexpected such as collecting modern watercolors. When the business in which he had invested went bankrupt, he paid its debts although he had no legal obligation to do so.

[41] John W. Davis, "Working-Class Make-Believe: the South Lambeth Parliament (1887-1890)," *Parliamentary History* 12 no. 3 (1993): 249-58.

[42] Caine's testimony on 2 March 1877, House of Lords select committee on intemperance.

[43] Ian Cawood, *The Liberal Unionist Party: A History* (I.B Taurus, 2012), pp. 24-25.

[44] Graham D. Goodlad, "Gladstone and His Rivals: Popular Liberal Perceptions of the Party Leadership in the Political Crisis of 1885-1886," in Eugenio F. Biagini and Alastair J. Reid, eds., *Currents of Radicalism: Popular Radicalism, Organised Labour and Party Politics in Britain, 1850-1914* (Cambridge University Press, 1991), p. 169.

[45] Caine to editor, 13 March 1887, in *Good Templars' Watchword*, 28 March 1887, p.199; Caine to editor, 25 Jan. [presumably misprint for July] 1887, in *Good Templars' Watchword*, 1 Aug. 1887, p. 483. In an undated memoir the Liberal Unionist Sir Henry James said: "W.S. Caine told me, towards the end of 1889, that he could not much longer stand being howled at and hooted at every Temperance meeting he attended, and should probably go back Gladstonian Liberalism, as he cared more for Temperance than Home Rule." Lord (G.R.) Askwith, *Lord James of*

Hereford (Ernest Benn, 1930), p. 190.

[46] *Good Templars' Watchword*, 11 July 1887, pp. 443-44; 18 July 1887, pp. 456-57.

[47] John Newton, *W.S. Caine* (James Nisbet, 1907), 191, 193-94, 316. Caine's papers do not survive. The old biography by Newton is supplemented by the entry in the *Oxford Dictionary of National Biography* which H.C.G. Matthews revised based on the original article by C.S. Woods. See also the obituary notice in *Abkari*, April 1903, pp. 43-50. After the collapse in 1893 of the iron company in which Caine was a partner, "he never seemed the same buoyant, strong man afterwards." Newton, *W.S. Caine*, p. 266. Caine had not played an active role in the business, but he promised to pay all the creditors from his own purse, about £40,000. Once wealthy, he died leaving just over £2,500. In the last eighteenth months of his life, he had a good-paying office as chairman of the United Kingdom Temperance and General Provident Institution. His financial difficulties forced him to sell many of his paintings. Obituary by John Stuart ("Memoir of a Valiant Leader") in *United Temperance Gazette* 8 no. 2 (June 1908): 52-53. His widow served in 1912-15 as president of the Women's Total Abstinence Union. For Caine's leadership in the fight against drink and drugs in India, see James H. Mills, "Cannabis in the Commons: Colonial Networks, Missionary Politics and the Origins of the Indian Hemp Commission, 1893-4," *Journal of Colonialism and Colonial History* 6 no. 1 (2005). Caine helped found the Anglo-India Temperance Association in 1888 and its journal *Abkari*, published beginning in 1890 and edited by Caine's private secretary (1892-1903) Frederick Grubb. For Grubb, see his twenty-page memoir, *Fifty Years' Work for India: My Temperance Jubilee* (H. J. Rowlings & Sons, 1942).

[48] *Alliance News*, 16 May 1888, Caine to Burns, 11 May 1888.

[49] *Hansard*, 3rd ser. CCCXXIV, cols., 1499-1500, 17 April 1888.

[50] Chapter 11 in Newton, *W.S. Caine*, is devoted to the 1888 compensation controversy.

[51] For the CETS, see the unpublished manuscript by Gerald Wayne Olsen, "Drink and the British Establishment--The Church of England Temperance Society, 1873-1919" (2003). Leading a CETS deputation to Ritchie, Canon Ellison asked that the compensation go the actual license holder only.

[52] Lambeth Palace Library, Church of England Temperance Society minutes, Legislative Subcommittee, 13 June 1888, Ms 2044, ff. 59-63. Later the memorandum summarizing the story was ordered expunged from the minutes. Although crossed out, the material is easily read. Caine's biographer John Newton said that from the time that he was acquainted with Caine (1890), he was open to compensation as part of a final settlement of the drink question. Newton, *W.S. Caine*, p. 215.

[53] Hussey probably was a Good Templar as he contributed to the National Temperance and Templar Home Mission Fund in 1885.

[54] *Parl. Deb.*, 3rd ser., CCCXVII, 28 June 1888, cols. 1582-83.

[55] Cosmo Bonsor discussed with temperance leaders in the House of Commons about the spending of the grant of new licenses. They were willing to support it for a single year only. Bonsor considered this "too short" a period. Guildhall Library, Meeting of Firms of the Court of Brewers Company. MS. 5468 f. 196, 21 June 1888. Bonsor wanted any new licenses to be a transfer of a license from another district.

National Trade Defence Association, M.B.1, f. 29-30, 8 Nov. 1889.

[56] Salisbury to Lady John Manners, 12 June 1888. Quoted in Marsh, *Discipline of Popular Government*, p. 128. Joseph Chamberlain regarded the Government as "very ill-judged in bringing forward the Licensing question again," but believed "the damaging effect would wear off, and would be forgotten by the time of the next General Election." E.W Hamilton journal, 25 June 1890, quoted in Davis, "The Role of the Liberal Unionist Party in British Politics, 1886-1895," p. 181.

[57] Harcourt to John Morley, 10 June 1888. Bodleian, Harcourt Ms 17, f. 35.

[58] *Parl. Deb.*, 3rd ser., CCLIII, 18 June 1880, col. 363. See also 5 March 1880, cols. 465-75; 15 May 1890, col. 1003.

[59] National Trade Defence Fund minute books, Fund committee, Nov. 8, 1889, fol. 29-30; 17 Dec. 1889, fol. 31.

[60] Crapster, "Our Trade, Our Politics," p. 333. Nearly all the Liberal Unionists supported Sunday closing. David W. Gutzke, *Protecting the Pub: Brewers and Publicans against Temperance* (Royal Historical Society, 1989). p. 100.

[61] Brewers' Company, Guildhall Ms 5468, f. 209. For the London and provincial licensed victuallers as opponents of Sunday closing, see the Parliamentary Committee of the Licesned Victuallers of the United Kingdom, *Sessional Report*, 1888.

[62] Harcourt to John Morley, 10 June 1888. Bodleian, Harcourt Ms 17, f. 36.

[63] *Parl. Deb.*, 3rd ser., CCCXXVIII, 28 June 1888, cols. 1589, 1590.

[64] *Parl. Deb.*, 3rd ser., CCCXXVIII, 28 June 1888, cols. 1590, 1591-1600.

[65] A.E. Dingle, *The Campaign for Prohibition in Victorian England: The United Kingdom Alliance. 1871-1895* (Croom Helm, 1980), p. 123. Dingle pointed out that Alliance members criticized Lawson for his support of the Liberal MP and wine merchant Mark Beaufoy.

[66] *Parl. Deb.*, 3rd ser., CCCXXVIII, 28 June 1888, cols. 1602-09.

[67] *Good Templars' Watchword*, 16 July 1888, p. 349. In this internal quarrel among temperance reformers, Malins agreed with Caine. See also Caine's letter to the editor, 26 June 1888, *Good Templars' Watchword*, 2 July 1888, p. 329.

[68] *Times*, 20 Nov. 1889, p. 10. Quoted in D.A. Hamer, *John Morley: Liberal Intellectual in Politics* (Clarendon Press, 1968), p. 244.

[69] Lawson to Whyte, 24 Nov. 1889, in Alliance minutes, 27 Nov. 1889.

[70] Lawson to Whyte, 26 Nov. 1889, in Alliance minutes, 27 Nov. 1889.

[71] National Liberal Federation, *Proceedings* (1889), p. 127. Originally the Federation planned to ask for the popular control of the liquor traffic. It could mean a referendum on reducing the number of licensed premises rather than local prohibition. See Henry Carter, *The English Temperance Movement: A Study in Objectives* (Epworth Press, 1933), pp. 212-18. For Lloyd George's role, see *Alliance News*, 13 Dec. 1889, p. 998.

[72] United Kingdom Alliance, Annual Report, in *Alliance News,* 17 Oct. 1890, p. 675.

[73] Unlike the 1888 proposal, the 1890 bill included Scotland as well as England and Wales.

[74] Guildhall Library, Brewers' Company minutes, 14, 19, 20, 28 March 1890. Ms 5468, ff. 242-48, 298. On Goschen and taxes on the brewers, also see W.H. Smith to Balfour, 13 April 1889. British Library, Add. 49696, f. 95b, 96b. W.H. Smith to

---

Akers-Douglas, 14 April 1889. U564 C25/83. The last of these archival references courtesy of David W. Gutzke.

[75] Smith to Goschen, 9 April 1890; Goschen to Smith, 9 April 1890. Quoted in Thomas J. Spinner, *George Joachim Goschen* (Cambridge University Press, 1973), p. 144. Ritchie said that the licensing proposals were much misunderstood. Ritchie to W.H. Smith, 14 May 1890. Hambleden papers PS 15/25.

[76] Ritchie, Cabinet memorandum, 2 April 1890. Public Record Office, Cab. 37/27. The county councils could not forbid new licenses for railway refreshment rooms, eating-houses, or hotels. Crapster, "Our Trade, Our Politics," p. 328.

[77] Salisbury to Goschen, 12 April 1890. Quoted in Spinner, *Goschen*, p. 144.

[78] Gutzke, *Protecting the Pub*, p. 105.

[79] 28 March 1890, Dudley W.R. Bahlman, ed., *The Diary of Sir Edward Walter Hamilton, 1885-1906* (University of Hull Press, 1993), p. 112. On 6 April 1890 (p. 113), he added that "brewers and licensed victuallers are awkward and noisy customers to deal with." According to Hamilton, Gladstone later (7 April 1891, p. 139) described "the proposal for compensating publicans" as "the greatest blunder he ever remembered to have been made in Parliament by a Chancellor of the Exchequer."

[80] William Borland to James Parker Smith, 16 May 1890. Quoted in Davis, "Role of the Liberal Unionist Party," p. 176.

[81] *Parl. Deb.*, 3rd ser., CCCXLIV, 12 May 1890, esp. cols. 705-06, 708, 09, 711-12.

[82] Smith to Caine, 5 May, 1890, quoted in Newton, *W.S. Caine*, p. 215.

[83] *Parl. Deb.*, 3rd ser., CCXLVIV, 7 May 1890, col.

[84] *Parl. Deb.*, 3rd ser., CCXLV, 12 June 1890, col. 749.

[85] Brewers' Society, National Trade Defence Fund committee minutes, 19 May 1890, f. 35; Guildhall Library, Brewers' Company minutes, 20 May 1890, Ms 5468, f. 259.

[86] J. Danvers Power, memorandum, 16 May 1890, apparently sent to W.H. Smith. Hambleden MSS, PS 15/26. Emily Smith was a daughter of Frederick Dawes Danvers.

[87] *Parl. Deb.*, 3rd ser., CCCXLIV, 15 May 1890, especially cols. 994-95, 1002-03. On the eve of Gladstone's speech Harcourt nervously told his son: "I *hope* we have got the G.O.M. up the mark." Bodleian, Harcourt Ms 157, f. 145.

[88] *Parl. Deb.*, 3rd ser., CCCXLV, 13 June 1890, cols. 934-35. The Irish nationalist T.M. Healy pointed out that Russell "was secretary to the Dublin Temperance Association, and a vehement opponent of the Licensed trade." With irony, Healy continued: "Devoid of the geniality and humour of his race, he sported a bilious face and splenetic manners." Healy, *Letters and Leaders of My Day* (Frederick A. Stokes, 1928) 1: 261, quoted in Davis, "The Role of the Liberal Unionist Party," 324. Davis inverted the words in the title of Healy's memoir.

[89] Churchill to Harcourt, 26 July 1890. Quoted in James B. Brown, "The Pig or the Stye: Drink and Poverty in Victorian England," *International Review of Social History* 18 (1973): 384.

[90] George Smith to Lord Mount Edgcumbe, 6 June 1890, forwarded to W.H. Smith, 7 June 1890. Hambleden MSS, PS 15/32. Quoted, without citing the dates of the correspondence, in Lord Chilston, *W.H. Smith* (Routledge and Kegan Paul, 1965), p. 324.

[91] *Brewers' Journal*, 15 May 1890; *Brewing Trade Review*, 1 June 1890 (weekly edition), Nov. 1895. For Walker, see David M. Fahey, "Brewers, Publicans and Staff in Late Victorian and Edwardian Licensed Trade Societies, Part II," *Brewery History* 181 (Winter 2019): 7-8; for Buxton, see Fahey, "E.N. Buxton (1840-1924)."

[92] For Chamberlain, see Joseph Chamberlain, *A Political Memoir, 1880-92*, ed. C.H.D. Howard (London, Batchworth, 1953), p. 289.

[93] Although most Liberal Unionists became indistinguishable from Conservatives, some defected either early (such as W.S. Caine) or late. A. Cameron Corbert (1856-1933), a Scottish MP, rejoined the Liberal Party in 1908 after twenty-two years as Liberal Unionist. T.W. Russell (1841-1920), an Ulster MP, was successively a Liberal Unionist and an Independent Unionist before rejoining the Liberal Party. He held office in a Liberal government and was rewarded with a baronetcy.

[94] *Alliance News*, 9 May 1890, p. 293. Caine at the consultative council of the United Kingdom Alliance, 2 May 1890, offered to consider compensation as part of a final settlement of the licensing question. Newton, *W.S. Caine*, p. 215.

[95] *Parl. Deb.*, 3rd ser., CCXLIV, cols. 729-30.

[96] *Parl. Deb.*, 3rd ser., CCCXLIV, 12 May 1890, cols. 717-43. Many Liberal Unionists in the country agreed with Caine about compensation. A Liberal Unionist M.P., holding a Scottish seat, received a letter from "a Radical, [who] worked at the last general election to defeat Mr. Gladstone and instal the Tories. Their compensation proposals will render that impossible at the next election. They are bound to bring in and pass if they can a local government Bill for Ireland, and that being done most temperance reformers amongst the Unionists will rather risk the return to power of Mr. Gladstone than retain the authors of compensation to publicans. The Government should remember that some of the strongest Unionists are Temperance reformers. Some of the keenest Radical Unionists in Glasgow are of that class. Any chance of carrying doubtful seats, and there are many such, depends upon the support of the Liberal Unionists. While these men will not make temperance propaganda an essential part of their support, they will make it a condition that the chance of temperance legislation in the future is not destroyed by the gratuitous concession of the principle of compensation." William Borland to James Parker Smith, 16 May 1890. Quoted in Davis, "The Role of the Liberal Unionist Party," p. 176.

[97] Harcourt to Lewis Harcourt, 14 May 1890. Bodleian, Harcourt Ms 151 f. 145.

[98] Chilston, *W.H. Smith*, p. 324. For Caine's circular letter, 11 June 1890, and the memorial, see Hambleden MSS, PS 15/35, 36.

[99] Alliance minutes, 11 June 1890. Caine agreed to the memorial on 10 June.

[100] William Borland to James Parker Smith, 16 May 1890. Quoted in Davis, "The Role of the Liberal Unionist Party," p. 176.

[101] West to Churchill, 17 May 1890. Churchill College, Lord Randolph Churchill papers, no. 3557.

[102] *Times*, 14 June 1890, p. 12.

[103] *Parl. Deb.*, 3rd ser., CCCXLV, 16 June 1890, col. 1046, 1051.

[104] *Parl. Deb.*, 3rd ser., CCCXLV, 16 June 1890, col. 1054.

[105] By this point the trade was willing to fund compensation provided that there was no time limit. A few years later (19 Jan. 1893) the *Pall Mall Gazette* interviewed

Cosmo Bonsor. Accepting that the burden of compensation would be borne by the trade, Bonsor said: "I told Mr. Ritchie on the night that the introduced his bill that it would fail because he proposed to put a burden on the ratepayers." In a subsequent *Pall Mall Gazette* interview (23 Jan. 1893) with Charles Walker, the chairman of the London publicans, Walker opposed any reduction in the number of public houses on the grounds that it would mean that "uncontrolled clubs" would multiply.

[106] According to the trade, the Government made a bargain with the brewers at a private meeting, on 19 June 1890, that the new license fees would be refunded, if the compensation clauses were not passed. Goschen later denied this. MS, 5468 d. 302, 12 June 1891 (private memorandum). Reference courtesy of David W. Gutzke.

[107] David Lloyd George to William George, 21 June 1890. Quoted in Herbert DuParq, *Life of David Lloyd George* (Caxton, 1912), 1: 112. Lloyd George devoted his maiden speech in the House of Commons to an attack on the purchase proposals.

[108] Arthur Elliott, *The Life of George Joachim Goschen* (Longmans, 1911), 2: 167. Joseph Chamberlain "had advised the Government to summon a meeting of the party and to endeavour to push [the licensing clauses] through." Chamberlain, *A Political Memoir, 1880-92*), p. 289.

[109] Chilston, *W.H. Smith*, p. 324.

[110] *Parl. Deb.*, 3rd ser., CCCXLV, 24 June 1890, cols. 1799-1803.

[111] Newton, *W.S. Caine*, p. 220. He resigned as whip and applied for the Chiltern Hundreds on 23 June 1890. The Government abandoned its compensation clauses on 26 June 1890.

[112] Cawood, *Liberal Unionist Party*, p. 59.

[113]. Caine to Whyte, 24 June 1890, in Alliance minutes, 19-25 June 1890.

[114] Caine to UKA, two telegrams, 26 June 1890; Caine to Whyte, 26 June 1890, in Alliance minutes, 26 June-2 July 1890.

[115] J. Martin Skinner to Whyte, 27 June 1890, in Alliance minutes, 26 June-2 July 1890.

[116] The Lord President of the Council referred to "the fanatical & conceited folly of Caine" in reporting the election results to his diary. *The Diary of Gathorne Hardy, Later Lord Cranbrook, 1866-1892*, ed. Nancy E. Johnson (Clarendon Press, 1981), p. 773.

[117] Henry Hibbert at UKA annual meeting in *Alliance News*, 24 Oct. 1890, p. 692. Family members persuaded Lloyd George not to campaign on behalf of Caine in Barrow. Caine had invited him to come. W.R.P. George, *Lloyd George: Backbencher* (Gomer Press, 1983), pp. 33-35.

[118] Harcourt to Caine, 3 July 1890. Bodleian, Harcourt Ms 218 ff. 20-31. Quoted in Newton, *W.S. Caine*, pp. 228-29. The Gladstonians won ten consecutive bye-elections from April to October 1890, so it was clear that the Liberal Unionist gamble for control of the Liberal party had failed. Douglas Reid Legg, "The Fourth Cabinet of William E. Gladstone, 1892-1894" (M.A. thesis, University of Notre Dame, 1957), p. 26.

[119] Caine to Chamberlain, 27 March 1892. University of Birmingham, Joseph Chamberlain papers, JC 5/10/10b. Caine was surprised that no other temperance supporter among the Liberal Unionist MPs joined him in resigning. Joining Caine in resigning was only an agent of Leonard Courtney in Cornwall. Wesley Ferris, "The

Liberal Unionist Party, 1886-1912" (Ph.D. dissertation, McMaster University, 2008), p. 241.

[120] H.V. Emy, *Liberals, Radicals and Social Politics, 1892-1914* (Cambridge University Press, 1973), p. 82.

[121] WSLUA minute book, quoted in Cawood, *Liberal Unionist Party*, p. 59.

[122] Quoted in Richard Shannon, *Gladstone: Heroic Minister, 1865-1898* (Allen Lane/Penguin Press, 1999), p. 504.

[123] Shiman, *Crusade against Drink in Victorian England* (Macmillan, 1988), p. 217.

[124] Michael K. Barker, *Gladstone and Radicalism: The Reconstruction of Liberal Policy in Britain, 1885-94* (Harvester Press, 1975), p. 210.

[125] John Morley, memorandum, 30 Dec. 1890, Harcourt papers, quoted in Barker, *Gladstone and Radicalism*, pp. 258-59. (comment on Gladstone to Arnold Morley, 26 Dec. 1890.)

[126] Harcourt to John Morley, 3 Jan. 1891, Harcourt papers, quoted in Barker, *Gladstone and Radicalism*, p. 210.

[127] Harcourt to Gladstone, 1 Jan. 1891. Bodleian, Harcourt Ms 11 f. 202. See also Arnold Morley to Gladstone, 30 Dec. 1890, 1 Jan. 1891. BL, William Gladstone papers, Add. Ms. 44254 ff. 63-64, 67-68.

[128] Gladstone to Harcourt, 2 Jan. 1891. Bodleian, Harcourt Ms. 11 f. 204.

[129] Caine to Gladstone, 24 Sept. 1891. BL, William Gladstone paper, Add. Ms. 44513 ff. 181-82.

[130] Lawson to Gladstone, 27 Sept. 1891. BL, William Gladstone papers, Add. Ms. 44513 ff. 183-86. Lawson's emphasis. "I would very respectfully suggest that it is unnecessary to raise that matter [compensation] at present."

[131] National Liberal Federation, *Proceedings* (1891), p. 92.

[132] Ibid., 103. There is a slightly different text in *Times*, 3 Oct. 1891, p. 10. Herbert Gladstone argued that at Newcastle his father had given in to the party as represented by Francis Schnadhorst, the secretary of the National Liberal Federation, and that he had made clear at Newcastle that the policy "was for the future and others rather than the present and himself." Herbert Gladstone to Robert Hudson (Schnadhorst's successor as Federation secretary), 10 March 1898. BL, Herbert Gladstone papers, Add. Ms. 46022, ff. 15-16.

[133] Lawson to Gladstone, 1 Dec, 1891. BL, William Gladstone papers, Add. Ms. 44513 ff. 284-87.

[134] Herbert Gladstone's memoir about his father (*After Thirty Years*, first published in 1928) has no index entry for licensing, temperance, or the Veto. The major recent biography is equally silent about alcoholic drink. H.C.G. Matthew, *Gladstone, 1875-1898* (Clarendon Press, 1995). According to Herbert Gladstone's book, the elder Gladstone "strongly disliked a teetotal dinner" such as one at Sir Wilfrid Lawson's (p. 44), date not mentioned.

[135] Quoted in Shannon, *Gladstone: Heroic Minister*, p. 508.

CHAPTER FOUR

THE LIBERALS AND LOCAL VETO

Less than a year after endorsing the Newcastle Programme, Gladstone formed his fourth and final ministry. The Liberals and their Irish allies had narrowly defeated the Unionist parties in the general election held in the summer of 1892. Although Irish Home Rule dominated the legislative program, the Parnell divorce case of 1890 encouraged the Liberal Party to consider other issues too.

Despite the Prime Minister's commitment at Newcastle and the pledges of all but a handful of Liberal MPs, the Government probably would not have introduced a prohibition bill except for Harcourt.[1] Harcourt was abrasive, ambitious, and many people believed opportunistic. Asquith complained about his "lack of any sense of proportion, his incapacity for self-restraint, and his perverse delight in inflaming and embittering every controversy."[2] Harcourt may have regarded temperance support useful in his quest to succeed the elderly Gladstone as party leader. As early as 1882, meeting a temperance deputation, he described himself as "practically a teetotaler. "[3] If so, he was a hard-drinking teetotaler. His son's journals for November 13, 1885, report that his father and he "had drunk about [three and a half] bottles of claret during the evening" and added "that is what comes of talking local option and temperance."[4]

By 1892, when he became chancellor of the exchequer, Harcourt was "a jovial, indeed a rather Falstaffian, figure, known as Jumbo, with a formidable temper which made him many enemies, particularly among his immediate colleagues." The author of this description, Peter Stansky, wonders in his *Oxford Dictionary of National Biography* article whether Harcourt would have been less abrasive, easier to work with if he gone to a public school instead of being privately tutored.

Limitations in parliamentary time made the priority awarded among electoral promises crucial. In the elections the advanced temperance party had failed to convince most Liberal candidates that it was a politically indispensable ally.[5] Harcourt grumbled about its "want of activity and zeal." Writing the prohibitionist W.S. Caine, Harcourt said: "I confess I don't know any of the other water drinkers who will do an hour's work for the cause."[6]

Liberal candidates complained that temperance organizations provided little help after they had demanded pledges that antagonized the drink trade. Caine offered to prove to any complaining Liberal candidate "that at least 30% of his canvassers and active workers are teetotalers." "It is our habit as an organization [the Alliance] to join the candidate's election committee, and work in connection with his party organization. Surely this is better than messing about as independent teetotalers. It doesn't show as well, but it *gets men in*."[7] Caine encouraged optimism about support for a Veto bill, despite the Irish Nationalists being "a sickly lot on all temperance legislation." Although the Good Templars and others might be unhappy about postponing Sunday closing, "my personal influence with the extreme men is considerable."[8]

Gladstone preferred a less controversial alternative to the Veto: transferring the existing licenses powers from the JPs to the County Councils.[9] A well-connected Liberal fortnightly, the *Speaker*, campaigned for this substitution, together with limited compensation and an auction of licenses to the highest bidder.[10] Recognizing this opposition, Caine lost confidence in the Government sponsoring a bill, but other Alliance stalwarts intended to press the Government hard. For instance, T.P. Whittaker told an Alliance meeting "to show more fight." "Those who made the loudest demand would be attended to first."[11]

Harcourt, the new Chancellor of the Exchequer, mobilized a section of the Cabinet on behalf of the Veto and other domestic reforms. At a dinner meeting in late October, Harcourt, Arnold Morley, James Bryce, H.H. Fowler, G.O Trevelyan, and Sir Arthur Acland decided to insist on a full domestic program including the Veto. Reluctantly Gladstone agreed to the enlarged legislative program.[12] He told a critic of the licensing bill "it had not been prepared to embody his views."[13] The Cabinet authorized a committee chaired by Harcourt to draft a Veto bill. Harcourt's committee enjoyed considerable freedom. The Newcastle Programme had avoided contentious detail, Gladstone had made no clear pronouncement on compensation, and the Chancellor of the Exchequer had the confidence of the principal prohibitionists. Caine suggested a private member's bill that the Government "eventually" would adopt.[14] Shortly after the Government had been organized Lawson promised Harcourt: "Bring in any Licensing Reform Scheme which you think would be either useful or popular. Keep compensation *out* of it, and keep the direct veto *in* it, and you will have the Temperance forces at your back."[15]

In search of a compromise on compensation Harcourt's committee studied the bills recently drafted by the moderate Westminster and Manchester temperance reform committees. Although the Cabinet committee rejected the Westminster scheme of limited money compensation ("which is understood to be the Liberal Unionist idea"), the committee showed interest in the Manchester proposal for a five-year time limit that delayed the exercise of the Veto to allow the owners of licensed property to accumulate a sinking fund.[16] Despite Harcourt's fears, when the advanced reformers were consulted, they did not characterize the time limit as something that would make them withdraw support. Caine said: "everything depends on what we are to get at the end of the five years." Later he confided to Asquith (1852-1928) that the temperance party would "take a time limit rather than lose the bill."[17] Although dismayed by the "abominable proposal" of a time limit, Lawson answered Harcourt noncommittally. He considered it the business of the Government to draft its own bill and the business of the temperance party to criticize any shortcomings in it.[18] Fearing private agreements that sacrificed the right of public criticisms, he discouraged the Alliance from sending a deputation to the Government to discuss the draft bill. "The discussions invariably drift into licensing propositions and then [the members of the deputation] get committed to some folly or other unless they are wary, which all of them are *not*."[19] This may have been a tactical error on Lawson's part. His caution, together with Caine's candid willingness to accept a time limit, emboldened the Cabinet committee to insert a time limit into its bill, one reduced in length from the Manchester proposal (five years) to three years.

The advanced temperance party had to swallow even larger concessions that left the meaning of Local Veto in the bill largely symbolic. Harcourt's committee decided to require a two-thirds' vote in a prohibition referendum rather than a simple majority. Numerous exceptions eroded the principle of the authority of local residents to prohibit the sale of drink. The Veto would not apply to the sale of drink in hotels, restaurants, eating houses, and railway refreshment rooms, "viewed as extensions of the drinker's home" or to those off-licenses such as wine merchants that had only excise licenses. The bill did affect other off-licenses that needed a license from the magistrates. Avoiding the places where the comfortable classes got their drink, the bill struck at public houses where the working classes drank. Consequently, enemies characterized it as a "Rich Man's Protection Bill" and a "Poor Man's Coercion Bill." The bill also accumulated secondary reforms to supplement the prohibitive veto.

The committee inserted a local option for Sunday closing in the bill despite the insistence of the temperance movement that Sunday closing be mandatory.[20] The attitude of the advanced temperance party toward Sunday closing is a reminder that local option was a tactic and not something liked for its own sake. National prohibition was politically impractical, so the advanced temperance party called for Direct Local Veto. Sunday closing existed on a national basis in Scotland, Wales, and most of Ireland, so the advanced temperance party regarded national Sunday closing as practical politics and consequently disliked making it subject to local option referendums.

Initially the committee also favored a parallel bill to create elected licensing authorities. To establish the principle of Local Veto without any extraneous issues Caine suggested the Government restrict the bill to Scotland that already had Sunday closing and elected licensing authorities. Harcourt rejected this "tempting" proposal.[21] It is unlikely that the advanced temperance party would have accepted it as adequate. Indeed, restive Welsh MPs wanted priority for a Welsh temperance bill.[22]

The drafting of the bill showed less than complete Liberal commitment to drastic temperance reform. The Cabinet committee often was divided on what to put in the bill. For instance, a consensus to drop a clause prohibiting new licenses rested on such conflicting motives as a belief in the necessity for new licenses, recognition of their negligible numbers, and reluctance to strengthen the monopoly value of existing licenses. Asquith, who was Home Secretary, spoke out for a strong bill, while Herschell, the Lord Chancellor, doubted that the House of Commons would support a drastic bill. Supposedly Harcourt admitted that the bill would be a dead letter in the unlikely event that it became law. Although he insisted that party honor required the attempt to enact a Veto bill, he gloomily hinted that unless the temperance party supported the Government proposals vigorously, it might be a reluctant, symbolic fight, "like a French duel."[23]

There still was a possibility doing a deal with the drink trade. C.H. Croxton Powell, a Liberal who formerly had been employed by a drink trade organization, asked that Harcourt consult Lord Burton about a reduction in the number of licenses with equitable compensation. Powell made the amazing claim that a majority of retail license holders were Liberals.[24]

The Liberal brewer Edward North Buxton wrote Harcourt a series of letters in November and December 1892 and again in May 1893.[25] Buxton hoped to replace the Veto is the Liberal program with a reduction in the number of licensed premises combined with money compensation provided by the trade. In his 23 November letter, Buxton argued that reduction in numbers after a five-year time limit (the Manchester bill) would confiscate millions of pounds of property in London alone. He favored an extension of the principle in the Westminster bill that surviving licenses that profit from the elimination of competition should pay into a fund to compensate those who lost their licenses. He said that this proposal was his alone, and he did not claim that other brewers would support it. "Nevertheless, it is on these lines that an equitable settlement will be found." In his December letter he suggested that it would be more accurate to call money compensation "'mutual insurance,' rendered possible by Act of Parliament." He added: "The purgatory of hot water in which the Trade are kept is worse than the furnace to which some would consign them." Buxton at this stage was still very much a Liberal partisan. "I profoundly distrust the Tories who, through Goschen and Ritchie, have done us more harm than enough." In his May letter Buxton called for a Royal Commission and argued that legislation had to deal with clubs and with the reduction in the number of licenses, combined with what he called the "betterment" principle of compensation. "Three men around a table could produce a workable scheme."[26] Years later the head of the London licensed victuallers' organization paid tribute to Buxton's "masterful tact, and his indomitable energy."[27]

Buxton was a public-spirited reformer who had served as a member of the London school board for seventeen years and as chairman in 1885-86. He was a Liberal member of the House of Commons briefly, 1885-1886. According to Elizabeth Baigent in the *Oxford Dictionary of National Biography*, he "supported free schools, legislation against the enclosure of the commons, the enfranchisement of long leaseholds, and disestablishment in Scotland and Wales." He was a wealthy and devout philanthropist, best known as a champion of public spaces for the recreation of ordinary people. He insisted that Epping Forest remain a forest and not become a park. As a young man, he had been a daring Alpine climber. Later he became a big game hunter. He was one of the first to suggest shooting animals with a camera rather than with a gun. He helped organize a society for the preservation of big game that, renamed, still exists today. As a vice-president of the Commons Preservation Society, he helped save Epping Forest and many other open spaces and footpaths for the public. As his final benefaction he gave Hatfield Forest to the National Trust.[28]

Harcourt could expect little help from Gladstone who neither liked nor understood the bill. The Prime Minister confusingly told the Queen: "the object of Sir Wm. Harcourt's Local Veto bill is to enable the rate payers of different districts to refuse public houses to any applicant and thereby reduce the number of public houses." With lack of enthusiasm, he added that the bill "is mixed up with questions of compensation and payments which make it rather a complicated measure."[29] He told a friend who complained about the lack of compensation that the bill did not express his own views.[30]

Despite the compromises embodied in the bill and the misgivings of the Government that sponsored it, the introduction of the Liquor Traffic (Local Control) bill marked the high point for the prohibitionist agitation in Britain. Harcourt presented the bill to the House of Commons on 27 February 1893.[31] It provided the local electors (including women) with two referendum options: in both England and Wales a prohibitive Veto or total closing which required a two thirds' majority for both adoption and repeal; and in England Sunday closing which required a simple majority. Scotland was offered parallel legislation. As a concession to license holders the Veto referendum would not take effect until three years after the enactment of the bill.[32] To appease the Irish Home Rulers the bill would not apply to their hard drinking country. Some Nationalist MPs were personally involved in the drink trade.[33] According to Sir E.W. Hamilton's diary, the day after Harcourt had introduced the bill he admitted privately that it was unlikely to become law and that if it did, "it probably will be a dead letter."[34] The Liberal MP and historian Herbert Paul described the bill as "perhaps the most unpopular measure ever brought into the House of Commons."[35]

In justifying the bill Harcourt had to pick his way carefully. Arguments based on the evils caused by drink and the drink trade raised doubts about the adequacy of the bill as a measure of temperance reform, while arguments based on local self-government suggested the need for the delegation of greater powers. Arguments that justified restrictions on local control undermined the principle of local option.

Harcourt said that the bill was not intended to prevent drinking. Instead, it authorized the local electors to prevent what he later called tippling, public drinking not part of a meal. It did not attempt to prevent the purchase of drink for consumption at home or at places construed as an extension of home such as hotels, restaurants, eating-houses, railway refreshment rooms, and clubs.

According to Harcourt, the means of local control was indispensable to the end desired, a responsible and self-disciplined people. "If the people are to be reformed they must be the authors of their own reformation." As a practical matter the law could not be ahead of public opinion, but localities with advanced attitudes need not tarry for the country as a whole. Harcourt argued that the question was one of areas. He wanted public opinion to be tested in the smallest area possible, the parish, with the largest electorate available, the municipal voters who included a few women (but who, as his critics noted, excluded many working men as they were not ratepayers). For the same reason, to keep in step with public opinion, he proposed that

Sunday closing be decided by local referendum rather than by statute. He admitted that in most parts of England, particularly London, public opinion was not ready.

Harcourt acknowledged that his bill was not a comprehensive remedy. He promised to supplement it later with a reform of the licensing laws that would include a popular licensing authority to replace the appointed magistrates in administering them. He tried to minimize the partisan and controversial character of his bill by comparing it with the bill that Lord Randolph Churchill had introduced as a private member in 1890.

Although the Opposition did not force a division, and Goschen denied that it opposed the bill from a party standpoint, the Unionists in the brief first reading debate rejected both the details of the bill and its principle. Despite *Sharp v. Wakefield,* the brewer Cosmo Bonsor claimed that licenses had an absolute right to renewal. He also argued that the bill would aggravate intemperance by encouraging unregulated clubs. In his maiden speech a Tory active in the Church of England Temperance Society, C.E. Tritton, advocated a reduction in the number of licensed premises instead of the Veto. T.W. Russell, a Liberal Unionist from Ulster, wanted both the Veto and reduction. Harcourt had told F.W. Farrar that the success of the bill depended to a large degree on CETS support. If the CETS insisted on "pecuniary compensation [then] we may bid a long farewell to any Temperance Legislation in this generation."[36]

Welsh Liberals preferred a bill for Wales alone, a bill that would distract from Harcourt's. Lloyd George told a Welsh reformer: "Raper & Co. [of the United Kingdom Alliance] came foaming and spitting" in protest and threatened not to support a Welsh bill if it came to a vote. [37]

Harcourt's bill completed the politicization of the temperance question. The drink trade and the advanced temperance party tightened their alliances with the respective major political parties. The licensed trade greatly strengthened its defense organization. The threat of prohibition aroused even the normally somnolent country publicans. Although the trade held protest meetings, particularly in London, it concentrated in 1893 on circulating petitions against the bill. They attracted more than a million signatures, twice that of the temperance petitions in support of the bill.[38] Temperance reformers lamented their limited financial resources and staff as compared with a wealthy trade and tens of thousands of public houses. At one point the Alliance had overdrawn its bank account by £3,000.[39]

In rejecting Harcourt's bill Unionist politicians happily combined their general principles with a stand popular in working-class constituencies. In Unionist eyes the Local Veto bill violated the rights of private property and of personal liberty, discriminated against workingmen, often voteless under Harcourt's bill, robbing them of the poor man's club by its attack on the public house, embodied the disgraceful practice of a party bartering the public trust for the votes of faddist minorities, and failed to provide real remedies for the problem of intemperance.

Reginald Mortimer, secretary of the Country Brewers' Society and manager of the National Trade Defence Fund, explained what he saw as the problem in an interview published in a new Liberal evening newspaper, the *Westminster Gazette*.[40] He argued that the bill did not let the people affected decide.[41] "Those who will vote on the question whether there is or not to be a public-house will be those who do not use the public-house and not those who do use it. Honestly, I never use the public-house, because I don't need to; but my man-servant often goes, and he hasn't got a vote." Despite Mortimer's argument, many working class and trade union leaders signed a petition in favor Harcourt's bill. They included John Burns, Havelock Wilson, J. Keir Hardie, Sam Woods, Ben Tillett, Joseph Arch, Robert Smillie, Pete Curran, and Tom Mann.[42]

Joseph Chamberlain, long an advocate of temperance reform, was prominent among the new allies of the drink trade. In a celebrated speech before an audience of more than ten thousand at Bingley Hall in Birmingham on 6 April he attacked the Alliance and the Veto and won the permanent friendship of the drink trade. The *Times*, 7 April, reported the speech as follows.

> There are three main objections to this Bill. In the first place it will be ineffective. It involves the *maximum* of inconvenience and the *minimum* of real temperance reform. It is invidious because it will press hard upon the working classes and it will not touch the propertied classes at all. In the third place it is unjust, because it destroys the means of sustenance of one great class of the community without giving them the compensation which has always been given in similar cases. And to that I will add one more objection, and that it is dishonest (hear, hear) because it is brought in to serve political exigencies (hear, hear)."

Chamberlain argued that if the government wanted to advance temperance it should provide a referendum for a reduction in the number of licensed houses and that if it wanted to be just it should provide money compensation for those who lost their licenses.[43] On 6 July 1894, he made clear his frustration with the Alliance. "I know of no organisation, either political or social, which, with so much money, has done so little good. It has done very little itself in the way of legislative reform, but it may congratulate itself upon having prevented anybody else from doing anything."[44]

While the Veto bill consummated the alignment between the advanced temperance party and the Liberal Party, it also exposed the disagreements that strained the relationship. Despite their enthusiasm over the introduction of a Government bill to authorize Local Veto, temperance MPs such as Lawson and Caine hinted that they would offer amendments to eliminate the exceptions to prohibition allowed in the bill and expressed regret over the absence of mandatory Sunday closing. Moreover, outside Parliament a few prominent advanced temperance reformers joined with moderates to draft a comprehensive temperance bill that had to be considered a rival to Harcourt's or at least a distraction.

The larger problem lay less in the prohibitionists being dissatisfied with Harcourt's bill than with their doubting the determination of the Liberals to press for its enactment. The lack of enthusiasm that much of the London press in London showed for the bill troubled the advanced temperance party. The new evening voice of metropolitan Liberalism, the *Westminster Gazette*, complained: "the present bill while calling out the permanent maximum of public opposition, does the very minimum for temperance reform."[45] Lawson warned Harcourt that it was imperative to dispel the rumors that the enemies of the bill spread that the Government did not intend to fight for the bill.[46]

The UKA preferred to lobby ministers and MPs through memorials and private letters, but when the drink trade attacked the bill with petitions and public meetings the Alliance had to reply in kind. Unfortunately for the UKA, the trade produced twice as many signatures as did the temperance societies even though the temperance people had many more petitions. (For the bill: 10,058 petitions with 610,760 signatures; against: 6,132 petitions with 1,163,359 signatures.) The battle of demonstrations had no clear victors. The temperance societies had more than ten times as many meetings, but they were mostly very small, while the licensed trade's were large. (For the bill: 4,040; against 302.) For instance, the trade held a monster protest demonstration at Hyde Park on 10 June.[47] The campaign on behalf of the bill strained the resources of the UKA.[48] The public agitation of the Alliance and kindred societies for the Government bill was designed to convince the Liberals that Local Veto would strengthen the party at the polls. In a struggle among priorities even sympathetic MPs needed continuous pressure from the electors.[49]

Despite the prolonged postponement of the second reading, Lawson resisted proposals to threaten the Government with a withdrawal of support.[50] He relied on Harcourt and his faith was at least partly justified. The Chancellor of the Exchequer startled the Cabinet by threatening to resign if the bill was not read a second time before Christmas.[51] When the

Veto was not mentioned in the Queen's Speech opening the autumn session the UKA sought labor support. At a meeting of the Trades Union Congress in Belfast 173 trade union officials and working-class MPs signed a memorial on behalf of the Veto. The memorial used the language of class warfare that offended right-wing members of the UKA such as (later Sir) George Livesey, president of the South Metropolitan Gas Company.

The Government abandoned its 1893 bill without a second reading. The advanced temperance party had to settle for the promise of another Veto bill sometime in the future, something offered on 7 December to a prohibitionist deputation by Gladstone and Harcourt.[52]

Throughout much of 1894 the advanced temperance party stood on tiptoes, hopeful, suspicious, impatient, frustrated. The UKA lobbied for a stronger bill than 1893's with no exceptions to prohibition.[53] Vetoists worried about the influence of Lord Rosebery (1847-1929) who had become Prime Minister in March upon Gladstone's retirement.[54] With Harcourt's encouragement, Sir Wilfrid Lawson wrote to Rosebery. "[The prohibitionists] ask for absolutely nothing more than that the magisterial veto on the issue of licenses should be popularized in accordance with the most elementary principles of self-government." Although Harcourt's 1893 bill "was not perfect in their judgment," they "vigorously supported" it. Lawson warned that it would be unfortunate politically "if once the prohibitionists got into their heads that the Government was not in earnest in this matter."[55]

Harcourt was preoccupied with his Progressive Budget that introduced the principle of graduated taxation.[56] In mid-April, the day after Harcourt had presented the budget, Lawson warned him about the slowness in introducing a new Veto bill. With characteristic vigor the Chancellor counterattacked:

> If my Budget proposals [which raised taxes on alcoholic beverages] have not satisfied the Temperance Party that I am prepared to fight and do battle with the Brewers, Distillers and all their crew, I can only say that they are even more unreasonable than I supposed them to be, and that is saying a good deal. Any veto bill must await the passage of the budget. If the temperance reformers distrusted the Liberal leaders, they could find another Government in which they have more confidence.

He was "dead sick" with "this constant distrust and menace" and with the factionalism within the temperance party. Harcourt blamed the impasse as much on the temperance party as on Unionist obstructionism. He pointed at the so-called Temperance Parliament promoted by Arnold F. Hills. It drafted a licensing reform bill, "under the patronage of Caine [Stafford Howard, Thomas Snape, Hugh Price Hughes, and others] from whom the Government might have expected a reasonable support." This temperance conference "must have the effect of greatly weakening our hands." Harcourt angrily told Lawson: "there is really no use in trying to help people who made it impossible to help them."[57]

Lawson tried to appease Harcourt. He had stood aloof from the Temperance Parliament that had aroused the touchy Cabinet minister's ire. He applauded Harcourt's budget as "the victory over Land and Liquor united."[58]

The UKA tried to pressure the Liberal leadership with manifestoes and deputations, a strategy that Lawson disliked as inexpedient.[59] Rosebery had offended the UKA by declining to receive a deputation when he visited Manchester where its headquarters were located. Early in May the Alliance issued a manifesto. Disclaiming any attempt to dictate to the Government or lack of confidence in it, the manifesto warned that discontent was rising in the constituencies.[60] Presumably Rosebery sought to mollify the temperance reformers when later in May he attacked the political power of the drink trade with much quoted vehemence: "If the State does not soon control the liquor traffic, the liquor traffic will control the State."[61] Despite the Prime Minister's appeasing rhetoric, the Government announced on 11 July that it would propose no Veto bill in 1894. It did promise that in 1895 the Veto, with two other measures, would share the highest legislative priority.

The year 1894 still had major shocks left for the prohibitionists to warn them that many prominent Liberals preferred to look elsewhere for a program of temperance reform. A new organization in favor of the Gothenburg Scheme asked Gladstone to join. Although the former Prime Minister declined for reasons of age, he praised the Gothenburg principle, the elimination of the profit motive from the retail sale of drink, as "the sole chance of escape" from widespread intemperance. Although he supported Local Veto, he doubted that it would be exercised enough to have much practical effect. He also questioned that the reduction in the number of public houses would diminish intemperance.[62] In public, Vetoists tried to minimize the damage of Gladstone's statement. Lawson and the UKA secretary James Whyte emphasized that Gladstone had not repudiated the principle of Local Veto and that Vetoists did not object to licensing schemes such as those of Gothenburg for those districts that did not want prohibition.[63] In a *Westminster Gazette* interview (5 Oct. 1894, pp. 1-2), T.P. Whittaker deplored the effect of Gladstone's letter after the Newcastle Programme pledge, a general election fought in part on the Veto issue, and the reassurances that Gladstone and Harcourt had given on 7 Dec. 1893. In private many Vetoists, Harcourt included, fumed.[64]

Reduction in number posed a more immediate threat to the Liberal commitment to the Veto than did the Gothenburg Scheme. Gladstone had derided reduction in numbers as "little more than an imposture," but as early as 1893 most of the Liberal press had urged that any Government bill include a local option of reduction, and by 1894 some Liberal leaders began to agree.[65] The Chief Whip, Tom Ellis, outraged Lawson when he used his speech as chairman of the public session of the UKA's annual meeting to argue that a reduction option would improve the prospects for the enactment of a bill that included Local Veto.[66] After Harcourt forwarded Lawson's letter to Ellis, Ellis said that Lawson had misinterpreted his remarks. He simply had said that he sympathized with "the very strong feeling *in Wales* for a power of referring to the local vote, the question of *reducing* [the number of] public houses." He "cannot understand why Lawson should object so testily to the mere expression of the complexity and difficulty of the problems."[67] In late October 1894 John Morley speculated that Harcourt might bolt the Rosebery ministry if he could be secure in the backing of a section of "the Temperance men."[68] At the beginning of November Harcourt got the Cabinet to agree to introduce a Veto bill in 1895 and to carry it to an early second reading.[69] Temperance reformers were in a funk. Caine and Malins warned that if Local Veto bill was not introduced and "*pushed,*" some temperance reformers might form their own prohibition party and others "sulk in their tents."[70] Later in the month Rosebery alarmed the Veto supporters in the Government with a speech in Glasgow in which he implied that he wanted to substitute a reduction bill on the lines of that proposed for Scotland by the backbencher MacLagen.[71] A Cabinet crisis seemed likely until it became clear that Rosebery wanted a reduction option added to the Veto rather than instead of it. Ironically on the day of Rosebery's speech a Cabinet committee had recommended the same thing.[72]

The reduction option caused endless headaches, both technical and political. How great would the reduction be? How would the licensing authorities select licenses for suppression? In the end, the reduction was one of a quarter of the total number of licenses and could be repeated in later referendums.[73] Licenses were to be voided in districts that voted by a simple majority for a reduction option, so that magistrates would not be inhibited by an assumption that existing license holders had a claim to favorable consideration.[74] It is hard to see how this would have overcome the real problem, a feeling of fairness rather than the letter of the law. The political problem came from Vetoists like Lawson who considered reduction vastly inferior to prohibition and dangerous as a distraction. When he had learned about the introduction of a reduction option, he had been "rather staggered."[75] From the Alliance standpoint the 1893 bill had been a compromise since it had allowed many exceptions to total prohibition and required a two-thirds' majority. Lawson agreed that if a further compromise was politically necessary, he would accept any bill which Harcourt said contained an effective prohibitive Veto, but he argued that the advocates of the reduction option wanted to wreck the Veto.[76]

In fact, the Cabinet had second thoughts about sponsoring any Veto bill. The belated soul-searching arose more out of considerations of political expediency than out of principle. For instance, the chairman of the Brigg Liberal Association warned the Prime Minister that Harcourt's bill had brought about the Liberal defeat in the Brigg bye-election. Poor villagers without money to spend on public houses had remained loyal to the Liberal Party, but the town workers, who drank regularly at public houses, had been seduced by propaganda that denounced the Veto as class discrimination.[77] The Liberal leaders also worried about the immediate problem of getting a majority in the House of Commons. Supposedly most of the Cabinet feared that Irish abstentions and other defections would prevent a Veto bill from carrying a second reading division.[78] Clearly, there was no hope of the House of Lords accepting the bill.

Although Lawson still relied on Harcourt, he worried about "traitors in the Government," critics of the Local Veto policy such as Tom Ellis and Herbert Gladstone (1854-1930), the former Prime Minister's son.[79] In January 1895 the National Liberal Federation, meeting at Cardiff, endorsed a local option for reduction as well as for prohibition, with a resolution proposing that ratepayers obtain "the power of deciding how many, if any," licenses be granted. The president of the Federation forwarded to the Prime Minister and the Chancellor of the Exchequer a statistical analysis of the general election of 1892 intended to prove the disastrous electoral power of the public houses and the danger of the present Veto policy.[80]

Harcourt predictably dismissed the case for appeasement as "one these ingenious calculations of what might have been if everything had been different." He saw no point in trying to mollify the publicans who were the natural enemies of the Liberal Party. Harcourt told a promoter of the so-called Westminster bill that he saw no advantage in private negotiations with interested parties and believed that his own bill "will command the largest amount of support from the real Temperance Party in the country."[81] He distrusted the motives of the wealthy Quaker philanthropist Joseph Rowntree (1836-1925) who had prepared the statistics. "Does he lust after the flesh pots of Gothenburg?" Harcourt could accept a reduction option but not the Gothenburg Scheme.[82] When on 23 January 1895, Harcourt told his Derby constituents that the next Government veto bill would include a referendum for reduction, he seized the opportunity to denounce the Gothenburg Scheme.[83] Joseph Malins, the head of the Good Templars, traveled to Scandinavia to collect evidence against the Gothenburg Scheme for Harcourt. Surprisingly for a militant prohibitionist, Malins was sympathetic to the idea of adding reduction to the Veto as a local option.[84]

It was not until 8 April 1895, that Harcourt introduced his Intoxicating Liquor Traffic (Local Control) bill.[85] Other than the local option for reduction the 1895 bill differed from that of 1893 by borrowing its electorate from the new Parish Councils Act that had enfranchised servants and lodgers, by allowing the repeal of prohibition by a simple majority, and by dropping the exception for eating-houses. Harcourt cited a new book by E.L. Fanshawe on American and Canadian licensing legislation to justify the practicability of local option and establish the precedents for the refusal to pay compensation. Sensitive to the claims made on behalf of the Gothenburg Scheme, Harcourt argued that the advance of temperance in Sweden and Norway owed more to the right of local option on the sale of beer than to the much publicized elimination of the profit motive in the retail sale of spirits.

Although Liberal fears of a first reading division did not materialize, the House of Commons debated the bill at greater length than in 1893. The former Solicitor General, Sir Edward Clarke, led the debate for the Opposition. Like several other speakers he characterized the new bill as a retreat from the previous one and questioned that the Government would ever press it for a second reading. He argued that the new reduction option contradicted Harcourt's position in 1893: that reduction in numbers could only be carried out by a popularly chosen licensing board as part of a comprehensive scheme. He reminded the House that Gladstone had criticized the assumption that a reduction in the number of licensed premises would reduce intemperance. Clarke complained that even under the new parochial franchise only a minority of the people affected would be eligible to vote. He criticized the neglect of the problem of drinking in clubs and elicited from the Chancellor the promise of a bill to regulate them. Clarke also questioned the need for temperance legislation of any kind. The progress of temperance had gone far without legislation, particularly among the upper and middle classes, and with the advance of popular education, additional improvement among the working classes might be expected. Whatever the laws, a residuum of drunkards would remain. In addition, Clarke questioned the assumption that drink was largely responsible for many social ills.

In a largely unmemorable debate Sir Wilfrid Lawson derided the reduction option as implying a want of confidence in the magistrates who had the power to refuse the renewal of unnecessary licenses. It was not the prohibitionists but instead "a few Members [of Parliament], a few newspaper editors, and a few philosophers, who sat up in attics and did not know anything about it," who had urged this addition to the bill. He hoped that with it they would be content and join him in working for the Government bill.

In his diary Sir Edward Walter Hamilton reported a conversation with Harcourt on 30 April in which the Chancellor was alternately optimistic and pessimistic. Harcourt was cheered by a report that the Church of England Temperance Society would support his bill, a claim followed by "professions of a longing [for the Government] to fall upon it," or, even more extreme, a wish that the Cabinet would refuse to let him proceed with the bill, so that he could resign.[86]

The bill never proceeded to a second reading. The parliamentary committee of the Church of England executive decided "with practical unanimity" to support a second reading at which time it wanted to amend the bill.[87] "Wesleyan enthusiasm in 1895 was especially striking for a supposedly non-political denomination: in the regional synods in May, only six hands were raised, two in Leeds and four in Lincoln, against support for the bill; and although the Wesleyan president was a Conservative, he was prepared to join the other connexional presidents in calling on all Methodists to rally behind the measure." [88]

In contrast, several Liberal newspapers such as the *Daily Chronicle* called for its abandonment as a matter of expediency.[89] On the other hand, the *Daily News* championed the bill.[90] Although the UKA was short on money for a campaign on behalf of the bill, it tried to generate pressure for it. The advanced temperance party held "the biggest indoor anti-liquor meeting" in its history on 25 May at Albert Hall. About 90,000 people had applied for tickets, but all but 10,000 of them had to be refused for want of room.[91]

In retrospect the drink trade may have been unnecessarily uncomfortable. The secretary of the major drink trade defence organization expected that the bill would pass or fail to pass a second reading vote by two or three votes, with the likelihood of defeat increasing as the months passed. H.A. Newton reported that the Liberal press considered the bill just in principle but politically inexpedient, while the Tory press considered the drink question worthy of consideration but that Harcourt's bill was on the wrong lines. Newton despaired: "Even on the ... [Tory] side ... there seemed to be a feverish desire that something should be done and of the multiplication of schemes there was no end."[92]

The Government lacked confidence that the bill could get a House of Commons majority. Even Harcourt admitted that the Government faced defeat on a second reading division. He argued that the popularity of Local Veto in the country would make an election on this question an asset for the Liberal Party. The Prime Minister doubted that anyone in the Government except perhaps John Morley shared the Chancellor's belief of the importance of the Veto bill and temperance in general as political questions. Rosebery favored making the powers of the House of Lords the paramount issues.[93] Sir Edward Hamilton described the proposal as a "Bill *pour rire*," a symbolic bill introduced just of laughs.[94] Wearied by internal disputes the Government seized the excuse of a defeat on a minor vote to resign on 22 June.[95] Its leaders could not agree among themselves on what issues to fight the elections that followed.

At the elections held in July 1895 the Liberal Party lost almost two hundred seats, a smashing defeat from which it did not recover for more than ten years.[96] Harcourt himself was defeated at Derby.[97] The Conservative campaign against Local Veto sought to make it an economic question. In Liverpool "canvassers announced that Local Veto would mean £33 million extra annual taxation and two million unemployed."[98] Many Liberals blamed not just Harcourt's personal defeat but that of the party on Local Veto.[99] Although many things contributed to the debacle, including Liberal disorganization, the Liberal press and political insiders generally focused on Harcourt's Local Veto bills. Kimberley grumbled to Ripon "this folly about local veto is in itself proof of [Harcourt's] utter want of judgment."[100] The drink trade was quick to call upon the victorious Unionists to present their case in Parliament.[101]

Herbert Gladstone told his father that he hoped no more would be heard about Local Veto; "I can't help feeling that defeat may be good for us."[102] Critics of the Liberal entanglement with Local Veto put much of the blame on it. Campbell-Bannerman (1836-1908) argued that Harcourt had underestimated the power of the Church and even more that of the drink trade. "The noisy fussiness of the Teetotallers is nothing against the steady pressure of the interest they attack."[103]

In letter of condolence to Harcourt, William Gladstone hinted in his usual cryptic style that the party should abandon the veto. "I do not feel sure that Local Option may not in the future do better propelled by independent action than by a Liberal Government."[104] Four years after the Newcastle Programme the Liberal commitment to Direct Local Veto looked in doubt. Worried prohibitionists considered packing the December 1895 conference of the National Liberal Federation with their supporters to block a rumored attempt to jettison the Veto.[105]

In the 1895 general election the Unionists represented the Local Veto bill as class legislation. For instance, Balfour (1848-1930) said: "The poor man, the man of moderate means, who gets his glass of beer--and surely he has a perfect right to get his glass of beer--at the publichouse [sic] will be prevented from doing so, while the rich man who supplies his consumption from the wholesale dealers, the member of the club, the person who has access to the railway station, will be entirely outside the [provisions of the bill]."[106]

Although politically discredited in most eyes, Local Veto clung tenaciously to the Liberal alliance. Its main champion in the Liberal Party, Harcourt, succeeded Rosebery as leader when the ex-Prime Minister abruptly resigned from his party post in 1896. The Liberals remained in Opposition for ten years. Not being in Government diminished the need for a clear decision. Although a few Liberals fought the Veto policy openly, many others who disliked it as an electoral liability preferred to let it fade into the shadows. Apparently, Haldane and Asquith worked out a licensing program in 1896 that dropped Local Veto and provided money compensation, but nothing was heard of it in public.[107]

That the general election of 1895 ended the Liberal Party support for prohibition referendums is clearer in hindsight than it was in the late 1890s. For half a decade the revolt against the Veto flared fitfully in apparent inconclusiveness. The call for the abandonment of the Veto challenged the legitimacy of pressure groups (so-called faddists) and the conception of politics embodied in the Newcastle Programme. Along with the Veto the National Liberal Federation itself faded into the background. In 1898 the Federation denied that its resolutions ever had constituted a program. Supposedly it was Gladstone's acceptance of particular resolutions that had constituted the Newcastle Programme.[108]

The *Westminister Gazette*, only a few weeks old when Harcourt introduced the first of his local control bills, led the anti-Veto agitation.[109] Its first editor, Edward Cook (during 1893-95), and his deputy and longtime successor (during 1895-1921), J.A. Spender, spoke out at a time when the Newcastle Programme and the first Government bill had silenced most Liberal critics of the Veto.[110] In 1893 Spender wrote a series of articles which embarrassed the United Kingdom Alliance, "Philanthropic Finance: A Forgotten Chapter in the Temperance Movement." He detailed the swindle perpetrated by Jabez Balfour who had bilked small investors, most of them foot soldiers in the temperance movement, and pilloried Dr. Dawson Burns, Balfour's brother-in-law and auditor of Balfour's corrupt Liberator Building Society until shortly before its collapse. For thirty-seven years Burns had been metropolitan superintendent of the UKA.[111] Although

Burns personally had done nothing wrong, and retained the confidence of the London Auxiliary, the executive committee of the Alliance forced him out of office.

After the general election of 1895 the *Westminster Gazette* sent a questionnaire to Liberal candidates to explore nine possible causes of the defeat, the Veto bill being the one that the newspaper listed first. Of the 74 successful candidates who expressed an opinion on Harcourt's bill, 54 called it harmful, 14 not harmful, and six helpful. Of the 157 unsuccessful candidates who gave definite replies, 134 found the bill harmful, 16 of no great harm, and seven helpful. Although the candidates emphasized the damage done among working-class voters, they believed that the bill was unpopular among all classes.[112]

Many of the candidates who replied to the *Westminster Gazette* agreed with Campbell-Bannerman that the political strength of the temperance party had been exaggerated. Shortly before the general election several correspondents of the *Daily Chronicle* had disparaged the temperance party's electoral work. The temperance reformers canvassed only their own people, lacked the tact to persuade doubtful voters, and had little money to publish local campaign literature.[113] An ardent prohibitionist had complained in private about the scarcity of funds. "We have scores of men who have got fat through our movement. Where are they now?"[114]

In the Annual Report for 1895 the executive committee of the Alliance defended Local Veto as a principle and as politically expedient. It had been made a scapegoat in explaining the defeat. In popular votes the Liberal defeat had not been a rout. The Liberal Party had been hurt by a variety of issues and organizational difficulties, particularly Independent Labour Party candidacies in the North. The drink trade had showed little increase in strength with one exception: the conversion of private businesses into joint-stock companies whose investors had an interest in the profits of the drink trade. If Liberal candidates had played up the Veto, they might have won over many of the electors who had failed to vote. These electors lacked strong partisan feeling. This "reserve force of the social reform army" would have responded to an appeal to "their desire for the security and purity of their homes."[115]

In a paper read at a prohibition convention in Newcastle in April 1897 W.S. Caine further argued that Liberal candidates closely identified with the Veto attracted the votes of a higher percentage of the registered electors than did other candidates. He cited his own defeat at East Bradford.[116] James Whyte, the UKA's general secretary, said at the same conference that the Liberal liquor traders and their friends had invented the myth of popular hostility to the Veto. In his analysis of the anti-Veto revolt he pointed to the "conspicuous" role of Mark Beaufoy, a wholesale wine merchant who sat as Liberal MP for South Kennington, of several Liberal brewers in the House of Commons (Sydney Evershed, H.T. Fenwick, Hugh E. Hoare, William McEwan) and of Courtenay Warner, a Liberal MP without licensed trade business connections.[117] In 1898 the Alliance Annual Report also blamed Henry C. Fulford (1849-1897), a Birmingham brewer and one of the few wealthy Liberals who did not secede from the Gladstonian party with Chamberlain. Fulford had been elected for Lichfield at the general election of 1895 but was then unseated by petition for violating electoral laws. Since he was ineligible to stand at the bye-election that followed, he supported Courtenay Warner who had lost his seat at the general election. As "a very rich and open-handed man," Fulford was influential with the Liberal agents, organizers, and local leaders in the Midlands. When he died, he left an enormous estate of more than £423,000.[118]

Liberal candidates and M.P.s and Liberal constituency associations became increasingly skittish about the Veto. When there was a bye-election at Bradford in 1896, the local Liberals rejected Caine's proposal to become a candidate again and even rejected his offer to come to the constituency to speak on behalf of the chosen candidate who once had been his campaign agent.[119]

Harcourt and the other Liberal leaders watched the Veto controversy in near silence, perhaps sympathizing with those demanding a new policy. In 1896 Harcourt rejected an invitation to preside over the annual meeting of the Alliance, perhaps out of irritation with Caine's work for a new non-partisan consensus temperance bill "Men like Caine and others decried the bill I introduced and in this state of things it is not surprising that we failed."[120] Lawson answered: "it is rather hard that we should all suffer for [Caine's] eccentricities."[121] Early in 1897 Harcourt refused the request of the prohibitionists for a reaffirmation of his commitment to the Veto. In declining to issue "a pronouncement *ex Cathedra*," he deplored "the great want of unanimity and coherence in the different sections of the Temperance reformers." "When the troops are a little more disciplined I shall be quite ready to carry my musket to the front."[122] That time never came. Although he never openly repudiated the Veto, Harcourt was out of the fight. He told Lord Kimberley that he had informed the temperance people that although he still adhered to "some popular control of licensing" after the general election defeat "he was no longer pledged" to his local option bill.[123]

Even Nonconformist ministers doubted the practicality of a party commitment to the Veto. The Congregationalist, Dr. J. Guinness Rogers, went further. He told the editor of *Daily News*: "to make Temperance Reform a question of party politics is to injure the Liberal party without benefiting the Temperance cause."[124]

The sputtering controversy burst into flame when Herbert Gladstone attacked the Veto policy at the Manchester Reform Club on 23 November 1897. In 1880, the year that he entered Parliament, he had favored local option of some sort but not Local Veto. He had no desire to close all the public houses and advocated compensation for the publican who lost his license for no fault of his own.[125] After the general election of 1885 he had decided "to throw in my lot with wholehearted extremists rather than seek in vain for support of a *moderate* measure from men whose moderation seems to be a snare and a delusion, a mere pretext for doing nothing at all."[126] Despite these bold words, the younger Gladstone's support for the Veto lacked zeal. A UKA official complained: "you never seem at home with us."[127] For instance, speaking at Holbeck in January 1894, young Gladstone had expressed a preference for a reduction in the number of public houses in proportion to population and some kind of compensation limited to publicans. He also worried that if Harcourt's bill became law, an unintended result "would be the weakening, if not the breaking up, of a great political Temperance organisation," while that of the drink trade "would remain in full force."[128]

In 1897 Herbert Gladstone argued that in the last general election the Veto had been the "heaviest burden" other than Irish Home Rule. He did not want the Liberals to abandon the Veto because it cost votes but because its electoral unpopularity showed that if the Veto were enacted it would be a dead letter. A two-thirds majority in a local referendum was impractical. Although he still accepted the principle of Local Veto, he considered the mitigation of drunkenness more important than any particular method. He proposed an alternative program of severe penalties for drunkenness, detention of habitual inebriates, increased powers for magistrates over physical accommodations to discourage mere drinking dens, and the reduction in the number of public houses in some ratio to the population. Affected license holders should be compensated "by free use of the time limit, and out of the proceeds of the enhanced values of the remaining licenses." He expected that the Royal Commission which in 1896 had been appointed to study the liquor problem would make practical recommendations that all reformers could support.[129]

Although shortly afterwards Harcourt inserted a brief reaffirmation of the Veto in one of his speeches, Liberals at large welcomed Herbert Gladstone's call for its abandonment.[130] The *Westminster Gazette* led the applause. After six weeks of vigorous debate in its correspondence columns, an editorial summed up the anti-Veto case. It revived the old charge, much resented by prohibitionists, that the UKA had obstructed Bruce's licensing bill in 1871. According to the editorial, it had been the best chance that the country had ever had for a fair settlement of the drink question. In its fifty years of existence the Alliance had failed to bring about prohibition, but it had "diverted most of the energy available to Temperance Reform." The Veto had been the veto of reform. Practical men could no longer allow it to obstruct practical reforms.[131] Once again, on 7 January 1898, the *Westminster Gazette* urged: "let us see that Local Veto is not the veto of reform."

Some provincial newspapers remained loyal to the old policy, notably the *Manchester Guardian* whose proprietor John Edward Taylor was a committed Vetoist. In London the Liberal press united in criticism of the Veto as a political liability. Cooke had moved from the *Westminster Gazette* to the *Daily News* as editor and brought his anti-Veto attitudes with him. The *Daily Chronicle* also had developed a distaste for "faddists." "Mr. Herbert Gladstone *touches the spot* when he says we must remember that we are Liberals first, and supporters of any particular reform afterwards. And Liberalism means any particular reform as far as it can be carried."[132] Praising Herbert Gladstone, the *Speaker* complained that prohibitionists "confuse principles with tactics." It pointed out: "In the England of our day Prohibition is an impracticable fad."[133]

The United Kingdom Alliance tried to minimize personal controversy with the ex-Prime Minister's son over his "extraordinary deliverance." In the first issue of the *Alliance News* after the speech the UKA weekly only reprinted the *Manchester Guardian*'s leader in defense of the Veto. Later a leading article in the Alliance's newspaper disputed the definition of the drink problem that Gladstone had put forward. He had characterized drunkenness as the evil to be attacked, but drinking short of drunkenness "produces evils as many and great . . . and, in fact, much more widespread and greater." Respectable surroundings would not alleviate the drink problem. The better class of drink shops did the greatest harm since they attract customers who would not patronize cruder ones.[134] The UKA newspaper supplemented its own cautious response by publishing letters and reprinted articles that answered Gladstone less gently. This caution sometimes ran thin. James Whyte, general secretary to the Alliance, gave a long interview with a reporter for the *Manchester Evening News*. Pointing out that large number of young teetotalers would soon be of age to vote, he said that "we [temperance reformers] do not care a snap for the Liberal party."[135]

The Alliance defended the Veto as moderate, effective, and democratic. Even where it lacked an immediate majority it would exert a wholesome influence and, in any event, it was the people's right to decide. Lawson explained that the Veto would be as effective as the people wanted it to be. "It combined the minimum of change in our legislation with the possibility (and no intelligent advocate of the veto goes further than that) of the maximum of reform."[136]

Other members of the advanced temperance party saw no reason to measure their words. T.P. Whittaker characterized as "absolutely untrue" Gladstone's charge that the Local Veto advocates had obstructed all other reforms. "if you can do nothing but carp and growl, grumble and complain, then, in the name of commonsense and humanity, cease caviling and get out of the way!"[137] Speaking at the Wesleyan West End Mission, Hugh Price Hughes referred to Herbert Gladstone's "treachery" and his "foolish" speech. Hughes blamed the 1895 electoral defeat upon "the extraordinary coalition between priests and publicans."[138]

Herbert Gladstone's attack on the Veto had disquieted the West Leeds constituency that he represented. Joseph Henry, his Ulster-born agent, regretted that Gladstone had gone out of his way to offend the prohibitionists, "who after all are the hardest workers in our party." Henry also doubted that the Veto had handicapped Gladstone in the last election and asked what sort of a party program Gladstone would leave the Liberals. "As I understand your position it is that unless we all agree upon a subject it ought not to be included in the liberal programme . . . . If that be so I am afraid the liberal party has no policy or any programme."[139]

Gladstone explained his position to his West Leeds constituents early in January 1898 in the schoolroom of a Baptist chapel, with Henry in the chair. Gladstone claimed that the Liberal Party was grounded "on a sandbank in a fog" and must be lightened by jettisoning its excess cargo of Local Veto. The Unionists had gained votes all over the country, votes that the public houses, aroused over the Veto, had mobilized. There was no possibility of a Veto bill being passed in the next ten or fifteen years, and in any event the large referendum majority required and the many exceptions to prohibition would make Harcourt's version of the Veto ineffective. In large cities it was unrealistic to abolish the public houses without offering an alternative to supply "the urgent wants of the people."[140] He minimized the problem of drunkenness. No more than five in a thousand population drank to excess.[141] In his manuscript notes for this speech but not in the published reports Gladstone protested against majority dictation in personal matters and pressure groups forcing a policy on parliamentary candidates.[142]

After this speech to his constituents the Vetoist anger against Herbert Gladstone redoubled. Leif Jones, an unsuccessful parliamentary candidate in the neighboring constituency of Central Leeds, belittled him as a self-exposed opportunist. The critics of the Veto who proposed other remedies misunderstood the drink problem. According to Jones, "the fault lies, not chiefly in the magistrates, nor in the police, nor in the licensed victuallers or their premises, nor even in the want of self-restraint on the part of the drinkers." Instead, "the root of the evil is in the nature of the drink that is sold." Only prohibition provided an adequate answer. The vigor with which the drink trade resisted the Veto bills showed that they expected the people would exercise their rights. If the Liberals proposed lesser reforms as Gladstone recommended, the drink trade would still oppose them, while the prohibitionists could no longer work with their old enthusiasm. All that could be said against the Veto in the 1895 general election was that it did not save the Government from its unpopularity on other issues. The long history of the Veto agitation, cited by Gladstone as a record of failure, in fact showed a continuous growth in support. "The future is in our hands."[143] Leif Jones, writing to Lady Carlisle, 3 January 1898: "My mind is full of Herbert Gladstone and my brain is a whirl."[144] The Alliance honorary secretary Samuel Pope said that he thought "Herbert Gladstone has done us good by raising a discussion as the righteousness of the Veto. Any reason [that he gives] that it is *inconvenient* to the party is simply contemptable."[145]

In still another speech on the Veto, delivered in Cambridge on 25 April 1898, Gladstone attacked "the pressure group tactics of the advanced temperance party. "It is a bad thing for this country if a certain number of individuals in a constituency have only to get themselves into what they call an association, and then go to a candidate and say, *Now if you won't vote for us we won't vote for you.* (Cheers) Candidates should lead more, and be led much less."[146]

In his Cambridge speech Herbert Gladstone also denied that the temperance party had provided the Liberals with its victory in the Plymouth bye-election in January 1898 as many temperance reformers claimed. Although it preferred to emphasize the justice of its cause, the UKA recognized the importance of being able to deliver or withhold votes. Votes had more influence with politicians than public meetings and manifestoes.[147] Consequently, its district agent for Plymouth, John Newton, sent Gladstone a detailed analysis of the election. The only difference between the election in 1895 that the Liberal candidate lost and the election in 1898 that the Liberal won lay in the improved discipline and organization of the local temperance party. Fifty temperance Liberals pledged themselves in writing to vote for the Liberal candidate only if he promised to support Harcourt's bill.[148] When he did so, and the Conservative candidate refused to do so, 58 Liberal Unionist and Conservative electors decided to vote for the Liberal candidate and 36 others decided to abstain. The total of the three groups was 202, 40 more than the 162-vote victory margin. And this did not count their campaign work among others. "Taking the country as a whole, if the Liberals cannot win with the Temperance men, they certainly cannot win without them."[149]

Replying, Gladstone denied that Newton had proved that Local Veto explained the victory at Plymouth. Undoubtedly the supporters of the Veto could weaken the Liberal Party by abstaining or by voting for the Unionists, but the theory of the temperance party and other pressure groups wrongly assumed that theirs was the sole issue, that all other Liberal votes came from "a fixed quantity of purely party men who care for nothing but for the return of the Liberal Party to office."[150] Gladstone might have added that it was easier to persuade electors to plump for one issue in a bye-election when the result could have no effect on the chances for a parliamentary majority than in the tougher competition of loyalties presented at a general election. Abstentions by temperance militants also could hurt the temperance party by angering Liberal partisans, as instanced by the Durham City bye-election held in June 1898.[151]

Probably a majority of Liberals, a substantial number of Liberal Unionists, and a few Conservatives agreed with Direct Local Veto in principle, but not many voters would ignore all other considerations to conform to the single-issue strategy of the advanced temperance party. When the Alliance introduced an independent temperance candidate to challenge Liberals connected with the trade or hostile to the Veto, the modest vote obtained showed the limits of the hardcore prohibitionist support. Independent candidates got 810 votes at Houghton-le-Spring in Durham in 1892 and 730 at South Kennington in 1895.[152] Early in the twentieth century a veteran UKA agent admitted that "historically and practically" a policy of independent candidates was "utterly suicidal and inane."[153]

Even abstention campaigns proved difficult to organize. In 1894 the Alliance tried to organize abstentions in Grantham in Lincolnshire where the Liberal candidate, a maltster, promised only neutrality on the veto. The UKA district agent learned that the temperance electors numbered only about 130. "Blinded by party prejudice," the chairman of the local temperance society, the treasurer of the Salvation Army, and various Dissenting ministers had pledged themselves to the maltster.[154]

When the Alliance tried to organize abstentions in Herbert Gladstone's constituency in 1900, the district agent could no longer collect subscriptions for the UKA in Leeds. He complained: "pious Wesleyans want to drown me, others prefer shooting me, the parsons have deserted me."[155] Out of diverse motives, "a brewery director, a licensed grocer, and eleven Nonconformist ministers" urged electors to vote for Gladstone.[156] The local licensed victuallers remained neutral in the contest between Gladstone and a Conservative candidate.[157]

A bye-election in 1899 in a Yorkshire constituency dramatically illustrated the limits of the power of the prohibitionists when other Liberals refused to stay put. In the past Sir John Austin, who was the Liberal member, had voted for Veto bills even though he was a maltster. In 1899 he voted against a private member's Veto bill for Scotland that had no chance of passage. Austin's constituency association rebuked him mildly, while the prohibitionists criticized him vigorously. The elderly baronet promptly resigned his seat and stood for re-election as an independent Liberal, defying his critics to fight him on the issue of Local Veto. Ironically thirteen years earlier the sitting Liberal member had broken with Gladstone over Irish Home Rule, and Austin had captured the seat as a party loyalist.

No election can be reduced to a single issue. The official Liberal candidate in the bye-election, Charles Roberts, the young son-in-law of the Countess of Carlisle, was like her was a zealous prohibitionist. He received support from those who considered Austin disloyal to the Liberal Party and those who objected to his vote against a bill to restrict ritualism in the Church. (In 1894 Austin had converted to the Roman Catholic Church. Roberts declared himself a Protestant.) Roberts, like Austin, supported trade union proposals such as the eight-hour day for coal miners.[158] Roberts was an outsider, while the well-known Austin enjoyed popularity with the working-class electors of an industrial constituency. More important, the Tories nominated no candidate of their own. Since they voted for Austin, he could poll fewer Liberal votes than Roberts and still win handily. Whatever the explanation for Austin's triumph, people concluded that he had called the Vetoists' bluff.[159] Austin was the only Liberal to vote against his party's attempt to add a time limit to Balfour's licensing bill in 1904.

The status of Local Veto as part of the official Liberal program survived only precariously in the years after the general election of 1895. Reaffirmations of the veto policy by Harcourt and a few other Liberal leaders meant little unless they reflected widespread popular enthusiasm. More and more politicians saw the Veto as an electoral liability and dared risk the toothless anger of the United Kingdom Alliance.[160] In 1896 the Veto disappeared from the program adopted by the National Liberal Federation. It seemed unlikely that a Liberal Government would ever press a Local Veto bill very hard, particularly after the elderly Harcourt resigned the leadership at the end of 1898.[161]

The annual meeting of the Alliance in November 1899 was silent at Lawson's request about the Veto as the shibboleth for electoral support. Militant prohibitionists, mostly Good Templars, were furious.[162]

The fading of the Veto commitment did not mean that the Liberal Party had abandoned other kinds of temperance reform. In "Notes on the Veto," perhaps prepared for a speech, Herbert Gladstone asked: "Is the Veto party ... the only temperance party?" He added: "Am not I a temperance reformer?"[163]

Notes

[1] For the pledges by MPs, see Emy, *Liberals, Radicals and Social Politics*, p. 44. Dingle, *Campaign for Prohibition*, p. 349, claims that all but five Liberal MPs had pledged themselves to Direct Local Veto.

[2] Quoted in Peter Stansky, *Ambitions and Strategies: The Struggle for the Leadership of the Liberal Party in the 1890s* (Oxford University Press, 1964), p. 111.

[3] Lewis Harcourt journals, 24 April 1882, quoted in Patrick Jackson, *Harcourt and Son: A Political Biography of Sir William Harcourt, 1827-1904* (Fairleigh Dickinson University Press, 2004), p. 92; Patrick Jackson, ed. *Loulou: Selected Extracts from the Journals of Lewis Harcourt (1880-1895)* (Fairleigh Dickinson University Press, 2006), p. 38. Jackson should be read with Peter Stansky's lengthy entry about Sir William Harcourt in the *Oxford Dictionary of National Biography* and with the book review *of Harcourt and Son* by William Lubenow, in *Parliamentary History* 26 pt. 2 (2006).

[4] Jackson, *Loulou*, pp. 110-11.

[5] Prohibition supporters had to drag other Liberals along. In 1892 the proprietor of the Manchester Guardian, John Edward Taylor, complained that his cousin, editor C.P. Scott, supported "milk and water temperance folks" instead of Local Vetoists. J.L. Hammond, *C.P. Scott of the Manchester Guardian* (G. Bell & Sons, 1934), p. 82.

[6] Harcourt to Caine, 1 Aug. 1892. Consulted at Stanton Harcourt.

[7] Caine to Harcourt, 2 August 1892. Consulted at Stanton Harcourt.

[8] Caine to Harcourt, 30 July 1892. Consulted at Stanton Harcourt.

[9] Gladstone, Cabinet minute, 19 Aug. 1892. BL, William Gladstone papers, Add. Ms. 44648 f. 2.

[10] "Temperance Legislation," *Speaker* (1892), pp. 273-74; "Real Licensing Reform," *Speaker*, 10 Sept. 1892, pp. 303-04; "Prohibition a Reform?," *Speaker*, 24 September 1892, pp. 363-65. The *Speaker* spoke favorably about advocates of the Gothenburg Scheme.

[11] Quoted in D.A. Hamer, *Liberal Politics in the Age of Gladstone and Rosebery* (Clarendon Press, 1971), p. 186.

[12] Lewis Harcourt, Journals, 27, 29 Oct. 2, Nov. 1892. Bodleian, Harcourt Ms. 387, unfoliated when consulted. Harcourt to Gladstone, 30 Oct. 1892. BL, William

Gladstone papers, Add. Ms. 4420, ff. 274-75. See also Harcourt to Gladstone, 16 July 1892. Quoted in Michael Barker, *Gladstone and Radicalism*, p. 237.

[13] 23 March 1893 in *Private Diaries of the Rt. Hon. Sir Algernon West*, ed. Horace G. Hutchinson (John Murray, 1922), p. 150. West told Gladstone that he "believed no good Licensing Bill would pass without some form of compensation."

[14] Caine to Harcourt 22 July 1892. Harcourt MS 220 f. 81.

[15] Lawson to Harcourt, 4 Aug. 1892. Bodleian, Harcourt Ms. 220, ff. 148-49. See also Lawson to Harcourt, 30 Sept. 1892. Bodleian, Harcourt Ms. 216, f. 109.

[16] Harcourt to Asquith, 28 Nov. 1892; veto committee minute, 28 Nov. 1892. Bodleian, Harcourt Mss., consulted when uncatalogued. See also draft bills. Bodleian, Harcourt Ms. 152.

[17] Harcourt to Caine, 28 Nov. 1892; Caine to Harcourt, 30 Nov. 1892; Asquith to Harcourt, 23 Dec. 1892. Bodleian, Harcourt Ms. 148, f. 28, Ms. 75, ff. 46-47, Ms. 148, ff. 19-20; Ms. 152, unfoliated when consulted. See also W.S. Caine, "The Attitude of the Advanced Temperance Party," *Contemporary Review* 69 (January 1893): 47-60. [Caine letter consulted at Stanton Harcourt]

[18] Lawson to Edward Pearson, n.d., in Alliance minutes, 30 Nov. 1892; Harcourt to Asquith, 19 Dec. 1892. Bodleian, Harcourt Mss., uncatalogued when consulted.

[19] Lawson to Whyte, 13 Nov. 1892, in Alliance minutes, 16 Nov. 1892. Emphasis in original.

[20] R. W. Perks to Harcourt, 6, 27 Feb. 1893. Bodleian, Harcourt Ms. 145, ff. 36-37, 47-48. As he was not a Sabbatarian, Lawson wished that Sunday closing was not in the bill at all. Lawson to Wright, 25 Feb. 1893. Bodleian, Harcourt Ms. 145.

[21] Harcourt to Sir G.C. Trevelyan, 2 Dec. 1892, Trevelyan to Harcourt, 4 Dec. 1892. Bodleian, Harcourt Ms. 92 ff. 148-149, 153.

[22] Lawson to Harcourt, 8 March 1893. Bodleian, Harcourt Ms. 145, ff. 80-81

[23] Opinions of Cabinet committee, including Asquith, 24 Dec. 1892; Harcourt to Herschell, 24 Dec. 1892. Bodleian, Harcourt Ms. 14, ff. 40-41, 42-43. Herschell, in his comment on the bill (20 Dec. 1892) said: "The strength of the Temperance party is, in my opinion, greatly overestimated by Liberals generally." In his response Harcourt said that he agreed.

[24] Powell to Harcourt, 26 July 1892. Harcourt 220 f. 94.

[25] Buxton to Harcourt, 23, 29 Nov., 7 Dec. 1892, 8 May 1893. Bodleian, Harcourt Ms. 148, fols. 21-25, 32-33, 34-37; Harcourt Ms. 146, fols. 48-50. See also Fahey, "E.N. Buxton (1840-1924)," p. 28.

[26] In his May letter Buxton said that brewers lend publicans between 50% and 60% of selling volume. His own firm typically had a profit around 10%.

[27] Charles Walker in *Licensing World*, 6 May 1899, p. 345.

[28] Fahey, "E.N. Buxton (1840-1924)."

[29] Gladstone to Queen Victoria, 28 Feb. 1893. Royal Archives, Windsor Castle, RA D 41/73. I must express my gratitude to her Majesty for her gracious permission to make use of materials from the Royal Archives at Windsor.

[30] *Private Diaries of the Rt. Hon. Sir Algernon West*, pp. 149-50, entry for 23 March 1893.

[31] For the full debate see *Parl. Deb.*, 4th ser., IX, cols. 476-530.

[32] Mark Beaufoy, a Liberal M.P connected with the wine trade, did not oppose the

bill, as he considered it relatively mild. Beaufoy to Harcourt, 6 March 1893. Bodleian, Harcourt Ms 145. Beaufoy had been elected pledged to vote for Local Veto and got the support of Lawson despite being a wine merchant. When Beaufoy decided that he could not vote for the Veto, a compromise was worked out with Caine. Beaufoy would abstain and not stand for reelection. In fact, he did stand in 1895 but was defeated. Hamer, *The Politics of Electoral Pressure*, pp. 278-80.

[33] John Hilton, the Alliance parliamentary agent, issued a public manifesto to the Irish Nationalists that embarrassed his employers. Alliance minutes, 19 July 1893. Hilton argued that it was not always practical to consult Manchester when decisions needed to be made in London. Hilton to Whyte, 25 July 1893. Alliance minutes, 26 July 1893.

[34] Hamilton diary, 28 Feb.1893. BL, Sir Edward Hamilton papers, Add.Ms 48659, f.121.

[35] *A History of Modern England* 5: 263, quoted in Crapster, "Our Trade, Our Politics," p. 347.

[36] Harcourt to Farrar, 1 March 1893. Bodleian Library, Harcourt papers, MS145.

[37] Lloyd George to D.R. Daniel, 8 March 1893. W.R .Lambert, *Drink and Sobriety in Victorian Wales c. 1820-c. 1895* (University of Wales Press, 1983), p. 235. David Robert Daniel (1859-1931) was appointed assistant organizer for the Alliance in north Wales in 1887.

[38] The temperance people pointed out that nearly half of its petitions came from public meetings and often bore the signature of only the meetings' chairman. Moreover, in the past, critics of the temperance movement had scorned petitions as meaningless, so the temperance party was slow to circulate petitions in favor of Harcourt's bill. It focused instead on organizing meetings. *Alliance News*, 21 July 1893. p. 500; *Alliance News*, 20 Oct. 1893, p. 703.

[39] *Alliance News*, 20 Oct. 1893, p. 709. The Alliance spent over £13,000 and employed during this crisis thirty agents. *Alliance News,* 27 Oct. 1893, p. 726.

[40] The *Westminster Gazette* began publication on 31 January 1893 with E.T. Cook as editor. When he moved to the *Daily News* three years later, J.A. Spender became editor. The *Westminster Gazette* had political influence much greater than its small circulation of perhaps 20,000 might suggest.

[41] *Westminster Gazette*, 28 Feb. 1893, p. 9.

[42] *Alliance News*, 20 Oct. 1893, pp. 710-11.

[43] *Times*, 7 April 1893, p. 11.

[44] Quoted in *Temperance Chronicle*, 10 Nov. 1899, p. 549.

[45] *Westminster Gazette*, 9 April 1893, p. 11.

[46]. Lawson to Harcourt, 10 April 1893. Bodleian, Harcourt Ms. 146 ff. 14-16.

[47] Harcourt outraged the trade, particularly the militant London publicans' organization. "We have learnt by bitter experience that we cannot trust any party absolutely; that they all regard the Trade as a cow to be milked or an ass to be burdened; but we have never before had a party leader who attacked us, out of sheer spite and vindictiveness, as Sir William Harcourt is doing and will continue to do as long as he remains in power." *Licensing World*, 25 May 1894.

[48] Annual Report, *in Alliance News*, 20 Oct. 1893, pp. 703, 709.

[49] Leif Jones, "How to Influence Governments," delivered at the International Congress on Alcoholism, 14 Sept. 1911. Quoted in G.B. Wilson, *Leif Jones (United Kingdom Alliance* [1948]), Appendix A., pp. 98-104.

[50] Lawson to Harcourt, 2 Sept. 1893. Bodleian, Harcourt Ms. 146, ff. 99-102.

[51] Bryce to Rosebery, 18 Aug. 1893. National Library of Scotland, Rosebery papers, Box 65. "Respectful silence" was the response of the Cabinet.

[52] *Times*, 8 Dec. 1893, p. 11.

[53] Lawson to Harcourt, 5, 9 Feb. 1894. Bodleian, Harcourt Ms. 147, ff. 16-20, 23-24. Harcourt to Lawson, 7 Feb. 1894, in Alliance minutes, 14 Feb. 1894.

[54] Harcourt to John Morley, 2 March 1894. Bodleian, Harcourt Ms. 26 f. 74. With Harcourt's approval, Lawson wrote to Rosebery. Harcourt to Lawson, 10 March 1894. Bodleian, Harcourt Ms. 147, f. 35. Lawson to Rosebery, 10 March 1894. National Library of Scotland, Rosebery papers, Box 68A.

[55] Lawson to Rosebery, 10 March 1894. National Library of Scotland, Rosebery papers, Box 68A. Harcourt to Lawson, 10 March 1894 (answering Lawson's letter of 9 March). Consulted when the correspondence was at Stanton Harcourt. Lawson wrote the Alliance that Rosebery had written him that the Cabinet had decided to "make every effort to proceed with the Bill during the present Session." Alliance minutes, 21 March 1894. Harcourt was less optimistic. "Harcourt cannot tell at all when he will get a chance of bringing in the Veto Bill. The Tories would not allow it to be brought in quietly and printed--so we must wait a bit, as we always have to do!" Lawson to James Whyte, 21 March 1894. Alliance minutes, 28 March 1894. Rosebery later told Caine that he expected that the bill would be introduced in 1894, "but he thinks it cannot be got through this year." Hilton to Whyte, 24 April 1894. Alliance minutes, 25 April 1894.

[56] In March 1894 Harcourt dealt with a minor temperance matter. Caine and Lord Roberts had asked Campbell-Bannerman to support the Army Temperance Association with a thousand pounds. Roberts said the Association has been "equal to adding two battalions of men to the Indian Army." Although Campbell-Bannerman ordinarily thought such societies should be self-supporting, in this instance he was willing to recommend five hundred pounds. Campbell-Bannerman to Harcourt, 7 March 1894. Harcourt concurred. Harcourt to Campbell-Bannerman, 7 March 1894. Consulted when the correspondence was at Stanton Harcourt.

[57] Harcourt to Lawson, 19 April 1894. Bodleian, Harcourt Ms. 147 ff 43-45.

[58] Lawson to Harcourt, 12 May 1894. Bodleian, Harcourt Ms. 147 ff. 50-51.

[59] Lawson to Whyte, 26 April 1894; Raper to Whyte, 26 April 1894; Lawson to Alexander McDougall, 29 May 1894, in Alliance minutes, 2 and 30 May 1894.

[60] For Rosebery's refusal, see Alliance minutes, 2 May 1894. For the manifesto, see Alliance minutes, 9 May 1894; McDougall to Harcourt, 11 May 1894, in Alliance minutes, 23 May 1894.

[61] *Times*, 24 May 1894, p. 6.

[62] Gladstone to Lord Thring, [no day] Sept. 1894, in *Times*, 19 Sept. 1894, p. 4.; 4 Oct. 1894, p. 7 The Gothenburgers had started their campaign with a meeting at Grosvenor House on 6 July 1894. The Bishop of Chester made Gladstone's letter public at a meeting in Aberdeen on 18 September 1894. In the autumn of 1895 Gladstone again endorsed the Gothenburg principle. Gladstone to Thomas Snape,

11 Sept. 1895, in *Times*, 5 Oct. 1895, p. 8. Alderman Snape made the letter public at a meeting in Chester on 4 October.

[63] Lawson to editor, in *Times*, Sept. 1894, p. 11; Whyte to editor, in *Times*, 25 Sept. 1894, p. 8; Whyte to Gladstone, 27 Sept. 1894, in Times, 20 Oct. 1894, p. 5.

[64] Harcourt to John Morley, 24 Sept. 1894. Quoted in Gardiner, *Life of Harcourt*, 2: 307.

[65] *Daily News*, 1 March 1893, pp. 4-5; *Daily Chronicle*, 7 March 1893, p. 4. See also *Star*, 9 April 1895, p. 1. Comparing the 1893 and 1895 bills, "exit local veto—enter local option."

[66] Lawson to Harcourt, 25 Oct. 1894. Bodleian, Harcourt Ms. 147, ff. 72-75, especially ff. 73-74.

[67] Ellis to Harcourt, 27 Oct. 1894, Harcourt papers, consulted when at Stanton Harcourt. Harcourt was frustrated with everything. He told Lord Spencer: "As you know I am not a supporter of this Government." Harcourt to Spencer, September 21, 1894, Gardiner, *Sir William Harcourt*, p. 300.

[68]. John Morley to Lord Spencer, 26 October 1894, in *The Red Earl: The Papers of the Fifth Earl Spencer, 1835-1910*, ed. Peter Gordon, 2 vols.; Publications of the Northamptonshire Record Society, vol. XXXIV (Northampton, 1986) 2: 248.

[69] Lewis Harcourt, Journals, 1 Nov. 1894. Bodleian Harcourt Ms. 411, unfoliated when consulted.

[70] Caine to Rosebery, 11 Nov. 1894. National Library of Scotland, Rosebery papers, Box #66C. Malins was staying with Caine at the time when he wrote to Rosebery. Caine emphasized how important temperance reformers were as constituency workers and that Rosebery had called them the backbone of the party. Speaking at Cardiff to the National Liberal Federation, on 18 January 1895, Rosebery recognized Welsh Nonconformists as the backbone of the Liberal Party too but went on to say: "I have come to the conclusion that the Liberal party is extremely rich in backbones. I do not suppose that it can have too many backbones, but my correspondence makes me feel that there is a multiplicity of backbones in the Liberal party, all preparing to be alienated if certain measures are not pushed forward."

[71] Lewis Harcourt, Journals, 16 Nov. 1894. Bodleian, Harcourt Ms. 412, unfoliated when consulted. John Morley to Harcourt, 16 Nov. 1894. Bodleian, Harcourt Ms. 26, f. 177.

[72] Veto committee minute, 14 Nov. 1894. Bodleian, Harcourt Ms. 147, ff. 94-95. Lewis Harcourt had lobbied his father on behalf of reduction. Dingle, *Campaign for Prohibition*, pp. 160-61.

[73] Harcourt to Sir Henry Jenkyns, 19 Nov. 1894; Lewis Harcourt, Journals, 20, 22, 23 Nov. 1894. Harcourt, Ms. 147, ff. 115-116; Ms. 412, unfoliated when consulted.

[74] Henry Spring to Rosebery, 20 Dec. 1894. National Library of Scotland, Rosebery papers, Box 96.

[75] Lewis Harcourt Journals, 24 Nov. 1894. Bodleian, Harcourt Ms. 412, unfoliated when consulted.

[76] Lawson to Harcourt, 25 Nov. 1894. Bodleian, Harcourt Ms. 147, ff 126-133.

[77] Henry Spring to Rosebery, 20 Dec. 1894. National Library of Scotland, Rosebery papers, Box 96. Inviting Rosebery to chair a meeting at Cardiff, a United Kingdom Alliance district superintendent acknowledged: "The Temperance Party was not

very powerful [at the last general election] but if they abstained from voting the Elections would have different results often times." He added: "we depend for our support upon the lower middle and the upper working classes." A. Sidney Davies to Rosebery, 11 December 1894. National Library of Scotland, Rosebery papers, Box #66C.

[78] Lord Battersea, reported in William Williams to executive committee, 24 Nov. 1894, in Alliance minutes, 28 nov. 1894.

[79] Lawson to Whyte, 16 Jan. 1895, in Alliance minutes, 16 Jan. 1895. Lawson referred to a letter of Ellis as "rotten" and called Herbert Gladstone "abominable." Lawson must have had in mind a speech that Herbert Gladstone delivered under the auspices of the Bramley Liberal Club. *Alliance News*, 4 Jan. 1895, p. 22. Herbert Gladstone said that at first he had opposed Local Veto on the grounds of practicality and political expediency, but that about ten years ago he announced that he would support Local Veto because the majority of the party favored it. He continued to support it. He went on to say that it was necessary in prohibition districts that "the just wants and necessities of individuals would always be respected." Most of the speech dealt with reforms that Gladstone considered politically practicable such as legislation for habitual drunkards. He gave priority to them over Local Veto. Previously teetotal, Ellis abandoned teetotalism in 1895 for reasons of health.

[80] Joseph Rowntree to Robert Spence Watson, 5 Feb. 1895, with supplementary statistics, enclosed with Watson to Rosebery, 7 Feb. 1895. National Library of Scotland, Rosebery papers, Box 72C. The Rowntree letter also was enclosed in Watson to Harcourt, 7 Feb. 1895. Bodleian, Harcourt Ms. 148, ff. 157-160. See also Joseph Rowntree and Arthur Sherwell, *The Temperance Problem and Social Reform* (1899; 7th ed., London, 1900), pp. 101-04.

[81] Harcourt to Francis William Fox, 31 Jan. 1895. Bodleian, Harcourt Ms 148.

[82] Harcourt to Watson, 11 Feb. 1895. Bodleian, Harcourt Ms. 148, ff. 161-62.

[83] *Alliance News,* 1 Feb. 1895, p. 73.

[84] Malins to A. Spencer Wells, 9 Nov. 1894; Malins to Harcourt, 15 Jan., 28 March 1895. Bodleian, Harcourt Ms. 147, ff. 87-93; Harcourt Ms. 148, ff. 97-99; Harcourt Ms. 149, ff. 36-37.

[85] For the full debate, see *Parl. Deb.*, 4th ser., XXXII, cols. 1161-1247.

[86] Bahlman, ed., *The Diary of Sir Edward Walter Hamilton, 1885-1906*, p. 297. According to Hamilton (11 May 1895, p. 299), Harcourt regarded "the lessening of the curse of drink" as "the great object of his life."

[87] *Temperance Chronicle*, 10 May 1895, p. 228. (Later Sir) E. Stafford Howard, MP, chaired the committee. Howard was one of a handful of MPs active in the CETS. Other MPs included Sir William Houldsworth and C.E. (Ernest) Tritton, both of them Conservatives.

[88] D.W. Bebbington, *The Nonconformist Conscience: Chapel and Politics, 1870 to 1914* (G. Allen and Unwin, 1982), p. 50.

[89]. *Daily Chronicle*, 30 April 1895, p. 4. Several years after the failure of Harcourt's bill, an anonymous prohibitionist offered a theory about the breakdown of Liberal support for local veto. Supposedly, the *Speaker* had begun an editorial campaign against Local Veto in September 1892, even before Harcourt had introduced his first bill. Later the *Daily News*, the *Daily Chronicle*, and the *Westminster Gazette* echoed

the demand to drop Local Veto from the Liberal party program. Joining the campaign were "the four Liberal brewers, Messrs. [Sydney] Evershed, [H.T.] Fenwick, [William] McEwan, and [Edward] Majoribanks [Lord Tweedmouth], with the contiguous interests represented by the [Mark] Beaufoys, and aided by the Liberal Whip, Mr. Herbert Gladstone, with one or two congenial spirits of the Courtenay Warner type." The writer added a reference to W.E. Gladstone's letter to Lord Thring in September 1894, "as if to bring the suspicion and fear of betrayal to a certainty." The writer also criticized Liberal Unionists who claimed to be temperance reformers. The treasurer of the Church of England Temperance Society, C.E. Tritton, went out of his way to denounce Harcourt's bill and to ridicule Sir Wilfrid Lawson. "Crucible," in *Temperance Register*, vol. 1, no. 1 (Jan. 1903): 19. E.T. Cook (1857-1919) seems like a representative anti-Local Veto journalist. After a couple of years as editor of the *Pall Mall Gazette*, he was editor of the *Westminster Gazette* from January 1893 until January 1896 when he left to become editor of the Nonconformist and Cobdenite morning newspaper, the *Daily News*, until January 1901, when he was dismissed because of his support for the South African war. He then became a leader writer for the *Daily Chronicle* for ten years. J. Saxon Mills, S*ir Edward Cook, K.B.E., A Biography* (Constable, 1921), pp. 154, 196, 218; *Oxford DNB*.

[90] *Daily News*, 27 May 1895, p. 6; 7 June 1895, pp. 4-5.

[91] Lawson to Harcourt, 26 May 1895. Bodleian, Harcourt Ms. 149, ff. 150-51.

[92] H.A. Newton, "The Position of the Trade before and after the General Election," *Brewers' Almanack* (1896), pp. 69-71. After the election, the Unionist MP George Curzon (Lawson's nephew) made new temperance proposals. *Licensing World*, 8 Aug. 1895, pp. 104-05.

[93] Sir Edward Hamilton, diaries, 30 April 1895. *Destruction of Lord Rosebery*, p. 244. According to Arthur Sherwell, James Bryce told him a few years afterwards that the Cabinet approved the 1895 bill only to "placate" Harcourt. "'Rough Notes' by Arthur Sherwell on an Ms of H. Carter re Origins of Gothenburg." Methodist Church Archives, Division of Social Responsibility. MA. 243. Quoted in Greenaway, *Drink and British Politics*, p. 222 n. 119.

[94] Hamilton diary, April 9, 1895, in *The Destruction of Lord Rosebery: from the Diary of Sir Edward Hamilton, 1894-1895*, ed. David Brooks (Historians' Press 1986), p. 237.

[95] For the trade, the National Trade Defence Fund was responsible for the elections except in London. The licensed victuallers' Central Board, which had the responsibility there, complained about its lack of funds. It applied to Brewers' Hall and to the Rectifiers' Club (the organization for distillers). Joint (Wholesale and Retail) Parliamentary Committee minute-book, 24 June 1895, 2 July 1895.

[96] The popular vote was not so one-sided. The United Kingdom Alliance argued that a system of proportional representation would have given the Unionists a modest majority of twelve seats. *Alliance News*, 18 Oct. 1895, p. 669. An Alliance agent who blamed the election defeat on Irish Home Rule described Local Veto as "only a side issue," a curious contrast to previous claims about its importance. Henry Hibbert to editor, 14 August 1895, *Bradford Observer*, reprinted in *Alliance News*, 23 August 1895.

---

[97] Patrick Cassidy, "Temperance and the 1895 General Election in the Constituency of Derby," *Midland History* 33 no. 1 (Spring 2008): 97-114. Cassidy points out that Harcourt's support for Direct Local Veto was not the only reason for his defeat at Derby. The *Alliance News* (19 July 1895, pp. 464) acknowledged the importance of the drink trade in Harcourt's defeat, but pointed to other reasons, for instance, the abstention of 200-300 Independent Labour Party electors who had voted Liberal in the previous general election and the neutrality of the Trades Council, the result of Conservative largess to unemployed in the previous winter, as well as more general causes such as the hostility of the Church to the Liberal Party education agenda. Contemporaries also noted that thousands of carriage mechanics working for the Midland Railway Company had been on short time for two or three years and that Irish electors voted Conservative because of the education question. James Firth to editor of the *Leeds Mercury*, 4 December 1897, reprinted in *Alliance News*, 10 December 1897. Paul A. Readman, "The 1895 General Election and Political Change in Late Victorian Britain," *Historical Journal* 42 no. 2 (1999): 471-72, reports that 72% of Liberal electoral addresses mentioned Local Veto, with a higher percentage in the more urbanized boroughs and London. The Liberals who emphasized the Veto depicted it as part of local democracy.

[98] Philip J. Waller, *Democracy and Sectarianism: A Political and Social History of Liverpool, 1868-1939* (Liverpool University Press, 1981), p. 159.

[99] For instance, Sir Hugh Kay Shuttlesworth to Spencer, 23 July 1895, cited in Stansky, *Ambitions and Strategies*, p. 179.

[100] Kimberley to Ripon 30 July 1895, quoted in Stansky, *Ambitions and Strategies*, p. 182.

[101] Sir Cosmo Bonsor to Lord Salisbury, 2 Aug. 1895. Christ Church, Oxford, Salisbury papers. The election, which was spread over more than three weeks in various constituencies, had not yet ended.

[102] Quoted in Sir Charles E. Mallet, *Herbert Gladstone: A Memoir* (Hutchinson, 1932), p. 56.

[103] Campbell-Bannerman to Rosebery, 20 July 1895. National Library of Scotland, Rosebery papers, Box 2. According to a prohibitionist publication, the general election reduced the number of teetotalers in the House of Commons from one out of every eleven to one out of every fifteen members. *Abstainers' Advocate*, March 1896 p. 37.

[104] Gladstone to Harcourt, 15 July 1895. Quoted in Gardiner, *Life of Harcourt*, 2:371.

[105] *Daily Chronicle*, 29 Nov. 1895, p. 5.

[106] Quoted in Readman, "The 1895 General Election and Political Change in Late Victorian Britain," p. 479. E.N. Buxton pointed out that the drink trade had fought the Liberals as hard in 1892 as in 1895. The difference was the resentment of workingmen against restrictions on their liberty in Harcourt's bill. Buxton to editor, *Times*, 2 Aug. 1895, p. 3.

[107] Haldane to Rosebery, 18 Sept. 1900, quoted in H.C.G. Matthew, *The Liberal Imperialists: The Ideas and Politics of a Post-Gladstonian Elite* (Oxford University Presss, 1973), p. 239.

[108] National Liberal Federation, *Proceedings* (1898), 40-42.

[109] The *Westminster Gazette* worked against the Liberal policy of denying financial

compensation. Following a statement in the *Times* that T.P. Whittaker, A.F. Hills, and other prominent temperance reformers were willing for compensation to be paid out of trade funds, the *Westminster Gazette* (7 June 1895, p. 3) interviewed Whittaker. Whittaker said that he had no enthusiasm for compensation and had no intention of pressing for it, but, speaking as an individual, he would accept the trade compensating itself under government auspices if there was legislation to reduce the number of licensed premises. In that case, it should not be an annual levy but only at the time of reduction. In the case of local prohibition, all that temperance reformers would accept would be a time-notice. W.S. Caine sharply criticized the editor of the *Methodist Times* for proposing compensation of extinguished licenses with charges imposed on the surviving licenses. *Methodist Times*, 13 June 1895, p. 377.

[110] Other political important London editors included H.W. Massingham at the *Daily Chronicle*, 1895-1899, and A.G. Gardiner (the biographer of Harcourt) at the *Daily News*. 1902-1919. The editor of the most important provincial Liberal newspaper, the *Manchester Guardian*, C.P. Scott served as editor from 1872 till 1929.

[111] *Westminster Gazette*, 21, 22, 25, 26, 27 July, 10, 15, 17 Aug. 1893, and related articles. See also Sir Linton Andrews, "J.A. Spender," in Sir Linton Andrews and H.A. Taylor, *Lords and Laborers of the Press* (Southern Illinois University Press, 1970), p. 73.

[112] Westminster Gazette, 13 Aug. 1895, pp. 1-2.

[113] *Daily Chronicle*, 30 May (p. 3), 1 (p. 6), 4 (p. 6) June 1895 (p. 6). Enclosed in Lawson to Harcourt, 20 June 1896. Bodleian, Harcourt Ms. 157, ff. 35-36.

[114] Jonathan Hargrove to Whyte, 12 May 1895, in Alliance minutes, 15 May 1895. Hargrove gave as his illustration the honorary secretary of the Alliance, Samuel Pope, QC.

[115] Annual Report, in *Alliance News*, 18 Oct. 1895, pp. 668-73 (quotations, pp. 668, 670, 672). Leif Jones acknowledged that in London and the south of England "there is some weakness and some dread of the [Local Veto] Bill," but he argued "the cure for it is not to run away, but to educate the backward South." Jones to editor, 22 Nov. 1896. *Westminster Gazette,* 23 Nov. 1896, p. 2.

[116] W.S. Caine, "The Last General Election," In Guy Hayler, ed., *The Prohibition Movement: Papers and Proceedings of the National Convention for the Prohibition of the Liquor Traffic, Newcastle-upon-Tyne, April 3rd to 9th, 1897* (Newcastle, 1897), pp. 59-62. In this paper Caine said that the trade spent more than £3,000 to defeat him, but in a contemporary estimate he said £300 or £400. *Bradford Observer,* 16 July 1895, p. 5. Elsewhere Caine minimized the impact of the trade on his defeat. Supposedly the trade counted for 200 votes in an election that he lost by 700 votes. *Daily Chronicle*, July 26, 1895, p. 7. See also *Alliance News*, 10 Dec. 1897, pp. 812-813.

[117] James Whyte, "The Prohibitionists in Politics," in Hayler, *The Prohibition Movement*, pp. 275-82. William McEwan, the Edinburgh brewer, was enormously wealthy. Ian Donnachie, "Men of Brewing: William McEwan," *Scottish Brewing Archive Newsletter* no. 5 (Summer 1985). See Mark Beaufoy to Rosebery, 31 May 1895. National Library of Scotland, Rosebery papers, Box 70B. For anti-Veto Liberal M.P.s, see Lawson to Whyte, 11 June 1895. Alliance minutes, 12 June 1895.

[118] *Alliance News*, 14 Oct. 1898, p. 662 (part of a section of the Annual Report called "The Revolt against the Veto," pp. 662-665); and the first number of *Temperance Register*, Jan. 1903, p. 19. Supposedly after Fulford's death, temperance reformers (led by the Cadburys) took over the Birmingham Liberal Association. Not being teetotalers, the agent and the secretary were fired. *Licensed Trade News*, 30 Oct. 1897, pp. 5-6. Its editor E. Lawrence Levy knew Birmingham well. See also *Times*, 20 Jan. 1897, p. 8. Fulford had been president of the East Birmingham Liberal Council and treasurer of the Birmingham Liberal Association. The family brewery was founded around 1872. Fulford was born in 1849. He had served as councilor in Birmingham.

[119] Hamer, *The Politics of Electoral Pressure*, pp. 289-290.

[120] Harcourt to Lawson, June 1896 [?]. Bodleian, Harcourt Ms. 233, f. 23. See also Harcourt to Robert Spence Watson, 22 Jan. 1897. Percy Corder, *The Life of Robert Spence Watson* (Headley, 1914), p. 272.

[121] Lawson to Harcourt, 22 June 1896. Bodleian, Harcourt Ms. 231, ff. 140-141.

[122] Harcourt to Watson, 22 Jan. 1897. Bodleian, Harcourt Ms. 233, ff. 23-24. Quoted in Corder, *The Life of Robert Spence Watson*, p. 272.

[123] *The Journal of John Wodehouse First Earl of Kimberley*, p. 447 (entry for 8 February 1897). Lawson continued to see Harcourt as the best hope of the temperance party. After Harcourt declined to preside over a temperance meeting in 1902, Lawson urged him: "Do not be too hard on our Temperance Brethren. They are not bigger fools than other Galileans, though they annoy you and me more." Lawson to Harcourt, 9 March 1902. Harcourt papers uncatalogued when consulted. Presumably the reference is to the sect of Zealots that followed Judas of Galilee.

[124] *Daily News*, 21 Oct. 1897, p. 5.

[125] *Temperance Chronicle*, 27 March 1880, p. 198; *Temperance Chronicle*, 18 Dec. 1880, p. 811.

[126] For a report of this speech with minor variation, see *Manchester Guardian*, 24 November 1897, p. 7; and *Alliance News*, 3 December 1897, p. 796 (the latter with the subtitle, "How the Local Veto Still Sticks in His Gizzard"); Herbert Gladstone to editor, 6 April 1894, in *Leeds Mercury*, 9 April 1894, p. 7.

[127] Henry Hibbert to Herbert Gladstone, 17 April 1896. British Library, Herbert Gladstone papers, Add. Ms. 46056 f. 171. Hibbert also wrote to Gladstone, 9 and 15 April 1896. British Library, Herbert Gladstone papers, Add. Ms. 46056, ff. 167-170. See also Mallett, Herbert Gladstone, p. 108.

[128] *Brewers' Almanack* (1895), p. 50.

[129] *Manchester Guardian*, 24 Nov. 1897, p. 4.

[130] For Harcourt, see Times, 26 Nov. 1897, p. 10. See also John Morley's defense of the Veto policy. Times, 10 Dec. 1897, p. 6.

[131] *Westminster Gazette*, 29 November 1897, p. 1; 7 Jan. 1898, p. 2. The first issue was reprinted in the *Alliance News*, 10 December 1897, p. 8.

[132] *Daily News*, 10 Dec. 1897, p. 4; Daily Chronicle, 4 Dec. 1897, p. 4.

[133] *Speaker*, 15 January 1889, pp. 67-68. *The Speaker*'s favorite scheme was disinterested management.

[134] *Alliance News*, 3 Dec. 1897, p. 800.

[135] *Alliance News*, 3 Dec. 1897, p. 797.

[136] *Ibid.*

[137] Whittaker to editor of the *Westminster Gazette*, 7 December 1897, in *Alliance News*. 17 December 1897, p. 827. The *Alliance News* gave the letter the subtitle, "A Few Plain Words to Critics of the Veto."

[138] *Alliance News*, 3 December 1897, p. 799. See also *Manchester Guardian*, 24 November 1897, p. 4. In an interview with the (Manchester) *Evening News*, James Whyte expressed confidence about the future. For instance, he cited the potential of the 142,000 Rechabites. 75% of adult Rechabites were under age 35, while 57% were under 25. The future promised many temperance voters. Reprinted in *Alliance News,* 3 Dec. 1897, p. 797.

[139] Henry to Gladstone, 9 Dec. 1897. British Library, Herbert Gladstone papers, Add. Ms. 46046 ff. 65-66. An ironmaster, Henry became Lord Mayor of Leeds in 1918.

[140] *Manchester Guardian*, 8 Jan. 1898, p. 8. The opening figure of speech did not appear in the newspaper report; it is quoted in Mallet, *Herbert Gladstone*, p. 161.

[141] *Brewers' Almanack* (1899), p. 53. The entry for this speech also mentioned the metaphor about the Liberal Party being "on a sandbank in a fog."

[142] "Notes on the Veto." British Library, Herbert Gladstone papers, Add. Ms. 46092 ff. 161, 168-69. See also Gladstone to Thomas Wilson, 2 May 1901, rebutting a letter by the Rev. Leonard M. Isitt. *Eastern Morning News*, 4 May 1901. "I maintained the right of those whose licenses might be removed to equitable consideration."

[143] Quoted in Wilson, *Leif Jones,* pp. 14-23. See also Leif Jones to editor, *Leeds Mercury*, reprinted in *Alliance News*, 14 January 1898, p. 25. Gladstone admitted that "good, kind temperance friends" had administered "hard knocks," but he believed in speaking frankly about Local Veto. Mallet, *Herbert Gladstone*, p. 161.

[144] Castle Howard, Ninth Countess of Carlisle papers, J23/100.

[145] Pope to McDougall, 26 Feb. 1898, in Alliance minutes, 2 March 1898.

[146] *Cambridge Independent Press*, 29 April 1898, p. 6. See also Gladstone to Calvert, 11 Oct. 1906, in which Gladstone reviewed his position on the Veto. Herbert Gladstone papers. Add. Ms. 46064, f. 84. In a letter to a constituent Harry Rogers (14 Oct. 1898), Gladstone did make the concession that he would be guided by his constituents if a Local Veto bill reached a second reading. Add. Ms. 46057, f. 72.

[147] E.C. Brambley to Whyte, 10 April 1894, in Alliance minutes, 11 April 1894. In this letter Brambley celebrated and explained the Liberal victory at Wisbech. The successful candidate (Arthur Brand) "told [Brambley] that Mr. [Cosmo] Bonsor declared in the Dining-room of the House of Commons that they (the trade) would not hesitate to spend £5,000 to win the seat."

[148] D.A. Hamer says the number was 150. *The Politics of Electoral Pressure*, p. 269.

[149] Newton to Gladstone, 11 June 1898. British Library, Herbert Gladstone papers, Add. Ms. 46057 ff. 55-56. Published with minor changes in *Alliance News*, 29 July 1898, p. 481. See also *Manchester Guardian*, 8 January 1898, p. 8; 10 January 1898, p. 6; 11 January 1898, p. 7; 12 Jan. 1898, p. 7; *Alliance News*, 21 January 1898, pp. 28-29, 36; Newton to Whyte, 29 Jan. 1898, in Alliance minutes, 26 Jan. 1898 [sic]. Newton had been a UKA district superintendent since 1887. *Alliance News*, 5 Nov. 1897, p. 735.

[150] Gladstone to Newton, 20 July 1898. British Library, Herbert Gladstone papers, Add. Ms. 46057 ff. 57-58. The Liberal candidate Mendl won despite anti-Semitic

and anti-foreign prejudice, as he was Jewish and his father had been born in Romania. *Morning Advertiser*, 6 Jan. 1898, p. 2; and leader, "The Roumanian Gentleman Who Desires to be the Radical Member for Plymouth," 7 Jan. 1898, p. 4.

[151] Hamer, *The Politics of Electoral Press*ure, p. 294.

[152] *Alliance News*, 21 Oct. 1892, p. 679; 16 July 1895, p. 5. See also Hamer, *The Politics of Electoral Pressure*, pp. 262-65.

[153] E.C. Brambley to editor, 16 Aug 1895, in *Daily News*, 19 Aug. 1895, p. 8. The letter was a contribution to the debate over the candidacies of the National Independent Temperance Party founded in 1905.

[154] Thornley to Whyte, 12 June 1894, in Alliance minutes, 13 June 1894.

[155] William Pearson to UKA, n.d., in Alliance minutes, 13 Oct. 1900. See also *Alliance News*, 4 Oct. 1900, pp. 630-31. Gladstone's support for compensation and grocers' licenses particularly angered Pearson. The militant Good Templars advised their members to abstain. Pearson to James Whyte, 25 September 1900, in Alliance minutes.

[156] *Alliance News*, 18 Oct. 1900, p. 661. Two Congregational, two Baptist, two Wesleyan Methodist, two Primitive Methodists, and one Methodist Free Church ministers published a letter in the *Leeds Mercury* in support of Gladstone's election. *Alliance News*. 4 October 1900, p. 631.

[157] *Licensing World*, 29 September 1900, quoted in *Alliance News*, 4 October 1900, p. 631.

[158] *Alliance News*, 19 June 1899, p. 411, 29 June 1899, p. 412. About 4,000 miners were electors in the constituency.

[159] *Alliance News*, 29 June 1899, pp. 411-13. See also Hamer, *The Politics of Electoral Pressure*, pp. 297-98. Austin was returned in the general election of 1900 as an independent Liberal. By this time his support for Irish Home Rule had cooled. He strongly supported the South African war: "in the division which followed the publication of the Spion Kop dispatches, he was the only member of the Opposition who voted with the Government and against his [Liberal] leader." Predictably the Conservatives once again refrained from opposing him with their own candidate and instead supported him against the official "Little Englander" Liberal candidate. Austin also got the support of the licensed victuallers. *Tablet*, 29 Sept. 1900, p. 26 (summarizing accounts in the *Yorkshire Herald* and the *Yorkshire Post*). The *Tablet* was a Roman Catholic newspaper. Austin did not stand for reelection in 1906, the year of his death.

[160]. See Frederic Dolman, "The Liberal Party and Local Veto," *Fortnightly Review*, Feb. 1899, pp. 249-58.

[161] Part of the reason for this resignation may have been that Harcourt's anti-Ritualism was controversial in the Liberal Party.

[162] Hamer, *The Politics of Electoral Pressu*re, p. 300.

[163] "Notes on the Veto" (probably 1897/98). BL, Herbert Gladstone papers, Add. Ms. 46092 f. 169.

CHAPTER FIVE

THE SEARCH FOR A SETTLEMENT

The fruitless struggle among pressure groups and political parties encouraged a search for a compromise to end the deadlock. A compromise settlement had special attraction for moderate reformers as they accepted that the sale of drink would continue and the necessity of compensation for dispossessed license holders. By the turn of the century the exhausting and precarious legislative stalemate helped persuade some of the leaders of the advanced temperance party and of the drink trade to support a compromise settlement, the advanced reformers out of a desire for half a loaf immediately, the drink traders out of a desire for security. They envisaged the nature of the compromise in conflicting ways.

The withdrawal of the licensing proposals introduced by successive Conservative and Liberal Governments in 1888-95 showed the futility of legislation that lacked a broad consensus of support. Without it any Government could expect strong resistance from the Opposition and dissension in its own ranks. The failure of the compensation schemes, together with *Sharp v. Wakefield*, showed that the trade could not obtain the security that it wanted except as part of a large measure of licensing reform. The Newcastle Programme and Harcourt's bills seemed to condemn the trade to perpetual struggle. The failure of the Local Veto bills showed that an emphasis on prohibition and a rejection of money compensation doomed reform legislation. The Unionists could not take satisfaction in the bitter stalemate. Many Liberal Unionists felt strongly about drink, and virtually all Ulster Unionists supported drastic temperance legislation. The Church of England Temperance Society was predominantly a Tory organization. Sir William Houldsworth, MP, a Manchester cotton spinner, helped organize a society of Conservative (and later Unionist) temperance reformers. Many country MPs who served their native districts as JPs favored a paternalist, restrictive policy toward the sale of drink. People in all political parties were exasperated by the harassing tactics of the advanced temperance party and alarmed by the swaggering power of the licensed drink trade. The temperance question seemed too dangerous politically and too urgent socially to leave unresolved.

Innumerable bills sought to find a politically practicable compromise. As early as 1883 Sir Wilfrid Lawson complained: "Everybody has now a licensing bill."[1] A decade later this was even more true.

Most compromise schemes combined an immediate reduction in the number of licensed premises and a miscellany of smaller reforms such as Sunday closing, together with a form of money compensation paid out of special taxes on drink or on licensed premises. The details which fleshed out this outline could make a particular compromise plan unacceptable to people who advocated a settlement on the same general principles. For instance, the Conservative proposals of 1888 failed because of the smallness of the reduction in numbers and the permanence of the right of compensation as well as because of the unrealistic hopes of both extreme temperance reformers and trade militants. Different compromise schemes looked for allies in different directions. A program designed to reconcile the trade with the moderate reformers usually excluded the prohibition Veto, while a scheme which hoped to unite moderate and advanced reformers had to offer at least a symbolic recognition of the principle of prohibition by local referendum, perhaps after a delay of several years or perhaps only for Scotland and Wales. The Gothenburg Scheme did not fit the general pattern for compromise settlements. Most of the advanced temperance party bitterly opposed it, and the trade could not consider monopoly versions that mandated the destruction of commercial ownership of the retail trade. Consequently, the revival of the Gothenburg Scheme must be left to a later chapter.

Lord Randolph Churchill (1849-95) drafted the first of the major compromise schemes that abounded in the 1890s. In the late 1880s he began to denounce "this destructive and devilish liquor traffic." He claimed that the brewers exploited the publicans and hinted that the brewers had forced the Salisbury Government to propose compensation in 1888.[2] He privately consulted Sir Wilfrid Lawson and Sir William Harcourt and urged the trade to support a settlement of the licensing question before the next general election.[3] Harcourt commiserated with Churchill about his task. Liquor legislation requires "a very nasty piece of navigation & any channel is full of sunken wrecks of all description."[4] A Conservative who appears to have disliked Churchill admitted that his bill "would satisfy almost entirely the Radical Temperance Unionists."[5]

Sir Algernon West (1852-1921), a moderate Liberal, played a considerable role in the making of Churchill's bill. West later was vice-chairman of the 1896-99 Royal Commission on the liquor licensing laws.

Leading brewers asked Churchill to draft a bill to settle the licensing question but were not happy with what he produced. Cosmo

Bonsor (1848-1929), a Conservative M.P., a major London brewer, and the treasurer of the National Trade Defence Fund, expressed frustration. "It has been my ambition to have a hand in settling the Licensing Question but I shall never try again."[6] Bonsor added that a trade meeting decided unanimously that the trade would not accept a bill that included the Veto and "a licensing authority elected specially for the purpose." If they were dropped from the bill and compensation was based on market value, the bill could be accepted in principle.[7] James Wigan (1832-1902) represented the country brewers in an interview with Churchill. He explained the difficulties blocking trade support for the bill. The big brewers could not deliver trade support: "the probable attitude of the retailers, and some of the smaller brewers, who would in spite of us, undoubtedly have opposed the Bill, and who no one section of our Trade, however powerful, can control." Wigan would gladly see a settlement, "if it could be effected without violent opposition, from within our own ranks."[8]

After Bonsor had read the printed text of the bill, he wrote Churchill with "plain speaking." "The bill as drafted would please nobody except the Teetotallers." The trade was being asked to endorse a bill without knowing what kind of compensation the Government would add to it. The result of this uncertainty would be "an agitation similar to that which killed Bruce's bill."[9]

Apparently, Churchill had a confidential meeting with the Liberal brewer Samuel Whitbread (1830-1915).[10]

The National Trade Defence Fund directed its secretary J. Danvers Power (1858-1927) to draft a bill that would allow prohibition of new licenses and thin out congested districts by allowing the transfer of licenses to other districts. In the end the Fund did nothing about its own confidential draft and refused to support Churchill's bill. Churchill's proposal, introduced in the House of Commons on 29 April 1890, combined local control of licensing with money compensation. The bill provided no details about compensation as it was a private member's bill, but he told the Church of England Temperance Society that he intended to finance compensation with increased license duties and confine compensation to the twenty years after the enactment of the bill. After receiving a copy of the bill, Ritchie complained: "in not dealing with compensation you are avoiding the real crux of the whole business."[11] The bill transferred the licensing authority of the justices of the peace to the county and county borough councils. In private Churchill admitted that he would have preferred creating ad hoc licensing boards but did not to avoid controversy.[12]

Although Churchill's bill never reaching a second reading, it reflected the growing interest in a compromise settlement. In part out of personal and political loyalties and in part out of a longing for a settlement, several leaders of the London trade cautiously backed Churchill. In early May Charles Walker (1836-1903), a prominent London publican and one of Lord Randolph's constituents, presided over a special trade meeting that approved the bill in principle. Bonsor attended this meeting.[13] On the following day a Liberal brewer, E.N. Buxton (1840-1924), asked Churchill for an interview.[14] Originally hopeful, in the end Buxton rejected Churchill's compensation offer of a period of years when licenses would be secure. "The more I consider the matter the more I should regret action of the principle of a 'ten years grace.' Almost any fate would be better than that, for Brewers at any rate. Certainly ten years of penal servitude would be more endurable than 10 years of such Purgatory as that." Buxton did agree with one part of Churchill's proposals. "I would without question prefer the existing powers of the magistrates should be transferred to the County Councils."[15]

Churchill quickly abandoned his efforts when he found support weak. Lloyd George described his efforts sardonically. "His, at the best, was a kind of mushroom teetotalism, which grew no one knew why or when and which has disappeared, how no one exactly knows."[16]

The bills of the Manchester and Westminster licensing reform committees and of the Church of England Temperance Society represent the approach to compromise most characteristic of the moderate reformers.[17] All three proposed a statutory reduction in the number of licensed premises in proportion to the local population. The Manchester and Westminster bills also allowed a prohibitive Local Veto.

The Manchester bill tried to combine the program of the CETS and the UKA. Manchester was the headquarters of the Alliance, and the UKA was well represented at the meetings in 1890 and 1891 that led to the Manchester bill. Many Gladstonian Liberals served on the Manchester committee. The honorary treasurer of the Alliance, (later Sir) W.J. Crossley (1844-1911), served the Manchester committee in the same capacity. Theodore Neild (1834-1929), then an Alliance member, also took part.[18] Nevertheless, after the bill had taken shape most Vetoists criticized it. Moderates, including individuals not otherwise associated with the organized temperance movement such as Manchester's Anglican and Roman Catholic bishops, dominated the committee. Several local MPs headed by Sir Henry Roscoe (1833-1915) introduced the Manchester bill in the House of Commons in March 1894. It provided for a reduction in the number of licensed premises to a proportion of one per thousand people in boroughs and one per six hundred in rural districts, ratepayers' referendums on Sunday closing and on hours of sales, and (by a hard to obtain three-fourths' majority) prohibition of most kinds of liquor licenses. Where licensing continued, licenses would be auctioned to the highest bidders. To ease the blow to the trade most provisions would not be implemented until five years after the bill's enactment.

Another group of moderates, mainly Liberal Unionists, organized a licensing reform committee in April 1891 at the Westminster Palace hotel.[19] Leonard Courtney (1832-1918) and several other MPs introduced the Westminster bill in the House of Commons in March 1894. It provided a statutory reduction in the number of licensed premises in proportion to population, one per thousand in urban districts, one per five hundred in rural ones, authorized a referendum to prohibit the sale of drink for on-premises and off-premises consumption, and created partially elected licensing boards to take over the powers of the licensing justices. The boards also would be empowered to shorten hours of sale, impose Sunday closing, and appoint licensing inspectors. The bill offered money compensation to those who lost their licenses for the purpose of reduction at the first licensing sessions after the enactment of the statute. The unspecified amount of compensation would be funded out of a special charge on license holders and clubs.

In 1891 the Church of England Temperance Society's executive committee adopted a series of resolutions recommending licensing reforms. Early in 1892, after consultation with the diocesan councils, the executive committee declared these resolutions to be CETS policy.[20] The resolutions urged ad hoc licensing boards elected by the ratepayers or, alternatively, as a second choice, licensing committees of the County Councils. They also asked for reduction in the number of licensed premises to one per thousand in towns and one per six hundred in the country, statutory Sunday closing, and special inspectors. In March 1893 the president of the CETS, Dr. Frederick Temple (1821-1902) bishop of London, introduced a bill in the House of Lords that embodied these resolutions. It provided money compensation restricted to the five years that followed the enactment of the bill. Each license holder would declare the value of his premises, a declaration that would provide the basis for the compensation if the license was not renewed and the basis for the levy to raise the money to compensate others if the license was renewed. In 1894 Dr. Temple introduced a similar licensing bill without the controversial elected licensing boards which many critics feared would draw the drink trade into local politics. In 1896 C. Ernest Tritton (1845-1918) introduced the CETS bill in the House of Commons.[21]

The CETS occupied a crucial position in the temperance movement. It was not representative of the Established Church since it was dominated by teetotalers who outnumbered the moderate drinkers of the "general section" three to one. Despite this, it enjoyed considerable influence among the clergy, particularly after Dr. Temple was elevated to the Primacy. Harcourt, who resented the CETS's rejection of prohibition and its support for money compensation, sneered that the CETS was a great deal Church and very little temperance. As the Manchester and Westminster committees never consisted of more than a handful of activists, the CETS provided moderate temperance reformers with their most powerful organization. Its prestige faded after 1895 when the CETS declined in membership, revenue, and sales of literature.

The Manchester, Westminster, and CETS bills stimulated discussion but aroused no widespread agitation in their behalf. Without the support of a major section of the advanced temperance party, no controversial licensing bill had much prospect of passage. The advanced temperance party contained most of the activists necessary to mobilize temperance sympathizers in the constituencies.

In the mid-1890s Arnold F. Hills (1857-1928), a wealthy London shipbuilder, attempted to unite the advanced temperance party with moderate reformers. Although a Conservative in politics, Hills was committed to reforms associated with the fringe of the Liberal Party.[22] He was president of the Federal Vegetarian Union and of the West Ham and District Temperance Union. Although a fierce opponent of trade unions, he was a paternalistic employer. For example, he financed a football team consisting of his workers that eventually became the West Ham professional club.[23] He had the financial resources to offer generous subsidies to the UKA and the CETS (for which he became co-treasurer), and other reform organizations and to underwrite the Ideal Publishing Union that published temperance and vegetarian journals, books, and pamphlets.[24] The *Licensed Trade News* harshly commented: "it is the shekels that attract men to him, not his transcendent ability."[25] To get his way, he often offered to write large checks. In 1901, when the football team became separate from the Ironworks, he offered to pay off its considerable debts if the players promised to become teetotalers.[26]

It was the Alliance that initiated the contact with Hills. "Mr. Hills is about in the prime of life, has wealth, and a generous disposition towards temperance work, and he is worth cultivating." In September 1892 Hills offered a thousand pounds as an initial contribution and £250 annually, if the Alliance could come to terms with the CETS on a common program. The Alliance representative asked for an immediate contribution and got ten guineas.[27]

Hills sometimes irritated his fellow reformers by the impetuosity with which he tried to manage their affairs. For instance, in February 1893 he proposed that the president of the British Women's Temperance Association (Lady Henry Somerset) should resign when the organization became divided between her supporters, who favored a broad program of social, moral, and women's suffrage reform, and her opponents, who included many of the other leaders of the British Women who wanted to concentrate exclusively on temperance. They later seceded to form the Women's Total Abstinence Union.[28]

In 1893-96 Hills underwrote the expenses of four United Temperance Conferences, or "Temperance Parliaments." His non-partisan approach to temperance legislation in practice relied heavily on Liberal Unionists. Leonard Courtney, a prominent Liberal Unionist, presided over the conferences in 1893, 1894, and 1896. Other Liberal Unionists (Andrew Johnston, Sir George Livesey, and Stephen Bourne) shared the chair in 1895, while W.S. Caine, who for several years had been Liberal Unionist chief whip, chaired the organizing committee. Hills served as honorary treasurer.[29]

A professional parliamentary draftsman prepared a complex licensing bill. Hills optimistically entitled it the United Temperance Bill. With modifications, it was presented to the four conferences. The bill combined a local option to permit a reduction in the number of licensed premises to one per thousand in towns and one per six hundred elsewhere, with a prohibitive Veto affecting all licenses and requiring a two-thirds' majority. It also proposed Hills' favorite reform–mandatory Sunday closing–and many other lesser reforms. It provided for a new licensing authority, half the membership being justices of the peace, the other half chosen by the County Councils. In the event of approval of a referendum for reduction the licensing premises which retained their licenses paid money compensation for a five-year period to those that lost their licenses. As the advanced temperance party vehemently disliked money compensation, Hills employed euphemisms, at first, "compensation for disturbance" and later "allocation clauses." Although licensed premises closed through Local Veto received no money compensation, the blow was softened for them by a five-year grace period until the end of which no Veto referendum would be held.[30]

Hills hoped that his "Parliaments" would give the United Temperance Bill a unanimous approval. A majority vote overriding a large minority would not establish the necessary consensus. Although parts of the bill received broad support, Hills could never get any kind of temperance majority for the compensation scheme that was part of his bill.[31]

Despite the dissension regarding compensation, Hills's "Parliaments" showed that willingness to compromise was widespread. The CETS deputation abstained to permit a unanimous vote in favor of Local Veto. Well-known prohibitionists rallied to the United Temperance Bill despite its emphasis on reduction and regulation and its restricted form of money compensation. This had precedent. In the 1870s and the early 1880s some prominent Alliance people in Liverpool, such as the wealthy Alexander Balfour (1824-86), had favored cooperation with the CETS to enact regulatory legislation.[32] Other than Caine, the Vetoist supporters of the United Temperance Bill in the mid-1890s included J.H. Raper, a former parliamentary agent of the UKA who, like Hills, was a vegetarian or at least mostly one.[33] Another was Dr. J. Dawson Burns, for thirty-seven years (until 1893) the metropolitan superintendent of the Alliance. Perhaps the most surprising was Joseph Malins, the Grand Chief Templar of the Good Templar Order in England. Although the Good Templars were noted for their militancy, Malins served as joint honorary secretary of the committee that had organized the conferences. When Hills organized the National United Temperance Council in July 1896, Malins took a seat on the executive committee. Caine and Malins privately had offered to compromise on compensation with the Salisbury Government in 1888.

Malins argued that his readiness to compromise showed his zeal for temperance. "I am more anxious for the destruction of the drink traffic than I am for any principle." He distinguished between Hills' compensation scheme and the Government bill that he had opposed. In the Salisbury Government's scheme compensation had been permanent, and the money insufficient to extinguish many licenses. In contrast the United Temperance Bill allowed compensation only for a limited number of years and guaranteed the closing of many public houses.[34]

Other prohibitionists disagreed. Lawson refused to take part in the conferences as he believed that they undercut Harcourt's local veto bills of 1893 and 1895. Despite the position of their leader, many Good Templars fought money compensation in any form. Some of them only took part in the "Temperance Parliaments" to sabotage Hills' program to unite the advanced and moderate temperance reformers by combining their programs. In 1896 Hills lamented that "no less than forty Good Templars took part in this rejection of re-union amongst the Temperance forces, and that the mover and seconder of the resolution for deletion were prominent members of their Central Executive."[35] The amendment to delete compensation had been moved by J. Martin Skinner (1852-1926), the electoral superintendent of the English Grand Lodge. A former UKA district agent. Guy Hayler (1850-1943), a Good Templar employed as secretary by the North of England Temperance League, seconded the amendment. John Kempster (1836-1916), a former editor of the *Good Templar's Watchword* and honorary secretary of the UKA's London auxiliary, also took a prominent part in the fight against the United Temperance Bill.[36]

The split in the advanced temperance party over the United Temperance Bill foreshadowed the more important division later in the decade over the Royal Commission on the Liquor Licensing Laws and its minority report. Not everybody took similar positions in the two controversies. T.P. Whittaker (1850-1919), a Liberal MP from Yorkshire, led the prohibitionists who wanted the Veto to remain separate from any discussion of general licensing reform. He did not want to encourage those who wanted to "tack other things" on Harcourt's bill such as reduction in numbers. Although Whittaker grew more sympathetic toward the United Temperance Bill when the fall of the Liberal Government destroyed whatever prospects Harcourt's bill once had, he continued to support Lawson in arguing that the UKA should not propose a bill for licensing reform, even if it might accept the same bill introduced under Government sponsorship.[37] Whittaker was willing for the drink trade to compensate itself under state auspices, although he had no special enthusiasm for such a scheme.

Despite defeat at his fourth "Temperance Parliament" Hills continued to agitate for the United Temperance Bill.[38] In July 1896 he founded the United Temperance Councils with himself as president of the National Council. The executive committee included the Good Templar Malins, E. Stafford Howard of the CETS, and Robert Rae, the veteran secretary of the National Temperance League. Existing local total abstinence societies were invited to join in federations that acted as county affiliates. The United Temperance Councils promoted a legislative program of reduction in numbers, direct local veto, and mandatory Sunday closing, while rejecting compensation out of public funds and municipalization of the retail trade (which Hills' ally Joseph Malins bitterly opposed). In later years the United Temperance Councils concentrated on promoting the strict enforcement of the existing licensing laws. Hills's purse enabled the National Council to recruit a staff of experienced temperance workers, such as, for instance, as secretary Charles Pinhorn (1848-1920), a Primitive Methodist preacher and retired metropolitan police inspector, who had been a Good Templar officer and a UKA district agent.[39] In addition Hills continued the Ideal Publishing Union and founded the *United Temperance Gazette*, an illustrated magazine.[40] Henry J. Osborn (1852-1941), a Good Templar who once had headed the UKA's press service, managed Hills' publishing house and edited the magazine.[41]

Hills's last great crusade was the Sunday closing campaign in 1898 and 1899.[42] He figured briefly in the agitation for Lord Peel's minority report and was treasurer of the Central Temperance Legislation Board that supported it. Deteriorating health and financial reverses forced him to withdraw from active temperance politics in the new century. He left an ambivalent legacy, a movement in favor of a compromise settlement, strengthened by the sympathy of respected prohibitionists, but, on the other hand, the suspicion of diehard Vetoists who resented rich men who sought to impose a compensation scheme.

Ironically, Lord Salisbury's Government accomplished what Hills could not. It redirected the energies of the bulk of the temperance party behind a single compromise program. The Unionist ministry made this possible by creating the Royal Commission on the Liquor Licensing Laws in April 1896.[43] In past years moderate temperance reformers and a few drink trade leaders had suggested an official inquiry. In 1893 F.W. Fox, a Quaker member of the Westminster committee, and E.N. Buxton, a Liberal brewer, asked the Liberal Chancellor of the Exchequer for a Royal Commission. Buxton sanguinely predicted: "three men around a table could produce a workable scheme."[44] In 1894, Charles Walker, the leader of the London publicans, called for a Royal Commission.[45] After the Liberal defeat in the general election of 1895, Sir William Houldsworth, MP, chairman of a Unionist temperance association, asked in the House of Commons for a select parliamentary committee to investigate the drink problem.[46] About the same time the Westminster committee asked A.J. Balfour, the leader of the Unionists in the House of Commons, for a parliamentary inquiry.[47] Late in 1895 the National Trade Defence Fund said that it would support the appointment of a Royal Commission provided that it investigated the licensing question in all its aspects.[48] In November 1895 representatives of various Christian denominations, under the chairmanship of the Bishop of London, recommended the appointment of a parliamentary committee of both Houses to inquire into several licensing issues.[49] Later the bishops of the provinces of Canterbury and York added their unanimous endorsement of a parliamentary committee. The Archbishop of Canterbury, Dr. E.W. Benson, opened a correspondence with the Prime Minister in mid-December.[50]

At first Lord Salisbury discouraged the idea. He complained that any official inquiry would be denounced by the trade as interference and by the extreme temperance party as delay of needed legislation.[51] In a subsequent letter Dr. Benson inadvertently altered his request by asking for a Royal Commission.[52] Nearly all temperance reformers preferred a parliamentary committee for reasons of speed.[53] Despite Salisbury's foreboding, Cosmo Bonsor assured the Government that the trade had no objection to an inquiry provided that a Royal Commission with limited terms of reference conducted it.[54] The Cabinet then unenthusiastically authorized the appointment of a Royal Commission on the condition that the moderate reformers and the trade could agree on the terms of reference.[55] It is unlikely that the Cabinet anticipated that the Royal Commission would propose that the State reshape the culture of drinking.

Salisbury and Balfour rebuffed a CETS deputation that asked the Government to sponsor a licensing bill in 1896, but in private Salisbury asked Balfour to take care of the Royal Commission at the next meeting of the Cabinet.[56] By coincidence about this time a Lib-Lab MP Henry Broadhurst asked for a Royal Commission on the tied house question. Later, assuming that he had inspired the creation of the Royal Commission on the Licensing Laws, he was puzzled why had not been appointed a member.[57]

Before the end of February 1896 all parties had agreed to an official inquiry. When Hills' "Temperance Parliament" collapsed regarding compensation after a final session on 20 and 21 February, a Royal Commission became the hope of the large majority of temperance reformers who hoped for a compromise settlement. The trade in turn got the form of the inquiry it favored–a Royal Commission–but not the terms of reference that it had submitted on 13 February. Instead, the terms of reference accepted by the Government were those proposed by the Westminster committee, "to inquire into the operation and administration of the laws relating to the sale of intoxicating liquors, and to examine and report upon the proposals that may be made for amending the aforesaid laws in the public interest," with the addition of a trade amendment, "due regard being had to the rights of individuals."[58]

The personnel of the Commission represented different interest groups. The temperance, the trade, and the less committed points of view each received eight seats, with care taken to represent special interests within each group, such as advocates of restrictive legislation as well as prohibitionists, publicans as well as brewers. The Government disappointed some groups. For instance, the Gothenburgers were denied a place.[59] So were workingmen's clubs.[60] Some Nonconformists had hoped for the appointment of a Nonconformist minister as an Anglican bishop had been appointed. The representation of Ireland raised problems. The trade objected to the choice of the O'Conor Don for the Irish neutral seat since he had led the movement for Irish Sunday closing. When he withdrew, shortly before Balfour announced the names of the commissioners on 21 March, the Government was left with an embarrassing vacancy for more than a week.[61] A minority in the trade criticized the defense societies for agreeing to a Royal Commission, while a few extreme temperance men–notably Lawson–belittled the large size of the commission and the principle of representation of interests which likely would doom the inquiry to an inconclusive minority reports.[62] Frederick J. Jayne (1845-1921), bishop of Chester, complained about the lack of a representative of the disinterested management of Gothenburg scheme.[63]

During the four-year life of the Royal Commission an articulate and forceful Yorkshire MP, T.P. Whittaker (1850-1919), emerged as the leader of the compromise-minded prohibitionists. He was the son of a well-known temperance evangelist, Thomas Whittaker, and a director of the temperance insurance company that had employed his father as an agent.[64] The younger Whittaker had been elected one of the numerous Alliance vice-presidents in 1892. He had begun to accept compensation as the price of temperance legislation prior to his Royal Commission appointment.[65] The *Pall Mall Gazette* was not his admirer. Supposedly Whittaker "occupied a monstrous amount of time in making friendly witnesses repeat what they had already said, and in trying to make hostile witnesses contradict themselves, without any success worth mentioning.[66]

The other prohibitionist members were W.S. Caine (1842-1903), president of the National Temperance Federation and a business associate of Whittaker's, often absent from the Commission while ill or traveling in India; Dr. Frederick Temple (1821-1902), president of the CETS, Bishop of London, and after December 1896 Archbishop of Canterbury, who similarly rarely attended Commission sessions; Sir Charles Cameron, Bt. (1841-1924), a newspaper editor, non-practicing physician and Liberal MP, who represented Scotland; and J. Herbert Roberts (later Lord Clwyd of Abergale) (1863-1955), a Liberal MP, timber merchant, and Caine's son-in-law, who represented Wales.

The non-prohibitionist temperance members were Sir William Houldsworth, Bt. (1834-1917), Conservative MP, Manchester cotton spinner, and president of the National Conservative and Unionist Temperance Association who in the past had advocated Sunday closing for England; the Rev. Hercules Henry Dickinson, DD (1827-1905), dean of the Chapel Royal, Dublin, who was Professor of Pastoral Theology at Trinity College, Dublin, and who from 1874 to 1903 headed the Church of Ireland temperance organization, represented Ireland and acquired a reputation as the Royal Commission's wit;[67] and William Allen (1870-1945), a young Liberal MP and member of the executive committee of the Tied-House Tenants' League which endeavored to protect publicans in tied houses from the demands of the brewers. His father had been a prominent member of the

United Kingdom Alliance and a devout Methodist.[68] Later the younger Allen embarrassed the temperance party when he was found guilty of fraud while floating stock for a Leeds brewery.[69] Neither Allen nor Houldsworth were teetotalers. According to Whittaker, only five of the temperance members were total abstainers, so there was another "temperance" member who was not a teetotaler, perhaps Dickinson.[70]

In the beginning (Alfred) Money Wigram (1856-1899) led the liquor contingent.[71] He was a Conservative MP, a member of the London firm of Reid's (later merged with Watney's and Combe's), a past Master of the Brewers' Company, and since 1895 treasurer of the National Trade Defence Fund. After he fell ill (dying on 13 October 1899), the leadership passed to Edward North Buxton (1840-1924) from another major London brewery, Truman's. Buxton was an active Liberal and a former MP, a member of the London school board, a public-spirited champion of parks and open spaces, and a big game hunter (first with guns and later with cameras). Several years earlier Buxton had proposed to Harcourt that the drink question be settled by a large reduction in the number of the licensed premises, with the owners to be compensated by the surviving license holders.[72] He was named to the Commission in mid-April 1898, on the resignation of the ailing Sir Frederick Seager Hunt, Bt. (1858-1904), a Conservative MP and London distiller, so he missed most of the taking of evidence. Leading members of the trade recognized the importance of persuading Buxton to join the Royal Commission. Cosmo Bonsor wrote him a personal letter "impressing on him the importance of his accepting the position." When Buxton agreed to serve, he did so on the condition that he "keep his independence of thought." He still believed "that some settlement was possible." On the Royal Commission he became "the leader of the Trade."[73]

The other trade members were Henry H. Riley-Smith (1864-1911), the head of John Smith Todcaster brewery in Yorkshire, chairman of the Country Brewers' Society, and later an unsuccessful Conservative candidate for Parliament (who on his death left an estate of approximately a half million pounds);[74] George Younger (later Viscount Younger of Leckie) (1851-1929), chairman of the Scottish brewery of George Younger and Sons, president of the Scottish Licensed Trade Defence Association, convener of the county of Clackmannan, and subsequently a Unionist MP and chairman of the party organization;[75] Samuel Young (1822-1918), an Irish Protestant, who was a wealthy distiller and a brewer; he was an anti-Parnellite Nationalist MP, with conservative views;[76] Henry Grinling (1854-1913), in politics a Liberal and in business a director of W. & A. Gilbey, a firm which supplied nearly 2,400 grocers and other off-license holders. He was a frequent contributor to the press on licensing issues;[77] Samuel Hyslop (1830-1901), former president of the Licensed Victuallers' National Defence League, a provincial organization, and mayor of Newcastle-upon-Lyme who had been considered for a Liberal nomination to Parliament; and Charles Walker (1838-1903), president of the Licensed Victuallers' Central Protection Society of London, Ltd., since its reorganization in 1892. Walker became notorious for his endless questions that exasperated friendly witnesses.[78]

The two most important neutral members were the chairman, Lord Peel (1812-1911), retired Speaker of the House of Commons, son of the famous Prime Minister, and a Liberal Unionist; and Sir Algernon West (1832-1921), a retired chairman of the Inland Revenue (1881-1892) and a former private secretary to William Gladstone, who was elected vice-chairman. West had once been interested in Lord Randolph Churchill's licensing bill.[79] For instance, on 12 May 1890, he had suggested to Churchill compensation for only five years, perhaps ten, and not the twenty years in Churchill's draft bill. West was the only "neutral" identified with the Gladstonian Liberals. One of the chairman's sons Sidney Peel served as secretary of the Commission.[80] Henry Somers Somerset, the son of Lady Henry Somerset, served as assistant secretary.

The other neutral commissioners–"Christians at large," as Lawson called them--[81]were Lord de Vesci (1844-1903), a Liberal Unionist and Lord Lieutenant of Queen's County, Ireland who represented the military interests;[82] the Earl of Jersey (1845-1915), a Conservative and Lord Lieutenant of Oxfordshire, who resigned in 1897; his replacement Lord Windsor (later earl of Plymouth) (1857-1923), a Conservative, Lord Lieutenant of Glamorganshire and former Paymaster General, who later became chairman of the pro-trade True Temperance Association (founded, 1908); John Lloyd Wharton (1837-1912), a Conservative MP and chairman of the Quarter Sessions of County Durham (described as "the best Chairman of Quarter Sessions in England") who had chaired in 1893-94 a departmental committee on habitual drunkards;[83] Andrew Johnston (1835-1922), a teetotaler opposed to prohibition, a former MP, and a Liberal Unionist, who was chairman of both the Essex Quarter Sessions and County Council and who had been instrumental in passing the wine and beerhouse act in 1869 (and was a cousin of the Liberal brewer E.N. Buxton); Johnston had chaired the third of Arnold Hills' United Temperance Parliaments; William Graham (1838-1899), a Conservative and barrister best known as counsel for the *Times* in the Parnell libel case;[84] and Alexander Morison Gordon (1846-1913), a Conservative and convener of Aberdeenshire.[85] Of the neutrals only West was a Liberal.

The *Pall Mall Gazette* complained that Roberts and Whittaker took up too much time, Roberts ineffectively. Whittaker was "a born cross-examiner" who took three hours of the Commission's time futilely trying to make Sir Harry Poland contradict himself. "On the other side Mr. Walker, though not of the same choleric temperament [as Whittaker], wasted nearly as much time." "He displayed an extraordinary faculty for setting up the backs even of friendly witnesses." The newspaper also complained that Grinling was "terribly long-winded."[86]

The Royal Commission constituted a major enterprise. Lawson glumly estimated that the cost to the Government would be forty thousand pounds.[87] At first the commission met every Tuesday and Wednesday. Later this was modified to every fortnight on the same days, eleven to four, with a short luncheon recess.[88] Many members were irregular in attendance. For instance, Caine was absent from November 1896 until March 1897 to visit India.[89] He was concurrently a member of a Royal Commission for Indian Finance. In the only important procedural dispute, the trade successfully opposed an interim report on clubs. The commission decided to allow British witnesses to refer to foreign evidence but did not invite foreign witnesses.[90] The trade worked hard to avoid internal divisions over such issues as clubs, grocers' licenses, and tied houses.[91] The UKA also chose discretion by not nominating Dawson Burns as a witness. His knowledge of licensing was encyclopedic but the Liberator investment scandal might have embarrassed the temperance reformers.[92] Both the trade and the temperance party organized special committees to prepare evidence. The Fund had a consultative committee, the Central Board a Royal Commission committee, and the Alliance a special committee. The temperance party accepted the proposal of the CETS to create a Central Temperance Evidence Board.[93]

Against the recommendation of the chairman, the Commission decided to take evidence in public.[94] Despite the bad acoustics in the Queen's Robing Room in the House of Lords, where the witnesses were questioned, reporters compiled detailed summaries that were widely published in the general press as well as in temperance and trade papers.[95] The official text of the minutes of evidence of the 259 witnesses filled eight substantial volumes.[96]

The weight of the testimony heard by the Royal Commission favored drastic licensing reform.[97] It was obvious that the Commission would recommend a substantial reduction in the number of licensed premises and unlikely that it would propose permanent, market value compensation. In reaction, the general committee of the Country Brewers' Society ignored the advice of its chairman Danvers Power and Royal

Commission member E.N. Buxton who urged restraint. The committee voted in July 1898 to oppose any plan for compulsory reduction without full compensation.[98] Perhaps alarmed by Buxton's conciliatory attitude, the licensed victuallers opposed "compromise or concession" at this time.[99] Late in 1898 when it appeared that the rest of the commission soon would adopt an unacceptable majority report the trade secretly drafted its own. Offering little in the way of compromise, the proposed trade minority report added compensation to the three reforms which the Chancellor of the Exchequer, Sir Michael Hicks-Beach, had urged in a speech at a dinner of the Country Brewers' Society, early in November: graduated license fees, reduction in numbers in overcrowded areas by the exchange of old licenses for new ones elsewhere, and the regulation of clubs. Cosmo Bonsor sent the Prime Minister a summary of the projected trade minority report on 6 November. It had been expected that Lord Peel would circulate his chairman's draft report on 9 November.[100] In fact, because of illness he did not do so until early in 1899. A full year elapsed between the completion of hearing of evidence (20 July 1898) and publication of the final reports (18 July 1899).

Lord Peel's appointment in 1896 had occasioned many tributes to his impartiality and moderation. The *Morning Advertiser*, which was controlled by London publicans, claimed: "no better chairman could possibly have been found."[101] During the course of the commission he was converted to temperance reform.[102] By late 1898 the drink commissioners feared that Peel and the other neutral commissioners would draft a report hostile to the trade. They kept their own report secret "until Peel has shown his hand."[103]

Charles Walker, who represented the London publicans on the Royal Commission, claimed to have recognized Peel's animus earlier. "Personally, I soon discovered that his sympathies were with the teetotal party--it became plainly evident by his apparent petulance and indifference to Trade witnesses as compared with his encouragement to those who favoured teetotal views." Allegedly, Peel received information from witnesses prior to their examination statements that he shared with nobody "except perhaps Mr. Whittaker." Supposedly, Peel "would not even allow the shorthand writers to take a full note of what was said," as shown by the "very large discrepancies between the official and unofficial minutes that appeared in newspapers.[104]

Lord Peel drafted his report without consulting any other of the commissioners. Whittaker remembered that his fellow temperance commissioners had "no inkling whatsoever" as to its proposals.[105] When the report was circulated early in February 1899, it surprised fellow commissioners by its severity toward the trade. Consequently, it offered the trade the opportunity to escape its isolation by joining with those who favored more limited reforms than did Lord Peel. Lord Peel recommended substantial statutory reduction in the number of licensed premises with only limited compensation and severe restrictions on those permitted to continue. The aggressiveness with which Lord Peel championed his plan offended many colleagues. Sir Algernon West complained that Peel told the Commission at its first meeting after it had received his draft "that whether [the other commissioners] agree to it or not, it was his report, and that *his* report was *the* report." West protested that Peel hurried the commission through the draft with procedural rules that hampered adequate discussion. Peel's casting vote as chairman, wielded after he had already voted as a commissioner, decided many issues.[106] Whittaker vigorously disputed West's account. Peel simply required that his draft report be discussed and amended in the order in which it appeared and not helter-skelter. There was a consensus on the first four parts of the draft report when Peel suffered another bout of illness that prevented discussion of the fifth and final part.

The illness of Peel in March forced a recess that enabled his opponents organized by West and Buxton to prepare an alternative plan for reduction in the numbers of licensed premises and the compensation of their owners. Some Liberals outside the commission wanted a unanimous report, supported by the trade commissioners, to force the Unionist Government to sponsor a licensing bill that might remove the drink question from politics. Apparently, Henry Gladstone, one of the former Prime Minister's sons, arranged a meeting between West, an old family friend, and Robert Younger, the brother of the brewer commissioner, in hopes of heading off an intransigent trade minority report.[107]

Upon the chairman's recovery, the new compromise report was submitted with majority support.[108] At this, on 12 April, the commission broke up. According to West, Peel resigned as chairman and tried to dissolve the commission. According to Peel's supporters, he simply withdrew. The majority sponsorship of the new plan amounted to a coup de main that make his continued attendance meaningless and humiliating.[109] Peel's anger was not unexpected. His opponents had made contingency plans. In the previous month Balfour had assured West that the chairman could not terminate the commission and that, if Peel withdrew, West should take the chair.[110] The majority report was largely written by Johnston and Wharton.[111] From the trade, only Buxton attended the meeting that prepared the report. In effect the commission divided into two overlapping groups, each writing its own report. The advanced temperance reformers supported the chairman, although they had known nothing about the contents of his draft until it was officially circulated. They received a few concessions from him.[112] The report that they signed with him was the minority report, but to borrow the former Speaker's prestige its friends called it Lord Peel's report.[113]

The two reports disagreed principally about compensation for the loss of licenses as a result of a general reduction in the number of licensed public houses.[114] The minority imposed a statutory reduction to a maximum of one per 750 persons in urban districts and one per 400 in the countryside. In contrast the majority left the decision about reduction to the justices.[115] Both reports compelled the license holders who retained their licenses to pay the money for the compensation of those who lost their licenses. The majority report proposed a permanent right of market value compensation whenever a license holder was denied renewal without being guilty of some offence. In the eyes of most temperance reformers this recommendation was twice damned. First, it created a permanent vested interest where before there had been annual licenses with no compensation for non-renewal. In the second place, the expense of market value compensation would slow the rate of reduction.[116]

In contrast the minority report emphasized that the compensation it offered was not a right, but instead something awarded out of grace and expediency, "a compassionate allowance." The basic concession took the form of a warning that after seven years the power to deny annual license renewals without compensation would be freely exercised. Money compensation would be allowed to license holders who were denied renewal during this seven-year time limit. The amount of compensation would be determined by multiplying the assessment of the premises for rates by the number of the remaining years of the period of warning, rather than market value if renewable indefinitely. This plan would have allowed fairly rapid reduction in England and Wales during the first seven years and as rapid a reduction as the justices desired afterwards. The minority report also recommended Local Veto for Wales in five years, for Scotland in seven years, and for England at some undetermined point in the distant future. The minority report altered the composition of the licensing authority by adding members of the County Council to the licensing justices. The minority report also disagreed with the majority by proposing the end of "mixed trading," that is, grocers' licenses. Later Buxton said that the Peel Report had strengthened the trade by driving the off-license holders into its ranks.[117]

In signing one or the other report or both nearly every commissioner saw himself as a realist making a painful compromise. The neutrals who signed the majority report apparently believed that only recommendations accepted by the trade members could be enacted. The *Daily Chronicle* thought this was true for West, de Vesci, Windsor, and Johnston.[118] The trade commissioners disliked some of the specific reforms in the majority report and the general tone of criticism.[119] When they signed the report, they had to accept the judgment that "it is undeniable that a gigantic evil remains to be remedied, and hardly any sacrifice would be too great which would result in a marked diminution of this national degradation." In recompense the majority report provided them with allies in the fight against Lord Peel's proposals. One trade commissioner Riley-Smith privately explained that a report signed only by trade members would lack influence.[120]

By adhering to Lord Peel's report the prohibitionist wing of the temperance party tolerated the delay of Local Veto and a diluted form of money compensation in order to get drastic reduction in the number of licenses and the elimination of the claim to a permanent vested interest.[121] Lord Peel had to make concessions to his advanced temperance allies. Allegedly his original draft had restricted Local Veto to Scotland.

Observing that many Local Veto stalwarts supported the minority report, A.F. Hills wistfully pointed out that they earlier had rejected his United Temperance Bill because it had postponed the Veto for England and had allowed a form of compensation. Hills regretted that Imperial Sunday Closing, that is, statutory Sunday closing, was omitted from Lord Peel's Report and considered it the highest priority for temperance reformers.[122]

The reluctance behind many trade and temperance signatures showed in official reservations and clarifications. Several trade commissioners rejected consensus reforms such as the outlawing of child messengers who fetched beer from public houses. The five prohibitionist members signed an addendum in which they affirmed their belief in the desirability of Local Veto and Sunday closing for England. One of them, T.P. Whittaker, appended a personal memorandum that was almost a hundred pages long, virtually a textbook for the statistical, historical, and philosophical study of the temperance question, in which he worked out a synthesis between Lord Peel's reduction scheme and Local Veto.[123] A Tory temperance commissioner (Houldsworth) signed Lord Peel's report but repudiated its distinctive mode of reduction and compensation. Two other moderate temperance commissioners managed to sign both reports by adding reservations to each of them.

Coincidentally, during that same April when the public heard rumors about the conflict within the Royal Commission, two social reformers published the findings of their massively researched private inquiry into the drink problem and recommendations for reforms.[124] Joseph Rowntree was a Quaker and a wealthy chocolate maker (and the father of the social investigator Seebohm Rowntree).[125] His Wesleyan Methodist collaborator, Arthur Sherwell (1863-1942), apparently did the research that Joseph Rowntree financed.[126]   This included trips to North America, Scandinavia and other countries over the course of a decade. *The Temperance Problem and Social Reform* sold more than 50,000 copies, more than 90,000 if one counts abridged versions. Between April 1899 and January 1901 there were nine printings of the full book which was over six hundred pages in length.[127] Rowntree and Sherwell said that they were "fully conscious that Temperance is no universal panacea. There are pressing economic questions which it cannot solve. But they hold that apart from Temperance the social problem will remain insoluble."[128] Any comprehensive reform had to include Direct Local Veto as "it enlists the enthusiastic support of a large majority of the Temperance party."[129] The Veto might work in rural areas. Believing that prohibition was impracticable in the larger towns and cities, they favored alternatives to it. They did not favor restriction alone. They thought that "constructive" policies were needed to supplement restriction. This led Rowntree and Sherwell to some variant on the disinterested management schemes pioneered in Sweden and Norway. Doing so would weaken the drink trade and its obstruction of reform.

In some ways the Rowntree and Sherwell book strengthened the movement in favor of a comprehensive compromise settlement and therefore smoothed the way for Lord Peel's report. On the other hand, *The Temperance Problem and Social Reform* competed with Lord Peel's report for moderate support.[130] Rowntree and Sherwell differed from the minority report by advocating the Gothenburg principle of non-commercial management of the retail trade. They rejected prohibition as ineffective.

Another influential analysis of the drink problem and recommendations for reform that appeared at the turn of the century was *The Heart of the Empire: Discussions of Problems of Modern City Life in England* (1901), edited by C.F.G. Masterman. It included an essay "Temperance Reform," by Noel Buxton and Walter Hoare, both of whom had brewing connections, that largely echoed Rowntree and Sherwell.

The turn of the century was a critical time for drink reform.

Notes

[1] Quoted in R.A. Jameson, ed., *Wisdom, Grave and Gay, Being Select Speeches of Sir Wilfrid Lawson, Bart., M.P., Chiefly on Temperance and Prohibition* (S.W. Partridge, 1889), p. 94. At the annual meeting of the United Kingdom Alliance, 16 Oct. 1883.

[2] Churchill at Walsall, 28 July 1889. Quoted in R.R. James, *Lord Randolph Churchill* (Phoenix, 1959), pp. 338-39. For his earlier opinion, see Churchill to H.L. Pratt, 7 Feb. 1884. Churchill College, Lord Randolph Churchill papers, no. 295. See quotations from Churchill's speeches, published in the *Alliance News*, 1 Feb. 1895, pp. 72-73, on the occasion of his death; and Charles Bailey, "Lord Randolph Churchill and the Liquor Question," *Pioneer: a Journal of Temperance and Social Progress* [Official Organ of the Temperance Committee of the Wesleyan Methodist Church, ed. Henry Carter], April 1915, pp. 82-83.

[3] Churchill to Lawson, 7 Dec. 1889; Lawson to Churchill, 14 Feb. 1890. Churchill College, Lord Randolph Churchill papers, no. 3345, 3410. Churchill to Harcourt, 24 Jan. 1890. Bodleian, Harcourt Ms 218, ff. 5-6. Harcourt to Churchill, 26 Jan. 1890. Churchill College, Lord Randolph Churchill papers, no. 3384.

[4] Harcourt to Churchill, 20 January 1890, Lord Randolph Churchill papers, 1/25/1384.

[5] George Smith to Lord Mount Edgecumbe, 6 June 1890, enclosed in Lord Mount Edgecumbe to W.H. Smith, 7 June 1890. Hambeden MSS, PS15/32.

[6] Bonsor to Churchill, 10 Jan, 1890. Churchill College, Lord Randolph Churchill Papers, no. 3369. J. Danvers Power, an official in the trade defence organization, had met with Churchill. Power to Churchill, 8 Jan. 1890. Churchill College, Lord Randolph Churchill Papers, no. 3365. Presumably Bonsor and another brewer, James Wigan, also attended this meeting. Bonsor to Churchill. 6 Jan. 1890. Churchill College, Lord Randolph Churchill Papers, no. 3360.

[7] Bonsor to Churchill. 10 Jan. 1890. Churchill College, Lord Randolph Churchill Papers, no. 3369.

[8] Wigan to Churchill, 18 Jan. 1890. Churchill College, Lord Randolph Churchill Papers, no. 3380.

[9] Bonsor to Churchill, 31 Jan. 1890. Churchill College, Lord Randolph Churchill Papers, no. 3390.

[10] Sir Algernon West to Churchill 14 Feb. 1890. Churchill College, Lord Randolph Churchill Papers, no. 3409.

[11] Ritchie to Churchill, 31 Jan. 1890. Churchill College, Lord Randolph Churchill papers, no. 3385.

[12] Churchill in *Parl. Deb.*, 3rd ser., CCXLIV, 29 April 1890, cols. 1698-1724; Lambeth Palace, Church of England Temperance Society, Legislative Sub-Committee, 25 Feb., 6 March 1890, MS 2044, ff, 73-75, 78-79. Churchill to Harcourt, 24 Jan. 1890. Bodleian, Harcourt 218, ff. 5-6.

[13] *Brewers' Journal*, 15 May 1890, pp. 295-97; *Brewing Trade Review*, 1 June 1890, weekly edition, pp. 260-62; Nov. 1895, pp. 305-06.

[14] Buxton to Churchill, 8 May 1890. Churchill College, Lord Randolph Churchill papers, no. 3536.

[15] Buxton to Churchill, 15 May 1890. Churchill College, Lord Randolph Churchill papers, no. 3550.

[16] *Parl. Deb.*, 13 June 1890.

[17] For summaries of the bills, see Royal Commission on the Licensing Laws, *Minutes of Evidence*, vol. 8, *P.P.*, 1899 (C. 90705), XXXIV, Appendices, p. 732 (synopsis), 733-36 (CETS), 736-43 (Westminster), 768-70 (Manchester). Brynmor Jones,

brother of the Alliance militant Leif Jones, was one of the sponsors of the Westminster bill. According to Leonard Courtney, the failure of Goschen's licensing proposals in 1890 led to the formation of the Westminster Licensing Reform Committee, composed mainly of Liberal Unionists. J. Fischer Williams and others, *Memories of John Westlake* (Smith Elder, 1914), Courtney, ch. 4, "Public Affairs," pp. 68-69.

[18] See Neild's obituary in *Monthly Notes* 19 (Feb.-March 1929): 24.

[19] James E.G. deMontmorency, *Francis William Fox* (Oxford University Press, 1923), pp. 27-30, 34-35. Sir William Houldsworth chaired the initial meeting.

[20] *Temperance Chronicle*, 7 Oct. 1892, p. 494. For the CETS and more generally the Church of England, see also Shiman, *Crusade against Drink in Victorian England*, pp. 99-109; and the work of Gerald W. Olsen, beginning with his doctoral dissertation, "Pub and Parish--The Beginnings of the Temperance Reform in the Church of England, 1835-1875" (Western Ontario, 1972) and continuing through articles such as "'Physician Heal Thyself': Drink, Temperance and the Medical Question in the Victorian and Edwardian Church of England," *Addiction* 89 (1994): 1167-76. Olsen contributed many related entries in *Alcohol and Temperance in Modern History: An International Encyclopedia*, ed. Jack S. Blocker, David M. Fahey, and Ian R. Tyrrell (2 vols., ABC-CLIO, 2003). I was fortunate to read Olsen's unpublished monograph, "Drink and the British Establishment--The Church of England Temperance Society, 1873-1919," in a draft dated 2003.

[21] CETS, *Our Legislative Policy, 1864-1908* (London, 1908), 7-9.

[22] *Oxford Dictionary of National Biography*, art. Hills; *Spartacus Educational*, art. Hills. For Hills's controversial industrial policies, see Bristow, "The Defence of Liberty and Property," pp. 291-92. In an obituary for Archbishop Temple, the organ of the Church of England Temperance Society described Hills' organization (the United Temperance Council) as "an honest but not very successful attempt to unite all sections of the Temperance army." *Temperance Chronicle*, 2 January 1903, pp. 6-7.

[23] Hills had been an outstanding athlete at Harrow and Oxford. Ironically, from 1906 he was almost entirely paralyzed. Alan G. Jamieson wrote the *Oxford Dictionary of National Biography* entry for Arnold Frank Hills (1857-1927). Hills's wealth had been reduced to a still substantial £60,000 by the time of his death.

[24] On the subsidies which he paid or offered, see, for instance, Lambeth Palace Library, Ms. 2048, CETS, finance committee minutes, 2 May 1899, fol. 36; *Temperance Chronicle*, 5 May 1899, p. 224; National Temperance League, executive committee minutes, 29 April, 26 Aug, 11, 25 Nov. 1897, National Temperance League, Joseph Livesey Memorial Library, Clegg-Livesey House, Sheffield (now at University of Central Lancashire); Frederick Cowley to James Whyte, 1 Oct. 1892, in Alliance minutes, 19 Oct. 1892; Hills to Whyte, 22 Sept. 1897, in Alliance minutes 29 Sept. 1897; Hills to Whyte, 2 Nov. 1897, in Alliance minutes, 3 Nov. 1897. Late in 1897 the Ideal Publishing Union took over the National Temperance Publication Depot that had been operated since the early 1880s by the National Temperance League and two League journals, the *Record* and the *Mirror*. Hills paid £2,500 for his acquisitions.

[25] *Licensed Trade News*, 25 March 1899, p. 5.

---

[26] Tony Collins and Wray Vamplew, *Mud, Sweat and Beers: A Cultural History of Sport and Alcohol* (Berg, 2002), p. 121.

[27] Frederick Cowley to Whyte, 1 Oct. 1892, in Alliance minutes, 19 Oct. 1892.

[28] *Our Position and Our Policy: A Reply to Charges Made against a Minority of the Executive Committee of the British Women's Temperance Association, by its President, Lady Henry Somerset, at the Annual Council Meeting, 1893*, Appendix XIX, pp. 147-49.

[29] Andrew Johnston, a teetotaler (and E.N. Buxton's cousin), had been a Liberal MP, Sir George Livesey, also a teetotaler, was president of the South London Gasworks. Stephen Bourne had retired as assistant principal of the statistical department. Board of Customs. He died at age 81. *Temperance Chronicle*, 14 Dec. 1900, p. 619.

[30] See the printed *Abstracts of Proceedings* for all four conferences and the verbatim *Report of Proceedings* for the conference in 1894. University of Wisconsin, Memorial Library, Guy Hayler collection, *Temperance Tracts*, vol. 16 (also available on microfilm).

[31] Hills had hoped to soften opposition from the drink trade. Country Brewers Society, parliamentary committee, 7 June 1893.

[32] For temperance in Liverpool, see Liverpool Vigilance Committee, *Licensing Administration in Liverpool: Summary of Reforms (1889-1898)* (Licensing Laws Information Bureau, 1899).

[33] J. Deane Hilton, *A Brief Memoir of James Hayes Raper* (Ideal Publishing Union, 1898), pp. 25-26. Raper was the UKA's salaried parliamentary agent, 1860-78, and continued to do this work unpaid until 1886. When he ceased to be a paid official, he joined the Alliance's executive. Hilton, *Brief Memoir*, p. 129.

[34] *Report of Proceedings* (1894), 84.

[35] Arnold F. Hills, "A Bad Blunder," *United Temperance Gazette*, June 1896, p. 51.

[36] Like Hayler, Kempster was a staunch Radical. He edited a newspaper circulated among the metropolitan police and ran a firm that printed temperance publications.

[37] Whittaker, *Report of Proceedings* (1894), pp. 26, 31, 69-70; *Abstract of Proceedings* (1895), p. 12; *Abstract of Proceedings* (1896), p. 10. See also *Methodist Times*, 13 June 1895, p. 377; UKA, Annual Report, in *Alliance News*, 23 Oct. 1896, p. 682. The last was a discussion of a proposal by A.F. Hills.

[38] Hills mixed his call for unity with repeated quarrels (for instance, his "Bad Blunder" editorial in the *United Temperance Gazette* in June 1896). He sometimes mixed money with criticism. His letter to the *Alliance News*, published in July 1896, pp. 450-51, was accompanied by a check for a £100.

[39] For Pinhorn, see *Standard Encyclopedia of the Alcohol Problem*.

[40] "The London United Temperance Council" [Typical Organizations Series], *United Temperance Gazette* 5 (1900): 33-40. See also Charles Pinhorn, secretary, National United Temperance Council, to Dr. Frederick Temple, 4 Nov. 1897. Lambeth Palace Library, Temple Papers, vol. 7, fol. 82.

[41] *Standard Encyclopedia of the Alcohol Problem*, art. Osborn; *Reformers' Year Book* (1902), 131-32. In 1903 Osborn purchased the Ideal Publishing Union from Hills. *United Temperance Gazette*, Dec. 1903, p. 149.

[42] The Central Association for Stopping the Sale of Intoxicating Liquors on the Sunday was organized in 1866. See Dawson Burns, "The Sunday Closing

Movement--Historical and Statistical," in Arnold F. Hills and others, *The Case for Sunday Closing, Compiled for the Service of the Sunday Closing Special Campaign* (Ideal Publishing Union, 1899).

[43] This account of the Royal Commission largely follows that in my article, "Temperance and the Liberal Party–Lord Peel's Report, 1899," *Journal of British Studies* 10 (1971: 132-59. Some details and citations have been omitted, while new information has been added, errors corrected, and arguments modified. For another analysis, see David E. Wright, "The British Liquor Licensing Question, 1895-1905" (Ph.D. dissertation, McMaster, 1972), ch. 6. Regrettably, Wright never published his dissertation in any form, although he did co-author an article on women and drink in Edwardian England. The dissertation is available online.

[44] F. W. Fox to Harcourt, 24 March 1893; E.N. Buxton to Harcourt, 8 May 1893. Bodleian, Harcourt Ms. 145 ff. 48-50. See also Bonsor to Harcourt, 27 Dec. 1892, Harcourt papers ("The purgatory of hot water in which the trade is kept is worse than the furnace to which some would consign them.") The Liverpool philanthropist and advocate of high license, William Rathbone, also asked for an official inquiry. Rathbone to Harcourt, 7 Jan. 1893. Bodleian, Harcourt 145, ff. 15-22. Rathbone had sponsored the private study of American and Canadian licensing legislation by E.L. Fanshawe published as *Liquor Legislation in the United States and Canada: Report of a Non-Partisan Inquiry* (Cassell, 1893).

[45] Charles Walker, 23 Oct. 1894, in *Licensing World*, 2 Nov. 1894, p. 277.

[46] Houldsworth, in *Parl. Deb.*, 4th ser., XXXVI, 20 Aug. 1895, col. 386.

[47] Leonard Courtney and others to Balfour, 10 Sept. 1895; Balfour to the hon. secretaries, Westminster committee, 7 Oct. 1895. *Times*, 23 Oct. 1895, p. 7.

[48]-*Licensed Trade News*, 2 Nov. 1895, p. 7; Brewers' Society, NTDF, general committee, 29 Oct. 1895, fol. 224.

[49] The meeting was held on 6 Nov. 1895. *Conference on Temperance Legislation, London House* ([London, 1895]). Lambeth Palace Library, E.W. Benson papers, vol. 146, fols. 341-42. See also *Times*, 8 Nov. 1895, p. 10.

[50] Benson to Salisbury, 16 Dec. 1895. Lambeth Palace Library, Benson papers, vol. 146, fols. 343-44. In his reply Salisbury referred to Benson's letter as dated the 17th. For another analysis of the role of the bishops, see John R. Greenaway, "Bishops, Brewers and the Liquor Question in England, 1890-1914," *Historical Magazine of the Protestant Episcopal Church* 53 (1984): 61-75.

[51] Salisbury to Benson, 19 Dec. 1895. Lambeth Palace Library, Benson papers, vol. 146, fols. 346-47.

[52] Benson to Salisbury, 20 Jan. 1896. Lambeth Palace Library, Benson papers, vo. 146, fols. 349-50. There was much subsequent correspondence on this point.

[53] Caine regretted the slower choice, a Royal Commission. Writing in 1897 to W. Rathbone, he said: "I do not see how we can report before 1899. We shall fulfill the main object with which we were appointed, viz: that of postponing to the next parliament all practical legislation on the Drink question." Caine to Rathbone, 8 June 1897, quoted in Greenaway, *Drink in British Politics*, p. 226.

[54] Bonsor to Salisbury, 30 Jan. 1896. Christ Church, Oxford, Salisbury papers, uncatalogued when consulted. The *Liberty Review* (7 and 14 March 1896), a proponent of the bill introduced by Lord Wemyss, disliked the appointment of a

Royal Commission. It sneered at the support for the Royal Commission by the big London brewers, "the old gang in Victoria Street." *Liberty Review*, 25 April 1896, p. 251.

[55] Salisbury to Benson, 5 Feb. 1896. Lambeth Palace Library, Benson papers, vol. 146, fols. 355-56.

[56] *Temperance Chronicle*, 14 Feb. 1896, pp. 68, 79-82. J.S. Sandars to Schomberg K. McDonnell, 13 Feb. 1896 (annotated by McDonnell, initialed by Salisbury). Christ Church, Oxford, Salisbury papers. Sandars had forwarded a letter from the brewer A. Money Wigram to A. Akers-Douglas and the terms of reference proposed by the trade. For the text of the trade terms of reference, see *Licensing World*, 21 March 1896, pp. 184-85.

[57] Broadhurst in *Parl. Deb.*, 4th ser., XXXVIII, 20 Feb. 1896, col. 716. See also his autobiography, *The Story of His Life* (Hutchinson, 1901), p. 164.

[58] deMontmorency, *Francis William Fox*, p. 32; NTDA, general committee, date?, fols. 241-42. On March 6, 1896, the General Committee of the National Trade Defence Fund voted to agree to a Royal Commission. *Manager's Report to the Subscribers for the Year 1896* (1896), p. 6.

[59] See Dr. Frederick Jayne, Bishop of Chester, to the editor, *Times*, 3 April 1896, p. 8. Lord Thring criticized Chamberlain for not helping his fellow Gothenburgers get a Royal Commission seat. Thring to Benson, 2 April 1896. Lambeth Palace Library, Benson papers, vol. 146, fols. 381-82.

[60] Balfour assured the head of the Club and Institute Union that having a member of the Royal Commission was less important than presenting evidence. Balfour to B.T. Hall, 21 Sept. 1896. George Temlett, *Clubmen: History of the Working Men's Club and Institute Union* (Secker & Warburg, 1987), pp. 95-96. Benjamin Tom Hall (1864-1931), a carpenter by trade, became secretary of the Club and Institute Union in 1893 at the early age of twenty-eight. He served until 1929. He was a member of the Fabian Society.

[61] Balfour in *Parl. Deb.*, 4th ser., XXXIX, 24 March 1896, cols. 522-24.

[62] On the trade, see *Liberty Review*, 21 March 1896, p. 187; 18 April 1896, p. 231. The criticisms of the Royal Commission provoked a break between the Central Board and the Liberty and Property Defence League whose secretary and parliamentary agent, Frederick Millar (1866-1929), edited the independent *Liberty Review*. Millar to Wemyss, 22 April 1896; Wemyss to Albert Deane, 8 May 1896. Cited in Edward J. Bristow, "The Defence of Liberty and Property in Britain, 1880-1914" (Ph.D. dissertation, Yale University, 1970), p. 154 n. 3. For Lawson, see his letter to the editor, *Times,* 3 April 1896, p. 231. In addition to being a strong individualist, Millar was a secularist. David M. Fahey, "Brewers, Publicans and Staff in Late Victorian and Edwardian Licensed Trade Societies-Part II," *Brewery History* 181 (Winter 2019): 9-10. Behind the scenes, the UKA was consulted about the choice of its unofficial representatives on the Commission. William Allen to UKA, 6, 7 March 1896, in Alliance minutes, 11 March 1896.

[63] *Times*, 3 April 1886, p. 8.

[64] *Dod's* lists him as a director beginning in 1898 and as chairman beginning in 1908. After graduating from grammar school (Huddersfield College), he went to work selling hardware and iron goods at the age of sixteen. He later edited newspapers

such as the *Daily Oracle*, 1889-92. He served as the M.P. for Spen Valley in the West Riding of Yorkshire from 1892 until his death in 1919.

[65] See an interview with Whittaker in *Methodist Times*, 16 May 1895, p. 315, and in *Westminster Gazette*, 7 June 1895, p. 3.

[66] *Pall Mall Gazette*, 28 March 1899, p. 2. The *Gazette* much preferred Caine "who was generally brief and to the point."

[67] Dean Dickinson had to cross the Irish channel repeatedly to attend Royal Commission meetings. Once when the weather was rough "he nearly threw up the Royal Commission." J.W. Leigh (dean of Hereford), *Other Days* (Macmillan, 1921), pp. 238-39. Dickinson and Walker were the members of the Royal Commission who were the most regular in attendance.

[68] *Alliance News*, 20 April 1899, pp. 248-49.

[69] *Times*, 7 Dec. 1899, pp. 3-4; 13 Dec. 1899, p. 3; 14 March 1900, p. 13. See also *Newcastle Guardian*, 9 Dec. 1899, p. 3; 16 Dec. 1899, p. 3; 30 Dec. 1899, p.2. Leaving Parliament, Allen volunteered for military service in the South African war. After a long gap, Allen returned to the House of Commons in 1931 as a National Liberal.

[70] T.P. Whittaker, "The 'Temperance' Reply to Sir Algernon West," *Nineteenth Century* (March 1900): 516.

[71] Ideally, Wigram wanted the trade to have had fourteen representatives, as he saw that many sections of the trade. The Government could not allow so many appointments. *Temperance Chronicle*, 3 April 1896, p. 157.

[72] Buxton to Harcourt, 23, 29 Nov., 7 Dec. 1892, 8 May 1893. Bodleian, Harcourt Ms. 148, fols. 21-25, 32-33, 34-37; Harcourt Ms. 146, fols. 48-50.

[73] Cosmo Bonsor in *Licensing World*, 5 May 1900, p. 325. Buxton testified at the Royal Commission on 29 June 1897 before he became a commission member. Showing his moderation, he said that he did not object to the requirement that new licenses pay the State for the monopoly value of licensed status. Nor did he oppose requiring licenses houses in growing districts to pay additional fees. *P.P.*, 1898 (C. 8694), vol. XXXVI, quests, 35,460-35,464, p. 310.

[74] At one point Riley-Smith supported retail organizations so strongly that his firm declined to subscribe to the Country Brewers' Society. *Brewing Trade Review*, Jan.1890, p. 4.

[75] See Ian Donnachie, "Men of Brewing, Viscount Younger of Leckie," *Scottish Brewing Archive Newsletter*, no. 6 (Winter 1985).

[76] He was the wealthiest Nationalist MP, dying with an estate worth £300,000. William B. Gwyn, *Democracy and the Cost of Politics in Britain* (1962), p. 136 n. 1.

[77] The Gilbey firm began its agency system the year after Gladstone had created grocers' licenses in 1860. Grinling was a cousin of the founder of the Gilbey company, Sir Walter Gilbey and his brother Alfred Gilbey, and the uncle of two other partners Henry Arthur Blyth and Sir James Blyth, Bt. Two Gilbey sisters married the brothers Henry Gold and Sir Charles Gold. Sir Herbert Maxwell, Bt., *Half-a Century of Successful Trade: Being a Sketch of the Rise and Development of the Business of W & A. Gilbey, 1857-1907* (W. & A. Gilbey, Ltd., 1907).

[78] *Pall Mall Gazette*, 28 March 1899, pp. 1-2; reprinted in *Licensing Trade News*, 1

April 1899, pp. 12-13; provoking the angry reply, "Fowling His Own Nest," *Licensing World*, 15 April 1899, pp. 295-96.

[79] Churchill College, Lord Randolph Churchill papers, West to Churchill, 7, 10, 14, 15, and 17 Jan.; 11, 14, and 18 Feb.; 12, 24 March; 12 and 17 May 1890. Numbers 3362, 3367, 3374, 3375, 3402, 3409, 3416. 3402, 3409, 3416, 3458, 3505, 3502, 3557.

[80] See his subsequent booklet, *Practical Licensing Reform* (Methuen, 1901).

[81] Russell, ed., *Sir Wilfrid Lawson*, p. 234. Seven of the eight neutrals were licensing magistrates and three were chairmen of quarter sessions. *Alliance News*, p. 694.

[82] Lord de Vesci was a son-in-law of the earl of Wemyss, a founder of the Liberty and Property Defence League, an organization hostile to prohibition. I owe several details about neutral members (de Vesci, Wharton, Johnston) to Wright, "The British Liberal Party and the Liquor Licensing Question," p. 241.

[83] *Brewers' Almanack* (1898), 65. Wharton had chaired an inquiry into habitual drunkards in the mid-1890s.

[84] His obituary in the *Times,* 7 Nov. 1899, p. 6.

[85] For Gordon's obituary, see *Aberdeen Daily Journal*, 19 March 1913, p. 5.

[86] *Pall Mall Gazette* 28 March 1899, p. 2.

[87] *Alliance News*, 17 April 1896, p. 249.

[88] *Alliance News*, 15 May (page?), 6 Nov. 1896, p. 717

[89] Newton, *W.S. Caine*, p. 279.

[90] Central Board, Royal Commission committee minutes, 15 Feb. 1897, 28 Feb. 1898. Central Board, United Parliamentary Council minutes, 15 Nov. 1898. Hilton to Whyte, 8 Feb. 1898, in Alliance minutes, 9 Feb. 1898.

[91] On clubs, see Royal Commission committee minutes, 27 July 1896; United Parliamentary Council minutes, 5 Nov. 1896. See also Benjamin Tom Hall, *Over Sixty Years*, pp. 225-26. The trade collected evidence about clubs but chose not to present it. On grocers, see Royal Commission committee minutes, 28 June 1897, 12 July 1898, and on tied Houses, Royal Commission committee minutes, 27 July 1896.

[92] The collapse in 1892 of the Liberator Building Society (the largest building society in the United Kingdom) and connected financial institutions impoverished many of the Nonconformists and temperance reformers who had invested in them. The founder of these companies, the swindler Jabez Balfour, had served for several years as a Liberal M.P. He was a son of the temperance reformer Clara Lucas Balfour, best known as the author of *Morning Dew Drops, or the Juvenile Abstainer* (1853). He was named after a celebrated Baptist minister, Jabez Burns, whose son Dawson Burns, also a Baptist minister, married the sister of Jabez Balfour. Dr. Burns (his title was honorific, conferred by Bates College in Maine) served as auditor for the Liberator for several years. His reputation was not helped by his brother-in-law's flight to Argentina to escape prosecution as a swindler. J.A. Spender, "Philanthropic Finance: A Forgotten Chapter in the Temperance Movement," *Westminster Gazette*, 21 July 1893, pp. 1-2; continued with different subtitles 22, 25, 26, 27 July and 3, 10, 15, 17 August 1893; and related articles such as the leader about Dawson Burns, "The Parnell of the Temperance Cause," appearing on 17 Oct. 1893. Burns replied on 9 June 1893, p. 3. In September 1893 the Alliance executive committee asked for Burns' resignation as metropolitan superintendent. When he refused, the executive

committee dismissed him effective at the end of the calendar year. Alliance minutes, 13 and 20 Sept. 1893; Burns to Whyte, 25 Sept. 1893, in Alliance minutes, 27 Sept. 1893; Burns to Whyte, 2 Oct.1893 in Alliance minutes, 4 Oct. 1893; resolution of special committee of the London Auxiliary, Alliance minutes, 18 Oct. 1893, and Whyte to an unhappy Kempster, 20 Oct. 1893. The conflict developed into a quarrel over London autonomy. See the printed invitation, dated 9 Nov. 1893, for a meeting of the London Auxiliary, 10 Nov. 1893, in Alliance minutes 8 Nov. 1893. George Livesey, unhappy about the class rhetoric of the Alliance, decided to pay his subscription to the London auxiliary and not to Manchester. Livesey to McDougall, 23 Nov. 1893, in Alliance minutes, 23 Nov. 1893. The parliamentary agent, John Hilton, took over Burns' duties in London. Alliance minutes, 20 Dec. 1893. Burns was a major figure in the Victorian temperance movement. For instance, he was honorary secretary of the London Temperance Hospital from its founding in 1871 until his death in 1909. Seymour J. Price, *From Queen to Queen: The Centenary Story of the Temperance Permanent Building Society, 1854-1954* (Franey & Co., [1954]), pp. 54-59, 128-29. There is an entry for Dawson Burns in the *Oxford Dictionary of National Biography* by Charlotte Fell-Smith, revised by Mark Clement. See also Karen E. Smith, "The Balfours and the Burns: Baptists Battling the Power of Strong Drink," *Baptist Quarterly* 45 no. 8 (Oct. 2014). For the brother-in-law, see David McKie, *Jabez: The Rise and Fall of a Victorian Scoundrel* (Atlantic Books, 2004).

[93] The Board spent £1,300 during its brief life. See the article by its secretary, A.F. Harvey, "Evidence Board," *United Temperance Gazette*, June 1900, p. 74. Harvey, the Board secretary, earlier had been assistant secretary of the CETS. He later was secretary of the Central Temperance Legislation Board and then the Temperance Legislation League.

[94] *Alliance News*, 15 May 1896, p. 305.

[95] For instance, Frederick Ernest Slee, a barrister in George Candy's chambers, served as a reporter for the *Morning Advertiser*. Minute book, Royal Commission committee, Licensed Victuallers of London, 11 Oct. 1897.

[96] The Royal Commission members asked over 74,000 questions. It cost the taxpayer almost £8,000. Greenaway thesis, p. 305.

[97] The Royal Commission did not take foreign evidence. Walker had suggested taking evidence from English-speaking lands. Minute book, Royal Commission committee, Licensed Victuallers of London, 24 February 1898.

[98] Country Brewers Society, grand committee, 4 July 1898.

[99] Royal Commission committee, Licensed Victuallers, Central Board, 12 July 1898. Those attending included three Royal Commission members Charles Walker and Samuel Hyslop, who represented the publicans, and a representative of the Gilbey wine interest, Harry Grinling. They agreed not to permit sectional differences interfere with trade unity, notably the publicans' dislike of grocers' licenses. Buxton to Harcourt, 23, 29 Nov., 7 Dec. 1892, 8 May 1893. Bodleian, Harcourt Ms. 148, fols. 21-25, 32-33, 34-37; Harcourt Ms. 146, fols. 48-50..

[100] Bonsor to Sir S.K. ("Pom") McDonnell, 6 Nov. 1898. Christ Church, Oxford, Salisbury papers, uncatalogued when consulted. The speech by Hicks-Beach was published in the *Alliance News*, 11 Nov. 1898, p. 738. For the date that the draft

report had been expected, see *Licensing Trade News,* 12 Nov. 1898, p. 6.

[101] *Morning Advertiser,* 1 April 1896, p. 4.

[102] For an obituary from a "realist" temperance perspective, see T.P. Whittaker, "The Late Viscount Peel," Temperance Legislation League, *Monthly Notes* 2 no. 11 (Nov. 1912): 1-2.

[103] Bonsor to Salisbury's private secretary, 6 November 1898. Quoted by Greenaway, *Drink and British Politics since 1830,* p. 62.

[104] *Licensing World,* 14 April 1900, p. 277.

[105] Whittaker, "The Late Viscount Peel," (Temperance Legislation League) *Monthly Notes* 2 no. 11 (Nov. 1912): 1.

[106] Sir Algernon West, "The Two Reports of the Licensing Commission," *Nineteenth Century,* Feb. 1900, pp. 260-74.

[107] Henry Gladstone to Herbert Gladstone, 16 Feb. 1899. BL, Herbert Gladstone papers, Add. Ms. 46045, ff. 193-94. "It is most important to get a unanimous report so as to give the Government no excuse for not dealing with the question." Reporting a speech by T.P. Whittaker, a trade newspaper wrote: "in the early stages of discussion on the report, Sir Algernon West told him (Mr. Whittaker) that he did not think that any report would carry weight in the country, and lead to legislation unless it had the signatures of the trade members." *Licensed Trade News,* 24 Feb. 1900, p. 11. See also Whittaker, "The 'Temperance' Reply," p. 514.

[108] According to a trade account, Peel had been angered by a rival report having been circulated. Supposedly Windsor, de Vesci, West, Johnston, and Buxton had written the report. "Lord Peel's Failure: Autocracy and Ill-Temper," *Licensing World,* 15 April 1899, pp. 296-97. The newspaper contrasted the role of a Speaker of the House of Commons, especially during a time of Irish obstructionism, with that of a royal commission chairman. The sense of command that made Peel a great Speaker made him a poor chairman.

[109] T.P. Whittaker, "The 'Temperance' Reply to Sir Algernon West," *Nineteenth Century,* March 1900, pp. 510-25.

[110] West had asked Balfour the legal status of a Royal Commission if its chairman withdrew. Balfour to West, 17 March 1899. BL, Balfour papers, Add. Ms. 49853, f. 60.

[111] West, "Two Reports, p. 265.

[112] Whittaker, "The 'Temperance' Reply," p. 514. According to a trade commissioner, Peel abandoned a local option referendum for public management (the Gothenburg Scheme) as a concession to the prohibitionists. George Younger, in *Parl. Deb.,* 4th ser., CXCIV, 21 Oct. 1908, col. 1239.

[113] The Home Office disappointed both factions in regard the printing of the report. On 2 June 1899, it rejected the suggestion (1 June 1899) of the Hon. Sidney Peel, secretary to the Royal Commission, that the minority report be printed first since the chairman was among the minority, and it told Sir Algernon West that he could not identify himself as vice-chairman when signing the majority report since his title did not come from the Crown. Public Record Office, H.O., 45/10151/20998/39.

[114] On July 18, the Majority and Minority Reports and related statements were published as *Parliamentary Paper* 1899 (C. 9379), XXXV. The seven thousand copies of the first edition sold out almost at once. *Licensing Trade News,* 29 July

1899, p. 7.

[115] Buxton argued that the scale of the reduction proposed in the Peel Report explained the inadequacy of compensation. *Licensing World*, 5 May 1900, p. 325. In his remarks at a banquet of the London publicans, Buxton outlined his own ideas for a settlement (pp. 324-25). Presiding at this annual dinner, Buxton and his brewery (Truman, Hanbury, Buxton and Company) showed great generosity. The brewery contributed £625, Buxton personally £155, two members of the Hanbury family, over £52 each, Gerald Buxton over £52, and other members of the firm smaller amounts.

[116] Lord de Vesci unsuccessfully attempted to persuade the majority to prohibit a mixture of trade. In Ireland persons who carried on other businesses in the same premises held ninety per cent of the licenses. *Licensed Trade News*, 13 May 1899, p. 10.

[117] *Licensing World*, 5 May 1900, p. 325.

[118] *Daily Chronicle*, 13 April 1899, p. 4. The newspaper apparently regarded the other neutrals--Gordon, Graham, and Wharton--as pro-trade.

[119] Two trade summaries are available in the papers of the National Trade Defence Fund, Staffordshire Record Office. (1) Reprinted from the *Manager's Report to the Subscribers for the Year Ended September 30th, 1899*, and bearing the title National Trade Defence Fund. This report includes a chronological list of events from 1895. D3163/2/1/1/ between folios 295 and 296. (2) Birmingham and Midland Counties Wholesale Brewers' Association, Report for 1899 (1900), reprinted from *Brewery Trade Review and National Trade Defence Association's Manager's Report* (1899). D3163/1/2/4/

[120] Country Brewers' Society, general committee, 1 May 1899. The Majority Report received final approval on 6 June 1899. *Licensed Victuallers' Official Annual* (1906), p. 150.

[121] Whittaker was not in love with reduction in numbers. In 1900, he told a world's temperance congress "complete closing for one day a week or for an hour or two earlier in the evening on all days is probably more effective in diminishing intemperance than a very considerable reduction in the number of licensed houses." Whittaker, "The Lessons Taught by Legislation for the Promotion of Temperance," in John Turner Rae, *World's Temperance Congress 1900* (Ideal Publishing Union, 1901), pp. 288-89.

[122] A.F. Hills, "Our Temperance Warfare," *United Temperance Gazette* 4 (Dec. 1899): 148.

[123] "Memorandum on Some Phases of the Liquor Licensing Laws, with Suggestions for their Amendment," *P.P.*, 1899 (C. 9379), XXXV, pp. 295-381.

[124] In April 1899 there also was a conference of socialist and labor elected officials, chaired by Sidney Webb, in Leeds. The conference considered prohibition a failure and Local Veto a class measure which would be inoperative where the drink problem was worst. Moreover, Local Veto left the private profit motive intact. The conference called for a maximum and minimum ratio of licenses to population, "high license," that is fees proportionate to actual value, representative licensing authorities instead of appointed ones, and municipal control of the drink trade. *Daily Chronicle*, 3 April 1899, p. 4.

¹²⁵ For Rowntree, see Anne Vernon, *A Quaker Business Man: The Life of Joseph Rowntree, 1836-1925* (Allen & Unwin, 1958); *Oxford Dictionary of National Biography*.

¹²⁶ There is only fragmentary biographical information about Arthur James Sherwell (1863-1942). Although raised in an Anglican family, young Sherwell trained to be a Wesleyan minister and at one point helped Hugh Price Hughes at his West London Mission. With a focus on urban poverty, Sherwell wrote *Life in West London: A Study and a Contrast* (1897). In 1899 he published with Joseph Rowntree, *The Temperance Question and Social Reform,* followed by many other books on the drink question, often as a co-author with Rowntree. Rowntree financed his research in North America and Scandinavia. A champion of disinterested management (the Gothenburg scheme), Sherwell was honorary secretary of the Temperance Legislation League. He served for twelve years as a Liberal MP, representing a Yorkshire constituency. First elected at a bye-election in November 1906, he resigned on the eve of the general election of 1918. He had alienated local Liberals. He opposed wartime conscription. After he left Parliament, Sherwell served on the Royal Commission on Licensing (England and Wales), 1929-1931. In his *Who's Who* entry he listed in first place among his recreations "bluebooks."

¹²⁷ Vernon, *A Quaker Business Man*, p. 134. There is a good summary of Rowntree and Sherwell by Greenaway, *Drink and British Politics since 1830*, pp 68-70.

¹²⁸ Rowntree and Sherwell, *Temperance Problem and Social Reform*, first edition, p. xiv.

¹²⁹ Rowntree and Sherwell, *Temperance Problem and Social Reform*, June 1900 edition, p. 512.

¹³⁰ Rowntree and Sherwell later published *State Prohibition and Local Option* [1900], *British "Gothenburg" Experiments and Public House Trusts* [1901], and *The Public Control of the Liquor Traffic* [1903]. "In the writing of two later volumes-- *Taxation of the Liquor Trade* (1906) and *State Purchase of the Liquor Trade* [1919]- -Joseph Rowntree did not actively participate." *Joseph Rowntree (1836-1925), A Typescript Memoir, Probably by Luther Worstenholm (Editor Northern Echo 1908-1926) and Related Papers* ([Joseph Rowntree Charitable Trust, ca. 1986). H. 1.

CHAPTER SIX

WHITTAKER AND LORD PEEL'S REPORT

It was quickly apparent that the majority report lacked popular and political appeal. The hopes of Sir Algernon West and the other neutral commissioners that they had produced a practicable scheme for legislation died stillborn. Before the general election what support the majority report attracted was mostly to create an obstacle to the minority report. The liquor trade would not work to obtain its enactment. The trade either clung to the status quo as the best of all attainable worlds or, in the case of a few militants, agitated for legislation to protect them from local temperance reformers seated on licensing benches. Salisbury took advantage of the lack of unanimity in the Peel commission to do nothing. The Home Secretary, Matthew White Ridley, announced on 8 November that no legislation based on the commission's recommendations was planned for the time being.[1] The repudiation of reform after a four-year inquiry galled reformers the more for taking place at a dinner of the Country Brewers' Society. After the general election a deputation led by Sir Algernon West and identified with the neutral signatories of the majority report waited upon the new Home Secretary, C.T. Ritchie, but to no immediate effect.[2] A CETS official complained: "The Royal Commission was the Government's own child, but when it finished its Report the Government would have nothing to do with it."[3]

In contrast to the oblivion into which the majority report sank, Lord Peel's Report provided the focus for a well-organized campaign managed by T.P. Whittaker, a Liberal M.P. who had long been identified with the prohibitionist wing of the temperance movement. Whittaker sought to convince Liberal leaders to adopt Lord Peel's temperance proposals as the party program, while attempting to unite temperance reformers of all stripes behind Lord Peel's report. Whittaker launched his campaign at a time when the Liberals had new leaders. Harcourt, the most important Liberal identified with Local Veto, had retired in December 1898. Sir Henry Campbell-Bannerman, an elderly Scot popular in the House of Commons, succeeded him as the Liberal Party leader. A few months later the chief whip, T.E. Ellis, died unexpectedly. He was only forty. Although Ellis had not always agreed with the UKA, there was no doubt that the young Welshman had been a vigorous supporter of temperance reform. In April 1899 Herbert Gladstone (1854-1930) was appointed chief whip.

As chief whip, Herbert Gladstone is best known for his secret agreement with Ramsay Macdonald in 1903 to let Labour candidates in two-member constituencies stand against Conservatives without a Liberal candidate dividing the anti-Conservative vote. The *Oxford Dictionary of National Biography* describes Herbert Gladstone as an "outstanding" chief whip whose public image was as "a placid, straightforward fellow, amiable and sensible." He was "a poor public speaker."[4] Family members regarded him as irritable.

Like his father, Herbert Gladstone lacked enthusiasm for legislation authorizing local prohibition.[5] His objective was party unity.

Herbert Gladstone had friends in the licensed trade, especially the licensed grocers. A Liberal M.P. who was a director of the Gilbey wine firm (much of whose business was through licensed grocers) reported to the party leader: "I have told all my friends for days past that [Herbert Gladstone] is the one man capable of pulling the party together." The Gilbey partners appreciated Gladstone's help. In 1904 Sir Walter Gilbey and Sir James Blyth said that they would lend carriages to transport voters on his request, "though they will refuse any one else." The chief whip tangled with "the temperance faddists" in York for rejecting "the smartest of my candidates," a distillery director. Gladstone grumbled that as a result they were "in my bad books."[6]

The temperance question provided one of the first issues to test the new leadership. For Herbert Gladstone the value of Lord Peel's Report lay as a slogan with which he could exorcize the stubborn ghost of Local Veto. He opposed any party commitment to the controversial proposals in the report. His principles, his personal connections, and his party responsibilities made him the natural intermediary between the remaining Liberal drink traders and Campbell-Bannerman. Despite its distilleries and breweries, the leader's native Scotland was a temperance stronghold, and he was committed to temperance reform. To break the impasse over temperance legislation, Campbell-Bannerman, "ever the political realist," was willing to make concessions at the expense of Local Veto.[7] In a speech at Hull on 8 March 1899, prior to the publication of the Royal Commission reports, he characterized temperance reform as one of the most important subjects of social reform, expressed his hope that the Peel commission would make proposals behind which reformers could unite, and warned against becoming "too pedantic, too obstinate in pursuing some particular method we may sincerely consider the best."[8]

Shortly after the publication of the reports Whittaker approached Herbert Gladstone. According to the chief whip's interview diary for 10 July, Whittaker recommended that party policy follow Lord Peel's Report closely. Whittaker proposed that the merits of the Veto for England be considered after the seven-year period during which compensation would be paid. Whittaker was not particular about the amount of compensation if the practice was temporary. Gladstone told him that "agreement on this basis was quite possible."[9] Other leaders such as Morley and Campbell-Bannerman were also receptive.[10] Vacationing at his favorite Marienbad spa, C-B reported to Gladstone that, although currently resting, he proposed that at the beginning of September he would "begin the perusal of Whittaker de Temperantia. For the present I find it enough to look at the outside of the volume."[11] This homework presumably was the lengthy memorandum that Whittaker had attached to the minority report.

In the autumn the tempo of political activity quickened despite the distraction of the Boer war. Early in November the Liberal leaders, in Campbell-Bannerman's words, "engineered this deal" with Whittaker. On 5 November, Whittaker wrote out the details of his plan for Gladstone. He urged that the Liberal leaders affirm their support for the principle of local control, including Direct Local Veto, and for the Peel recommendations as a basis for the practical first steps of legislation in the entire United Kingdom. The leaders of the temperance movement then would reply with public statements of electoral support. Whittaker argued that temperance unity would be made possible by combining in a single program direct popular control and licensing reform through more efficient regulation.

Although he accepted a few years of compensation, Whittaker remained a prohibitionist. Like Whittaker, W.S. Caine had signed Lord Peel's minority report, together with a supplementary statement asking for Local Veto. Whittaker's proposal to the Liberal leaders asked for more than Caine and the Good Templar leader Malins had sought in 1888 during the fight regarding compensation. They had not demanded a promise from Ritchie to enact Local Veto after a delay of a few years. If prohibitionists like Caine and Malins had been willing to consider a deal on compensation without any promise about Local Veto, it was reasonable for Whittaker to hope the temperance party could accept a few years of compensation as part of Lord Peel's Report. As he saw it: "Legislation on the lines of Lord Peel's report would prepare the way for the enactment of Direct Popular Control in England. It would reduce the number of public houses and diminish their profits (by Taxing them more heavily), and thereby curtail the political power of the trade."

Whittaker predicted that all the prominent temperance men, with the possible exception of Sir Wilfrid Lawson, would support Lord Peel's report as an immediate electoral program.

> All that is needed to carry the full approval and hearty support of Temperance men in their various constituencies–and it is essential–is that they be convinced that the revised policy is not intended to be a mere item in a long programme of pious opinions, but is put forward by the Liberal Leaders earnestly and whole-heartedly and with the determination to give prompt legislative effect to it when they return to power.[12]

In other words, temperance reform had to be made a clear priority.

Campbell-Bannerman made the desired temperance declaration ten days later, on 15 November, in a speech at Manchester, the UKA's headquarters city. In his speech he justified the change in policy to advanced temperance reformers by pointing to the long failure to secure legislation. They had been perfectionists rejecting imperfect bills that would have accomplished much good, such as that introduced by H.A. Bruce in 1871. He argued that Lord Peel's Report presented a worthwhile body of legislatively practicable reforms.

> In Lord Peel's proposals the friends of temperance have a code of reform which may be rightfully adopted as meeting the immediate necessities of the case. And in saying this, I take upon myself to appeal to those stalwart upholders of licensing reform, to those men who with much effort and sacrifice, with toil and storm, have advanced the cause of direct popular control–to appeal to them not to accept any compromise–I won't ask them to do so, and not to renounce any principle but to view with favour a scheme which would undoubtedly work immense good immediately, which would pave the way for effecting in after years those future and more complete reforms which they have at heart.

It was impossible to ignore that in England there was reluctance about Local Veto that did not exist in Scotland and Wales. It was only realistic to recognize that the public wanted compensation given to those whose licenses were suppressed. "I have not the view to push any particular scheme or nostrum or notion of my own," he concluded, "but I want to enforce on you that the time has come and the occasion offers for a serious and concentrated and practical effort to cope with the evils which we all deplore."[13]

The London papers did not fully report the speech, but the *Manchester Guardian* did. As soon as it reached Whittaker, he congratulated Campbell-Bannerman and gave him the text of a Temperance Manifesto, responding to the appeal for unity behind Lord Peel's report, for which he was collecting signatures.[14] Campbell-Bannerman, very pleased with his *demarche*, proposed to Gladstone that the temperance section of his speech be reprinted for wide circulation. "I think that what I said is (though I say it myself) judicious and sufficiently full."[15]

In alarm, the chief whip protested that the Manchester speech tied the Liberals too closely to the Peel proposals. It was impractical tactically to restrict compensation as narrowly as had Lord Peel when even the advanced temperance stalwarts Caine and Whittaker accepted compensation in principle. Gladstone predicted that if a Liberal majority in the House of Commons passed a bill providing only meager compensation the House of Lords would force an election on the issue and that the Liberals would lose. He feared that "without an adequate amount of grease we shall not be able to overcome the friction of the trade in the next or almost any election." He also reported that the reaction to Campbell-Bannerman's speech by the Liberal brewer E.N. Buxton. Buxton questioned whether he could stand for Parliament on a party platform which included Lord Peel's Report, but being "very reasonable" and having read only the abridged *Times* report, he promised to read a full account before reaching a decision. For Buxton, a time limit made any compensation scheme unacceptable.[16] Gladstone urged Campbell-Bannerman to clarify the party's temperance program during his next speech in Birmingham.[17]

Meanwhile the friends of Lord Peel's report launched their public campaign on 21 November at the inaugural meeting of the Central Temperance Legislation Board in London.[18] Lord Peel had been scheduled to take the chair. When illness prevented him from attending, he sent a long letter in which he declared that in the drink question "it had come to be a struggle for mastery between the State and a trade." The main thrust of the letter and of the meeting was that the minority recommendations provided a program of reform which "a vast and growing mass of thoughtful and moderate opinion" would support.[19] Disagreeing, the Alliance and the Good Templars withdrew from the Central Board to which they had briefly belonged.[20]

Three days later Campbell-Bannerman returned to the issue of temperance. He criticized Home Secretary Ridley for having pronounced against any immediate legislation and urged that at a minimum the Government implement those recommendations on which the two reports agreed. Despite Gladstone's plea, Campbell-Bannerman said nothing to modify his support of Lord Peel's Report that might mollify the small group of drink traders who considered themselves Liberals.[21]

The Temperance Manifesto that Whittaker had promised was published on 7 December. Its thirty signatories, most of them MPs or divines, called on the temperance party to rally behind the Liberal Party in return for its commitment to the minority report. The signers included politicians such as David Lloyd George and Dr. R. Spence Watson, clergy and Nonconformist ministers such as Dean F.W. Farrar and the Rev. Hugh Price Hughes, eighteen of the Alliance's honorary vice-presidents, and both its honorary secretary and its honorary treasurer.[22]

Campbell-Bannerman's Manchester speech and the Temperance Manifesto in response to it alarmed a variety of Liberals who disliked Lord Peel's Report as too weak or too strong. Sir Wilfrid Lawson led a section of advanced temperance men who protested the failure of Campbell-Bannerman and the manifesto signatories to insist on Local Veto for England and also denounced compensation.[23] These enemies of the manifesto were pleasantly surprised that Campbell-Bannerman greeted Whittaker's declaration coolly. Those who considered the Lord Peel's Report too extreme also complained. On the day of the publication of the manifesto Sir Algernon West, "simply horrified," warned Herbert Gladstone that the adoption of the minority report would alienate the grocers and the moderates.[24]

Gladstone needed no persuasion. He had obtained a promise of Asquith's support to modify Campbell-Bannerman's Manchester declaration.[25] Lord Tweedmouth, Lord Kimberley, and Lord Spencer also joined the chief whip in the effort to disassociate the Liberal Party from Lord Peel's Report. In a speech at Peterborough on 6 December Spencer spoke in favor of Liberal support for those recommendations on which the Royal Commission had reached a virtual consensus. Although Spencer did not want to embarrass Campbell-Bannerman by a public disagreement and said that he personally could support Lord Peel's Report, he told the party leader that "I confess to feeling somewhat keenly that we must not have another liquor difficulty in our way" and that "it does not seem safe to pin ourselves absolutely" to the minority report, particularly over compensation.[26] Campbell-Bannerman hoped that temperance acceptance of some kind of compensation paid by the trade to itself might "soften the stubborn opposition of the trade in England."[27]

The day after the publication of the manifesto Gladstone cautioned Campbell-Bannerman about the danger that it would be interpreted as expressing the agreement of the Liberal leadership with the temperance movement on behalf of the specific proposals of Lord Peel's Report. Gladstone insisted that the report be modified to provide adequate compensation, "the all important point." He also deplored the abolition of grocers' licenses implied by the endorsement of Lord Peel's report. The Liberals might lose the support of the grocers and wholesale distributors represented by the Gilbey interest.[28]

Campbell-Bannerman replied the next day with a mixture of conciliation and stubborn conviction. His reference at Manchester to Lord Peel's proposals as a "code of reform" had been given a more precise meaning than he had intended. He had never committed the party to the enactment of all the Peel recommendations. He had emphasized the need for a politically practicable program and had disavowed any claim of offering an infallible nostrum. He disputed Gladstone's argument about compensation and about grocers' licenses. The proposal for full compensation paid by the trade through the earmarking of a tax simply revived Goschen's plan. Furthermore, "in Scotland we are all against Grocers' Licenses which are the worst cause of evil—-drink being hawked about the country districts in vans which call at men's doors with tea, bread, etc. and 'lead captive silly women'."[29]

Liberal leaders such as James Bryce continued to press Campbell-Bannerman to retreat from his Manchester speech. Bryce reported that E.N. Buxton was indignant "that after he screwed up the other representatives of beer on the Commission to accept the Majority Scheme of Compensation the benefit of having nailed them to that should be lost."[30] Whittaker wanted to publish the Manchester speech in tandem with a summary of the Peel recommendations that, in Gladstone's opinion, would aggravate the confusion over what Liberal policy was.

Gladstone worried that: "At present the fat is all in the fire so far as the Liberal Liquor traders are concerned. The enclosed [from Charles Gold] is a sample. If it is thought we are going for the abolition of Grocers Licenses in England, I am afraid the result will be rather disastrous." Gold, the retiring Liberal MP for Saffron Walden, was the brother-in-law of the head of the Gilbey firm and one of his partners. It was very doubtful whether Gold and the rest of the powerful Gilbey clan would back the new party candidate, Armine Wodehouse, Lord Kimberley's son (and Matthew Arnold's son-in-law), in the general election. (In fact, young Wodehouse was elected for the seat at the 1900 general election.) "*We cannot afford* to lose the Gilbeys and all their grocer clients, the Whitbreads, Eversheds, Buxtons, Beaufoys, and other men like [the wealthy landowner] Adeane who are more or less associated with the trade." He implored Campbell-Bannerman to present party commitments only in terms of general principles without any endorsements of the specifics of Lord Peel's Report. Surprisingly, the chief whip said that this was Whittaker's opinion too. Gladstone urged that the policy for England and for Campbell-Bannerman's native Scotland be sharply distinguished.

> The sooner you make it clear that Veto for England is postponed the better. It will bring the parties of Lawson and Whittaker into conflict and will help us with our brewers and all moderate Liberal reformers. The [Lawson] battleaxe will have first to descend on the heads of the nearest 'traitors' in this case Caine and Whittaker. For the Peel Reporters are the men who threw the Veto overboard.

Gladstone considered it "absolutely essential" that Campbell-Bannerman repeat the interpretation of the Manchester speech that he had stated in his letter of 9 December in such a form that it could be officially circulated. He hoped that the declaration would include a passage on the lines of Campbell-Bannerman's Direct Veto memorandum which had arrived in the morning mail.[31]

Campbell-Bannerman wrote back in some puzzlement. He had not retained a copy of the letter of 9 December, and he was not sure what the Direct Veto memorandum that Gladstone referred to was supposed to be. He assumed that it was the draft of his reply to Lawson. Campbell-Bannerman protested that he had not committed the party to details, only to reduction in the number of licenses, compensation, and popularizing the composition of the licensing authorities. Furthermore, "the word grocer never issued from my lips, nor did I think of him." He was "quite content to leave the grocer alone, if our (Scotch) Van mischief could be dealt with by regulation." He had said nothing to upset the Liberal liquor traders. They could not expect the party to abjure Local Veto and local control. All that could be done had been done. The Veto had been postponed for England and compensation had been provided. He hoped that his forthcoming speech in Aberdeen would clarify everything.[32]

Before Aberdeen the chief whip received a desperate letter from Wodehouse who feared that he would have to withdraw as the candidate for Saffron Walden. Gold had categorically refused to support him out of anger with the party over grocers' licenses.[33] Gladstone remained optimistic that he could "mollify the clan." Buxton helped arrange a meeting with Gold. Meanwhile he worked out an understanding with Buxton that he explained to Campbell-Bannerman. "He would be content if we could take the line of a 'generous' measure of compensation payable by and through the trade without any specific plan, and with the Peel report as a *general basis* without committal to detailed recommendations."[34] Gladstone did not tell Campbell-Bannerman one detail about the interview that he entrusted to his diary: Buxton "evidently does not care much about grocers' licenses."[35] Lord Kimberley also wrote Campbell-Bannerman to protest about grocers' licenses and, more generally, the "song of triumph" resounding among the advanced temperance reformers.[36] Lord Spencer complained that what Whittaker wanted lacked consistency. The Veto was "only nominally preserved even in Peel's Report," but Whittaker's memorial sought to graft the Veto onto the minority report.[37]

In his speech at Aberdeen on 19 December Campbell-Bannerman once more grasped the nettles of the drink question. He said of the signatories of Lord Peel's Report that "it is by taking their report as a basis, without necessarily adhering to all their precise and detailed recommendations, that I believe the greatest practical amount of good will be done." The difference in public sentiment justified Scotland and Wales advancing toward Local Veto at a faster rate than England.[38]

Two days later Campbell-Bannerman explained to Gladstone and to Lawson that the Aberdeen speech before a Scottish audience had not proved to be the proper vehicle for the exposition of England's temperance policy that he had promised them. He added, to Gladstone, that he thought he had said enough to ease the fears of "our tender brewers." On the intervening day Lawson complained about the postponement of Local Veto for England. He received the tart advice in reply that the only worthwhile reforms are those that can be enacted. "I am weary of doing nothing in order to attain perfection."[39] Pleased with the Aberdeen speech, Gladstone still hoped that the party could adopt the majority report's recommendation on grocers' licenses. He reported that in the end Gold had consented to support Wodehouse, but that he had warned that the licensed grocers would be organized into a strong association to defend their interests.[40]

Campbell-Bannerman remained doubtful about the importance of pleasing the Liberal drink traders and their friends. He preferred to foster the new moderation of the advanced temperance reformers who had rallied to Lord Peel's Report. He told Lord Spencer that "Edward Buxton, Algie West, & Co." really wanted the Liberals to repudiate the Local Veto principle. "*We cannot do it*: all we can do is to delay or postpone it in England under cover of passing it for Scotland and Wales." Instead of appeasing the remaining Liberal drink traders and their sympathizers, the Liberal Party needed the support of people like Whittaker, whom he called "the reasonable extremists," to isolate diehard Vetoists and opponents of compensation.[41] "It seems to me having got these 'reasonable extremists' in tow, our only chance of success in the matter is to use them and stick to them."[42]

Perhaps Campbell-Bannerman was a more realistic politician than his chief whip. The section of the drink trade that identified with the Liberal Party was small and likely in a few years to disappear altogether. Did

Gladstone continue to conciliate the drink trade because he personally sympathized with the trade protests? It does not seem to have been realistic to expect that the Liberals could expect much political advantage from accommodating the trade. The grocers had no affection for the public houses and their brewer masters, so they might be kept in the fold. The Liberal brewers and maltsters who grumbled over the party alliance with the temperance reformers were too few to matter in a general election. [43]

One half of Whittaker's grand strategy, the capture of the Liberal Party for Lord Peel's report, ended in a substantial but incomplete success. In March 1900 the National Liberal Federation adopted the resolution which Whittaker proposed, in which it "re-affirms its declaration in favour of the urging of an effective reform in the laws relating to the liquor traffic, and believes that Lord Peel's minority report of the Licensing Commission furnishes, in the main, a basis for practical legislation in the immediate future in which all temperance reformers should combine and concentrate."

Joseph Rowntree seconded Whittaker's motion.[44] He was the co-author of a popular new book, *The Temperance Problem and Social Reform* that appeared just before the rival Royal Commission reports. The organ of the Church of England Temperance Society later called it "the most valuable book, perhaps, that has ever been written on Temperance."[45] On the basis of research in the United States, the book argued that prohibition was impractical in the big cities where the drink problem loomed the largest. The book sometimes was seen as offering an alternative to Lord Peel's Report because of its sympathy with the Gothenburg principle of disinterested management. Presumably Rowntree could support Lord Peel's Report tactically because he believed that by weakening the drink trade it would make Gothenburg a realistic next step in public house reform.[46]

Gladstone had delayed an insurmountable breech with the remaining Liberal liquor traders, and the trade in turn had weakened the Liberal adherence to the details of Lord Peel's report. In 1900 Gladstone could tell Buxton that he considered the trade's test questions for parliamentary candidates "reasonable." Buxton pressed the chief whip for a "clear declaration" from the Liberal leadership on the drink question.[47] Fighting his own two-front campaign, Buxton warned the trade against rallying as a bloc behind the banners of its Unionist friends. In that event the Liberals might fall completely under temperance influence.[48] Prohibition was dead, but reduction schemes made compensation a central issue. Urging trade unity, Buxton insisted upon defense of the licensed grocers despite the hostility of licensed victuallers toward their competitors.[49]

A loose endorsement of Lord Peel's report served as the foundation of Liberal licensing policy for more than a decade. Nevertheless, Buxton could hope that the existence of a handful of Liberal liquor traders and Liberals sympathetic to the licensed trade might provide insurance that could prevent a Unionist election defeat from becoming a trade disaster. Sixteen such Liberals were elected in 1900 with the help of trade neutrality.[50]

In the general election of 1900 Gladstone told his West Leeds electors what Gilbey and Buxton wanted to hear. Although he supported Lord Peel's report as a basis for legislation, he disagreed with it on two important points. Gladstone rejected the abolition of grocer's licenses. He accepted instead the recommendation of the majority report that licensed grocers be under the authority of the licensing authority. Second, and more important for Buxton and his friends, Gladstone regarded seven years of financial compensation as too little. Provided that the compensation came from the trade and its customers, Gladstone advocated what he called "full compensation." Without it, "there will be very little chance of any sensible and adequate temperance legislation for many years to come."[51]

The Liberal commitment to Lord Peel's report was problematic. The other part of Whittaker's grand strategy, temperance unity, suffered its defeats too, but considering the obstacles that it faced, its successes remain impressive. The British temperance movement comprised a myriad of organizations and policies and prickly personalities. Fundamentally the temperance party was divided between those who wanted to reform the drink trade and those who wanted to prohibit it. The difference should not be exaggerated. Many licensing reformers were teetotalers, and some of them accepted the principle of Local Veto, while virtually all prohibitionists simultaneously worked for reform of the licensing laws. The difference was one of priorities. For prohibitionist activists, Local Veto had assumed a symbolic importance beyond the closing of a few public houses in teetotal enclaves. Enactment of the Veto would legitimize the prohibitionist ideology, stigmatize the trade, and anathemize in the name of civilized society the evil of drink.

Whittaker scored initial successes in consolidating the temperance movement. To provide the Peel commission with temperance witnesses the principal organizations had cooperated in sponsoring the Central Temperance Evidence Board. Whittaker captured this body and transformed it into a Central Temperance Legislation Board pledged to Lord Peel's Report. Whittaker had little difficulty in persuading moderate reformers such as the leaders of the Church of England Temperance Society. The minority report gave them much of what they wanted and omitted what they opposed. In fact, the CETS had noticeably strong representation in the leadership of the new Board.[52] The architect of a previous unity campaign,

A.F. Hills, predictably appeared as the first honorary treasurer of the Central Temperance Legislation Board.[53]

Whittaker wanted the support of moderate drinkers who worried about excessive working class drinking. The active role Lord Peel played in the Board strengthened the appeal to those who did not look upon drink as intrinsically evil but feared the effect of heavy drinking on the country. Peel was not a teetotaler, and he had a reputation as moderate and practical man. As a result, his vehemence made a strong impression. In his letter to the inaugural meeting of the Board, he described the drink problem as "a supreme hindrance to the prosperity of the nation."[54] In the psychological unease at the turn of the century a great many thoughtful people agreed with Peel's subsequent diagnosis that the drink evil "was eating into the physical condition of our race, sapping our moral stature, and affecting our nervous system." "Surrounded as the country was by envious, and it might be, hostile, neighbors, we must keep ourselves clean and pure at home if we wished to face the trade competition which was becoming more and more pressing."[55] The reforms which he proposed "were not only enjoined and sanctioned by the Christianity which they professed and by the morality which they preached, but they were enforced upon them by the merest, lowest utilitarian principles of social and domestic expediency."[56]

The resistance to Lord Peel's report within the temperance movement came from a section of advanced reformers. Twenty-eight years earlier William Gladstone's Government had abandoned an ambitious program of reduction and local control when the prohibitionists failed to rally heartily behind a bill that they thought was good but not good enough. In 1899 the problem differed from that in 1871. The prohibitionists themselves were divided. Many of them, partly out of the memory of 1871, vigorously supported Lord Peel's Report. The prohibitionist commissioners signed it, the Temperance Manifesto endorsed it, and advanced temperance reformers tended to trust a report with such an impressive roster of sponsors. Many Alliance stalwarts took positions in the new Board. John Hilton, the Alliance's parliamentary agent, became an honorary secretary. Whittaker argued persuasively against the tactical folly of "headlong rushes at the strongest positions when flanking movements are obviously possible and necessary." "The more closely the habits of the people are touched and interfered with, the more necessary it is that the legislation should have the distinct approval of public opinion."[57] In a reminder of the Whittaker teetotal heritage, T.P.'s father Thomas Whittaker, JP, a pioneer itinerant temperance lecturer, died on 20 November.[58]

A hard core of opposition remained which eventually split the advanced temperance party. A young Welsh reformer, David Lloyd George, although pleased that most temperance people had rallied to Lord Peel's Report, acknowledged: "a few temperance leaders are likely to buck over the traces."[59] Sir Wilfrid Lawson was seventy years old in the year that Lord Peel's Report was published. Most of Lawson's old friends regarded him as too rigid and politically unrealistic. The *Methodist Times*, edited by Hugh Price Hughes, dismissed Lawson's opposition. "He has never been the real leader of the United Kingdom Alliance, though he has made a very amiable and witty figurehead."[60] Lawson decried the campaign waged in the report's favor, although in relatively circumspect language designed to avoid a lasting rupture. "I keep as much as I can from antagonism with the 'Peel liners' but our people are getting rather perplexed [and, pleading to Harcourt] want a lead on the old straight path."[61] Lawson's less judicious allies denounced the adherents of the report as men who had abandoned their principles for the sake of expediency.

The temperance opposition to Lord Peel's report found its organizational base not in the badly divided UKA but in the English and Scottish grand lodges of the Independent Order of Good Templars.[62] For instance, the Good Templar John Kempster was outspoken in arguing against making Lord Peel's Report the basis for temperance reform unless concessions were made about Local Veto in England and compensation was eliminated.[63] Even among the Good Templars there was a minority that wanted to accept Lord Peel's report. The English grand lodge briefly joined the new Central Temperance Legislation Board that had been created to support Lord Peel's Report. The grand lodge hoped to persuade the Board to endorse Direct Local Veto and Sunday closing. When that proved impossible and Board membership seemed to commit members to compensation, the grand lodge executive unanimously voted to withdraw.[64] The English grand lodge rejected the minority report only after a spirited battle for almost eight hours at the annual meeting at Southampton in April 1900. In another grand lodge debate in 1901, a dissident said that the Good Templars were "more equally divided than any of the other great Temperance organisations" and questioned the political practicality of rejecting Lord Peel's Report as an immediate program.[65]

The Grand Chief Templar, Joseph Malins, supported the policy of keeping a distance from Lord Peel's Report, but he urged a spirit of charity toward opponents. Although the Good Templars could not endorse the Peel Report, "they may not fight against."[66] Malins had been absent from England on a round-the-world tour of foreign lodges before the controversy over Lord Peel's Report had become bitter. On his return voyage, Malins wrote from Ceylon to recommend that the grand lodge withdraw from the Legislation Board which it did on 5 February 1900. (Ironically many years earlier Malins had joined his close ally Caine in an abortive secret plan for a compromise that would have allowed a kind of compensation.)[67]

A smaller and more aristocratic bastion of anti-Peel sentiment was Lady Carlisle's circle.[68] The Countess of Carlisle was important for the prestige of her title, her money, and her organizational ability. Her circle included her sometime secretary, Leif Jones (later Lord Rhayader), her son Geoffrey Howard (1877-1935), and her son-in-law Charles H. Roberts (1865-1959), all of whom became MPs.[69] In 1903 Lady Carlisle replaced Lady Henry Somerset, a proponent of Lord Peel's Report, as president of the National British Women's Temperance Association.

The United Kingdom Alliance remained neutral with apparently a substantial majority for a time sympathetic toward Lord Peel's Report. Other than its president Sir Wilfrid Lawson, Lady Carlisle's faction, and most Good Templars, nearly all the well-known prohibitionists enthusiastically supported the report. Indeed Whittaker "only invited prominent pronounced U.K. Alliance men to sign" his Temperance Manifesto.[70] In a letter to one of these signatories, Canon Edward Lee Hicks, Lawson sadly acknowledged that "what has filled me with a surprise beyond my expression is that so many of my best friends should have left the 'solid basis' [of Local Veto and no compensation] and taken their stand on something else."[71] The Good Templar John Kempster bitterly regretted that the majority of the Alliance executive committee and most of the district superintendents backed the report (and he could have mentioned that the general secretary supported the report as well).[72] The veteran prohibitionist Dawson Burns accepted a seat on the executive committee of the new Board.[73] Lawson was pleased that the official test question that the Alliance sent to parliamentary candidates spoke only about the Veto and was silent about Lord Peel's Report. "Bravo! Resolution all right. Alliance attending to its own business and leaving humbugs to attend to theirs. It's a gleam of light in the darkness."[74] After the general election of 1900 the district superintendents with near unanimity reported that the rank-and-file members of the Alliance "strongly" favored Lord Peel's Report, although with the important condition that the Veto supplement it.[75] In 1901, Lawson said: "I do not see the wisdom of our grand old Prohibition body--the U.K.A., taking up the additional duty of regulating the liquor traffic, but I am in a minority on the point."[76]

Two features of Lord Peel's report condemned it in the eyes of those who rejected it: financial compensation for at least some license holders and postponement of Local Veto, for a stated number of years in the case of Scotland and Wales, indefinitely in the case of England and Ireland. The report also omitted compulsory Sunday closing for England. Probably the opponents most hated the compensation clauses because they appeared to them to establish a principle that created a legal vested interest in license renewal. For many reformers, compensation was an endowment of sin similar to compensation paid to slave-holders at the time of emancipation in 1833. For others, it was a practical barrier to license reduction and prohibition. Lawson denied that a scheme that contained any form of compensation could be called a compromise. In an analogy which he often repeated, he said that he was willing to take half a loaf or even less when he could not get an entire one, but only if it was composed of wholesome food and not if it were a poisonous mixture of chalk and sawdust blended with a little flour.[77] He would not be a party to legislative recognition of the principle of financial compensation on the pretense that only the trade paid the tax that furnished the money.[78] Local Veto, the other threatened shibboleth, had been the dream of the prohibitionists for more than a generation and the policy of the Liberal Party since the Newcastle Programme. To give the enemies of Local Veto in the Liberal Party a pretext to drop this commitment was unthinkable. It would be the abandonment of years of hard work in exchange for lesser reforms that had no guarantee of enactment.

In their rebuttal the advanced temperance friends of Lord Peel's report emphasized that they too disliked the provisions for compensation and the postponement of the Veto. The reporters claimed to be realists in advocating unity at the next general election aligned with moderate reformers. Whittaker had no illusion about reduction in numbers as a temperance panacea. He believed that "complete closing one day a week or for an hour or two earlier in the evening on all days" would reduce drinking more effectively.[79] If the Liberals triumphed and introduced a temperance bill based on the report, the advanced temperance men could then fight to amend the bill to make it a better one. If they failed, the enactment of a bill similar to Lord Peel's Report would still constitute a major step forward. At most one out of every seven electors was a prohibitionist, so it was a practical necessity to provide an electoral program acceptable to at least three of the non-prohibitionists. The disunity within the temperance movement threatened to destroy the possibility of any reform whatever.[80]

The bitterness of the attack on the report arose from the feeling among many ordinary prohibitionists of exploitation by Liberal politicians and by self-anointed temperance leaders. The North of England and the Celtic fringe were impatient with the lukewarm spirit of London and the Home Counties and irritated by the condescending skepticism of the metropolitan Liberal press and the Liberal front bench. The Liberal Party seemed to take the electoral zeal of the advanced temperance reformers for granted. Despite fiery platform rhetoric even the small band of MPs who claimed to represent them in Parliament commonly behaved as comfortable members of the club called compromise. As a token of this laxity prominent teetotalers served wine at their own tables to non-abstaining guests.[81] Many prohibitionists called for less compromise and not for more. For instance, E. Tennyson Smith, a Good Templar, organized the Temperance Ironsides in 1896 to urge the expulsion of drink sellers from church memberships.[82]

There was a throbbing resentment over the domination of a few rich men in a movement composed largely of the lower middle classes and workingmen, particularly when the financial patrons tried to force the movement into unacceptable compromises. Guy Hayler, a Good Templar and general secretary of the North of England Temperance League, was a staunch Radical whose father had been a Chartist and two of whose sons would be conscientious objectors during the First World War. He complained: "for some time past an effort has been made by this very small but wealthy section of the Temperance party to capture this movement and its advocates in support of methods directly opposed to the very principles and policies upon which the Temperance movement is founded." For Hayler, the chief villain was A.F. Hills, who in the name of temperance unity had done much to promote disunity.[83] Lord Peel's Report suspiciously resembled the old United Temperance Bill. Hayler looked on the manifesto published by the thirty prominent temperance men as further proof of the alienation of the alleged leadership from the rank-and-file and of a political deal between the Central Temperance Legislation Board and the Liberal Party.[84]

Savage attacks on themselves for their own moderation by extreme purists who refused to tarry for Local Veto and demanded national prohibition aggravated the anger and frustration of Vetoists who rejected Lord Peel's Report. A small national prohibition wing of the movement rejected the electoral pragmatism of support for friendly candidates of the major political parties and endorsed only its own ad hoc candidates. Good Templar dissidents in England organized the National Prohibition Party in 1899. The affiliated Scottish Prohibition Party followed in 1901 and after the First World War elected a member of the House of Commons, defeating Winston Churchill.[85] Still other Good Templars were active in the National Independent Temperance Party, formed in 1905, which supported major party candidates as well as its own.[86] The agitation by these mostly Good Templar splinter groups made it very difficult for the Good Templar leadership to accept the report or to mute its opposition.

The most dramatic expression of the conflict within the advanced temperance party was provided when the Scottish Good Templars, led by their grand secretary Tom Honeyman, a former railroad engineer, opposed W.S. Caine's candidacy in the West of Scotland constituency of Kilmarnock Burghs. For half a century this veteran prohibitionist had spent his time and money on a broad spectrum of Nonconformist, Indian reform, and temperance activities. In 1898 the Liberals of Kilmarnock Burghs adopted Caine as their candidate. In the beginning of 1900 as a signatory of the manifesto, Caine found himself treated as a traitor to the prohibitionist cause. On 3 February a special session of the grand lodge of Scotland met at Kilmarnock and passed a resolution that declared that "only such Parliamentary candidates as favour an immediate Veto, and are opposed to compensation, will receive the Good Templar Order's support at the next election." The Scottish grand lodge circulated thousands of copies of a hostile tract, "Mr. Caine's Confession of Faith," in the constituency.[87]

Misunderstanding worsened the dispute. The proportion between the population and the maximum number of licensed premises allowed by Lord Peel's Report permitted an increase in licenses in Scotland; sometime this was misrepresented as compelling an increase.[88] Irritated, Caine assumed a more personal attack than had been intended. The Kilmarnock special grand lodge meeting had been scheduled before the Temperance Manifesto precipitated the crisis within the advanced reform ranks, and the Kilmarnock resolution was identical with that of others by Good Templars throughout Scotland.[89] A minority of Good Templars in fact favored Lord Peel's Report as an electoral program. Caine bitterly advised a body of such Good Templar friends, the Inverness and Black Isle Lodge, that the Grand Lodge pamphlets were "full of mis-statements, which can only be the result of ignorance and incapacity to understand the Royal Commission report." "You want to make a change in your Grand Lodge Executive. You appear to me to have extremely incompetent people in charge, and they are leading the Order into a bog."[90]

Caine already had decided to withdraw his candidacy. In a letter read at a meeting of the Kilmarnock Liberal Federation on 2 April 1900, he explained that "the Grand Lodge of Scottish Good Templars have taken up a most extra-ordinary and unexpected attitude toward my candidature." "They are flooding the constituency with personal attacks on myself, and I must either descend into an unseemly and acrimonious contest or withdraw altogether." He continued: "the declaration at the delegates' meeting of the 23rd [of March] by a member of the Kilmarnock Liberal Association who is also an officer of the Grand Lodge [J.B. King, assistant grand secretary], that he would be compelled to assume a hostile attitude towards my candidature, convinced me that the action of the Templar authorities were no idle threat."[91] Probably Caine's cool reception in Glasgow on 23 March when he addressed the Scottish Temperance League also influenced his decision.[92]

After the Liberal defeat in October 1900 at the general election the controversy over Lord Peel's Report for the time being lost its point, if not its edge. A wealthy executive council member and its treasurer, W.J. Crossley, sent his annual subscription of 500 guineas "to show there is no ill-feeling," but added he could not accept making the Veto a test question in the future when the Veto was not a politically realistic program. "I feel it unmanly to allow myself to be led any longer to give my time and money where my judgment tells me we are on wrong lines."[93] On 5 December 1900, at its general meeting the UKA agreed to disagree. With two or three dissenting voices it was resolved, on Whittaker's motion, "that this Council heartily welcomes the Report of the Minority of the Royal Commission on Licensing, and pledges itself to give the recommendations of the Report a cordial yet discriminating support, whilst reiterating the declaration that no legislation can be adequate which does not confer upon the people of the United Kingdom power to veto the grant or renewal of licenses for the sale of intoxicating liquor in their respective localities."[94] The underlying conflict was not dead, as indicated by an amendment, which received one vote, to omit from the resolution the word "cordial." It was merely "a kind of armed neutrality."[95] The dispute over policy eventually led to the practical secession from the Alliance of many supporters of Lord Peel's Report, including numerous substantial subscribers. In March 1901 the Alliance blamed its deficit of nearly £3,400 as partly the result of the conflict over Lord Peel's report.[96] Frustrated by what he considered a "policy of 'drift'," Whittaker declined to speak at public meetings held in conjunction with the annual Alliance conference.[97]

In two 1901 bye-elections local temperance people asked the Alliance to keep quiet to help the Liberal candidates. At Monmouth Boroughs the candidate "wished them not to show their hands," while at Bury the local temperance men also were anxious that the drink question not be prominent in the campaign.[98] This was painful advice for the Alliance to hear.

In the short run, Whittaker's strategy of 1899 had failed and had been destined to fail. Even if the Liberals and the temperance movement had rallied solidly behind Lord Peel's report, the war that broke out in South Africa in the autumn of 1899 would have thwarted their efforts. The war guaranteed the victory of the Salisbury Government in the Khaki election of 1900 and the postponement for half a decade of the return to power of the Liberals and their opportunity to legislate.[99]

Campbell-Bannerman considered as a temporary tactic Liberal support for the proposal offered by the bishops, legislation incorporating proposals that the Royal Commission majority and minority reports had in common. He told Gladstone:

> I had a talk last week with Harcourt about it: he is very reasonable. He suggested the Bishops' Resolution, moved by Whittaker. I think a less combative mover would be preferable .... I saw no trace of parental jealousy on account of Local Option.[100]

In the longer run, the strategy helped make reduction in numbers the central question in temperance politics. In 1901 the Central Temperance Legislation Board and its Scottish counterpart convened impressive public meetings in its behalf.[101] Lord Peel's report was the first compromise settlement to arouse widespread support among both moderates and many advanced temperance reformers. It remained the bedrock of Liberal policy in the Edwardian epoch, although Balfour's Licensing Act of 1904 forced acceptance of substantial money compensation to dispossessed pubs.

As Ian Packer reminds us, "temperance did not seem like an 'old' agenda to many Liberals in the 1900s, but one that was strikingly relevant." The Liberal Party added brewers to its "demonology as a privileged group who benefited at the public expense." "[T]he twin appeals to democracy and anti-elitism" targeted the brewer and not the humble publican.[102]

Notes

---

[1] *Times,* Nov. 1899, p. 7. Although this chapter draws on my article, "The Liberal Party and Lord Peel's Report," some of my judgments have changed. I am now more appreciative of Campbell-Bannerman's political realism and skeptical about Herbert Gladstone's.

[2] *Times*, 17 Jan. 1901, p. 10. In fact, Ritchie drafted a bill to enact points recommended by both the Royal Commission majority and minority. C.T. Ritchie, 30 Jan. 1901. Cab 37/56 (31 Jan. 1901). The Cabinet did not proceed with this bill.

[3] Rev. A. Haigh, in *Temperance Chronicle*, 16 Nov. 1900, p. 566.

[4] Iain Sharpe, review of Kenneth D. Brown, *The Unknown Gladstone: The Political Life of Herbert Gladstone, 1854-1930*, in *Reviews in History*, May 2018.

[5] "Outstanding" is the judgment of H.C.G. Matthew in the entry he wrote for the *Oxford Dictionary of National Biography*. Wright, "The British Liberal Party and the Liquor Question," p. 223, emphasizes the significance of Herbert Gladstone's appointment for his friends in the licensed trade. For a negative view about Herbert Gladstone as chief whip, see Francis Neilson, "The Land Values Movement in Great Britain," *American Journal of Economics and Sociology* 18 (April 1959): 225. Neilson (MP, 1910-1916) thought that Gladstone was dominated by his deputy

Richard Causton, later baron Southwark, who "had one idea ... and that was to find constituencies for men who were looking for knighthood."

[6] Charles Gold to Campbell-Bannerman, 14 April 1899. Gladstone to Campbell-Bannerman, 3 Sept. 1899. BL, Campbell-Bannerman papers. Misplaced catalog details. W.M. Crook to Gladstone, 6 Feb. 1904. BL, Herbert Gladstone papers, Add. Ms. 46024, f. 74.

[7] The phrase about Campbell-Bannerman's political realism was used in a different context by A. J. A. Morris in the *Oxford Dictionary of National Biography.*

[8] *Times*, 9 March 1899, p. 6. This speech worried the Good Templars. Grand Lodge of England, *Journal of Proceedings* (1899). pp. 30-31.

[9] Gladstone diary, 20 July 1899. BL, Herbert Gladstone papers, Add. Ms. 4683 f. 34. Gladstone had at least three other meetings with Whittaker (13, 31 July, 3 August 1899, fols. 30, 38, 40). Gladstone and Campbell-Bannerman met with E.N. Buxton on 15 May (fol. 11); Gladstone met with S.H. Whitbread, the Liberal brewer, on 8 August (fol. 42). The diary cited consists of abstracts of Gladstone's interviews as chief whip. At a meeting with Herbert Gladstone on 13 July 1899, Whittaker optimistically "hinted that Lawson would not stand in the way" of a settlement based on the minority report.

[10] Morley to Harcourt, 20 August. 1899. Bodleian, Harcourt Ms 32, f. 160.

[11] Campbell-Bannerman to Gladstone, 27 Aug. 1899. BL, Herbert Gladstone papers, Add. Ms. 45987 f. 14. On another occasion, Campbell-Bannerman described Whittaker, "excellent fellow as he is," as "too much of a combatant." Campbell-Bannerman to Harcourt, 23 Jan. 1901. Stanton Harcourt, Harcourt papers, uncatalogued when consulted. Other people described Whittaker as a no-nonsense Yorkshireman.

[12] Whittaker to Gladstone, 5 Nov. 1899; BL, Campbell-Bannerman to Gladstone, 14 Dec. 1899. BL, Herbert Gladstone papers, Add. Ms. 46057 ff, 206-11; Add. Ms. 45987 ff. 59-60. Campbell-Bannerman to Spencer, 19 Dec. 1899. Quoted in H.W. McCready, "Chief Whip and Party Funds: The Work of Herbert Gladstone in the Edwardian Liberal Party, 1899 to 1906," *Canadian Journal of History* 6 no. 3 (December 1971): 297. The letter from the Spencer archives is also quoted in the thesis by Wright, "The British Liberal Party and the Liquor Question," p. 294, where Campbell-Bannerman describes his "long conference" with Whittaker. (As Wright did not list the Spencer papers in his bibliography, he presumably got the material from McCready who was his thesis advisor.) Spencer preferred making the party's legislative priority the points where the Majority and Minority Reports agreed and then as much of Lord Peel's Report as practical. Spencer to Campbell-Bannerman, 10 Dec. 1899. BL, Campbell-Bannerman papers, Add. Ms. 41229, ff. 73-74.

[13] *Manchester Guardian*, 16 Nov. 1899, p. 9.

[14] Whittaker to Campbell-Bannerman, 17 Nov. 1899. BL, Campbell-Bannerman papers, Add. Ms. 41235 ff. 110-11.

[15] Campbell-Bannerman to Gladstone, 17 Nov. 1899. BJ, Campbell-Bannerman papers, Add. Ms. 41235 f. 142.

[16] Gutzke, *Protecting the Pub*, p. 133. Gutzke says that a time limit was the only kind of compensation that temperance reformers could accept.

[17] Gladstone to Campbell-Bannerman, 18 Nov. 1899. BL, Campbell-Bannerman

---

papers, Add. Ms. 41215 ff. 144-50. See also Gladstone diary, 17 Nov. 1899, for his meeting with Buxton. BL, Herbert Gladstone papers, Add. Ms. 46483 f. 49.

[18] Representatives of the societies that had supported the Central Temperance Evidence Board created the new Board. Several staunch prohibitionist organizations that initially had joined soon left because of reservations over the Minority Report: the United Kingtom Alliance, the National Temperance Federation, the Scottish Permissive Bill Association, the Good Templars, and the United Kingdom Band of Hope Union. *Temperance Chronicle*, 4 May 1900, pp. 216. The new Board was organized at the headquarters of the Central Temperance Legislation Board with E. Stafford Howard as chairman of its executive committee. He was active in the CETS and had been a member of the committee promoting the Westminster bill. A.F. Hills was treasurer. There were three honorary secretaries: John Hilton, parliamentary agent of the Alliance, Francis Fox, a Quaker who had helped promote the Westminster bill, and F. Eardley Wilmot, the CETS secretary. *Alliance News*, 12 Oct. 1899, p. 653. A.F. Harvey, CETS assistant secretary, was secretary (that is, salaried and not honorary) of the new Board. *Temperance Chronicle*, 15 Nov. 1899, p. 553. Harvey was in his late twenties. He continued as secretary through subsequent reorganizations. He was still general secretary of what was the Temperance Legislation League in the 1920s when the *Standard Encypedia of the Alcohol Problem* wrote its article about him. In 1898 Harvey was honorary secretary of the Special Sunday Closing Campaign, organized by A.F. Hills,

[19] *Times*, 22 Nov. 1899, p. 11.

[20] Malins wrote from Ceylon on 4 January 1900 to the executive in favor of the IOGT withdrawing from Central Board. *Good Templars' Watchword*, 5 Feb. 1900, p. 67.

[21] *Manchester Guardian*, 25 Nov. 1899, p. 5. This text seems more probable than that in the *Times*.

[22] *Times*, 7 Dec. 1899, p. 6; *48th Report of the Executive Committee of hte United Kingdom Alliance ... for the Year ending September 30th, 1900*, p. 13. The list of signatories included: W.S. Caine, H.J. Wilson MP, R.A. Allison MP, Thomas Burt MP, John Wilson MP (Durham), Robinson Souttar MP, John Colville MP, J. Herbert Roberts MP, John Wilson MP (Gowan), William Crosfield, Fred Maddison MP, Joshua Rowntree, David Lloyd George MP, Sam Woods MP, Dr. R. Spence Watson, the Rev. Charles Garrett, Alderman George White, Robert Cameron MP, F.A. Channing MP, the Rev. Dr. Alexander McLaren, Prebendary William Barker, the Rev. Dr. John Clifford, the Rev. C.F. Aked, J. Herbert Lewis MP, Alexander Guthrie, and Thomas P. Whittaker MP. According to his biographer, Caine was "largely responsible" for the manifesto. Newton, *W.S. Caine*, p. 285. The MPs Roberts and Lewis were his Welsh sons-in-law. In addition to the signatories, prominent supporters of the Gothenburg system included the Baptist ministers F.B. Meyer and John Clifford. Bebbington, *Nonconformist Conscience*, p, 49.

[23] Lawson to Campbell-Bannerman, 7 Dec. 1899. BL, Campbell-Bannerman papers, Add. Ms. 41235 ff. 130-33. T.P. Whittaker's father died late in 1899. Thomas Whittaker was a teetotal pioneer who had converted Lawson's father to total abstinence.

[24] West to Gladstone, 7 Dec. 1899. BL, Herbert Gladstone papers, Add. Ms. 46057

ff. 225-26.

[25] Asquith to Gladstone, 27 Nov. 1899. BL, Herbert Gladstone papers, Add. Ms. 46057 ff. 225-26.

[26] Spencer to Campbell-Bannerman, 10 Dec. 1899. BL, Campbell-Bannerman papers, Add. Ms. 41229 ff. 73-74. See also *Times*, 17 Dec. 1899, p. 2. Spencer's younger brother Lord Althorp had endorsed the principle of compensation if not from current public funds. C. Robert Spencer to Herbert Gladstone, 10 Aug. 1989. BL, Herbert Gladstone papers, Add. Ms. 46057, ff. 64-65.

[27] Campbell-Bannerman to Spencer, 19 Dec. 1899. Spencer papers. Quoted in Wright, "The British Liberal Party and the Liquor Question," p. 298.

[28] Gladstone to Campbell-Bannerman, 8 Dec. 1899. BL, Campbell-Bannerman papers, Add. Ms. 41215, ff. 158-61. The Gilbey firm served 2,374 agents in England (out of about 7,700 off-licenses). *Licensing World*, 16 May 1897, p. 317. In 1886 the National Federation of Off-Licensed Holders' Association was organized with a Gilbey partner as president. By 1900 it had about 12,000 members. Gutzke, *Protecting the Pub*, p. 137.

[29] Campbell-Bannerman to Gladstone, 9 Dec. 1899. BL, Campbell-Bannerman papers, Add. Ms. 41215 ff. 165-67.

[30] Bryce to Campbell-Bannerman, 16 Dec. 1899. BL, Campbell-Bannerman papers, Add. Ms. 41211 ff. 75-76.

[31] Gladstone to Campbell-Bannerman, 12 Dec. 1899. BL, Campbell-Bannerman papers, Add. Ms. 41215 ff. 169-72. Gladstone's emphasis. Gladstone spoke with Whittaker on 7 December. BL, Herbert Gladstone papers, Add. Ms. 46483 f. 53.

[32] Campbell-Bannerman to Gladstone, 14 Dec. 1899. BL, Campbell-Bannerman papers, Add. Ms. 41215 ff. 178-79.

[33] Wodehouse to Gladstone, 16 Dec. 1899. BL, Herbert Gladstone papers, Add. Ms. 46057 ff. 232-35.

[34] Gladstone to Campbell-Bannerman, 18 Dec. 1899. BL, Campbell-Bannerman papers, Add. Ms. 41215 f. 185. Gladstone's emphasis.

[35] Gladstone diary, 18 Dec. 1899. BL, Herbert Gladstone papers, Add. Ms. 46483 f. 55.

[36] Kimberley to Campbell-Bannerman, 17 Dec. 1899. BL, Campbell-Bannerman papers, Add. Ms. 41221 ff. 180-81.

[37] Spencer to Campbell-Bannerman, 15 Dec. 1899. BL, Campbell-Bannerman papers, Add. Ms. 41229 ff. 75-76.

[38] *Times*, 20 Dec. 1899, p. 6. The press did not appear interested. Asquith complained that although he had spoken on the same lines as had Campbell-Bannerman at Aberdeen, "not a syllable of what I said [on temperance] has been reported." Asquith to Campbell-Bannerman, 20 Dec. 1899. BL, Campbell-Bannerman papers, Add. Ms. 41210, f. 180.

[39] Lawson to Campbell-Bannerman, 20 Dec, 1899; BL, Campbell-Bannerman to Gladstone, 21 Dec. 1899; Campbell-Bannerman to Lawson, 21 Dec. 1899. BL, Campbell-Bannerman papers, Add. Ms. 41235, ff. 152-56; Add. Ms 41215 ff 186-87, Add. Ms. 41235 ff. 157-59.

[40] Gladstone to Campbell-Bannerman, 22, 23 Dec. 1899. BL, Campbell-Bannerman papers, Add. Ms. 41215 ff. 188-89.

[41] Campbell-Bannerman to Spencer, 12 Dec. 1899. Quoted in Hamer, *Liberal Politics in the Age of Gladstone and Rosebery*, p. 21 n. 1. Campbell-Bannerman's emphasis. See also Campbell-Bannerman to Spencer, 19 Dec. 1899. Quoted in McCready, "Chief Whip and Party Funds," p. 397.

[42] Campbell-Bannerman to Spencer, 19 Dec. 1899. Quoted in Wright, "The British Liberal Party and the Liquor Question," pp. 329-30.

[43] The subsequent development of Gladstone's position on compensation can be traced in his 18 September 1900, declaration to this West Leeds constituents that "subject to the compensation coming out of the trade and consumers, I am ready to say it should be full compensation to those who are dispossessed by public authority." *Leeds Mercury*, 19 Sept. 1900, p. 3. Still later, on 16 January 1901, Gladstone was a member of the deputation that urged the Unionist Home Secretary to consider a series of licensing reforms including "equitable compensation." *Times*, 17 Jan. 1901, p. 10.

[44] "Until at least 1880 JR [Joseph Rowntree] does not appear to have been a teetotaller, though his consumption of alcohol was very moderate. At Yorkshire Quarterly Meeting in 1889 he countered Friends who claimed that poverty was due solely to 'the drink', but he came to suspect that it was a contributory cause and, with Arthur Sherwell, set out to discover some hard facts; these found expression in the temperance problem and social reform (1899), a book which ran through an enviable number of editions." http://www.rowntreesociety.org.uk/joseph-rowntree-1836-1925.

[45] *Temperance Chronicle*, 3 July 1904, p. 336.

[46] National Liberal Federation, *Proceedings* (1900), p. 84.

[47] Gladstone diary, 31 Jan., 1 Aug. 1900; Buxton to Gladstone, 9 Oct. 1901. BL, Herbert Gladstone papers, Add. Ms. 46483 ff. 58, 76, Add. Ms. 469507 f. 130. The trade remained neutral in Gladstone's own constituency during the 1900 general election.

[48] *Licensed Trade News*, 10 Feb. 1900, p. 11. I have modified what I said in my 1971 article after reading Gutzke, *Protecting the Pub*, p. 134.

[49] Gutzke, *Protecting the Pub*, p.141.

[50] Gutzke, *Protecting the Pub*, pp. 145-47.

[51] Quoted in *Leeds Mercury*, 19 Sept. 1900, p. 3.

[52] For the leadership, see E. Stafford Howard, *Why the Church of England Temperance Society Supports Lord Peel's Report* (CETS, 1901); E. S. Stafford to F. Eardley-Wilmot, n.d., Eardley-Wilmot to Randall Davidson, 10 July 1900. Davidson Papers, Lambeth Palace. I owe these references to Greenaway, *Drink and British Politics*, pp. 229-30. The rank and file of the CETS may not have shared the enthusiasm of the leadership for Lord Peel's Report.

[53] Hills' National United Temperance Council was not dead. In June 1905 it issued a new program that included a five-year period when licenses would be renewed except in cases of misbehavior and a form of Local Veto, first for new licenses only during the five-year time limit and then for all licenses.

[54] *Times*, 22 Nov. 1899, p. 11.

[55] Peel at Dundee, 1 Oct. 1901. *Alliance News*, 10 Oct. 1901, p. 642.

[56] Peel at the conference of the Ely Diocesan Temperance Society, Cambridge, 1

March 1900. *Abstainers' Advocate*, April 1900, p. 43.

[57] Whittaker, "The Lessons Taught by Legislation for the Promotion of Temperance," in J.T. Rae, ed., *The World's Temperance Congress of 1900* (n.d.), pp. 287, 291.

[58] For the older Whittaker, see Janette Lisa Martin, "Popular Political Oratory and Itinerant Lecturing in Yorkshire and the North East in the Age of Chartism, 1837-60" (Ph.D. thesis, University of York, 2010).

[59] Transcript, *North Wales Observer*, 19 Jan. 1900 ("Notes of the Week" column). Beaverbook Library, Lloyd George papers A/9/2/3. Now at House of Lords Record Office.

[60] Quoted in *Temperance Witness*, March 1900, in an article by Guy Hayler, "The Present Crisis." Hayler supported Lawson's position on Lord Peel's Report and disagreed with those who diminished Lawson's importance. John Kempster, the editor of the newspaper published by the Grand Lodge of England and its Grand Electoral Superintendent, was another outspoken critic of the Peel Report. In contrast, the Alliance general secretary James Whyte appears to have been sympathetic to Lord Peel's Report. See the interview with him in the *Western Daily Mercury*, 24 March 1900, reprinted in *Temperance Chronicle*, 6 April 1900, p. 159.

[61] Lawson to Harcourt, 5 Aug. 1900. Harcourt papers, uncatalogued when consulted at Stanton Harcourt. Later he told the Alliance executive council "I do not see the wisdom of our grand old Prohibitory body--the U.K.A., taking up the additional duty of regulating the liquor traffic, but I am in a minority on the point." Lawson to McDougall, 18 Jan. 1901, in Alliance minutes 23 Jan. 1901.

[62] Other less important societies rejected the Peel minority report. For instance, the North of England Temperance League voted unanimously against it (6 January 1900). *Temperance Witness*, March 1900.

[63] Kempster to editor, 6 Nov. 1899, in *Alliance News*, 9 Nov. 1899, p. 1899; Kempster, "Twenty-One Reflections upon the Minority Report," (Glasgow) *Good Templar*, Supplement (January 1900), p. ii; Kempster, "The Compensation Scheme," (Glasgow) *Good Templar*, Supplement (January 1900), pp. ii-iv.

[64] J. M. Skinner, "The Position of the Grand Lodge of England," (Glasgow) *Good Templar*, Supplement (January 1900), p. iv; *Good Templars'Watchword*, 26 April 1900, pp. 259-60.

[65] J.H. Musk, in *Good Templars' Watchword*, 22 April 1901, p. 183. See also Musk in *Good Templars' Watchword*, 26 April 1900, p. 259.

[66] Malins to A.F. Harvey, 20 May 1899, in *Good Templars' Watchword*, 7 May 1900, p. 223.

[67] *Alliance News*, 26 April 1900, pp. 259-60; *Temperance Witness*, March 1900, pp. 2-3; *Good Templar's Watchword*, 22 April 1901, p. 183; Malins to A.F. Harvey, 20 May 1899, and Malins to a friend, n.d., in *Good Templars' Watchword*, 7 May 1900, p. 223.

[68] David M. Fahey wrote the *Oxford Dictionary of National Biography* entry for Rosalind Frances (born Stanley) Howard, Countess of Carlisle (1845-1921). She was president of the National British Women's Temperance Association from 1903 until her death. In 1892 she became the first woman elected president of the North of England Temperance League.

---

[69] In his parliamentary campaign in 1900, Roberts kept aloof from the Veto. "I considered it was tactically wiser during the contest to fight the other side not specifically on the Veto, but on the broader question" of Tory failures to do anything for temperance. Roberts to Whyte, 9 Oct. 1900, in Alliance minutes, 10 Oct. 1900.

[70] Whittaker to Campbell-Bannerman, 9 Dec. 1899. BL, Campbell-Bannerman papers, Add. Ms. 41235 f. 135.

[71] Lawson to Hicks, 2 Nov. 1900. Quoted in Fowler, *Life and Letters of Edward Lee Hicks*, pp. 196-97.

[72] Kempster to Whyte, 9 April 1900, in Alliance minutes, 11 April 1900. Kempster specified John Hilton, parliamentary agent, and John Newton, a district agent (later Caine's biographer). The general secretary James Whyte himself favored Lord Peel's Report, despite its compensation proposals. Whyte, interviewed in *Western Daily Mercury*, 24 March 1900. Cited in *Temperance Chronicle*, 6 April 1900, p. 159. The Alliance executive committee thought that Lawson and his supporters were being unrealistic. A memorandum labeled private asked: "Is Harcourt's Bill really alive in the minds of Temperance Reformers, or in the minds of Politicians?" Alliance minutes, 20 June 1900.

[73] Burns to editor, 11 Nov. 1899, in *Alliance News*, 16 Nov. 1899, p. 755. Perhaps being sidelined by the Alliance affected Burns' decision. As a result of his perceived involvement in his brother-in-law's Liberator scandal, he was not proposed as a Royal Commission witness, and he was ousted from his position as superintendent of the Alliance's London auxiliary.

[74] Lawson to Whyte, 27 Sept. 1900 in Alliance minutes, 3 Oct. 1900.

[75] Joint meeting of the executive committee and the district superintendents, 3 Dec. 1900, in Alliance minutes, 3 Dec. 1900.

[76] Lawson to McDougall, 18 Jan. 1901. Alliance minutes, 23 Jan. 1901.

[77] Lawson to the editor of the *Manchester Guardian*, 11 Aug. 1900. Reprinted in *Alliance News*, 6 Aug. 1900, p. 520.

[78] Lawson at the Metropolitan Templar Federation on 10 August 1900. *Alliance News*, 16 Aug. 1900, p. 518.

[79] Whittaker, "The Lessons Taught by Legislation for the Promotion of Temperance." Whittaker's recommendation that shortening hours be a major method of obtaining temperance anticipated World War I policy.

[80] Caine to the editor, 15 Feb. 1900. *Alliance News*, 22 Feb. 1900, p. 115. Caine and John Colville, MP, at the Scottish Temperance League, Glasgow, 23 March 1900. *League Journal*, 31 March 1900, p. 196.

[81] For instance, see the criticism of A. Cameron Corbett, MP, president of the Scottish Permissive Bill and Temperance Association, for serving wine to his non-abstaining guests. *Prohibitionist*, April 1906, p. 18. Apparently, Lawson had served drink at his home for many years after he had introduced the Permissive Prohibitory Bill. See *Parl. Deb.*, 3rd ser., CCXXXII (14 March 1877), col. 161; Lawson to editor, 13 Aug. 1886, in *Times*, [day?], Aug 1886; Lawson to Harcourt, 24 Nov. 1897, Harcourt papers, uncatalogued when consulted. Inviting Harcourt to his home in Cumberland, Lawson added the caution, "the establishment NOW conducted on strictly Temperance lines." Lawson's emphasis. The Countess of Carlisle served wine to her guests until 1903 when she was elected president of the National British

Women's Temperance Association. Lady Dorothy Henley (Lady Carlisle' daughter), *Rosalind Howard* (Hogarth Press, 1958), p. 109; Joseph Malins in *White Ribbon*, Oct. 1921, p. 151. Lady Dorothy Henley had married a brewer in 1913.

[82] For Smith, see his memoirs, *From Memory's Storehouse* (London, [1925]). Tennyson Smith (1850-1925) worked for temperance in Australia and New Zealand as well as in Britain. In 1896 he founded the *Temperance World and Prohibition Herald*. Ironically, even stricter prohibitionists attacked him as too indulgent toward the Liberals.

[83] It must have been painful for prohibitionists to see Hills hire activists from their own ranks. For instance, after serving the Alliance for upwards of thirty years, its Rochdale district agent resigned to take an appointment with the United National Temperance Council in London. Scholfield to McDougall, undated, in Alliance minutes, 1 May 1901. It was hard for the Alliance to break with Hills completely, because he was a generous contributor. In 1901 he claimed to be financially embarrassed because the South African war had prevented him from being paid for a railroad that he was building in the Cape Colony, but he still sent the Alliance a subscription for £250.

[84] Guy Hayler, "The Present Crisis," *Temperance Witness*, March 1900, pp. 4-5. About Hayler, see "Temperance Internationalism: Guy Hayler and the World Prohibition Federation," *Social History of Alcohol and Drugs* 20 no. 2 (Spring 2006). The article need correction on one point. The source of Hayler's independent income from the early 1900s was an inheritance received by his wife.

[85] The Scottish Prohibition Party was founded in Dundee by fifty Good Templars and their friends. W.M. Walker, "The Scottish Prohibition Party and the Millennium," *International Review of Social History* 13 (1973): 359. See also *Prohibitionist*, March 1904, p. 7; May 1904, pp. 17-18.

[86] *Prohibitionist*, June 1905, pp. 50-51.

[87] *Good Templar*, May 1900, Supplement, p. 1. Includes Caine's letter to his election agent that explained his withdrawal. The tract also appeared as an article in the *Good Templar*, April 1900, pp. 54-55, over the initials of the office of Past Grand Chief Templar. A letter critical of Caine by James Winning, published in the *Alliance News*, 10 Oct. 1901, p. 643, led to an angry and frustrated letter to Alliance secretary Whyte by the Baptist minister Charles F. Aked. Aked to Whyte, 19 Oct. 1901, in *Alliance News*, 30 Oct. 1901. Aked argued: "harm is being done by allowing the Alliance News to be used as it has been used for some considerable time now." For Aked, see Karen E. Smith, "Charles Frederic Aked (1864-1941): 'A Fighting Parson' for Social Reform," *Baptist Quarterly* 50 no. 1 (2019).

[88] Caine at the Scottish Temperance League, Glasgow, March 23,1900; *League Journal*, 31 March 1900, p. 195.

[89] Honeyman to the editor, 3 March 1900. *Alliance News*, 8 March 1900, p. 148.

[90] Caine to George Young, district electoral superintendent, 26 March 1900. *Highland News*, as quoted in *League Journal*, 7 April 1900, p. 217. Caine's opposition to the South African war contributed to his decision to withdraw. *North British Daily Mail*, 30 March 1900, p. 4. See also "The Withdrawal of Mr. W.S. Caine from the Kilmarnock Burghs," (Glasgow) *Good Templar*, Supplement (May 1900), pp. 1-2; "Mr. Caine's Withdrawal" [letter by R. Semple], (Glasgow*) Good*

Templar, Supplement (May 1900), p. 2. Unhappy with Caine, Semple sneered about "the many kaleidoscopic changes of his public life. Finally, see "Mr. W.S. Caine and the Executive," (Glasgow) *Good Templar,* Supplement (July 1900), pp. 13-14.

[91] Caine to secretary of the Kilmarnock Burghs' Liberal association, n.d., quoted in *Alliance News*, 5 April 1900, p. 216; Caine to James Wyllie, n.d. *Kilmarnock Standard*, 7 April 1900, p. 5. Caine's replacement as Liberal candidate, Dr. A. Rolland Rainy, with difficulty got Templar support. He told his father, Principal Rainy (28 Sept.1900), "all but the impossible temperance people are with me." Mrs. A. [Annabella Matheson] Rainy, *Life of Adam Rainy, M.P.* (James Maclehose & Sons, 1915), p. 179. Rainy lost the 1900 election but was victorious at the Liberal landslide in 1906.

[92] *League Journal*, 23 March, 1900; 31 March 1900, pp. 194-203; 7 April 1900, p. 217. Speaking with Caine in favor of Lord Peel's Report, were John Colville, MP, Prof. Murdoch Cameron, MD, and the Rev. George Gladstone (1842-1910). The *League Journal*, organ of the Scottish Temperance League, endorsed Lord Peel's Eeport on 7 April 1900 (p. 216). Caine did not lack allies in Scotland.

[93] Crossley to Whyte, 1 Nov. 1900 in Alliance minutes, 7 Nov. 1900. This single subscription constituted about five percent of the total Alliance income. Did Crossley get what he wanted? The printed text of general council resolutions, 5 December 1900, included a clause that does not appear in the final text that appeared in the *Alliance News*: "and, further, resolves that the policy to be adopted at Parliamentary elections be left to the judgment of the Executive [committee]--to deal with each case on its own merits." Alliance minutes, 28 Nov. 1900. Although generous toward the Alliance, Crossley was in a position to do more if he had wanted. Earlier in 1900, Crossley gave £60,000 to construct a new building for the Manchester Consumption Hospital. Crossley was the chairman of its board. *Alliance News*, 5 April 1900, p. 218.

[94]-*Alliance News*, 7 Dec. 1900, p. 779. Whittaker pointed out the hollowness of Lawson's claim that the Alliance always stayed clear of licensing reform. Lawson himself favored legislation to tighten the restrictions on the sale of alcohol to children.

[95] Newton, *W.S. Caine*, p. 299. See also *Alliance News*, 7 Dec. 1900.

[96] On the Alliance's financial difficulties being partly the result of the conflict over policy, see Alliance minutes, 27 March 1901. The Alliance experienced an overdraft of nearly £3,400. It forced staff reductions and diversion of energy to fund raising such as a great bazaar in 1903. Two district agents (Scholfield and Brambley) who did not collect enough subscriptions to pay their salaries and expenses were dismissed.

[97] Whittaker to Whyte, 16 Aug. 1901. Alliance minutes, 16 Aug. 1901.

[98] J. Tertius Phillips to Whyte, 13 April 1901; J.H. Musk to Whyte, 30 April 1901, in Alliance minutes, 17 and 30 April 1901.

[99] In 1901 Caine unsuccessfully entreated Chamberlain to support legislation to increase the power of the licensing magistrates, "avoiding such controversies as compensation and compulsory reduction." Caine hoped that Chamberlain recognized "the width and depth of strong Temperance sentiment prevailing in the

ranks of the Unionist party." Caine to Chamberlain, 7 Nov. 1901. University of Birmingham, Joseph Chamberlain papers, JC 11/39/17.

[100] Campbell-Bannerman to Gladstone, 4 Feb. 1901. BL, Campbell-Bannerman papers, Add. Ms. 41216, f. 78.

[101] *Alliance News*, 14 Feb. 1901, pp. 105-07; *Temperance Chronicle*, 15 Feb. 1901, pp. 78-81; Scottish Temperance Legislation Board, *Legislative Temperance Reform for Scotland, Lord Peel's Proposals* (Edinburgh, 1901). Queen Victoria's death forced the postponement of these meetings at Manchester and Edinburgh after they had been earlier postponed because of the ill-health and family bereavement of Lord Peel. The Edinburgh meeting was matched by a Vetoist meeting at Glasgow.

[102] Ian Packer, *Liberal Government and Politics, 1905-15* (Palgrave Macmillan, 2006), p. 112. See also Packer's article, "Religion and the New Liberalism: The Rowntree Family. Quakerism, and Social Reform," *Journal of British Studies* 42 no. 2 (April 2003): 236-57.

CHAPTER SEVEN

THE RISE OF DISINTERESTED MANAGEMENT

In the 1890s and the early 1900s there was a revival of interest in the Gothenburg Scheme, sometimes called disinterested management.[1] There were many variants on the Gothenburg Scheme. Its core principle was to eliminate or drastically reduce private profit from the retail sale of drink under a system of local control. All versions drew strength from a belief that a new policy was needed. Why? to free the country from the parliamentary deadlock over temperance, the apparent failure of the prohibition agitation, dissatisfaction with reduction in numbers and regulation as an adequate remedy, a resentment over the irrationality of the State bestowing huge economic advantages on private persons through the grant of licenses, and, most important, a conviction that drinking was too entwined with working class social habits for entirely negative legislation to end intemperance. The Gothenburgers hoped to undermine the drink habit by reforming the public house with the help of temperance-minded managers while at the same time offering an alternative non-alcoholic social life. Most Gothenburgers believed that effective temperance reform could come only after the destruction of the political and financial power of the drink trade.

In the last years of the century the Gothenburg principle reemerged from the obscurity in which it had languished since 1877 when Joseph Chamberlain had decided that it was impracticable to fight for it.[2] Beginning in the early 1890s the Bishop of Chester, Dr. Frederick Jayne, familiarized the educated public with the Gothenburg idea.[3] He wanted to raise the public house from a mere drinking den to a status comparable to the old coaching inn, comfortable, wholesome, and attractive. Philanthropic investors would receive only a small fixed return on their capital in licensed property, publicans would receive a salary unrelated to drink sales and also receive most of the profits from food and non-alcoholic drinks. Dr. Jayne's Gothenburg houses would accept a variety of reforms such as shortened hours that the commercial drink trade would resist to protect profits. The bishop's Gothenburg houses would provide newspapers, games, music, and temperance drinks. They would be more than a place to consume alcohol.[4]

In addition to writing letters to the *Times*, magazine articles and pamphlets, the bishop organized a series of conferences to which he invited prominent sympathizers. Early in 1894 Chamberlain reaffirmed his support for the Gothenburg principle at a well-publicized meeting held at Grosvenor House, the London mansion of the Duke of Westminster.[5] Later in the year a large conference in Aberdeen heard Dr. Jayne read a letter from William Gladstone in which the former Prime Minister declared that the Gothenburg principle offered "the sole chance of escape" from widespread intemperance.[6] In the same letter Gladstone described local option as "no more than a partial and occasional remedy." He added: "the mere limitation of numbers ... is little better than an imposture."

Harcourt's son Lulu complained: "Mr. G. has practically thrown himself into the arms of Chamberlain on this question ... but the financial aspects of the Gothenburg system make it impossible."[7] Harcourt himself said: "Mr. G has managed to make what seems to me a fatal mess of the temperance question." He asked: "Does anybody believe that the real temperance people are going to accept a State traffic in drink *a la Gothenburg*."[8]

To the further embarrassment of Liberal leaders and prohibitionists, Gladstone also sent a letter of support to another Gothenburg conference held in Chester in 1895.[9] He doubted the sufficiency of Local Veto. In a letter to Alderman Snape he also said that he had "a poor opinion" of a reduction in the number of licensed premises as a solution to the drink problem. He regretted the failure to give "free trade" in licenses "a fair trial." He was one of the last defenders of "free trade" in drink licenses.[10]

Unfortunately for Dr. Jayne nothing resembling a popular movement rallied to his side, no political party took up his case, and no leading politician lent active support. Chamberlain gave only a few kind words, as did the retired Gladstone. Gothenburg appeared politically unprofitable. Chamberlain did say he would like to see an experiment in a town or district with 50,000 inhabitants.[11] In an interview published in the *Westminster Gazette* the prohibitionist T.P. Whittaker said he had no objection to an experiment "subject to the proviso that no backward step be permitted." He also had no objection to licensing reform as long as there was no compensation from public funds.[12] Somewhat surprisingly, the Liberal brewer E.N. Buxton said he had no personal objection to a small-scale experiment on the lines of the Bishop of Chester's proposals to which he added a caution, "under reasonable conditions."[13]

The Bishop of Chester struggled on. In 1893 he introduced the Authorized Companies bill in the House of Lords. Like most moderate reform proposals, it included reforms such as reduction in numbers and excluded Local Veto, but unlike the others his would have permitted the licensing justices to experiment with grants of local license monopolies to non-commercial regulated companies. The Authorized Companies bill attracted even less attention than did the Manchester and Westminster bills, which were introduced in the House of Commons and which emphasized reduction in numbers and the United Temperance bill, which was debated out-of-doors as a basis for a compromise between moderate reductionists and advanced Vetoists, and much less attention than the Government bills introduced by the Liberal ministry in 1893 and 1895.

With legislation unlikely, the Gothenburgers sought another route. In 1896 the Bishop of Chester created the People's Refreshment House Company in association with Major (later Lt. Colonel) H.J. Crauford who had experience in the management of military canteens.[14] The Association managed a small number of public houses to provide practical evidence for non-commercial management as a method of temperance reform. The bishop's objective was "reform rather than abolition." A few years later a larger, like-minded movement, Lord Grey's various companies, swallowed up Dr. Jayne's organization.

British Gothenburg experiments multiplied after the conversion of Lord Grey (1851-1917). In 1899 residents of a district of Northumberland where he was the principal landowner asked him to obtain a new public house for their convenience. After the licensing justices granted Lord Grey a license, a brewer offered him ten thousand pounds for the newly licensed house, a dramatic proof of the monopoly value that the licensing authorities had gratuitously awarded. Shocked, Grey decided that the search for large profits in the commercial sale of drink had aggravated intemperance. As Lord Lieutenant, he wrote the licensing justices of Northumberland on 6 September 1900, to recommend non-commercial management of the retail sale of drink. The letter was published in the *Times*.

In the next year Lord Grey organized a trust house company in Northumberland that acquired public houses to be run on Gothenburg lines.[15] Scornful of ordinary temperance societies, the *Financial Times* (1 June 1901) praised Lord Grey's trust house. "The idea strikes us as an excellent one."[16] Under his inspiration autonomous public house trust companies sprang up in other counties and a few large towns with the support of other landed aristocrats, Anglican bishops, and Unionist politicians. It also obtained the support of intellectuals such as the economist Alfred Marshall. Lord Grey himself was a Liberal Unionist. The refusal of the Unionist Government to legislate based on the reports that the Royal Commission on the Liquor Licensing Laws submitted in 1899 stimulated this non-statutory approach to reform. Lord Grey's version of the

Gothenburg principle required no legislation. It needed only the leadership of public-spirited men of means. Privately, some leaders of the trust house movement described the no legislation approach as a temporary tactic and expected parliamentary support after the trust houses had proved themselves.

Within a half dozen years there were almost forty public house trust companies which controlled more than 200 licensed houses. After a brief period of friction, the Bishop of Chester's organization became affiliated with Lord Grey's, with the older society providing managerial expertise. A Central Trust House Association, founded in 1901, acted as a national propaganda organization.[17] After Lord Grey became Governor General of Canada in 1904, the young Lord Lytton stood in as leader of this phase of the Gothenburg movement.

Unlike other Gothenburgers the trust house supporters asked for no monopoly in the sale of drink. They offended their fellow Gothenburgers by applying for the grant of new licenses and by seeking to make the trust houses attractive places for people to spend their leisure, thus tempting them to frequent public houses when they might otherwise have stayed outside. Trust house Gothenburgers belonged to local and sometimes to national elites, generally supported Unionist parties and included few teetotalers or veteran temperance reformers.[18] Rarely located in the large towns and cities where the problem of intemperance loomed the largest, the trust houses consisted mainly of isolated rural public houses and small country hotels. Although the trust houses sought to make their pubs attractive, they did not emphasize this in order not to offend more temperance-minded Gothenburgers.[19]

The Bishop of Chester, Lord Grey, and their adherents demonstrated that the Gothenburg principle had appeal beyond the ranks of ordinary temperance activists and that the Gothenburg principle was compatible with very different definitions of the drink evil. The bishop and the peer wanted to civilize the public house. They did not despise it as a necessary evil, although Dr. Jayne wanted to encourage non-alcoholic refreshments. Although widely respected, the Bishop of Chester, Lord Grey, and their Unionist friends lacked weight in national politics. They were too few to count on a controversial question. Their trust house proved unprofitable and unable to provide funds for public purposes. Lord Grey's original Northumberland trust scheme went into liquidation in 1923.[20]

The main body of Gothenburgers or at least their leaders had deeper roots in the temperance movement. Teetotalers who wanted ultimately to eliminate the drinking of alcoholic beverages shaped their thinking. This version of the Gothenburg principle became important in public debate from

1899 when Joseph Rowntree, a Quaker chocolate manufacturer, and Arthur Sherwell, a Wesleyan social reformer, published *The Temperance Problem and Social Reform*.[21] This massive volume of over 700 pages, fact-filled and irenic in spirit, went through nine printings in two years and became one of the most influential books in the history of the British temperance agitation.[22] For instance, Gladstone's Liberal Unionist nephew Alfred Lyttelton told his wife that he was "tremendously impressed" and hoped that "the wisdom of these wise men touches the vast body of fanatics and sillys, who make up so much of the temperance party."[23]

The *Daily Chronicle*, a Liberal newspaper, argued on April 14, 1899: "Local Veto and Prohibition are discredited." The newspaper called for an educational campaign based on Rowntree and Sherwell with the objective of reforming the public house, the place where the working class met for social intercourse. It was not enough to reduce the number of public houses. "The only road to reform seems to us to lie in the transfer to the public authorities of the public-houses themselves, to be conducted under the public supervision." Rowntree and Sherwell advocated the reformed public house as part of rational recreation for the working class and the source of funds for other kinds of rational recreation.

The Labour politician J. Keir Hardie characterized *The Temperance Problem and Social Reform* as "the beginning of a new epoch of the temperance movement."[24] For the first time, drink and temperance reform were placed firmly in the context of general social reform. Previous temperance reformers simply had blamed social ills on drink to justify the priority that they claimed for temperance legislation. A few socialists and social reformers had spoken out in favor of municipalization of the sale of drink like all monopolies. For instance, the Independent Labour Party in 1895, a Fabian tract in 1898, and the book by the Fabian E.R. Pease in 1904 had sought to eliminate profit-based public houses. But these socialist proposals had not been rooted in careful research and analysis. They were merely ideologically justified opinions.[25] In contrast, Rowntree and Sherwell assembled a huge body of data and built a persuasive fact-based case. It can be associated with the so-called New Liberalism of the late 1800s and early 1900s.[26]

What was unique about Rowntree and Sherwell is that they were both part of the traditional, teetotal temperance movement—insisting that the test of a scheme of temperance reform was its ability to make "a considerable reduction in the national consumption of alcohol" and also part of the turn-of-the-century social efficiency reform movement that argued that the problem was not just drinking in itself but the impact on family income and the danger to physical and mental efficiency "in the industrial competition of nations."[27]

Rowntree and Sherwell argued for a complex interrelationship between intemperance and social ills afflicting the working class, with cause and effect impossible to separate neatly. They tried to answer in some detail the question "why do men drink?" They were not content to invoke moral weakness and temptation. Avoiding polemical rhetoric, Rowntree and Sherwell marshaled masses of official statistics, quotations from experts, and detailed observations from their own investigations in Britain and overseas. They earned a reputation for scholarly thoroughness and scientific objectivity rare among writers on temperance, and they stimulated readers with their cautious optimism. They did not consider temperance a panacea for all social ills or legislation a sufficient solution to the problem of drink. But they did believe that legislation was indispensable and that to succeed it had to respond to the needs that the beer shop and the public house had served. Only by raising the character of the working population could social reform succeed. For Rowntree and Sherwell the major problem that had not been solved in any English-speaking country was that of drink in the big towns. They looked to Scandinavia for the answer or rather for the principle that was the basis for the answer.

Rowntree and Sherwell had no confidence in a policy that simply repeated the traditional temperance programs, whether of education or of legislation to restrict drinking places. Despite changing attitudes toward drinking by the churches, by the medical profession, and other elites, *"the per capita consumption of alcohol in the United Kingdom is greater* [in 1899] *than it was in 1840,* when the Temperance reform was in its infancy," with a peak in 1876 and after a decline for a few years, a rise again in the 1890s.[28] Like everyone interested in temperance, Rowntree and Sherwell favored a reduction in the number of licensed houses, but they did not see such a reduction in itself as having any radical impact on intemperance. Scotland had a much lower density of public houses than England and Wales but a worse reputation for heavy drinking. Rowntree and Sherwell begrudgingly acknowledged that since Local Veto "enlists the enthusiastic support of a large majority of the Temperance party, [it] must necessarily form part of any great measure of licensing reform which is to receive their united support,"[29] but they doubted that it would have much practical effect outside rural districts. By insisting that the majority in favor must be at least two-thirds of those voting, they assured the truth of their own prediction that the Veto would be little more than a symbol.

For licenses that survived reduction in numbers and Local Veto, Rowtnree and Sherwell saw two alternatives. The first—high license—whether by bidding for licenses or by raising statutory fees, would not end the danger that the drink trade posed to the public life of the nation. Moreover, by concentrating the trade in the hands of the most wealthy and the most able, it might make the trade more powerful in politics. By raising the cost of operations, it might make the trade more zealous in expanding drink sales. Rowntree and Sherwell therefore adopted the other choice, that of eliminating private profit from the retail sale of drink, "taking the Trade out of private hands."

Rowntree and Sherwell looked to Scandinavia both for general principles and for empirical evidence about how the principles worked in large towns. The two reformers did not take over the details of the Scandinavian schemes. Indeed, they disliked some parts of the plan followed in the Swedish port of Gothenburg that had given its name to the general notion of taking the retail trade out of the hands of private businessmen. In both Sweden and Norway, the Gothenburg principle was confined to spirits as that was the preferred drink of the urban working class. Beer was considered almost a temperance drink, although in rural areas it sometimes was prohibited by local option. In both Sweden and Norway, the Gothenburg principle was operated through private philanthropic companies that received only limited profits on the capital that they had invested. In their 1899 book Rowntree and Sherwell preferred municipal management. Under pressure from those who feared the drink trade's corruption of local politics or who worried that the sin of selling drink would contaminate the body politic, they subsequently made company management their proposal. In Norway some profits and in Sweden all profits went directly to local purposes. Rowntree and Sherwell insisted that all local profits go into a central fund and that localities benefit in proportion to their population and not according to local drink sales. Moreover, they wanted profits to fund counter attractions which was not the case in Scandinavia. Of the two main Scandinavian schemes, Rowntree and Sherwell preferred that of Bergen in Norway where the drinking bar was an austere, unappealing place without seats for customers ("perpendicular drinking") rather than the scheme in Gothenburg itself which gave its name to all British plans to eliminate private profit from the retail sale of alcoholic drink. At Bergen there were no tables or chairs, no newspapers, no private compartments, and no women employed other than the landlord's wife.

What Rowntree and Sherwell borrowed from Scandinavia and saw as the heart of any Gothenburg system were three things: the elimination or rather the reduction of private profit in the retail sale of drink, combined with the notion of local control under the general statutory supervision of the central government, and the existence of a local monopoly of the not-for-profit management of the retail drink trade.[30] For Rowntree and

Sherwell, Gothenburg-style drink shops would be a grudgingly offered, "least harmful safety-valve" for stubborn drinkers, not an encouragement or a temptation for any casual or new drinkers.[31] Restrictions abounded: no credit sales, no barmaids, no "adventitious attractions" (such as music), no accommodation for clubs or benefit societies, no screens or partitions to prevent inspection from outside, and no back or side entrances on passages which were not public thoroughfares.[32] Rowntree and Sherwell strongly opposed the drink trade. They believed it obstructed temperance reform, acted as a powerful political force against the public good, and received large monopoly values through licensing without any payment.

The Gothenburg public houses would exist only in those localities that freely chose them. Supervisory legislation enacted by Parliament would authorize local public house monopolies on a permissive basis. Moreover, the Gothenburg companies would cooperate with local opinion when it wanted additional restrictions such as shortened hours, a reduction in the number of licensed houses, and complete prohibition without compensation.[33] The profits of the sale of drink, which Rowntree and Sherwell estimated at 20% of sales, would go into a national fund, from which localities would draw in proportion to their population to supply counter attractions to drink.[34]

Rowntree and Sherwell saw their proposals not as a complete solution but as "a reasonable basis for co-operation" and therefore politically practicable. It was necessary, they thought, to bring together the moderate and advanced reformers as well as "all other earnest citizens" who were interested in social reform. The reforms were to be constructive, that is, providing counter attractions as well as to be restrictive. "They would reach as far as the progressive spirit of the community had penetrated, and be consistent with further advance."[35] The restrictive principles appealed to advanced temperance reformers, that of counter attractions to the enlightened public in general. The Gothenburg Scheme was supposed to broaden the basis of support for temperance legislation by recognizing the need for a safety-valve for the availability of drink in the big towns and the need for counter attractions.

Unlike most temperance reformers Rowntree and Sherwell were interested in causes of intemperance other than that of temptation. Although they claimed that the most important reason for intemperance was "the arrangements under which the sale of drink is placed in the hands of those who seek to stimulate their consumption to the utmost," which was an argument for the Gothenburg principle, they also pointed out reasons which social reformers outside the temperance movement emphasized, "the monotony and dullness–too often the active misery–of many lives," and "the absence of adequate provision of social intercourse and healthful recreation." Rowntree and Sherwell insisted on counter attractions in the belief that "the public house problem is largely—by no means entirely—an 'entertainment of the people' problem," with "its roots in ordinary social instincts as well as in depraved and unenlightened tastes."[36] Concurrently, they argued that temperance assisted other social reforms. Although "no universal panacea," temperance was needed to provide the alert and responsible people capable of joining in other reforms. "Apart from Temperance the social problem will remain insoluble."[37]

Like the Bishop of Chester, Rowntree and Sherwell strongly favored improved recreational opportunities for the working class, but unlike him they rejected any association of drink with wholesome leisure. Recreation and social interaction would be offered in places free from alcohol but subsidized by the profits of drink shops. Drink-free People's Palaces would provide winter gardens for free promenade and music, indoor concerts and entertainments, rooms for games and reading, art galleries, arts and crafts exhibitions (including local handicrafts), popular lectures, social and recreational clubs (including boys' clubs to fight hooliganism), benefit societies, and gymnasiums. Supposedly physical training would increase economic efficiency by at least a fifth. Attractive temperance cafes would be located in the People's Palaces and elsewhere.[38]

A major difference between the trust houses of Earl Grey and the bishop of Chester and the Gothenburg ideas of Rowntree and Sherwell is that the former operated independently of legislation while the latter required a statute to provide a local monopoly for public houses operated without a profit motive.[39] The alliance of Rowntree and Sherwell with the militant temperance reformer Whittaker made it difficult to unite with the trust house movement.

Politically Rowntree and Sherwell took chances. Their version of the Gothenburg scheme offended advanced reformers who believed that it increased the complicity of the public in the sale of drink and disparaged the practical effect of the Veto. Most advanced reformers also resented the acceptance of financial compensation of the drink trade. Rowntree and Sherwell also risked offending people outside the temperance movement by representing the commercial drink trade as the enemy of the public welfare and incapable of reform within the profit system. Rowntree and Sherwell took a further risk by offering their ideas in considerable detail, probably to show that many of the criticisms of other versions of the Gothenburg principle could be avoided by a carefully drafted scheme.

Rowntree and Sherwell were simultaneously part of the traditional teetotal temperance movement (as they insisted that the test of a scheme of temperance reform was its ability to make "a considerable reduction in the national consumption of alcohol,"[40] not just of gross drunkenness) and also part of the turn-of-the-century social efficiency movement (which saw the problem as the impact of drinking on family income and the danger to physical and mental effectiveness "in the industrial competition of nations.")[41] Thus, they were able to rally to temperance reform a body of people who had stayed aloof earlier and yet continued to have credentials with at least part of the advanced temperance movement. Rowntree and Sherwell kept their distance from Lord Grey's trust house movement in part out of disagreement with some of its principles and out of fear that commercial interests might take over the trust houses. Equally important, they thought that the trust house Gothenburgers were unnecessarily divisive in antagonizing the Local Veto people. Temperance reform could not be carried with only the traditional temperance reformers, but it also could not be carried without them.

The timing of the publication of *The Temperance Problem and Social Reform* helped and hurt the prospects for a favorable reception. Rowntree and Sherwell's book appeared in April 1899, a few weeks before the publication of the reports of the Royal Commission on the Licensing Laws, when the press was filled with rumors about conflict among the commission members. Certainly, the interest in temperance reform stimulated by the controversy provided Rowntree and Sherwell with an audience that might consider them more objective than the divided Royal Commission, but a book by private individuals could not easily compete with official reports for political support.

Later in 1899 the Liberal Party leadership and a coalition of moderate and advanced temperance reformers endorsed the minority report. The failure of the Liberals to win the general election of 1900, the refusal of the Unionist Government to legislate based on the majority report or of the points of agreement between the two reports, and the division within the advanced temperance party provided opportunities for Rowntree and Sherwell. Lord Peel's Report turned out to be a transitional step toward a drastically different answer to the drink question than the Royal Commission had considered. Some temperance supporters of the minority report joined Rowntree and Sherwell to suggest granting a kind of compensation beyond what Lord Peel's Report had conceded. In a few years some of the warmest supporters of the minority report, including T.P. Whittaker and Lord Peel himself, sought to add to it a slightly modified version of Rowntree's and Sherwell's Gothenburg proposals. As the major modification, private philanthropic companies replaced municipalization as the method for disinterested management. The price of dropping municipalization was alienating many in the labor movement.

In 1899 exponents of professedly practical reform urged the temperance party to accept new policies to win moderate allies and to defer ultimate ideals to press for ameliorative legislation that had a strong chance of being enacted and implemented. For a couple of years Lord Peel's minority report rallied broad support. Championed by T.P. Whittaker and many leading prohibitionists, Lord Peel's Report strained the unity of the advanced temperance party, but the reporters and their critics managed to agree to disagree, if only barely so. Afterwards, the more controversial Gothenburg-centered proposals of Rowntree and Sherwell attracted the enthusiasm of Liberals who doubted the practicability of Local Veto. Lord Peel's Report in effect became incorporated in the Rowntree and Sherwell program, but with reduction in numbers becoming less important than the Gothenburg principles.

T.P. Whittaker was the most influential convert to Rowntree's and Sherwell's version of Gothenburg.[42] As early as 1894, when temperance reformers had been forced by Gladstone's letter to the Bishop of Chester to express an opinion on the Gothenburg principle, Whittaker had showed himself open-minded. Although he thought that most of the advantage of the Scandinavian system could be obtained by reducing the number of licensed houses and their hours of sale, he did not object to experiment "subject to the proviso that no backward step be permitted."[43]

In his lengthy memorandum attached to the reports of the Royal Commission, Whittaker had offered relatively sympathetic, if unenthusiastic, words about Gothenburg. "While the [Gotheburg] system cannot be regarded as a complete or even the best available remedy for the evils of our drinking system, there are, *as compared with any ordinary licensing system*, a sufficient number of good points about it to render it desirable that where the liquor traffic is to be carried on the people of the locality should have the option offered them of placing the sale of drink under the control of persons who would have no interest in pushing it."[44] In proposing the management of the drink trade by the local authority as one option of local control, he insisted that local government electors ratify the creation of any public management scheme proposed by the local authority, that there be no increase in the number of licensed houses, and that no drink profits accrue to the local district.[45] Elsewhere Whittaker criticized Rowntree and Sherwell's book, not for its advocacy of the Gothenburg scheme, but for its contention that prohibition had been ineffective where it had been tried, notably, in North America.[46] Whittaker never abandoned his belief in prohibition. For instance, in 1913 he supported the licensing act that allowed Local Veto in Scotland.

After the publication of a controversial temperance manifesto in October 1903, Whittaker wrote a substantial pamphlet, *Some Frank & Friendly Words to Temperance People* that appeared in December 1903. He emphasized that the Temperance Manifesto never mentioned municipalization. "So far as I am personally concerned, I am not an enthusiastic advocate of disinterested local management." (p. 22) He was willing to allow localities to adopt disinterested management subject to safeguards. He emphatically rejected giving localities a direct financial interest in running public houses. Whittaker sharply criticized private schemes for disinterested management such as the bishop of Chester's and Lord Grey's.

The Bishop of Chester's scheme is objectionable because it would make liquor shops attractive by allying themselves with amusements and innocent recreation, and would also thereby make it easy for people to go to them who now hesitate and refrain. Lord Grey's Trusts are to be deprecated because they tend to increase the number of licensed premises by inducing licensing justices to grant new licenses to them where they otherwise would not grant them at all, and by persuading local authorities to continue licensed houses for them which would otherwise by abolished. (p. 21)

Probably Whittaker first accepted the Gothenburg principle out of expediency, as a way of gaining allies and of weakening the political influence of the brewers, and only later became convinced that it was the most practicable method of reform. Increasingly, he seemed to consider the Gothenburg scheme as being as much of a reform as urban workingmen would accept for the foreseeable future. At a temperance congress held in 1900, Whittaker explained that public opinion dictated what kind of temperance legislation was practicable, not simply to put on the statute book, but to enforce after enactment. "[I]t is essential to have public opinion strongly behind liquor legislation," he argued,

> because it is legislation which closely affects the customs, prejudices, and appetite of the people. The more closely the habits of the people are touched and interfered with, the more necessary is it that the legislation should have the distinct approval of public opinion. The grades of interference are numerous. Reduction in the number of public houses does not materially interfere with what is termed the convenience of the public—they can still get what they want. Shortening of hours does so rather more, but not any great extent. The vast majority do not use public houses during the early hours of the morning and late at night. Total closing on Sunday touches a large number, many more than such closing with an exception for off-sale for dinner and supper beer.. Abolition of drinking bars and mere drinking places would interfere with many, but still with far fewer than total closing of all licensed premises in the district would. Local veto would interfere with a large number in a locality, but

with fewer *in the locality* than total prohibition over the whole country would. With local veto in force in a locality, household supplies could be obtained elsewhere and brought in. The more extensive and complete the restriction, the greater the interference and consequently the greater the temptation to violate the law, and the greater the necessity for a strong public opinion behind it.[47]

Whittaker seems to have considered a Gothenburg scheme as a safety-valve that would accommodate non-abstainers and allow the maximum of reform possible while drink continued to be sold and consumed.[48] Later he identified the major obstacles to temperance legislation as "the fact that probably three-fourths of the men of England and Wales are occasionally or regularly buyers and consumers of intoxicants" and "the widespread direct personal financial interest there is in the sale of drink."[49] The Gothenburg scheme would compromise with the first kind of opposition and attack the second. Whittaker also agreed with Rowntree and Sherwell that reduction in numbers did not offer an adequate solution. Indeed, the reduction in numbers that the licensing justices had implemented informally throughout England and formally in the Birmingham Surrender Scheme had made more drastic reforms more difficult by increasing the value of surviving licensed property. Whittaker pointed out, for example, that between 1852 and 1902 the consumption on beer and spirits per "on license" had grown by fifty per cent.[50] Whittaker considered magisterial discretion more important than reduction in numbers because a variety of reforms could be imposed by the magistrates through the threat of the denial of license renewal. In the summer of 1902 Whittaker visited Norway to study the Bergen system of public management. In the same year he began to advocate disinterested management as part of a larger program of temperance legislation beginning with his speech at the annual meeting of the British Temperance League.

He may have clung to a faint hope about winning over the Alliance. In 1902 he suggested that the Alliance "clear the air" by having the General Council discuss "compensation, municipalization, Lord Grey's scheme and the like" to decide "what should be our broad lines of policy as an organization." Although nominally willing to have the General Council discuss anything, Lawson ended his comment on Whittaker's letter with a chilly sneer. "As to what should be 'our broad lines of policy as an organisation', I thought that had been settled when the Alliance was formed half a century ago."[51] Despite what Lawson said, the Alliance had quickly climbed down from its original demand for national prohibition.

In 1901 disinterested management, at least as a basis for local experiments, received support in a thoughtful essay written by members of great brewing families traditionally connected with the Liberal Party. Noel Buxton and Walter Hoare contributed the chapter, "Temperance Reform," in a volume edited by C.F.G. Masterman, *The Heart of the Empire: Discussions of Problems of Modern City Life in England*.[52] Buxton and Hoare acknowledged "a balanced opinion must always be unexciting" but that is what they tried to offer. They began by arguing that diagnosis of the problem, not the prescription, is "the real difficulty." Few publicans push drinks on reluctant customers, and "a rowdy [public] house is very exceptional--at least in London." Drinking there is much the same as at a dinner party of the rich: "conversation accompanied by drink." Drunkenness at the pub is rare. Buxton and Hoare were more distressed by the waste of scant resources by the poor than by their getting intoxicated. The two authors thought that a "final solution" had become possible now that "the prohibitionist agitation has failed." They credit Rowntree and Sherwell and the Royal Commission "for persuading reformers to abandon a purely vetoist policy." Buxton and Hoare offered detailed suggestions for licensing reform, but they clearly preferred what they called "public management." They distinguished between two ideals: the intrinsically evil public house "treated simply as a necessary safety-valve" (a view they associated with Arthur Sherwell); and converting "the tavern into an acceptable and useful resort" (an approach that they attributed to the Bishop of Chester). Although Buxton and Hoare considered "the success of the Scandinavian system ... entirely beyond question," they thought that experiments in England needed to be made before it could be made general there. Control over managers, who have no financial motive in selling drink, was a crucial advantage to public management.

The Gothenburg principle clearly had emerged as a major policy option in British temperance politics when the so-called National Temperance Manifesto was published in October 1903. The timing resulted from knowledge that the drink trade was pressuring the Government for legislation to protect it from the magistrates who were refusing to renew the licenses for large numbers of public houses. The National Temperance Manifesto was drafted and circulated "to provide a rallying-point for that great mass of reasonable temperance and earnest non-abstaining opinion which must be kept together if disaster is to be avoided." [53]

The Manifesto sought to rally temperance and social reformers behind a program that combined a Rowntree-Sherwell Gothenburg scheme and the major proposals of Lord Peel's report, while appeasing prohibitionists with a nod toward Local Veto. The manifesto included reduction in numbers and Local Veto as well as a statutory system of mutual insurance to provide the trade with financial compensation for an unspecified number of years. In 1903 for many people compensation was the most important part of the manifesto. Before the supporters of the manifesto had completed gathering signatures, Good Templar opponents of the Gothenburg scheme and of compensation denounced the manifesto in a circular letter issued early in October and printed in the *Good Templars' Watchword*. They emphasized the role in the genesis of the manifesto of Whittaker and of Lady Henry Somerset, until that year the president of the National British Women's Temperance Association.[54] This seems like an exaggeration. More likely, Rowntree and Sherwell inspired the drafting of the manifesto. Although Whittaker's signature was invaluable in attracting that of others, he had been in the United States during much of the period when signatures were being collected. Veto diehards sometimes called the manifesto the Whittaker-Sherwell manifesto.

The *Birmingham Daily Post* published an unauthorized summary of the manifesto and a partial list of signatures.[55] This forced the manifesto leaders to show their hand prematurely. On 20 October 1903, the *Daily News* published the official text of the manifesto with the names of the 190 persons who to that date had signed it and without the additional signatures that Whittaker, who had just returned from America, had hoped to obtain.[56] In addition to Whittaker, Lady Henry Somerset, Rowntree, and Sherwell, the signatories included people associated with temperance reform such as Lord Peel; the president of the National Temperance League, the Rev. J.W. Leigh, Dean of Hereford; Dr. Frederick Jayne, Bishop of Chester; the honorary treasurer of the UKA, W.J. Crossley; politicians such as the former president of the National Liberal Federation, Dr. R. Spence Watson, the Liberal Unionist Leonard Courtney, the Lib-Lab MP John Burns, and the Independent Labour Party leader J. Keir Hardie; philanthropic businessmen such as George Cadbury and W.H. Lever; writers such as J.A. Hobson, Mrs. Humphry Ward, and Sir G.O. Trevelyan; physicians such as Sir Thomas Barlow and Sir Victor Horsley; and a huge phalanx of Anglican bishops, Nonconformist divines, and moderate temperance reformers.[57] But for his death earlier in the year W.S. Caine's name might have lent weight to the manifesto.[58] He had spent part of 1902 on a voyage to South America intended to improve his health and for the same purpose had travelled to the south of France in the middle of March, 1903.

The manifesto was not solely a Gothenburg document, but it brought the Gothenburg principle into a consensus program accepted by many moderate reformers and some prohibitionists. The manifesto offered moderate prohibitionists Local Veto and the assurance that a local plebiscite would be required before any Gothenburg experiment would be implemented.

The manifesto employed the expression, disinterested management, which emphasized the elimination of the profit motive, rather than public management, which for many people implied municipalization. In their book *The Temperance Problem and Social Reform* Rowntree and Sherwell had preferred municipalization. Hereafter, they accepted philanthropic companies limited to a small dividend on capital, somewhat like the philanthropic companies which provided model working class housing.

When the press broke the story about the manifesto, the United Kingdom Alliance's annual meeting was in session. The meeting adopted resolutions against municipalization and liquor monopolies by public companies, but the executive committee resisted pressure to denounce the manifesto directly. The UKA needed manifesto supporters as allies against an expected Government compensation bill. Consequently the *Alliance News* published without comment the pro-Manifesto speech that Whittaker and Lady Henry Somerset had delivered before the Bradford branch of the National British Women's Temperance Association.[59] This reluctance to antagonize the Gothenburgers provoked the anger of the new NBWTA president, the Countess of Carlisle who regarded the manifesto as "heretical poison."[60] Around the turn of the century Lady Carlisle and her Naworth Castle group—which included her son the Hon. Geoffrey Howard, her son-in-law Charles H. Roberts, and her former secretary Leif Jones, all soon to become Liberal MP's—emerged as a force in the advanced temperance party. Lady Carlisle's circle and the Good Templars refused to mute their criticism of the manifesto out of mere expediency.[61] Soon they would take control of the UKA.

Lady Carlisle made her case to the Alliance's secretary James Whyte on 25 and 28 November 1903 in a pair of long letters transcribed in the Alliance minutes (2 December 1903). She protested that when the *Alliance News* published the speeches of Lady Henry Somerset and T.P. Whittaker it had failed to provide an editorial critique. "Good Temperance people are floundering not knowing which is the safe path in this fog." In the first letter she reported that Lady Aberdeen tried on 17 November to get the Women's Liberal Federation executive to receive a deputation in favor of the Somerset-Whittaker Manifesto. Lady Aberdeen was the Federation's president. Lady Carlisle persuaded the committee to refuse to see the deputation at that time or in a month, Lady Aberdeen's compromise suggestion.

Lady Carlisle contrasted the Alliance's timid unwillingness to offend the Manifesto's champions, out of fear of dividing the temperance party, with the attitude in Scotland. Even the "least advanced" organization there, the Scottish Temperance League, answered the Manifesto "with no uncertain sound." Lady Carlisle criticized the secrecy in which the manifesto had been devised and the signatories solicited. "Mrs. Bertrand Russell [the American-born Quaker, Alys Pearsall Smith], when challenged on the secret methods which she and Lady Henry [Somerset] had pursued, said that 'secrecy was necessary to their propaganda, as if it had been carried on openly, the Prohibitionists would have baulked them.' Was there ever such as confession?" Lord Peel, Arthur Sherwell, and Lady Henry Somerset fought the Alliance because it stood for Local Veto. In contrast, Lady Carlisle considered Whittaker "a sincere Prohibitionist" who adhered to the Manifesto only "to get his big Compensation scheme floated." The manifesto people "are still determined to persuade the 'moderates' that we are extremists who must be mistrusted." She worried that Asquith and others weak on temperance might dominate the next Liberal ministry. In a postscript, Lady Carlisle reported that the Scottish Temperance Legislation Board, organized to promote Lord Peel's Royal Commission proposals, had adopted the Manifesto as its new program. As a result, the representatives of the Scottish Temperance League, the Free Church of Scotland, and the Wesleyan synod quit the Board. The parallel Board in England has "resisted attempts to capture it." Finally, Lady Carlisle reported that Mrs. Bertrand Russell had tried to get Beatrice and Sidney Webb to sign the Manifesto. They refused because the compensation proposals would divide the temperance party.

Enemies of the manifesto were pleasantly surprised when the Liberal leader Campbell-Bannerman dismissed it as a "hocus-pocus" scheme. The Scottish Good Templar Tom Honeyman told Leif Jones that Campbell-Bannerman "showed more insight than we gave him credit for."[62]

In an interview in the *Good Templars' Watchword*, Joseph Malins distinguished between Lord Peel's Report and the manifesto. He said the former "was largely a great scheme for reducing licenses." The Good Templars and most temperance organizations had "approved generally of the Peel Report, but they did not regard Compensation as a vital part of the Report." They uncompromisingly opposed compensation. The manifesto would make reduction without compensation impossible for an undefined number of years, whereas the Peel Report allowed compensation for only a transitional period. He was resolutely opposed to the other principal proposal in the manifesto, replacing private ownership of the retail drink trade with municipal or public ownership. Malins also minimized the manifesto signatures of prominent MPs and ministers. Whatever their public renown, most of the signatories stood were not active members of "the great Temperance organizations.[63] In another interview, originally published in the *Christian Endeavour*, Malins pointed out that no more than a half dozen officers of "the forty national and denominational Temperance bodies" had signed the manifesto.[64] He criticized the manifesto promoters for adding to the names of those who had signed as individuals the organizations that they served.

The initial response of so-called moderate reformers was unenthusiastic. The organ of the Church of England Temperance Society said: "it is doubtful whether any good will come of the publication of the manifesto." It feared further division among temperance supporters.[65] Later the newspaper added: "there is nothing in it to which we object, but there is still the doubt in our minds as to the wisdom of such a memorial at the present moment."[66]

The manifesto was an attempt to influence Liberal Party policy. Initially it failed. Campbell-Bannerman reacted unenthusiastically. When a pro-Veto deputation interviewed him, he affirmed him support for the Veto and his objection to the State being involved in a compensation scheme ("although he thought the trade should make the compensation arrangements for themselves"). He hinted that he would favor a time notice. He gratified the deputation by describing the manifesto as "hocus-pocus." The Scottish Good Templar who reported on the interview sneered in the same letter about the audience for a talk by Lord Peel and Lady Henry Somerset's manifesto as "largely composed of those who run after a real live Lord."[67]

Whittaker was a fighter, described by an associate as "one of the fiercest individuals that I know."[68] In December 1903 he hit back at his critics in a pamphlet, *Some Frank and Friendly Words to Temperance People (and Incidentally Some Others)*. Whittaker complained that some temperance reformers refused to learn from history. They alienated non-abstainers by a policy of obstruction. Only a combination of abstainers "who supply the motive power, the energy, the enthusiasm and the political scheme"[69] and the non-abstainers who have the numbers could enact major reforms. Moreover, some reformers make the Veto a shibboleth without remembering that it was itself a compromise—"a lowering of the flag"—adopted when the original goal of the Alliance, "the Total and Immediate Legislative Suppression of the Liquor Traffic," had appeared impracticable.[70] Whittaker insisted that experience taught that reformers should "seize the possible" as "stepping stones" to more complete reforms.[71]

Whittaker explained why only individuals had been asked to sign the manifesto. The experience of the United Temperance Conferences of the mid-1890s had showed that it was impossible to get organizations to agree to a common program.[72] The timing of the manifesto he explained as the result of a crisis. The Government had been pressed by the licensed trade to introduce a licensing bill that would provide security for licensed property against magisterial discretion. The manifesto provided an alternative to the Government bill, "to provide a rallying-point for that great mass of reasonable temperance and earnest non-abstaining opinion." Whittaker explained that a violation of confidence forced premature publication of the manifesto. He had expected to ask more individuals to sign after his return from America.[73]

Whittaker remained loyal to the Veto in principle although he regarded it politically impracticable. Leif Jones, a diehard Vetoist, recognized the distinction between Whittaker and Arthur Sherwell, the former being "an erring friend" and the latter "at heart a foe–indeed almost an open one."[74] Less kind to Whittaker, another diehard compared Whittaker disrupting the temperance movement to Joseph Chamberlain splitting the Liberal Party.[75]

The licensing crisis of 1903-04 temporarily forced temperance reformers to make their priority opposition to the Government's proposals to strengthen the legal status of license holders. Despite some tactical restraint during this battle the Alliance and its friends could not stomach disinterested management and dismissed the claim that management by private philanthropic companies was different from municipalization. A private meeting between the members of the Alliance executive and supporters of the National Temperance Manifesto in November 1904 could find no basis for a common legislative program in the wake of the passage of Balfour's Licensing Act.

In May 1905 the smoldering quarrel burst into flames. A circular letter signed by Lady Henry Somerset, David Lloyd George, T.P. Whittaker, Dr. John Clifford, a prominent Baptist minister, Alexander Guthrie (1845-1914), an Alliance activist best known as chairman of the Liverpool Vigilance Committee in the 1870s and 1880s,[76] Joseph Rowntree, and Arthur Sherwell condemned the effort by unnamed temperance societies (presumably the UKA and the Good Templars) to obtain pledges from parliamentary candidates to oppose any legislation authorizing experiments by disinterested management companies. "As many earnest Temperance Reformers are of the opinion that permissive powers to try such experiments ought to be given, along with other options, in any future comprehensive measure of licensing reform, we sincerely hope that you will refrain from pledging yourself, in advance, against any limitation of the scope of future legislation." The circular pointed out that the National Temperance Manifesto had proposed "disinterested Company Management (not muncipalization), under explicit statutory safeguards" and that the manifesto had "received wide and influential support."[77] Probably Sherwell was the instigator of the circular, although at the time Lawson accused Guthrie and Lady Henry Somerset.[78]

Later in 1905 Whittaker tightened his alignment with Rowntree and Sherwell.[79] In November Whittaker and other converts to disinterested management superseded the Central Temperance Legislation Board, a federation of temperance societies which supported Lord Peel's report, in order to create the Temperance Legislation League, which consisted of individuals (not societies) committed in essence to the program of the old Board, plus disinterested management.[80] At the 20 November meeting that created the League no debate over its program was permitted and no amendments could be entertained. There were several dissentients to the resolution creating the League. Canon W. Barker strongly opposed setting up a new organization. He "complained that, invited to a conference, they had been presented with a policy that they were not allowed to discuss."[81]

The League's first pamphlet claimed: "Disinterested Management is not proposed as a rival nor a substitute for any other method of Temperance Reform." Rather "it is merely supplementary."[82] Unlike the manifesto, the League excluded municipalization explicitly (which resulted in several Labour MPs, who had signed the manifesto, withholding their support). The League supported Rowntree's and Sherwell's proposals for People's Palaces funded by liquor profits. In 1906 Whittaker said that the core of the League's program was "full and unfettered discretion in the licensing authority, and a wide local option."[83] Although the League supported the principle of Local Veto for public houses and beer shops (not for hotels, restaurants, and off-licenses), it asked in 1907 for a local prohibitive Veto for Scotland only. In the same year it asked for a Veto on new licenses for England. Many adherents of the League merely tolerated the Veto to appease prohibitionists.

A few prohibitionist supporters of the old Board, such as John Hilton, the Quaker parliamentary agent of the UKA, who had served the Board as an honorary secretary, rejected disinterested management.[84] Whittaker was willing to lose such old allies to strengthen his connection with moderates. Other adherents of the old Board opposed the change in policy not in principle but as divisive, notably H.J. Wilson, a member of the Board's executive and Liberal MP for Sheffield.[85] At first the *Temperance Chronicle*, organ of the CETS, also complained about the demarche as dubious tactics, but later the CETS executive unanimously endorsed the League's program.[86] The coup could not be stopped because the old Board's dominant figures were behind it, notably, Whittaker, who was the vigorous chairman of the executive, Lord Peel, who was titular leader as president, and G.W. Brown, the honorary treasurer, who helped fund the new organization. The Board officers assumed the same offices in the new League. Alexander Guthrie became co-treasurer. A.F. Harvey of the CETS. became secretary.[87] The League won the active support of Rowntree and Sherwell that the Board had lacked. Sherwell became an honorary secretary, as did the trade unionist J.M. Hodge. Rowntree joined the executive committee. In 1910, Rowntree replaced Whittaker as chairman.

For Rowntree and Sherwell this was a matter of tactics. The authors of *The Temperance Problem and Social Reform* doubted the effectiveness of the key proposal in Lord Peel's Report, reduction in numbers, and wanted the Gothenburg principle that was not in the report.[88] The League succeeded in attracting a majority of the most eminent and the most affluent temperance reformers. Twenty-four Alliance vice-presidents, elected to their honorific positions because of their prestige or their wealth, joined the League. The League also attracted prominent people who would not have been comfortable on a UKA platform, such as Sir W.H. Houldsworth, the Unionist MP who had been a member of the Royal Commission on the Liquor Licensing Laws, the Bishop of Winchester, and the Roman Catholic Archbishop of Westminster.[89]

The advanced temperance party liked to argue that the leaders of the disinterested management party spoke for nobody but themselves and that most advanced temperance reformers remained loyal to Direct Local Veto. On 12 December 1905, a conference of national and regional temperance organizations voted to reject municipalization and public management and to reaffirm their support for the Veto.[90] Late in 1906, probably in October or November, an anonymous pamphlet published a repudiation of the policy of the League signed by some of the signatories of the National Temperance Manifesto of 1903. In response, Arthur Sherwell claimed that of thirty-one persons listed in the pamphlet, thirteen had never signed the policy of the League (which was not identical with the manifesto), while another thirteen in fact had not withdrawn. Thus, out of approximately 10,000 persons who had endorsed the League's policy, only five had withdrawn, including some who had done so under pressure and not because they had changed their minds.[91]

The Alliance and the League both claimed to represent the mainstream of British temperance reform. The UKA accused the proponents of disinterested management of heresy and divisiveness. In rebuttal, after ransacking the public record for the past half century, the League found statements sympathetic to disinterested management or at least expressing neutrality: in the *Alliance News*, in the annual reports of the UKA, in speeches by such Alliance stalwarts at W.S. Caine, Samuel Pope, F.R. Lees, and J.H. Raper, all deceased.[92] In response the League, the *Alliance News* said that although such "old stalwarts" may have favored it "academically," they did not support it actively, "It was never a real living issue in their time."[93]

In 1869, the Alliance's executive committee published as part of its annual report praise for disinterested management: "Pending the adoption of total prohibition, your committee would gladly see the friends of licensing reform intent on carrying out the Gothenburg scheme."[94] The League pointed out that in the parliamentary debate over Chamberlain's Gothenburg resolution in 1877 Sir Wilfrid Lawson had spoken and voted in favor of the proposal.[95] In 1894 when William Gladstone had written supportively to Lord Thring, a promoter of the Bishop of Chester's Gothenburg proposal, Lawson and the UKA secretary, James Whyte, had minimized the conflict between the Gothenburg principle and Local Veto. For instance, in a letter to the *Times* in September 1894, Lawson said: "Mr. Gladstone is in favour of giving communities the option of 'Gothenburg' when they decline to avail themselves of the Option of Prohibition. Why Prohibitionists should carp at Mr. Gladstone for this I cannot quite see." Testifying before Lord Peel's Royal Commission, Whyte further argued that public houses conducted by private companies on the Norwegian model might be an improvement, especially in country places.[96] At the annual meeting of the Alliance in 1894, Lawson emphasized that the Veto was not incompatible with licensing reform. In reference to the Bishop of Chester's version of the Gothenburg principle, Lawson had declared: "We want all plans tried. So long as the people do not object, we don't object."[97]

Lawson resented the insinuation that he had ever been well-disposed toward allowing an option of disinterested management. Undoubtedly tactics had made him take a conciliatory line in 1877 and 1894. In his memoirs he admits the reason for his voting for Chamberlain's resolution. Lawson "had no faith at all in any of these nostrums for making a bad trade a source of good; and was yet unwilling to object to anybody trying any scheme in which they believed."[98] By the early 1900s the Gothenburg had become a major rival to the Veto and consequently Lawson had become less indulgent toward the Gothenburgers. In June 1905 he protested the publication of his earlier remarks.[99] Shortly before his death Lawson complained to Canon Hicks: "It is the 'wise men' who are the plague of my life--the men who want to go round instead of to go straight."[100]

The divisions in the temperance party appeared vividly in an exchange of letters in the short-lived Liberal daily, the *Tribune*, in August and September 1906. John H. Roberts was an organizer for the new National Independent Temperance Party, committed to field candidates in constituencies for which the major parties had not nominated a Vetoist.

Roberts urged future historians to explore the parallel between T.P. Whittaker and Joseph Chamberlain. Supposedly, except for want of loyalty each would have inherited the leadership of his party, in the case of Whittaker that of the temperance party, in that of Chamberlain the Liberal Party. Roberts sardonically compared the meetings of Whittaker's Temperance Legislation League, adorned with bishops and baronets, with Chamberlain's Tariff Reform League, where the sometime Radical hobnobbed with his new ducal friends. Allegedly Whittaker had been corrupted by the spirit of compromise which made up the parliamentary atmosphere, his increasingly aristocratic connections, and his Roseberyite views on the Empire.[101] A Good Templar active in Roberts' party, E. Tennyson Smith, less politely described the League's disinterested management proposals as "conceived in treachery, brought forth in deceit, and . . . nurtured on misrepresentation and sophistry."[102]

In Whittaker's reply in the *Tribune,* he offered a different reading of recent temperance history. He contended that the uncompromising Vetoists were the out-of-step minority. After most temperance people had accepted Lord Peel's Report as an immediate program, the extremists managed to take over the governing committees of large temperance organizations (presumably he meant the UKA and the National Temperance Federation) and had forced out the moderates. Whittaker identified the extremists as the Good Templars John Kempster, Guy Hayler, and Joseph Malins, together with Lady Carlisle and "her immediate surroundings," obviously with Leif Jones, her sometime secretary in mind, and probably her son Geoffrey Howard and her son-in-law Charles Roberts.[103] Malins had supported the United Temperance Conferences and had been moderate about Lord Peel's Report since for him compensation was a matter for compromise. But he had been a bitter opponent of the Gothenburg scheme since the mid-1890s.[104] According to Whittaker, once imposing organizations had declined into "very much a stage army" after their capture by the extremists and their adoption of obstructionist policies that offended most other reformers. They withdrew from such organizations. Another temperance reformer described the shrunken veto faction as "the fanatical remnant.[105] In a subsequent pamphlet Whittaker added that Sir Wilfrid Lawson had only become a pronounced opponent of disinterested management after the death in May 1897 of J.H. Raper, for many years the UKA's parliamentary agent. Afterwards Lawson had fallen under the influence of extremist counselors.[106] Writing in 1905, Whittaker said "up to five or six years ago the inclusion of the option of Disinterested Management, with the option of Local Veto, was approved by practically all the prominent Temperance leader and the United Kingdom Alliance.[107] He mentioned, in addition to Raper, Samuel Pope, F.R. Lees, and W.S. Caine.

Whittaker argued that the Veto was not enough because few large towns would make use of it. Also "something more than mere licensing reform–fewer houses, shorter hours, Sunday closing, a reformed licensing authority, and the like . . . is required," as shown in the case of Scotland where these reforms existed, and the liquor problem remained at least as serious as in England. Whittaker wanted "a policy of full and unfettered discretion for the licensing authority, and a wide local option." The "great lesson of the history of liquor legislation in the United States" is that legislation "which closely touches the habits, prejudices, and life of the people" requires the support of local opinion. To restrict the role of drink to the minimum Whittaker said that private profit in the sale of drink had to be eliminated and local electorates had to be allowed the option of disinterested management as well as the prohibitive veto and were more likely to vote for the former than the latter. The sale of drink could be reduced by three-quarters and still allow enough profit to finance counter attractions to drink (what he called "indoor parks") to offer the social life usually available only in public houses.

Whittaker made clear why he endorsed the Gothenburg policy which was much more controversial with his old prohibitionist friends than was Lord Peel's Report. "That portion of [the League's] policy which the more extreme and impracticable of our Temperance friends object to is that which attracts our non-abstaining supporters. They attach little or no importance to local veto as a practical remedy, but they do welcome and value proposals to eliminate the stimulus of private profit from the trade, and to introduce counter attractions to the public-house." Whittaker favored a policy of inclusion:

> the League was formed in order to organise and consolidate that great mass of practical and moderate Temperance opinion which realises the necessity of carrying with it all the earnest opinion of the country, which is genuinely in favour of what is really practicable in Temperance reform.

The Temperance Legislation League had more money and more energy than the United Kingdom Alliance in the early twentieth century. In 1906 it distributed nearly a million pamphlets and tracts and supplied speakers to 700 meetings.[108] Whittaker and his literary associate Alexander MacCullum Scott (1874-1928) wrote innumerable letters to the editor and pamphlets to inculcate the League point of view. The Whittaker-Scott partnership was important enough to attract the hostility of the *Licensing World's* cartoonist.[109] Whittaker emerged as the leading figure in the temperance movement. As an appropriate symbol he received a knighthood in July 1906, the month of the death of the veteran president of the UKA, Sir Wilfrid Lawson.[110]

The Gothenburgers showed considerable flexibility in their program and avoided the policy of "all or nothing" which they accused the Alliance of having followed.[111] In private communications with the Liberal Government in September 1906 Whittaker had urged legislation granting the local option of the Gothenburg principle, but by November 1907 he dropped this proposal as politically impracticable. Although committed to legislation for disinterested management as an eventual objective, the League made its priority the payment of monopoly value by all license holders, not just holders of new licenses. Supposedly the exaction of monopoly value would clear the way for disinterested management and other reforms that existing vested interests hindered. For Whittaker, Rowntree, Sherwell, and their allies the monopoly value became of central importance. (Curiously, *The Temperance Problem and Social Reform* had lacked enthusiasm for high license that in effect the exaction of monopoly value was.)[112] Balfour's Licensing Act of 1904 had brought the exaction of monopoly value into the political arena by a requirement that new licenses pay a sum equivalent to the advantage of a licensed status. Although new licenses were few and the requirement only a gesture to appease temperance-minded Unionists, if applied to old licenses the exaction of monopoly value would become a drastic system of high license which would devastate the owners of licensed property.

For the temperance reformers the object was not to collect revenue. Reformers wanted to extinguish what remnant of equitable right to renewal might survive the time limit that the Liberals promised to enact to phase out the right to compensation created in 1904. The League feared that when the expiration of the time limit restored the old legal status of licensed property, the justices might be reluctant to refuse to renew public house licenses. Payment of monopoly value was intended to destroy the special profit gained simply from having a license, so a license in itself would be without value. Supposedly, knowing this would ease the inhibitions of the licensing authorities. (That anything would have reduced the status of license renewals to an equality with applications by newcomers seems dubious.) The transfer of monopoly value to the public allegedly would enable the public to regain full control over licensing. For the League the taxation of the monopoly value meant the destruction of a major argument against disinterested management and a great weakening of the financial basis for the political influence of the drink trade. In the final stages of the drafting of the Liberal Government's licensing bill, introduced in 1908, the League did not press for the Gothenburg principle. Instead, Arthur Sherwell told the

National Liberal Club, on 2 December 1907, of the critical importance of the policy that all licenses pay monopoly value. Publishing its final proposals for the bill in that month, the League excluded Gothenburg while including monopoly value.[113]

The League did not get the exaction of the monopoly value because the House of Lords defeated the Liberal bill, but the climate of opinion in favor of the Gothenburg remained strong. Indeed in April 1908 the future Unionist prime minister Andrew Bonar Law privately characterized disinterested management as "the only really effective way in which the cause of temperance can be helped by legislation."[114] After the passage of the Scottish Temperance Act in 1913 that the House of Lords wanted to amend to provide an option of disinterested management, the Gothenburg movement began to evolve into State Management, a response perhaps to the increasing control of the brewers over the retail trade.[115] Perhaps too this shift pointed up a large element of expediency in all local option agitations. When a national solution appeared possible, arguments about local self-government faded away. In his version of State Purchase, David Lloyd George championed disinterested management during the First World War. After the Second World War the Labour Government experimented in the "new towns" where no vested interests stood in the way.

A brief comment on the Gothenburg system in Sweden. Its genesis owed more to the Crown and municipalities desiring revenue than to philanthropic motives. It was confined to the sale of hard liquor and rarely existed outside large towns. In rural areas prohibition often existed or other restrictions did such as allowing only the sale of beer and wine (or just beer) as part of meals. Heavy drinking in rural districts was confined to special occasions such as a wedding that might be celebrated for a whole week. Despite the law, hard liquor was available everywhere through a kind of black market, as were potent patent medicines. By the time that Rowntree and Sherwell wrote, the Gothenburg system was dying. It was unpopular with poor people who complained that it had destroyed taverns that had been sites of working-class culture. Both manufacturers of alcoholic drink and militant temperance reformers, notably the Good Templars, attacked the Gothenburg system. Despite praise for it in other countries, it had a bad reputation in Sweden as financially exploitative. By the 1890s British advocates of disinterested management, other than a few socialists, avoided municipalization.

In 1917 the Gothenburg system was replaced in Sweden by the centralized Bratt system. Until 1955, the Swedish government rationed the sale of alcohol drink.[116]

Notes

[1] See David W. Gutzke, "Gentrifying the British Public House, 1896-1914," *International Labor and Working-Class History* 45 (Spring 1994): 29-43; Gutzke, "Gothenburg Schemes/Disinterested Management," in Jack S. Blocker, David M. Fahey, and Ian R. Tyrrell, eds., *Alcohol and Temperance in Modern History* (ABC-CLIO, 2003); David M. Fahey, *Temperance Societies in Late Victorian and Edwardian England* (Cambridge Scholars, 2020), pp. 43-52; Robert Thorne, "The Movement for Public House Reform, 1892-1914," *Diet and Health in Modern Britain*, ed. Derek J. Oddy and Derek S. Miller (Croom Helm, 1985). See also John R. Greenaway, "The 'Improved' Public House, 1870-1950: the Key to Civilized Drinking or the Primrose Path to Drunkenness?," *Addiction* 93 no. 2 (Feb. 1998): 173-81, and his other publications. For Frederick Jayne, Bishop of Chester, see Frances Knight. "Recreation or Renunciation: Episcopal Interventions in the Drink Question in the 1890s," in Stewart J. Brown and others, ed., *Religion, Identity and Conflict in Britain* (Routledge, 2016). For Lord Grey, see Brian Bennison, "Lord Grey's Public House Reform," *Tyne and Tweed Issue (Journal of the Northumberland Local History Society)* 48 (1993-94): 68-72. I thank David W. Gutzke for a copy of Bennison's article. Excerpted documents can be found in Malleck, ed., *Drugs, Alcohol and Addiction,* vol. 3.

[2] He proposed the Gothenburg scheme as part of an outline of a political program. Chamberlain to Salisbury, 29 Oct. 1894. Garvin, *Life of Chamberlain* 2: 616.

[3] Arthur Shadwell identifies a rector in Warwickshire as the pioneer of disinterested management in England. At the time that Shadwell published *Drink, Temperance, and Legislation* (Longmans, 1903), the clergyman had operated the Boar's Head for more than a quarter century.

[4] Jayne to Chamberlain, 27 May, 13, 17 June, 3, 6, 10 July 1894. University of Birmingham, Joseph Chamberlain papers, JC 5/47/3, 4, 6-9.

[5] Joseph Chamberlain and others, *Public House Reform: Report of the Grosvenor House Meeting (July 6th, 1894)* (Chester, n.d.).

[6.] Gladstone to Lord Thring, [no day] Sept. 1894, in *Times*, 19 Sept. 1894, p. 4. As early as 1876 Gladstone had requested Alexander Balfour to write a pamphlet in favor of the Gothenburg scheme. Dingle, *Campaign for Prohibition*, p. 75.

[7] Louis Harcourt's journals, 28 Sept. 1894. Consulted at Stanton Harcourt. Earlier Joseph Malins had provided Harcourt with information about the Gothenberg scheme as his request. Malins had already been to Sweden and Norway three times since 1880 and was about to leave for a fourth visit. Bodleian, Harcourt MS147, Malins to A. Spencer Wells, 9 Nov. 1894.

[8] Quoted in Barker, *Gladstone and Radicalism*, p. 252.

[9] Gladstone to Thomas Snape, 11 Sept. 1895, in *Times*, 5 Oct. 1895, p. 8.

[10] Gladstone stood by his commitment to the principle of local option (as he called Local Veto), but he did not think that it was sufficient. *Alliance News*, 11 October 1895, p. 657.

[11] Chamberlain's interview in the *Birmingham Daily Mail* as reported in *Times*, 28 Sept. 1894. Bodleian, Harcourt MS 156.

[12] *Westminster Gazette*, 5 Oct. 1894. Harcourt MS 156.

[13] Buxton in *Times*, 2 Jan. 1895. Bodleian, Harcourt MS 155. Harcourt collected a mass of clippings and data about the Gothenburg Scheme.

[14] In the same year (1896) the Scottish Threefold Option Alliance was organized. It advocated local votes on reduction, disinterested management (these two requiring a simple majority), and prohibition (requiring a two-thirds majority).

[15] Lawson sneered about "the 'Grey' Goose Scheme--the latest dodge for propping up the [drink] traffic." Lawson to Hicks, 7 Aug. 1901. Alliance minutes, 14 Aug. 1901.

[16] Bennison, "Lord Grey's Public House Reform," p. 69.

[17] Reginald Cripps, *Public House Reform, with a Brief Account of the Public-House Trust Movement* (Church of England Temperance Society, Depot, [1901]; A. MacCullum Scott, "Temperance Legislation: History of the Movement," *Reformers' Year Book* (1907), p. 199; Reginald Cripps in testimony taken on 1 April 1930, in *Minutes of Evidence taken before the Royal Commission on Licensing (England and Wales)* (London, 1929-31), pp. 915-16; [Grey] to Oliver Williams, 11 July 1901. University of Durham, Department of Palaeography, 4th Earl Grey papers, uncatalogued when consulted. There are abundant tracts published by Earl Grey's organization at Durham. Cripps was secretary of the Central Public House Trust Association [organized in 1901] since 1917 and secretary of the People's Refreshment House Association, Ltd., since 1901.

[18] Humbler people also supported Gothenburg trust houses. For instance, the shareholders of the Brechin Bolag in eastern Scotland, organized in April 1900, included shoemakers, insurance agents, bleachfield workers, librarians, photographers, police constables, and even distillery workers. Charles McMaster, "The Brechin Bolag," *Scottish Brewing Archive Newsletter*, no. 6 (Winter 1985).

[19] Gray to C.N. Cumming, 25 Sept. 1901. University of Durham, Department of Paleography and Diplomatic, Earl Grey Papers (4th Earl).

[20] Other trust house companies that combined developed into a high quality hotel chain, with 181 trust hotels in 1971 when it merged with Forte.

[21] In his entry in the *Oxford Dictionary of National Biography*, Robert Fitzgerald called Rowntree "one of the Victorian and Edwardian period's most successful businessmen." Rowntree had put forward part of his scheme several years earlier. Joseph Rowntree, *A Paper on Temperance Legislation Read at a Conference of the Friends' Temperance Union of London, February 3rd, 1892.*

[22] Favorably reviewed, it went through six printings in the first eight months and two more in the following year, followed by a cheap edition in 1901, for a total of 90,000 copies sold. Rowntree published with Sherwell several other books: *British "Gothenberg" Experiments and Public-House Trusts* (Hodder & Stoughton), *Public Control of the Liquor Trade*, *The Taxation of the Liquor Trade*, and *State Purchase of the Liquor Trade*.

[23] Lyttelton to his wife Edith, 24 May 1899, quoted in Edith Lyttelton, *Alfred Lyttelton: An Account of His Life* (Longmans, 1917), p. 227.

[24] Joseph Rowntree and Arthur Sherwell, *British "Gothenburg" Experiments*, p. 162.

[25] For an introduction to the debate over drink, society, and economics, see James

---

B. Brown, "The Stye or the Pig: Drink and Poverty in Late Victorian England," *International Review of Social History* 18 (1973): 380-95.

[26] Relevant to this discussion is Ian Packer, "Religion and the New Liberalism: The Rowntree Family, Quakerism, and Social Reform," *Journal of British Studies* 42 no. 2 (April 2003): 236-57. It looks at a younger Rowntree generation.

[27] *British "Gothenburg" Experiments and Public-House Trusts* (Hodder and Stoughton, 1901), pp. 4 (quotations),128.

[28] *Temperance Problem and Social Reform*, p. 2.

[29] *Temperance Problem and Social Reform*, p. 512.

[30] *Temperance Problem and Social Reform*, p. 518.

[31] *Temperance Problem and Social Reform*, p. 507.

[32] *Temperance Problem and Social Reform*, p. 596. They did not favor the kind of reformed public house that would attract young teetotalers with entertainment and amenities. Instead, they wanted, parallel to the Gothenburg houses, entirely separate non-alcoholic People's Palaces. *Temperance Problem and Social Reform*, pp. 391-92.

[33] Originally Rowntree and Sherwell were committed to localism. In contrast, during World War I they favored a national version of disinterested management.

[34] *Temperance Problem and Social Reform*, p. 743.

[35] *Temperance Problem and Social Reform*, p. 599.

[36] *Temperance Problem and Social Reform*, p. 603.

[37] *Temperance Problem and Social Reform*, p. xiv.

[38] *Temperance Problem and Social Reform*, pp. 572-85.

[39] Reporting a talk with Sherwell, Colonel H.J. Crauford to Lord Grey, 4 April [no year], and reporting a talk with Rowntree, Crauford to Grey, 26 July [no year]. Sherwell concurred with Lord Grey about the inexpediency of raising in the current Parliament a dual option of veto and management. Sherwell to Lord Grey, 20 March 1903. University of Durham, Department of Paleography and Diplomatic, Earl Grey Papers (4th Earl), uncatalogued when consulted.

[40] *British "Gothenburg" Experiments*, 128.

[41] *British "Gothenburg" Experiments*, 4.

[42] Leif Jones, a militant prohibitionist, regarded Whittaker as an erring friend, while he saw Sherwell as a foe. Although Whittaker was willing to postpone and supplement Local Veto, he still wanted the Veto eventually. Sherwell did not. Jones to Lady Carlisle, 8 Aug. 1907. Castle Howard, Ninth Countess of Carlisle papers, J23/100. On another occasion Leif Jones called Whittaker "a hot tempered blunderer." Jones to Lady Carlisle, 4 Nov. 1908. Castle Howard, Ninth Countess of Carlisle papers, J23/100.

[43] Interview with Whittaker in *Westminster Gazette*, 5 Oct. 1896. Bodleian, Harcourt MS 156.

[44] Whittaker, "Memorandum on Some Phases of the Liquor Licensing Laws, with Suggestion for their Amendment." C.9076, XXXV, p. 334.

[45] Royal Commission on Liquor Licensing Reform, *PP*, C. 9379, 1899, *Memorandum*, 325 (part of section entitled, "Municipalisation or the Gothenburg System," pp. 312-25, 342).

[46] See "The Rise of Disinterested Management," *Prohibitionist*, Sept. 1906, pp. 68-70.

[47] Whittaker, "The Lessons Taught by Legislation for the Promotion of Temperance," in John Turner Rae, *The World's Temperance Congress of 1900* (Ideal Publishing Union, n.d.), 287.

[48] Whittaker visited Norway in 1902. Whittaker to Whyte, 9 Sept. 1902. Alliance minutes, 10 Sept. 1902.

[49] Whittaker, *Temperance Reform and State Purchase: Some Lessons of the Past* (3rd ed., Temperance Legislation League Pamphlet, B Series, No. 28) (Temperance Legislation League, [1919?]), p. 4.

[50] Whittaker, *Some Frank and Friendly Words to Temperance People (and Incidentally Some Others)* (Temperance Legislation League Pamphlets) (Farrington, 1903), p. 29 note.

[51] Whittaker to Whyte, 7 Aug. 1902; Lawson to Whyte, 9 Aug. 1902, in Alliance minutes, 13 Aug. 1902.

[52] Reprint edition, ed. Bentley B. Gilbert (Harvester Press, 1973), pp. 165-210. Noel Buxton worked for the family brewery from 1889 to 1904. His uncle E.N. Buxton encouraged him to stand for Parliament as a Liberal in 1900. In 1905 Herbert Gladstone found him a usually Tory seat that he won. Mosa Anderson, *Noel Buxton: A Life* (George Allen & Unwin, 1951), pp. 27, 31, 35.

[53] Whittaker, *Some Frank and Friendly Words to Temperance People*, p. 32. See also *Alliance News*, 19 Nov. 1905, p. 776. The text of the Manifesto and an account of its critics, notably the National Temperance Federation, appear conveniently in Scottish Temperance *Annual* (1904), pp. 120-25. See David M. Fahey, *Temperance Societies in Late Victorian and Edwardian England*, pp. 46-52.

[54] *Good Templars' Watchword*, 10 Oct. 1903, p. 487. See also Joseph Malins to unknown correspondent, 2 Oct. 1903, in Alliance minutes, 7 Oct. 1903. Malins pointed out the signatories had been chosen for their prestige and not for their expertise on temperance legislation. Although Malins also said that temperance societies had not been consulted, the National Temperance League's executive committee by a "mem. con. vote," that is, unanimously allowed its secretary, John Turner Rae, to sign the Manifesto and later left him free to join the committee of the Temperance Legislation League, organized to promote the Manifesto program. Livesey library (Sheffield), National Temperance League minute book, 22 Oct.1903 (#2079), 23 Nov. 1905 (#2474).

[55] *Birmingham Daily Post*, 19 Oct. 1903, p. 2. Although one of the recipients of the Manifesto had shown it to Malins, he denied disclosing it to the *Post* because it had been marked "Strictly Private and Confidential." When the *Post* asked him for a copy, he refused, but he did give the newspaper a letter of the president of the Primitive Methodist conference rejecting the Manifesto program. *Good Templars' Watchword,* 31 Oct. 1903.

[56] *Daily News*, 20 Oct. 1903. See also *Times*, 21 Oct. 1903. Whittaker, *Some Frank and Friendly Words to Temperance People* (1903), p. 34.

[57] Whittaker, *Some Frank and Friendly Words*, p. 24. Later signatories included the historian G.P. Gooch, Francis W. Fox, one of the authors of the Westminster bill, and Alderman T. Vesey Strong, J.P., chairman of the London Temperance Hospital. *Times*, 6 Nov. 1903, p. 4. For Nonconformist support for disinterested management, see Bebbington, *The Nonconformist Conscience*, p. 49.

---

[58] Years earlier Caine nearly bankrupted himself by paying the debts of a company with which he was associated, something he was not legally bound to do. As a result, he left an estate of barely £2,500.

[59] Whittaker's wife Emma (d. 1938) and W.S. Caine's wife Alice (d. 1918) were active in the rival, single-issue Women's Total Abstinence Union and not the larger organization headed successively by Lady Henry Somerset and the Countess of Carlisle.

[60] Lady Carlisle to Whyte, 25 Nov. 1903. Alliance minutes, 2 Dec. 1903. In 1901 Lady Carlisle, head of the executive committee of the major Liberal women's organization since 1891, had been "elbowed out" of office and replaced by Lady Aberdeen. Lady Carlisle to Mrs. Reid, 15 May 1901. Castle Howard, Ninth Countess of Carlisle papers, J23/336. On 17 November 1903, Lady Carlisle got the executive committee of the Women's Liberal Federation to refuse to admit the Manifesto deputation that Lady Aberdeen had invited and which was waiting outside the door of the committee room. Lady Carlisle was Women's Liberal Federation president again in 1906-1914.

[61] See *Good Templar's Watchword*, 31 Oct. 1903; and interview with Joseph Malins, in *Good Templar's Watchword*, 7 Nov. 1903, 26 Dec. 1903.

[62] Tom Honeyman to Leif Jones, 25 Nov.1903. Castle Howard, Ninth Countess of Carlisle papers, J23/242.

[63] *Good Templars' Watchword*, 26 Dec. 1903, pp. 614-15. Malins said that Lady Henry Somerset left the presidency of the National British Women's Temperance Association to promote the Manifesto.

[64] Reprinted in the *Good Templars' Watchword*, 7 Nov. 1903, p. 530.

[65] *Temperance Chronicle*, 30 Oct. 1903, p. 532. Earlier the newspaper had expressed sympathy with the version of the Gothenberg scheme presented by Rowntree and Sherwell in their book, *Public Control of the Liquor Traffic*. It described as "fascinating" the chapter that described the destruction of the political role of the drink trade in Sweden and Norway. *Temperance Chronicle*, 29 May 1903, p. 264.

[66] *Temperance Chronicle*, 6 Nov. 1903, p. 544.

[67] Tom Honeyman to Leif Jones, 24 October 1903, 25 Nov. 1903. Castle Howard, Ninth Countess of Carlisle papers, JJ23/242.

[68] A.S. Rowntree to M.K. Rowntree, 7 Sept. 1910, in *The Letters of Arnold Stephenson Rowntree to Mary Katherine Rowntree, 1910-1918*, ed. Ian Packer (Cambridge University Press for the Royal Historical Society, 2002), p. 42.

[69] *Some Frank and Friendly Words*, p. 28.

[70] *Some Frank and Friendly Words*, p. 26.

[71] *Some Frank and Friendly Words*, p. 26.

[72] *Some Frank and Friendly Words*, p. 34.

[73] *Some Frank and Friendly Words*, p. 34.

[74] Leif Jones to Lady Carlisle, 8 Aug. 1907. Castle Howard, Ninth Countess of Carlisle papers, J23/100.

[75] John H. Robert to editor, 6 Sept. 1906, in *Tribune*, 8 Sept. 1906, p. 9.

[76] Obituary, in *Monthly Notes* 25 (Jan.-Feb. 1935), 12-16. Guthrie's commitment to temperance in everything led to the nickname, "Alexander the Less." Waller, *Democracy and Sectarianism*, p. 108.

[77] *Disinterested Company Management: Correspondence between Sir Wilfrid Lawson, Bart., M.P., and Mr. Alexander Guthrie* (1905]). .11. Annotated as received from Joseph Malins on 8 June 1905, there is a copy in Alliance minutes, 21 June 1905. See also Arthur Sherwell's questions to Leif Jones, on 9 July 1930, in *Minutes of Evidence taken before the Royal Commission on Licensing (England and Wales),* quests. 20, 243-30, 354 (p. 1725).

[78] Lawson to Guthrie, 23 June 1905, in *Disinterested Company Management,* p. 10. "One really knows very little who pulls the string in these matters and probably it is as well that one does not know."

[79] For a sketch, see Arthur Sherwell, "Sir Thomas Whittaker," *Monthly Notes* 9/11-12 (Nov-Dec. 1919): 55-56. Sherwell described him (p. 56) as "a fearless, and often a blunt, fighter." Historians have written little about the Temperance Legislation League, and the *Oxford Dictionary of National Biography* lacks entries for its two major figures, Whittaker and Sherwell.

[80] For the text of the final Board meeting (15 Nov. 1905), see *Temperance Chronicle,* 24 Nov. 1905, p. 581. See also *Good Templars Watchword,* 2 Dec. 1905, p. 571. The Board had lost to the new League its president (Peel), its chairman (Whittaker), and its treasurer (G.W. Brown) who was its main source of funds. The main opponent of dissolution was Henry J. Wilson, MP. Dawson Burns remained an honorary (that is, unpaid) secretary of the Central Temperance Legislation Board until October 1904. Alliance minutes, 26 Oct. 1904. In a *Tribune* interview with John Hilton, the Alliance parliamentary agent who had been one of the Board's honorary secretaries, claimed that not all who adhered to the League agreed about disinterested management. Twenty-four Alliance vice-presidents (an honorary position) had endorsed the League. *Licensed Trade News,* 8 Sept. 1906, p. 3.

[81] *Alliance News,* 23 Nov. 1905, p.761. For the policies of the League, see *Scottish Temperance Annual* (1906), p. 159. For public correspondence and resolutions against public management, see pp. 159-219.

[82] *Licensing Problem: The Option of Disinterested Management* (Temperance Legislation Pamphlets, No. 1) (ca. 1905), 17.

[83] T.P. Whittaker, *Temperance Reform* (Temperance Legislation League Pamphlets, No. 6) (London, 1906), 3.

[84] Unlike many of the people who had been associated with the Board, Hilton was a man of modest mean who left an estate of about £977.

[85] *Temperance Chronicle,* 24 Nov. 1905, pp. 574-75, 581; John Hilton, interview in *Tribune,* 31 Aug. 1906, p. 8. See also *Alliance News,* 23 Nov. 1905, p. 761.

[86] E. Stafford Howard to Archbishop Randall Davidson, 20 Feb. 1906. Lambeth Palace Library, Davidson Papers, T. 2. The Archbishop declined to endorse the League's program in a form which would commit him to all its proposals as they included Local Veto which he disliked. Davidson to Whittaker, 3 March 1906. Lambeth Palace Library, Davidson Papers, T.2. In 1907 Davidson signed a memorial in favor of disinterested management. *Temperance Chronicle,* 29 March 1907, p. 145.

[87] Alfred Francis Harvey (b. 1870) had been assistant secretary of the CETS and secretary of the Central Temperance Legislation Board, 1898-1905, at which point

he became general secretary of the Temperance Legislation League. He still held that office in the mid-1920s. *Standard Encyclopedia of the Alcohol Problem.*

[88] Joseph Rowntree, *The Licensing Problem and Fundamental Principles in Licensing Reform* (Temperance Legislation League, Pamphlets No. 4) (London, [1906]), 3-4; Arthur Sherwell at National Liberal Club, 2 Dec. 1907. Sherwell also disagreed with Whittaker's advocacy of a representative element in the local licensing authority.

[89] League supporters included well known people such as Frederic Harrison, Sir J.T. Brunner, Sir John Gorst, L.G. Chiozza-Money, Gen. Booth of the Salvation Army, Prof. W.J. Ashley, George Cadbury, J. St. Loe Strachey, Joseph Rowntree, B. Seebohm Rowntree, and Philip Snowden. List in Archbishop Davidson's papers. T.2 Lambeth Palace. Booth's signature surprised Malins. *Good Templars Watchword*, 26 Dec. 1903, p. 414.

[91] Sherwell, in *Temperance Chronicle*, 26 Nov. 1906, pp. 565, 568-69. Thirty-eight Alliance vice-presidents supported the new League.

[92] *Licensing Problem: The Option of Disinterested Management* (Temperance Legislation League, Pamphlets No. 1 (London, ca. 1905), Appendix.

[93] *Alliance News*, 8 September 1908, p. 572.

[94] Quoted in Williams and Brake, *Drink in Great Britain*, p. 100.

[95] "The Late Sir Wilfrid Lawson and Disinterested Management," *Monthly News* 20 (July/August 1930).

[96] Royal Commission, *Parliamentary Papers c. 9076, 1898 (Precis of Evidence)*, 67400-67402.

[97] *Times*, day? Sept. 1894, p. 11. The Alliance once smiled at disinterested management because it thought "the transition from such a scheme to one of Prohibition, would not be a very difficult task." Annual Report (1869), quoted in Carter, *The English Temperance Movement*, p. 198.

[98] Russell, ed., *Sir Wilfrid Lawson: A Memoir,* pp. 129-30.

[99] Lawson to Lady Henry Somerset, 29 June 1905, in *Alliance News*, 23 Aug. 1906, p. 536.

[100] Lawson to Hicks, 30 April 1906. Quoted in Fowler, *Life of Edward Lee Hicks*, p. 197. A few days later he added: "There are scores and scores of our excellent, but silly sheep, who would be delighted to browse on Sunday closing, barmaids, or 'reversal' [of the 1904 legislation]. The Veto would solve all these problems." Lawson to Hicks, 10 May 1906. Fowler, *Life of Hicks*, p. 198.

[101] John H. Roberts in *Tribune*, 6 Sept. 1906, p. 9. Whittaker was much less the all-around Radical than Lawson had been. During the South Africa war Whittaker stood aloof from the pro-Boer faction. Koss, *Nonconformity*, p. 33. In 1906 an ardent Conservative described him as "one of the best type of Radical members," which is to say not too Radical. *The Modernisation of Conservative Politics: The Diaries and Letters of William Bridgeman, 1904-1935*, ed. Philip Williamson (Historians' Press, 1988), p. 29. In 1909 he vehemently criticized the "People's Budget." In the first of the 1910 general elections, his Labour Party opponent in a three-way contest called Whittaker "the greater Tory" than the Conservative candidate. *Yorkshire Observer*, 11 Jan. 1910 quoted in Neal Blewett, *The Peers, the Parties and the*

People: The British General Elections of 1910 (University of Toronto Press, 1972), p. 219. In the "coupon" election of 1918 Whittaker was reelected as a Coalition Liberal. (Ironically, he had strongly opposed the original 1915 coalition.) When a Coalition Liberal, he supported an elected upper house. While others favored keeping some of the original members of the House of Lords, he vigorously opposed bishops as members. *Real Old Tory Politics: The Political Diaries of Sir Robert Sanders, Lord Bayford, 1910-35*, ed. John Ramsden (Historians' Press, 1984), p. 90 (5 Oct. 1917), p. 99 (2 Feb. 1918). "His feeling against the Church is very real and bitter." On many issues Whittaker was a moderate, no surprise for a Wesleyan, sometime editor of a business newspaper *(Daily Oracle*, 1889-92) and a successful insurance executive (managing director of UK Temperance and General Provident Institution since 1898 and later its chairman).

[102] E. Tennyson Smith, quoted in *Licensing World*. 29 Sept. 1906, p. 203.

[103] T.P. Whittaker, 30 Aug., 4 Sept. 1906, reprinted with supplementary material as *Temperance Reform: A Policy of Inclusion: Who Has Changed Front?* (Temperance Legislation League, Pamphlets No. 6) (London, 1906).

[104] For instance, see Malins, testifying on July 6, 1898, in Royal Commission on Liquor Licensing, *Minutes of Evidence*, vol. 8, *PP* (C. 9075, 1898, vol. XXXIV, quests. 71,938-72,098 (pp. 643-53) and Appendix XII (pp. 760-67).

[105] Oliver Williams (?) to Whittaker, (date?). University of Durham, Department of Paleography, 4th Earl Grey Papers, uncatalogued when consulted. Williams was secretary to the Central Public-house Trust Association.

[106] Whittaker, *Temperance Reform: Who Has Changed Front?* (reprinted from the *Tribune,* 4 Sept. 1906), (Temperance Legislation League pamphlet, No. 6), p. 13.

[107] Whittaker, *Temperance Reform: Who Has Changed Front?*, p. 11.

[108] *Temperance Chronicle*, 8 Feb. 1907, p. 61.

[109] Alexander MacCullum Scott was a Liberal MP and then a Lloyd George Coalition Liberal MP from 1910 to 1922. Two years later he joined the Labour Party. He had been an early ally of Winston Churchill whose biography he wrote. Cameron Hazlehurst contributed Scott's entry in the *Oxford Dictionary of National Biography*. Scott died relatively young in an airplane accident. For an example of Scott as a temperance exponent, see the *Reformers' Year Book* (1907), "Temperance Legislation: History of the Movement," pp. 196-99, and "A Practical Policy," pp. 199-201.

[110] When I traced one of Whittaker's daughters and her children to Argentina, they told me that they did not have his papers but that she remembered his nickname, Lord Drinkwater.

[111] Whittaker, "Lessons of the Past."

[112] *Temperance Problem and Social Reform*, p. 602. Rowntree and Sherwell were emphatically in favor of high license by the time of the publication of their book, *The Taxation of the Liquor Trade* (1906).

[113] *Times*, day? Dec. 1902.

[114] Andrew Bonar Law to unnamed correspondent, 2 April 1908. Beaverbrook Library, now at the House of Lords Records Office, Bonar Law Papers, 18/8/7.

[115] [Arthur Sherwell], "Prohibition and its Sequel," *Monthly Notes* 22 (Oct. 1932).

---

[116] This paragraph is based on Per Franberg, "Drink and Drinking Culture in 19th Century Sweden--Some New Perspectives" (unpublished paper, 1987). See also chapter one, "The Swedish Snaps," in Kettil Bruun and Per Franberg, eds., *Den Svenska Supen. En Historia om Brannvin, Bratt och Byrakrati* (Drink in Sweden. A History of Brandy, Bratt and Bureaucracy). (Stockholm, 1985); and Franberg, "The Social and Political Significance of Two Swedish Restrictive Systems," *Contemporary Drug Problems* (Spring 1985).

Alliance News, 1923
*Leif Jones

Stirling District

RT. HON. SIR H. CAMPBELL-BANNERMAN (R)

1895—Rt Hon Sir H. C.-Bannerman (R)	..	2786
S. McCaskie (C)	..	1653
Majority	..	1133
1892—Campbell-Bannerman (R)	.. ..	2791
Hughes (LU)	..	1695
Majority	..	1096

Representation Unchanged

RT. HON. HERBERT J. GLAD-
STONE (R)

1895—Rt Hon H. J. Gladstone (R)	.. ..	6314
Colonel North (C)	..	6218
Majority	..	96
1892—Gladstone (R)	.. ..	5974
Greenwood (C)..	.. ..	5621
Majority	..	353

Representation Unchanged

Herbert Gladstone

Cumberland (Cookermouth)

SIR WILFRID LAWSON, BT. (R)

1895—Sir W. Lawson (R)	.. ..	4259
T. Milvain, Q.C. (C)	.. ..	4018
	Majority	241
1892—Lawson (R)	.. ..	4599
Scott Napier (C)	.. ..	3828
	Majority	71

Representation Unchanged

Sir Wilfrid Lawson

THE RT. HON. THE MARQUIS OF SALISBURY
Prime Minister and Foreign Secretary

Lord Salisbury

National Portrait Gallery (by permission)
Whittaker

John Newton biography
WS Caine

Thomas Jones biography
David Lloyd George

Blanche Dugdale biography
Balfour

J.A. Spender and Cyril Asquith biography
Asquith

Alchetron encyclopedia
Arthur Sherwell

CHAPTER EIGHT

BALFOUR'S LICENSING ACT

Early in the twentieth century the prolonged stalemate over major licensing legislation came to an end.[1] A drastic change in the administration of the old laws forced a change in the laws themselves. The licensing justices long had enjoyed great discretionary powers, repeatedly reaffirmed by the courts but seldom exercised. Numerous licensing committees refused large numbers of renewals to reduce the number of public houses. The old status quo broke down without any new legislation. The magisterial reduction movement (by what the trade called the biased bench) threatened to do in a few years what the organized temperance movement had failed to achieve in several generations of agitation: close large numbers of licensed premises and cripple the trade financially. It was the licensed drink trade rather than the temperance party that had to appeal for legislation. The status quo no longer would protect its interests.

In retrospect, it was the publication of the reports of the Royal Commission and the minutes of evidence that preceded them, educating the public to the need for drastic licensing reform, which created the climate of opinion that forced the passage of Balfour's Licensing Act. The Unionist Government showed no immediate enthusiasm for licensing legislation based on even the moderate majority report, but in its indifference the Government was out of step with the mood in the country and even that in Parliament. In May 1900 Salisbury secured the defeat in the House of Lords of a resolution in favor of the recommendations common to both reports by a margin of only 45 to 42.[2] Its sponsor the Bishop of Winchester (and future Archbishop of Canterbury), Dr. Randall Davidson, proved more successful three days later when the Upper House of Convocation of the Province of Canterbury approved the same resolution. The trade objected to this stratagem of the moderate reformers who picked out reforms proposed in both reports for piecemeal legislation. The trade complained that it had offered its concessions as a part of a general settlement providing security for the future.[3] The trade suffered additional embarrassment later in 1900 when several beer drinkers in Manchester and elsewhere in the North of England died during the "arsenic in beer" scare. In addition, the high prices that the brewers had paid in building their tied house empires, combined with sluggish beer consumption, left the drink trade financially weakened.

Early in 1901, after the general election had shelved Lord Peel's report, Sir Algernon West led a deputation which urged C.T. Ritchie to sponsor legislation on the lines of the majority report. The new Home Secretary responded with decided coolness.[4] As a consequence, in March 1901 the Bishop of Winchester (Randall Davidson) introduced three bills for minor licensing reforms, all of which died, although the Government expressed sympathy for his bill about habitual drunkards. Davidson was a lifelong abstainer. In the same year the Government reluctantly allowed facilities for a private member's bill in the House of Commons to protect children from drink. The bill touched no vital trade interest and was amended to make it even more innocuous. The promoters of the bill changed the definition of the age of protected children. By a one-vote margin a grand committee weakened the bill. As amended, the bill changed from one to prevent children from entering a public house to one that required sealed containers to prevent children under fourteen from sipping the alcohol they fetched for adults.[5] The Sale of Intoxicating Liquors to Children Act, popularly known as the Child Messengers' Act, although accepted by the brewers, angered the provincial retail trade. It also symbolized the kind of consensus reform that no Government could easily refuse. The chairman of the provincial licensed victuallers' society might choose to describe the bill as an insult to the publican and "one of the most stupid Acts that was ever proposed to the House of Commons," but the bill became law with little House of Commons opposition.[6] A licensed victuallers' newspaper argued that in retrospect the 1901 legislation hurt the trade, despite Government assurances to the contrary. It "sensibly decreased the drawings of thousands of licensed houses, and drove the jug and bottle trade into the hands of the off-license holders."[7]

The pressure on the Government for a licensing reform bill increased when Joseph Chamberlain, opening a temperance hall in Birmingham in October 1901, platitudinously suggested that reformers concentrate their efforts on the enactment of a few limited reform. Temperance leaders chose to interpret Chamberlain's remarks as a statement of Government policy or at least of a personal commitment by the powerful colonial secretary.[8]

Ritchie had been quietly at work on a limited licensing bill. This was the last drink-related bill that was the result of the initiative of a minister rather than the Government as a whole. Ritchie was more sympathetic to temperance reform than his predecessor Ridley had been. In January Ritchie had asked the Cabinet for authority to prepare a bill. "A large number of our supporters are committed to Temperance reform of some kind; and among them are to be found many of the most influential and moderate men of the party." In November he circulated a memorandum outlining his proposed amendments of the law controlling habitual drunkards and revising licensing administration. He also stated his intention of adding a scheme for the regulation of clubs. At the end of the month, he announced in public that the Government would sponsor "a very considerable measure of temperance reform" but revealed none of its contents.[9] Trade leaders were alarmed about his reluctance to consult with them, but when the bill was introduced in January the brewers considered it too unimportant and too popular to fight. Speaking at Perth to the Scottish Licensed Trade Association, Harry George Younger (1866-1940) advised the trade to bend before the demand for reform as it did not endanger the trade's survival. He added that, despite the large Unionist majority in the House of Commons, "there was, he did not know why, a growing antipathy to their trade."[10] The bill angered the publicans by strengthening the penalties that would fall on them for the sale of liquor to intoxicated persons.[11] A publicans' newspaper complained about "a fresh series of petty restrictions."[12] The off-license holders, led by the Gilbey interest, also resented the provisions that subjected their wine and spirits business to magisterial supervision.[13] As they carried little weight in trade politics or with a Unionist ministry, the mostly Liberal off-licensees could be sacrificed to the forces of reform.[14] Ritchie proved more conciliatory with the working class clubs that the Working Men's Club and Institute Union represented.[15] On balance, Ritchie's Licensing Act of 1902 passed through Parliament with little controversy.[16] Perhaps the greatest immediate effect of the legislation was the elimination of many "bogus" clubs that were common in London.[17]

In June of the same year the Court of Appeal reaffirmed in the Farnham case the right of the licensing justices to deny license renewals to advance the policy of reducing the number of licensed premises. It established that the discretion of the justices was administrative, not narrowly judicial, that the justices themselves could initiate the objection to renewal, and that they were not personally liable for the expenses incurred when a license holder appealed to Quarter Sessions.[18] Apparently fearing that the House of Lords might add its judicial authority to this decision, the National Trade Defence Association purchased the rights and obligations of the Licenses Insurance Corporation and Guarantee Fund, Ltd., which had insured the Farnham license holders against non-renewal, and then suppressed the application for appeal.[19]

Because of the coincidence in time, license holders often blamed the Licensing Act of 1902 for stimulating licensing benches to adopt the local reduction schemes that appeared in the brewster sessions in 1903. In fact, the Licensing Act of 1902 had little connection with magisterial reduction.

Another major influence behind the magisterial reduction movement was the Birmingham Surrender Scheme. Other licensing benches, notably Liverpool's, already had substantially reduced the number of licensed premises with the aid of street improvements and slum clearances that had destroyed many public houses and beer shops.[20] Moreover, some benches insisted on a surrender of two or more old licenses as a condition for granting a new license. Brewers agreed to exchange small, unprofitable houses for new houses in districts with growing populations.

In Birmingham the possibility of a general reduction in numbers, made in cooperation with the trade and consequently without appeals to Quarter Sessions, became a reality with the development of a local form of compensation. Birmingham clearly had too many licensed premises. There was a licensed house for every 217 persons or one for every 140 persons over the age of fifteen. Under pressure from a licensing committee headed (1893-1903) by Arthur Chamberlain (1842-1913), the colonial secretary's brother, the major Birmingham brewers agreed to a voluntary reduction in the number of licensed premises. A few local brewers motivated by a strong communal spirit owned nearly all the licensed houses. The Birmingham press championed the reduction scheme. From 1898 through 1903 the Birmingham Surrender Scheme brought about the surrender of 183 licensed houses out of 2163, including thirteen pre-1869 beer shops protected from magisterial discretion. The direct cost of £173,000 was borne by a limited property company comprising very few breweries: nine in 1897, seventeen in 1899, and thirteen in 1903, which subscribed funds to compensate those who surrendered their licenses. In return, the justices cooperated with the trade on such matters as approving structural alterations. Prominent Birmingham brewers warmly supported this cooperative plan of reform, despite friction over the number of surrenders in the summer of 1901, the increasing prices demanded by owners of free houses and by brewers who did not subscribe to the Property Company, and apprehension by drink traders in other parts of the country about the precedent.[21]

The criticism in both the majority and minority reports of the Royal Commission that there were too many licensed premises, the Farnham case of 1902 in which the courts reaffirmed the discretionary powers of the justices, and the Birmingham Surrender Scheme combined to encourage licensing justices to initiate reduction plans. In the brewsters session of February and March 1903 the number of licenses refused renewal was more than three times what had been normal. The licensing committees refused to renew 639 licenses of which Quarter Sessions restored at least 159 on appeal. At least another 350 were surrendered, nominally voluntarily, under pressure. That about 400 licensing benches discussed reduction for the future disturbed the trade even more than actual non-renewals and forced surrenders.[22] In Birmingham the local scheme of compensated surrender soured when Arthur Chamberlain urged a great new reduction of 500 licenses over three years and denounced any statutory compensation that would restrict magisterial discretion. The shareholders at Holt brewery revolted. The Birmingham publicans and their customers already had been angered by his prohibition of air gun clubs sponsored by public houses. In October 1903, the full magisterial bench defeated Arthur Chamberlain for reelection as chair of the licensing committee by a vote of 40 to 20. He also was removed from the licensing committee altogether.[23]

Arthur Chamberlain could be a difficult man. The official history of the company that he guided to great success described him:

> [He had an] ascetic appearance and grave demeanor [and] his most striking characteristics were an almost pathological probity, a faculty of detachment which at times came perilously near ruthlessness, and a fervent conviction that of all sins Intemperance was by far the most deadly. The reaction he evoked in those around him varied from violent resentment to reluctant respect.[24]

As the justices took up the reduction campaign, a sense of urgency weighted upon the trade. Unless the Unionist Government intervened, the situation seemed hopeless as the refusals to renew were legal. It was not enough for the trade to block hostile legislation. It needed a statute. Furthermore, the trade was relatively isolated. In the battle against Local Veto, it could rally the support of tens of thousands of working-class electors who considered prohibition to be class legislation, an affront to their liberties as Englishmen. When the justices winnowed the numbers of licensed premises the public answered with a yawn the trade's cry of confiscation by a supposedly "biased bench."[25] The pub-drinking classes faced only the inconvenience of taking their custom to another licensed house across the street, while the educated and propertied classes who feared the effect of excessive drinking on the national interest sympathized with reduction to diminish temptation. The justices symbolized a tradition of responsible, conservative-minded paternalism unlike the faddist Radicalism of the prohibitionists. In addition, the Unionist Government was tottering, the party torn by the emotional issue of tariff reform and identified with policies unpopular with large sections of the electorate such as "Chinese slavery" in the Rand, the Taff Vale decision, and the Education Act of 1902.

The licensing crisis of 1903-04 illustrated the strengths and weaknesses of the trade alliance with the Unionist Party. It was easier to get the Unionist leaders to stop hostile legislation than to sponsor a friendly bill. Despite frantic trade appeals for help, the Government initially took a hands-off attitude. It argued privately that the widespread exercise of magisterial discretion to reduce the number of licensed premises was legal, although unusual, and that the Unionist promise of statutory compensation applied only to reduction imposed by Parliament.[26] As the Prime Minister told the King: "The action, though novel, at least in degree, seems to be legal, and it is not easy to see what remedy can be applied."[27]

The Home Secretary, Aretas Akers-Douglas, met on 21 January with "some of the more sensible members of the trade."[28] Frightened and angry, the general committee of the National Trade Defence Association voted on 20 February to press for legislation.[29] Many trade meetings clamored for statutory protection.[30] On 23 February a prominent Yorkshire brewer threatened that: "we mean to have a Compensation Bill, and unless the Government do justice to this trade they will find opposed to them a huge and solid phalanx of common sense and public opinion."[31] The Government lost seats at Woolwich and Rye on 11 and 18 March. Some members of the trade (for instance, the Beer and Wine National Defence League) actively opposed the defeated Unionists, while the trade in general was "lukewarm."[32] Labour defeated the Conservatives in two-candidate contests. In the case of Woolwich, the Labour victory was one-sided, with the Labour candidate receiving 61% of the vote. In the 1900 general election and in a 1902 bye-election the Conservative candidates had been uncontested.

When Balfour received a trade deputation on 18 March, he chided the justices in hopes of discouraging further extensive license reduction. The temperance party protested in the name of both reform and constitutional propriety. Despite this controversy Balfour had avoided any promise of legislation.[33] When months passed and tariff reform threatened to bring the Liberals to power, the trade grew nervous. On 6 May the National Trade Defence Association voted that it would oppose a bill that included a time limit to compensation. The resolution was not made public but was to be used by a brewer MP, John Gretton, "in his discretion."[34] As late as 26 May a Cabinet minister, St. John Brodrick, shocked the trade by hinting that no legislative remedy was justified.[35] Many brewers already suffered from grave financial problems, the result of having purchased licensed premises at extravagant prices, a decline in the consumption of beer after 1900, and intense competition that depressed retail prices.[36] Some members of the drink trade suspected Free Trade Unionists of hostility.[37]

Under these circumstances the trade began to accept the necessity of paying for its security. It had welcomed the memorial which Sir Ralph Littler, chairman of the Middlesex Quarter Sessions, published in the *Times* on 19 February in favor of statutory compensation paid out of taxes on the trade which would permit the reduction movement to continue with greater equity.[38] Littler circulated this memorial among benches of justices to enlist their support and invited all chairmen of Quarter Sessions and the surviving members of the Royal Commission to a conference which meet in London on 23 March under the chairmanship of the Archbishop of Canterbury. This distinguished assemblage unanimously approved trade self-compensation "to facilitate a considerable reduction."[39]

Another conference, held in May and chaired by Sir Wilfrid Lawson, met in London to defend the right of magisterial discretion, sidestepping the question of compensation.[40] This limited program attracted the support of A. Cameron Corbett, J. Herbert Roberts, T.W. Russell, Lady Carlisle, Leif Jones, Arthur Chamberlain, Dr. John Clifford, Sir Robert Reid, Canon Hicks, and Guy Hayler. Although not present, T.P. Whittaker and Lord Peel wrote letters of support.

In 1903 two private member's bills that sketched alternative approaches toward providing the trade with security attracted attention. J.G. Butcher's bill required compensation from a statutory fund underwritten by the trade but otherwise left the discretionary powers of the justices intact. On 23 April this bill received a substantial majority on a second reading division. The trade preferred another bill introduced on 7 April by Sir William Hart-Dyke. It suspended the power of the justices to refuse renewals until Parliament provided for compensation unless one of several specified offenses had been committed. The trade also liked a bill that had absolutely no chance of enactment. In 1903 Lord Wemyss introduced in the House of Lords a bill that the late Lord Bramwell had drafted after the *Sharp v. Wakefield* decision. The bill would have given all licensed premises the same right of renewal enjoyed by the pre-1869 beerhouses. The Government declined to grant any of these private members' bills time on the parliamentary schedule.[41] The trade showed its anger and frustration through protest meetings such as those at Birmingham on 11 June, at Derby on 15 June, and at Burton upon Trent on 16 June. Almost five thousand temperance reformers rallied against the bills offering the trade security in a meeting on 17 July at Albert Hall. The bishop of London, A.F. Winnington-Ingram, presided over the evening demonstration.

In April Joseph Chamberlain cynically had told his constituency agent that a suspensory bill would force the trade to work vigorously for the Unionists at the next general election. "If we do all we are going to do for them, before the General Election, they will have nothing to fear, and they will not work for us out of mere gratitude."[42] On 16 June the Cabinet provisionally decided on a temporary suspensory bill.[43] The Prime Minister did not tell the trade. He merely advised the NTDA that he agreed that the problem was a pressing one. He added, with regret, the Government lacked time to do anything in the present parliamentary session.[44] The trade was left dangling. Seven weeks later Balfour told Parliament that the Government would introduce a licensing bill early in the session of 1904 and hoped that Parliament could act before the appeals from the next brewster sessions.[45] The trade bitterly compared its situation to that of the temperance party in 1892-95 when a weak Liberal Government promised the Veto but did not press its proposals.[46]

In private negotiations the Government offered the trade a temporary bill that would have suspended for five years the discretionary powers of the justices to refuse license renewals. As a gesture to temperance reformers no new licenses would be granted except in return for the surrender of two existing ones. "It is quite clear that we cannot at the present time [propose] any large compensation scheme."[47] Though the London brewers initially accepted this proposal, the country trade rejected it. By the beginning of 1904 the brewers united behind a demand for legislation without a time limit.

The Home Secretary prepared another suspensory bill without a time limit. He argued with his colleagues that the Government could accept an amendment to limit the suspension of magisterial discretion to some specified number of years.[48] At the same time moderate reformers in the Unionist Party protested any tampering with the powers of the magistrates.[49] Balfour decided to drop suspension of magisterial discretion and take the other route, compensation. He emphasized that he could not afford to alienate the trade.[50] Austen Chamberlain, the former colonial minister's son, had helped draft the Cabinet's suspensory bills. The young Chamberlain said that Balfour personally outlined the licensing bill that the Government proposed in 1904.[51] The claim by A.K. Russell that Balfour's licensing bill was "known to have been drafted in the offices of the Trade Defence League" is puzzling and undocumented.[52] In March an Exeter Hall rally against compensation and reducing the discretionary powers of the licensing justices had the support of most of the bishops.

The much delayed Government bill, introduced late in April 1904, allowed magistrates in England and Wales their traditional discretionary authority to refuse to renew licenses provided that compensation was paid, but licensing justices had to refer to Quarter Sessions the denial of licenses simply to reduce their number. Quarter Sessions were given the discretionary power to impose a levy on the trade for this purpose. As the bill set a maximum limit to the levy, the pace of reduction was necessarily restrained. If a particular Quarter Sessions chose not to impose a levy, licensing benches in that county would have no funds for compensation and would be unable to refuse renewals for the purpose of reduction. The dispossessed license holders would be paid the market value of their licensed property as it existed prior to the enactment of the bill. As part of the price the trade was to pay for the bill, it eliminated the right that pre-1869 beerhouses had to renewal and required that any new public houses pay a large fee for the monopoly value acquired through licensed status, so that Balfour might conciliate his temperance-minded followers. The bill did not include off-licenses, although many country brewers wanted them included.[53] Unionist reformers unsuccessfully asked for another much larger concession, that the trade's new statutory right to compensation be restricted by the addition of a time limit.

The trade supported the bill but only as the best it could get. E.N. Buxton, for instance, said "we look to this Bill without enthusiasm," while Edward Johnson, chairman of the organization of London publicans, concluded a speech by acknowledging "they felt that a compromise must be accepted, and so they must take the method of funding the compensation as a matter of expediency."[54]

Militant temperance reformers were powerless during the debate over Balfour's bill. A biography by her son-in-law reports that in a single month Lady Carlisle posted 4,400 letters and leaflets from her home in the fight against the bill.[55] Such efforts were irrelevant. Other than the Church of England Temperance Society, the organized temperance movement had scant influence with Balfour's MPs.

The debates on the licensing bill can be summarized around four topics: (1) the general Government case for the bill, (2) compensation and time limit, (3) magisterial discretion and local control, and (4) the procedural issue of closure by compartments. In a ritual dance between Government and Opposition, the debates ratified what Balfour had decided. Balfour benefitted from "his inexhaustible skill as a debater."[56]

Balfour stated the position of the Government during the first reading debate on 20 April. He admitted the irrationality of the present licensing system, and he deplored the growth of monopoly values that had resulted from virtually automatic renewal of annual licenses over a long span of years, but he argued that in the case of existing licenses it was an established fact that had to be recognized. A system of trade mutual insurance under State auspices would allow magistrates to decide on the renewal of licenses in the public interest with the knowledge that the legitimate interests of license holders were to be secured by compensation. The bill did not prevent the reduction of the number of licenses by the justices but separated such reduction from injustice to the individual license holder.

Balfour argued that the bill contributed to temperance reform in three ways. It enabled the magistrates to close pre-1869 beerhouses, prevented the growth of monopoly values in the future by requiring recipients of new licenses to make full payment for the profit derived from licensed status, and allowed magistrates in Quarter Sessions to deny license renewal for reasons of reduction in number with a sense of justice which at present the lack of compensation prevented.[57] Balfour criticized the Opposition for trying to "render the tenure of the publican insecure," when the public interest was served instead by attracting the most responsible sort of men into the trade.

> You will never get rid of the public house from this country, and, I frankly admit it, I do not think you ought to get rid of it. What, then should you aim at? You should aim surely at this ideal, that the public-house which you have should be kept respectably, should be kept by respectable persons, and should be kept in a manner which will make those who frequent them obey the law and conform to the dictates of morality.[58]

Privately, Balfour argued that social changes mattered more for temperance than legislation. He told a Presbyterian minister active in Scotland's temperance movement "that the change we are most in need of is a change of sentiment and habit more than of licensing laws." Balfour much regretted that in Scotland people drank whiskey and not beer. In other private letters, Balfour contended that the Government bill did not block further reform. [59]

The Opposition ridiculed the claim that the Government bill should be seen as a temperance bill. The genesis of the bill was enough to make that improbable, a trade deputation in March 1903 demanding protection from licensing magistrates. Opposition MPs acknowledged the value of Clause Four, securing for the public the monopoly value of new licenses. They also welcomed the new authority of the magistrates to refuse renewal of pre-1869 beer shop licenses, though minimizing its importance as such licenses were already diminishing in number for commercial reasons. Despite these concessions the Opposition argued that the net effect of the bill was to strengthen the trade against subsequent reform efforts.[60] Campbell-Bannerman lamented that the licensed trade had "almost become an estate of the realm."[61]

In the argument on behalf of its compensation scheme the Government emphasized two points: the necessity in fairness for compensation for old licenses and the reasonableness of providing the money through a trade levy in what amounted to a mutual insurance scheme. It further contended that this form of compensation made a time limit of the kind proposed by the Opposition unjust, since after its expiration a license holder who had paid the levy during the time limit could lose his license with no compensation at all. The Government argued that a time limit would be fair only if the compensation scheme was funded by public moneys or if licenses were given security against non-renewal during the time limit, so that the license holder could put aside a depreciation fund.[62] The Government knew that the Opposition was opposed to compensation from public funds and would reject any suspension of magisterial discretion.

On 26 July, Campbell-Bannerman protested: "What a perfect farce and imposture the whole proceeding is." The Opposition for the most part would have accepted some form of compensation from trade sources. The objection was to the specifics of the Government scheme. Most of the Opposition considered a trade levy under statutory auspices merely a disguised tax diverted from general revenue purposes and would have preferred the trade to make voluntary arrangements without State involvement as in Birmingham. More important, the Opposition objected that the amount of money was inadequate for a significant reduction and the right of compensation was to be permanent rather than for a transitional period only. The maximum rate of the levy was too low, the Quarter Sessions were free to omit it altogether, the Government estimates of the cost of compensating houses at market value was unrealistically low, and the Opposition favored a much more drastic scheme of reduction than the Government envisaged.[63] The Opposition argued that the Government had intentionally provided inadequate funds to safeguard the trade from magisterial discretion.

The Opposition was more anxious for a time limit than for any other amendment. Without a time limit the compensation clauses provided a great obstacle to later experiments and reforms. Balfour denied that Parliament could tie the hands of its successors, but contradicted himself by adding that if a later Parliament wished to act justly it would have to pay back the compensation levy. A time limit with reduction carried out during it and financed by the trade was fair in the judgment of the Opposition. It was an insurance scheme that provided benefits during a given period of time. Those who received no compensation during the time limit benefitted by retaining their licenses throughout the time limit and by adding part of the patronage of those who lost their licenses. License holders were financially capable of paying a levy during the time limit and simultaneously accumulating the depreciation fund for the possibility of a later loss of the license. The Opposition did not make specific counter proposals, and the attitude toward compensation varied with every speaker. Asquith claimed that he was against compensation but for a "solatium." The practical distinction was unclear other than his tenderness for the feelings of the advanced temperance party. No one's statements sounded more ambiguous than those of the Liberal leader, Campbell-Bannerman. Liberal amendments seemed to fish for votes rather than to express a principled alternative.

The absence of a time limit drew criticism from staunch supporters of the ministry.[64] Many temperance-minded Unionists argued that some kind of time limit to compensation was desirable, and in the Upper House of Convocation the bishops unanimously endorsed the principle of a time limit. Balfour, who had already cuffed the ears of the justices, denied that the opinion of the clergy had any special claim to regard in this matter that was one of finance.[65] Nevertheless, the Government worried about the Church of England's criticism of the bill. "The Archbishop and his colleagues were as unsteady as they could be."[66] At a meeting of the Church of England Temperance Society on May 6 the Archbishop of Canterbury called for a time limit. The Solicitor General, Sir Edward Carson, hinted on 9 May that the Government might accept a time limit amendment in committee.[67] On the following day the maverick Tory newspaper, the *Pall Mall Gazette*, expressed a widespread opinion when it endorsed the principle of a "liberal" time limit. It said the Archbishop of Canterbury's proposal of a time limit of twenty years did the license holder no injury. The trade, already unhappy with some parts of the bill (some called it a Mutual Burial Fund), made it clear that it would not continue to support the Government on it if a time limit to money compensation was added.[68] Sir Edward Carson, who managed the bill, repudiated the possibility of a time limit on 10 May, a repudiation that Balfour confirmed the following day.

The trade resented the hostile position of the Established Church. Some breweries canceled their usual contributions to Church charities, and early in June the Yorkshire brewers passed a resolution in favor of Church disestablishment.[69] Though pointing out that the Yorkshire resolution did not express a general trade policy, the *Licensed Trade News* warned the Church that it "is playing with a two-edged sword when it plays with vested interests, dallies with time limits, and rejects compensation."[70]

The attempt to add a time limit to compensation was handicapped by the introduction of the amendment at an inappropriate stage of the bill. With the Government resolutely opposed, any amendment was doomed, so this tactical error did not much matter. On 7 June the preferred amendment of temperance-minded Unionists and the Opposition to create a fourteen-year time limit failed, as did a second, more drastic amendment for a seven-year time limit. Unionists in favor of a seven-year time limit included Sir W.H. Houldsworth, A. Cameron Corbett, T.W. Russell, and Winston Churchill. The last three named soon changed parties. On the fourteen-year time limit other Unionist MPs supported the attempt to amend the bill, such as the CETS stalwarts C.E. Tritton and Sir John Kennaway.[71] Later the Opposition supported new amendments which Unionist MPs had drafted. H.E. Duke's modest proposal to make explicit that Quarter Sessions acted as an administrative body and not as an exclusively judicial one carried on a thin House on 6 July by a vote of 132 to 124. On July 11 Houldsworth proposed that after a period of fourteen years houses denied renewal would be compensated only by the return of their previous compensation contributions. This amendment, intended to accelerate the pace of reduction, failed by a fairly close vote, 250 to 209.

Perhaps the strength of support for Houldsworth's amendment encouraged the Government to choose to announce its major concession, accepting an amendment to Clause Four that provided for the payment of the monopoly value acquired by new licenses. In the original clause the justices could have accepted the surrender of old licenses in payment of the monopoly value, the new license could have been renewed indefinitely, and if denied renewal the new license would have been paid compensation. The revised clause required that the monopoly value be paid in money to go for relief of local rates and that the life of the new license not exceed seven years which precluded compensation for non-renewal.[72] The licensing justices were assigned power to decide to grant new licenses. In the original bill it had been Quarter Sessions. On 15 July the National Trade Defence Association unanimously condemned this amendment but to no avail.[73]

The Government wanted to mollify its reform wing, and for most of the trade the new licenses seemed too few to be more than a symbol. Despite this common attitude, at a meeting of the NTDA general committee the Liberal brewer E.N. Buxton said that he would rather have no bill at all than one with the payment of monopoly values by new licenses. He feared that in the future the precedent would be used against the trade and to encourage municipalization of the retail trade. Probably Buxton had in mind the disinterested management or Gothenburg scheme. Trade leaders wanted a statute to protect licensed property from the magisterial reduction movement too desperately for hypothetical dangers to matter. When the bill was introduced, Buxton had said that the trade looked upon it "without enthusiasm" but would work for it to secure parliamentary acceptance of the principle of compensation.[74]

A minor phase of the controversy over compensation concerned its division among the parties who suffered loss. The Opposition claimed that the Government bill gave the brewers too much and the publicans too little and attacked the tied house system which often transformed the publicans into exploited agents of the brewers who owned or controlled license property. The attack embarrassed the Government which made minor concessions, but it failed to divide the retail trade from the wholesalers which was what the Liberals presumably had intended.

The effect of the bill on magisterial discretion attracted more concern than anything other than the lack of a time limit. The Government insisted that the magistrates retained their discretionary authority, but the Opposition argued that the requirement of compensation for non-renewal of licenses other than licensees guilty of statutory offenses, together with the enlargement of the powers of Quarter Sessions by the creation of a permissive compensation levy necessary for reduction in numbers, effectively crippled the licensing committees. Most Liberals favored a change in the composition of the licensing bench to make it more representative of the people, but they stressed that whatever its composition the local authority was in the best position to make decisions because it was local. The possibility of uncompensated non-renewal without restriction on the grounds for the decision or the number of houses affected had been the weapon by which the licensing benches had forced many local improvements. For instance, in many localities the sale of liquor to children had been prohibited by the justices for years before parliamentary legislation mandated the reform. As T.P. Whittaker said on 9 May: "the reduction of licenses, though desirable, was not a great end in itself; but the power to deal with the licenses was of vital importance."[75] The complaint that the bill undermined magisterial discretion touched a sensitive nerve in the Unionist Party, particularly for the country members. Many Unionist backbenchers, including the eminent ex-minister Joseph Chamberlain, spoke in favor of alterations to safeguard the powers of the justices.

The Opposition maintained that the licensing benches had used their discretionary powers moderately, that the magistrates, most of them Unionists, were moderate men, and that only in Birmingham and Liverpool had substantial reductions taken place. In 1903, out of 911 licensing districts in England and Wales only ten districts refused renewal of more than three houses for all causes, including licensing offenses. The bill assumed a problem that did not exist. The Opposition suspected that the true object of the bill was less that of compensation than the crippling of magisterial discretion, not merely in matters of reduction, but in matters of administratively imposed reforms.[76]

The procedural debate over closure by compartments appears to have been relished by both sides of the House.[77] On 1 July Balfour got his chance to twit the Opposition about parallels with closure by compartment in William Gladstone's ministries and bemuse the House with philosophic reflections on the necessity of providing the conditions for a Government to carry out its legislative program when it was of reasonable length. In fact, the problem of lack of time was largely the Government's fault as it had not introduced the bill until 20 April. The Opposition gravely warned the House that the enactment of the licensing bill under the coercion of the guillotine would carry no moral weight with a future Liberal Government and that the precedent of overriding the right of minorities to participate in the making of legislation might soon work against the Unionists. Only a few Unionists opposed the Government on the guillotine resolution. One who did was Sir John Gorst, a Free Trader and a former head of the national Conservative constituency organization. He did so on the ground that the guillotine was inappropriate for social legislation. He angrily remarked that he "did not know whether closure had not been imposed even in the Cabinet itself."[78]

A modern scholar, John P. Mackintosh, has argued that closure by simple majority to end debate and the guillotine or closure by compartments for successive clauses as a specified time was reached were insufficient to enable the Government to pass the licensing bill over the determined opposition it evoked. In his history of the Cabinet, Mackintosh points instead to the increased Government control over parliamentary time, the result of the adoption of the Standing Orders of 1896 which allocated a fixed number of days to the Committee on Supply, and even more the result of the Standing Orders of 1902 which left private members with only Friday afternoons. The new Standing Orders permitted the Government "to arrange virtually all the business of the House and fix the times by which motions were to be carried." After this revision of parliamentary procedure that Balfour had arranged, the Opposition could no longer force by obstruction the modification or withdrawal of legislation that it intensely disliked. It could only present a case before public opinion. A Government with a working majority and steady nerves would not even be swayed by bye-election defeats.[79] Frustrated by the inability to do anything but build up a record for a perhaps distant general election, the Opposition tended to consider the frequent use of closure to end debate as unconstitutional. On 6 July a large meeting of backbench Liberal MPs chaired by J.E. Ellis considered disruptive tactics that evening when the guillotine fell for the first time. Aware that the Liberal front bench would not countenance such tactics, the meeting declined to adopt a policy of disruption. But when Balfour tried to speak that night he was shouted down.[80]

The cavalier attitude of the Prime Minister and of Akers-Douglas, the Home Secretary, toward the debates intensified the bitterness over the guillotine and over the unwillingness of the Government to consider major amendments. Balfour and Akers-Douglas were criticized for their slack attendance and their shallow grasp of the technicalities of licensing law. The

Home Secretary appeared uncertain how reduction would aid temperance, although this was a major pillar supporting the Government's case. Balfour contributed little to the debates except on the first reading and on the proposal to adopt the guillotine. The licensing debates furthered the reputation of only one of the Unionist ministers, Sir Edward Carson, the Solicitor General, who did most of the work of managing the bill in the Commons, and who, within the small limits in which he could maneuver, tried to accommodate critics.

The debates meant less than the maneuvers that had preceded the bill's introduction in Parliament. After 1903 and early 1904 the events of mid-1904 in the House of Commons and out-of-doors seemed anticlimactic. Once the Cabinet had decided on the contents of the bill its majority of almost a hundred forced the bill through with minimal regard for critics, whether they wanted the bill amended or would have been satisfied only by its defeat or withdrawal. By the time the bill was introduced the pressure groups had had their day. Although the trade failed to get the bill which it would have drafted, the National Trade Defence Association decided on 28 April, eight days after the Government bill had been introduced, to support it. The bill afforded the trade the security it had sought so desperately and that outweighed what the trade considered the defects of the bill. The pressure groups on the other side had little impact. Neither the attempt to impose a time limit to compensation nor that to defend magisterial discretion could rally enough Unionists behind an amendment opposed by the party leadership to defeat the Government. Unionist MPs did not make good rebels. Despite party divisions on the tariff and the crumbling morale in the face of likely defeat in the next general election, party discipline held. The Licensing Act of 1904 was the last important legislative achievement that Balfour conjured out of his dying Parliament.

In the sedate atmosphere of the House of Lords the divisions within the Unionist Party showed more clearly than in the Commons that was disciplined by fiercer partisanship and by party electors. Lord Peel offered an amendment for a time limit as did the Archbishop of Canterbury, the latter in the particularly generous form of twenty years which struck many moderates as very reasonable. Lord Rosebery said that his own belief was that compensation to the trade should be entirely met by a time limit. Dr. Randall Davidson pointed out on 1 August that "the elementary truth that, if we are greatly to reduce the drinking of alcoholic liquor, somebody must be the poorer for our doing so, is often forgotten in dealing with this matter."[81] The interests of temperance conflicted with the interests of the trade, and the vested commercial interest had to yield before the good of the country. Peel's amendment and the Archbishop's both failed. Lord Grey succeeded in getting minor concessions in behalf of the Gothenburg trust movement, but the House of Commons rejected the amendments as violations of its privileges in finance.[82] Late in the debate, Lord Balfour of Burleigh, who presided much of the time, and who had neither voted against the second reading nor offered any amendment, sharply criticized the bill. He argued: "the maintenance of the absolute discretion of the Bench is the very keynote of all temperance reform."[83] Like many other Unionist temperance reformers he was a Free Trader. Four years later he explained that he would have spoken against A.J. Balfour's bill even more strongly except that he did not want his criticisms to be attributed to his break with the Government over tariff reform.[84]

The former Liberal prime minister, Lord Rosebery, who had a moderate reputation, spoke vigorously against the bill. On 5 August, he told the House of Lords: "it is tolerably evident that it is not much use to intervene in this debate or to attempt to bring any conviction to the serried battalions that it behind the Government."

On 11 August, the House of Lords approved the bill without a division.

The attitude of trade combined relief with frustration over the price that it had paid for the legislation.[85] Bad business aggravated the general malaise. For instance, per capita beer consumption had declined nearly 15% from 1899 to 1905. Customers tended to buy cheaper beers than had been typical, and the sale of less profitable bottled beers ate into draft beer turnover.[86]

Fortunately for the trade, the Kennedy Judgment (July 1906) slowed the rate of reduction that a fixed levy could support by including the wholesale profits of the brewers in the market value of tied houses.[87] On the other hand, the local administration of the Licensing Act did not always win plaudits from the licensed trade.[88] On the basis of his study of Salisbury, Ed Garman concludes the decisions of the justices often were arbitrary.

By 1915 about ten per cent of on-licenses had closed with compensation and another three per cent without compensation. Nearly all the compensation money went to the brewers, some making a profit from the closure of their tied houses. Only eleven per cent of compensation money went to the publicans who had lost their businesses.[89]

By the Second World War the compensation levy and magisterial reduction had become rare, but about 25,000 on-licenses or a third of the total existing in 1904 had been suppressed. In 1959 Parliament repealed the requirement that new licenses pay for the monopoly value that licensed property enjoyed.[90] By the twenty first century the number of public houses in England and Wales had declined considerably and continued to decline.

The reason was that the pubs had become unprofitable.

All segments of the organized temperance movement disliked Balfour's licensing bill, although with different intensities and for different reasons. This opposition of temperance activists bothered the Government little, so long as it could find a majority in Parliament and make a case before the electorate that the bill constituted a reasonable settlement of the licensing question. Despite the futility of the effort, the temperance party carried on a vigorous protest. George B. Wilson of the Alliance published a letter in the *Daily News*, 20 April 1904, "The 'Trade' and Parliament," that argued material interests were behind support for the bill. He listed as shareholders 167 peers, 129 MPs, and 880 titled personages.[91] The Wesleyan Methodists, who had been divided over the education bill, were united in opposing Balfour's licensing bill.[92] Temperance reformers held major demonstrations against the "Brewers' Endowment Bill" on 7 May at Trafalgar Square, on 28 May at Albert Hall, and on 25 June at Hyde Park. On this last occasion demonstrators marched from over seventy staging areas. The marchers were met by "three van-loads of drunkards' children in their native costume." Resolutions against the bill were adopted at innumerable smaller meetings in the provinces such as at St. George's Hall in Liverpool and the Coliseum in Leeds. The demonstration in Birmingham saw ten thousand people march while twenty thousand cheered them along the route.[93] Anti-bill tracts were circulated by the million. For instance, the relatively small North of England Temperance League sent out 250,000 parcels of propaganda literature weighing ten tons.[94] One of the many books attacking the bill was written by the Joseph Rowntree and Arthur Sherwell, *Public Interests or Trade Aggrandisements*, a collection of letters and articles that had appeared in the daily press and as pamphlets. The organ of the Church of England Temperance Society praised its "close reasoning, based upon a careful study of existing conditions" that, despite its moderation in language, concluded in "strong convictions as to the danger of the licensing measure now before Parliament."[95] The Earl of Carlisle, a Liberal Unionist who was rarely active in the temperance cause, published a series of letters in the *Temperance Chronicle* attacking Balfour's bill.[96] So strongly did the UKA feel that its executive committee apparently sanctioned the plan to disrupt the House of Commons as a protest against the Government's imposition of the guillotine.[97] The Liberal leader, Campbell-Bannerman, did not permit this.

The chronic disunity of the temperance party probably had no effect on the licensing crisis of 1903-04. It did have importance for the future when a Liberal Government would have to consider how to react to the new status quo. In 1903 the divisions over Lord Peel's Report complicated the Liberal and temperance fight against the Government and the drink trade. The supporters of the minority report accepted compensation under certain circumstances. Whittaker participated in Sir Ralph Littler's conference that unanimously endorsed statutory compensation accompanied by a substantial reduction in numbers. By 1903 the opponents of Lord Peel's Report had secured control of the UKA. In this they were aided by the growing alignment of the supporters of the minority report with the advocates of the Gothenburg scheme of disinterested management. Though some of the rising generation in the UKA wanted to take their stand on opposition to any compensation, most of the Alliance leaders preferred to emphasize the defence of magisterial discretion. They hoped to win the cooperation of the Peelites, knew that the Liberal leaders considered a defense of the discretionary powers of the justices the best tactics, and expected that the Government would sidestep the explosive compensation issue by proposing the suspension of magisterial discretion. Lawson first agreed with these tactics of the Alliance executive council but then rallied instead to the policy of emphasis on no compensation.[98]

Through its belated enthusiasm for magisterial discretion the Alliance won a new ally, Arthur Chamberlain. He had denounced Littler's memorial in favor of statutory compensation. He associated himself so closely with the advanced temperance party that he was denied reelection to the licensing bench. At a conference on 15 May 1903, organized by the UKA, he said that he would cast his vote against his brother's party. He argued that by the logic of its criticism of the licensing justices as unrepresentative of public opinion the Government should support local option. It was not the trade but the victims of the trade that deserved compensation. He asserted that the nation, confronted with the desperate competition from the United States and Germany, needed temperance reform for its physical and mental progress. Above all, temperance was needed for the well-being of the working class. In implied criticism of his brother, the former Colonial Secretary, he concluded that:

> if we could drive this into the minds of our people we would have done more than if we had added even a whole continent to the Empire. (Loud cheers.) An empire over black men and an empire over yellow men is not equal to an empire over ourselves. (Loud cheers.)[99]

The presence of Arthur Chamberlain cheered the advanced temperance party, but it did not compensate for the loss of T.P. Whittaker. Although his absence at the May meeting was explained by another commitment, his estrangement from the Alliance had become almost complete. In the early twentieth century the UKA lost its primacy in the temperance movement, and its political influence rapidly dwindled. When a Liberal Government planned temperance legislation to undo Balfour's Licensing Act of 1904, the Alliance could not credibly claim to speak for the temperance party. The militants who re-established their control over the UKA had won a hollow victory. Liberal leaders such as Asquith were inclined to regard men such as Whittaker and Sherwell as representing "the best and sanest opinion" in the temperance party.[100]

After Whittaker's death, Sherwell published excerpts from a letter that Whittaker had written a correspondent in August 1904 in which he recognized that Balfour's bill had changed the situation for temperance reform. He derided as

> useless to talk of repeal, in the sense that this measure can be wiped off the statute book and the *status quo ante* be restored. When a large saleable value has been allowed to grow up and be extensively dealt in, all over the country and over a long period of time, the difficulty of destroying it without compensation or commutation of some kind became practically insurmountable. Now that value has been created a legal property and given a Parliamentary title, it is impossible to take it away without compensation in some form or other. Even if a House of Commons would do it the House of Lords would never consent.

He added: "Parliament has decided that what is practically full compensation must be given. It will not be possible to go back on that." Considering a time limit to compensation, he said that getting it enacted "will depend entirely on the length of it." He continued: "It will be no use thinking of anything like seven or ten years. That would only be to delude ourselves and others. It will have to be quite double that."[101]

Notes

[1] For a succinct account, see Greenaway, *Drink and British Politics since 1830*, pp. 77-81. More detailed is Paul Jennings, "'Grasping a Nettle': The 1904 Licensing Act," in Mark Hailwood and Deborah Toner, eds., *Biographies of Drink: a Case Study Approach to Our Historical Relationship with Alcohol* (Cambridge Scholars Publishing, 2015), pp. 30-48.

[2] *Parl. Deb.*, 4th ser., LXXXII, 8 May 1900, cols. 1004-40.

[3] The parliamentary committee of the Country Brewers' Society rejected a proposal that the trade request legislation "on the lines of the Majority Report" to forestall legislation by a future Liberal Government. Country Brewers Society MB 6, 6 Nov. 1901. The proposal was first offered by Danvers Powers on 10 Oct. 1901

[4] *Times*, 17 Jan. 1901, p. 10.

5 Prior to the 1901 legislation: "(a) children of any age might buy beer and spirits for consumption off the premises, (b) children of thirteen and upwards might buy beer and drink beer on the premises, (c) children of sixteen and upwards might buy and drink either beer or spirits on the premises." Williams and Brake, *Drink in Great Britain,* p. 11.

6 E. Morrall in *Licensed Trade News,* 1 May 1902, pp. 7-9.

7 *Licensing World,* 20 Jan. 1906, p. 51.

8 Caine to Chamberlain, 31 Oct. 1901; Chamberlain to Caine, 4 Nov. 1901. Quoted in Newton, *W.S. Caine,* pp. 295-98. Caine to Chamberlain 7 Nov. 1901. University of Birmingham, Joseph Chamberlain papers, JC 11/39/17.

9 Ritchie, Cabinet memoranda, 30 Jan., 9 May, 15 Nov. 1901. PRO, Cab. 37/56, 57, 59. Salisbury to Edward VII, 19 Nov. 1901. Royal Archives, Windsor Castle, RA R22/60. For Ritchie's announcement that there would be a bill in 1902, see *Times,* 29 Nov. 1901, p. 6.

10 Misplaced Younger source, probably a drink trade newspaper. See also George A. Croft and Henry A. Newton to Ritchie, 17 Dec. 1901; J.A. Longley (for Ritchie) to Newton, 30 Dec. 1901; [Newton to ?, n.d.]. *Licensed Trade News,* 13 Jan. 1902, pp. 7-8. For the low-key attitude of the brewers after the bill was introduced, see *Licensed Trade News,* 8 March 1902, p. 5; 26 April 1902, pp. 5-6; 10 May 1902, pp. 5-6; 12 July 1902, pp. 5-6.

11 H. George Robinson to the editor, 20 Aug. 1902. *Morning Advertiser,* 22 Aug. 1901, p. 2.

12 *Licensing World,* 20 Jan. 1906, p. 51.

13 Beginning in 1882, the licensing justices could refuse licenses for grocers to sell beer.

14 Sir Walter Gilbey to Gladstone, 25 Feb. 1902. BL, Herbert Gladstone papers, Add. Ms. 46059 ff. 134-35. James Blyth (Lord Blyth) to Gladstone. BL, Herbert Gladstone papers, Add. Ms. 46059 ff. 171-73. See also *Country Brewers' Gazette,* 27 March 1902. This brewers' newspaper was critical of the negativism of the Federation of Off-License Holders. *Country Brewers' Gazette,* 24 April 1902.

15 Benjamin Tom Hall, *Over Sixty Years: The Story of the Working Men's Clubs and Institute Union* (Club and Institute Union, 1912), pp. 236-37; Working Men's Club and Institute Union, *Annual Report* (1902), 5-7. The Union treasurer (later Sir) Herbert Praed was also chairman of the Association of Conservative Clubs.

16 The trade was unenthusiastic. Se the executive committee of the National Trade Defence Association, M.B. 2, f. 30-31, 3 April 1892. Courtesy of David W. Gutzke.

17 Williams and Brake, *Drink in Great Britain,* p. 14.

18 (Sir) Alfred T. Davies, *The Licensing Problem and Magisterial Discretion* (3rd ed., Licensing Laws Information Bureau, 1902). Boulter v. Kent J.J or the Dover case (1897) had already established that the licensing justices could act on their own knowledge and were not bound by the rules of a court that acted solely on sworn evidence. They did not need to assign a reason for denying a license renewal. Wilson, *Alcohol and the Nation,* p. 108.

19 *Brewing Trade Review,* Oct. 1903, p. 376. The big brewers did not want to repeat their mistake in the case of *Sharp v. Wakefield* when they had stood aside. There has been occasional large-scale license reduction earlier, as for example, 65 licenses at

Blackburn in 1882. *Temperance Chronicle*, 19 June 1903, p. 308. The reduction in the number of Blackburn pubs was partly the result of building Queen's Park.

[20] Liverpool Vigilance Committee, *Licensing Administration in Liverpool: Summary of Reforms (1889-1898)* (Licensing Laws Information Bureau, 1899); Sir William B. Forwood, *Recollections of a Busy Life* (Lee and Nightingale, 1910), pp. 206-07. In 1904 the Liverpool Licensing chairman, Sir Thomas Hughes, said that in his fifteen years in office some 500 licenses had lapsed, mainly in demolition areas. *Times,* 24 March 1904. In the 1890s there was an average reduction in licenses of 24 per year on all grounds. There was also stricter law enforcement and a decline in prosecutions for drunkenness, the latter apparently the result of a less drunkenness and not lax standards. Charles H. Roberts, *Time Limit and Local Option* (2nd ed., P.S. King and Sons, 1908), pp. 23 f.

[24] See also Waller, *Democracy and Sectarianism.* Many people in the drink trade disapproved of the cooperation of Birmingham brewers with a surrender scheme and applauded the "No Surrender" policy of the Liverpool brewers. "A Tale of Two Cities," *Licensed Trade News*, 8 Sept. 1900, pp. 5-6.

[21] For the Birmingham Surrender Scheme, see *Licensed Trade News*, 24 Sept. 1904, pp. 11-12; *The Birmingham Surrender Scheme: Statement Issued by Directors of the Birmingham Property Co., Ltd.* (Birmingham, 1904); Arthur Chamberlain, *Licensing in the City of Birmingham–Birmingham Surrender Scheme* (2nd ed., dated 1 Oct. 1902); Arthur Chamberlain, "The Birmingham Surrender Scheme," *National Review*, May 1902, pp. 396-409. See also by brewers W. Waters Butler in *Licensed Trade News*, Special Supplement, 6 Dec. 1902, pp. I-iii; Joseph Ansell in *Brewers' Journal*, 15 March 1902, p. 139; Edward and Joseph Ansell in *Times*, 13 Nov. 1913, p. 20. The Good Templar leader, Joseph Malins, offered a retrospective in a letter to Leonard Page, 3 Nov. 1925. Quoted in Malins (the younger), *The Life of Joseph Malins*, p. 143 note.

[22] Of the 639, 414 were for public houses, 152 for beer shops, and 73 for other licenses. *Times*, 29 June 1903, p. 8. On 350 surrenders, see Roberts, *Time Limit and Local Option*, p. 28; National Trade Defence Association, *The Licensing Question: Points to be Considered in Connection with any Proposed Legislation* (N.T.D.A., 1904). In Liverpool the reduction movement began much earlier in response to the decision of the House of Lords affirming the discretionary authority of the licensing justices in the Sharp versus Wakefield appeal. Samuel Smith boasted: "our borough was the first to put in practice this version of the law" and praised the leadership of Sir Thomas Hughes (1838-1923). *My Life-Work* (Hodder and Stoughton, 1902), p. 293.

[23] *Licensing Trade News*, 16 Jan. 1904, p. 5; 30 Jan.1904, p. 5. Although Chamberlain described his successor Alexander M. Chance as "the nominee of the brewers," he was a teetotaler and a member of the Church of England Temperance Society. See also Joseph Malins, "The Late Mr. Arthur Chamberlain: A Reminiscence how Clubs and Grocers' Licenses came under Restriction," *Good Templars Watchword*, 1 Nov. 1913, pp. 517-18.

[24] *Under Five Flags: The Story of Kynoch Works, Witton, Birmingham, 1862-1962* (1962), p. 29, quoted in *Oxford Dictionary of National Biography.*

[25] *Licensed Trade News*, 23 Aug 1902, p. 6.

[26] A. Akers-Douglas to Cecil E. Kingsford, 2 Feb. 1903. Kent Record Office, Chilston papers, U 564 CL, p. 7. Akers-Douglas was sympathetic with the publicans "who will be turned adrift having lost their capital and in many cases too old to enter into fresh occupations." In contrast, he believed "the brewers are by no means in so bad a plight" as their surviving licenses would acquire more business.

[27] Balfour to Edward VII, 19 Feb. 1903. Royal Archives, Windsor Castle, RA R23/43.

[28] John S. Sandars to Balfour, 20 Jan. 1904. BL, Balfour papers, Add. 49762 f. 45, 46.

[29] *Brewers' Almanack* (1904), p. 51.

[30] For example, see 28 Feb. 1903, pp. 159-62.

[31] H.H. Riley-Smith at Yorkshire Brewers' Association, 24 Feb. 1903. *Licensing World*, 25 Feb. 1903, p. 165.

[32] *Licensed Trade News*, 14 March 1903, p. 9; 28 March 1903, p. 11.

[33] *Times*, 19 March 1903, p. 10. See also Balfour to Edward VII, 17 March 1903; Akers-Douglas to Edward VII, 18 March 1903. Royal Archives, Windsor Castle, RA R23/58, 77.

[34] National Trade Defence Association, M.B. 2, f.109. Courtesy of David W. Gutzke.

[35] *Licensed Trade News*, 30 May 1903, p. 7. Some members of the Liberal League wing of the Liberal Party imagined that the Liberals could gain trade support without sacrificing their principles. William Allard to Rosebery, 17 Feb. 1903. National Library of Scotland, Rosebery papers, Ms. 10,169 ff. 3-4.

[36] Sir Sydney O. Nevile, *Seventy Rolling Years* (Faber and Faber, 1958), pp. 60, 271; John Vaizey, *The Brewing Industry, 1886-1951* (Pitman, 1960), pp. xii, 12-13, 15-17.

[37] *Licensed Trade News*, 30 May 1903, p. 7; 26 Dec. 1903, p.5.

[38] *Times*, 19 Feb. 1903, p. 5. Although this method of compensation had been supported by trade members of the Royal Commission in its Majority Report, it had many opponents in the trade. Gutzke, *Protecting the Pub*, pp. 154-55.

[39] For details, see Ralph Littler, *Compensation in Licensing* (Butterworth, 1st ed., 1903; 4th ed., London, 1908), pp. 8-9. The resolution did not specify any time limit for compensation. Whittaker voted for the resolution. Caine was absent, on his deathbed.

[40] *Alliance News*, 21 May 1903, pp. 336-59.

[41] The Home Office staff disliked all three bills. PRO, H.O. 45/10283/106324; H.O. 45/10283/106776/no number, H.O. 45/10284/106986/1-2. The Government also considered making Brewster Sessions a court which would have to act judicially based on sworn evidence and not "act entirely upon their own prejudice." John S. Sandars to Balfour, 15 Jan. 1904. BL, Balfour papers, Add. 49762 ff. 23-25.

[42] Conversation of Chamberlain with C.A. Vince, 17 April 1903. Garvin and Amery, *Life of Joseph Chamberlain* 5:173. Chamberlain was more politic in an exchange of correspondence with the Birmingham trade. See W. Waters Butler and others to Joseph Chamberlain, 18 August 1903, and Chamberlain's reply, 22 August 1903, in *Licensed Trade News*, 26 Sept. 1903, pp. 6-7.

[43] Balfour to Edward VII, 16 June 1903. Royal Archives, Windsor Castle, RA R23/68.

[44] John Brickwood and H.A. Newton to Balfour, 17 June 1903; Balfour to Brickwood, 18 June 1903; Balfour to [Brickwood], n.d. *Licensed Trade News*, 27 June 1903, p. 11.

[45] Balfour in *Parl. Deb.*, 4th ser., CXXVII, 6 Aug. 1903, cols. 150-51.

[46] *Licensed Trade News*, 16 April 1904, p. 5.

[47] Akers-Douglas, Cabinet memorandum, 3 Dec. 1903. PRO, Cab. 37/67. The Home Secretary planned to meet with "our friends in the Trade" to see if they would accept a bill that made concessions to the temperance party. Sandars to Balfour, 14 Jan. 1904. BL, Balfour papers. Add. Ms. 49762/20. A speech delivered in West Gloucestershire by Sir Michael Hicks-Beach, 8 Dec. 1903, to a meeting of licensed victuallers and beer retailers prefigured parts of the eventual Government bill. Although acknowledging that drink trade was "a necessary and permanent trade," Hicks-Beach pointed out that there was a strong feeling in favor of reducing the number of licensed premises and that the money for compensation of those that lost their licenses would have to come from the trade. "As they were asking Parliament ... to guard them against a real and great danger, they must be prepared to give something as well as take something." Worcestershire Records Office, St. Aldwyn papers, D2455/PC/PP/65 fols. 43-44. See also the prohibitionist fears at this juncture. R.A. Jameson, "Mr. Balfour's Bargain with the Brewers," *Alliance News*, 17 December1903, pp. 846-47. Jameson was editor of the *Alliance News*.

[48] Akers-Douglas, Cabinet memorandum, 2 Feb. 1904. PRO, Cab. 37/68. Balfour preferred a temporary bill. Balfour to Sandars, 17 Jan. 1904. BL, Balfour papers, Add. 49762, f. 35b, 36, 37b.

[49] Sandars to Balfour, 20 Jan. 1904. B:, Balfour papers, Add. Ms. 49762 f. 45. See also Balfour to Sir John Kennaway, 17 Jan. 1904; Balfour to an unnamed bishop, 3 March 1904. Balfour papers, Add. Ms. 49856 ff. 47-49, 62-63. Balfour's defense of the Government as a friend of reasonable temperance reform in a letter to an unnamed correspondent, 2 Aug. 1904, was printed as a party leaflet. *The Licensing Bill, 1904. The Views of the Prime Minister* [National Union–No. 338] (1904).

[50] Balfour to Sandars, 17 Jan. 1904. BL, Balfour papers, Add. Ms. 49762 ff. 35-38.

[51] Chamberlain thought that the final bill was modeled on the Birmingham Surrender Scheme devised by his uncle. Austen Chamberlain, *Down the Years* (Cassell, 1935), p. 209. Balfour likely was influenced by Hick-Beach (St. Aldwyn) who was consulted, although this Free Trader was no longer in the Government. St. Aldwyn to Balfour, [no day] Aug. 1908. BL, Balfour papers, Add. Ms. 49695 f. 167. St. Aldwyn had anticipated the Government bill in important respects, on 8 Dec. 1903, in a speech before a West Gloucestershire trade society. There is a typed copy of the letter at the Gloucestershire Records Office, Earl St. Aldwyn papers, D2455/PCC/12.

[52] A.K. Russell, *Liberal Landslide: The General Election of 1906* (David & Charles; Archon, 1973), p. 30. It is possible that a trade official influenced a single clause. H.H. Riach, joint agent of the Eastern and Southern Counties district, National Trade Defence Association, claimed that "negotiations" with the Government improved the bill from the retailers' point of view. "The clause which was most important, and which did so much good, was drafted in the office in which he sat--not drafted, it was true, just as it stood now, ... for it had been knocked about a great deal, but it

was ... left with the Home Secretary ---[after his Government colleagues had] made a few minor alterations to it, [they] added it to the bill." *Licensed Trade News*, 16 Nov. 1904, p. 9. Riach (1847-1919) was an Oxford graduate and a barrister, who retired as a district agent in 1908 because of ill health. In the following week (26 Nov. 1904) of the same newspaper this similar passage appeared: "With regard to the Licensing Act of 1904, he [Riach] could safely say that a considerable amount of the good that the Trade was able to do in passing that was due to the personal acquaintance that happened to exist between one or two of their officials and one or two members of the Government. There was also a great deal to be done through the private secretaries of members, and therefore he said that they had more to do with the under-ground working of Parliament than anyone would believe, who had not seen their work. In the passing of the Act they had brought before the Government again and again, the important points, and as to those negotiations he could not enter into them fully, as it would be a breach of confidence. But he could say this, that the clause which was the most important, which did so much good, was drafted in the office in which he sat." Quoted in United Kingdom Alliance (1905) for 1906 election campaign, Campaign Leaflets, no. 7, *The Passing of the Licensing Act and the Threats of the Trade*.

[53] Based on reading reports of trade meetings, Crapster concluded: "the local societies were less enthusiastic about the [1904] bill than were the national organizations, while the Trade press was the most favorable of all." Basil L. Crapster, "Our Trade, Our Politics: A Study of the Political Activity of the British Liquor Industry, 1868-1910" (Ph.D. dissertation, Harvard University, 1949). p. 377.

[54] *Licensed Trade News*, 30 April 1904, p. 10. As late as May 1903, Buxton considered standing for the parliamentary seat at East Herts as a Liberal. A deputation that brought the invitation to Buxton was introduced by Sir Walter Gilbey, Bt., of the great wine company. *Chelmsford Chronicle*, 1 May 1903, p. 6. Late in 1909 he announced that he would vote for the Conservative candidate for Parliament. *Aberdeen Journal*, 31 Dec. 1909, p. 6.

[55] Charles H. Roberts, *The Radical Countess: The History of the Life of Rosalind, Countess of* Carlisle (Steel Brothers, 1962), p. 91.

[56] Entry in *Oxford Dictionary of National Biography* by Ruddock Mackay and H. C. G. Matthew.

[57] The provisions about new licenses were among the many parts of the 1904 bill that the trade disliked. National Trade Defence Association, *The Licensing Question: A Plea for Patience* (NTDA, 1907), p. 5.

[58] *Parl. Deb.*, 4th ser., CXXXIII, 20 April 1904, col. 740.

[59] Balfour to Dr. James Paton, 25 Oct. 1901. Add. 49854, f. 156b. Courtesy of David W. Gutzke. Balfour to unknown correspondent, Jan. 1904. BL. Balfour papers, Add. 49856, f. 51b. Balfour to Canon F.D. Cremer, 13 June 1904. Add. 49856, f. 128. Balfour also warned Cremer against identifying the church with the enemies of the bill. "Nothing can be worse for the Church than to ally itself with injustice." Later Balfour indicated that he would erect on his Lowland property "a public-house on the {Gothenburg] Trust principle, if I thought I could thereby induce my countrymen to drink beer instead of spirits." Balfour to T. Taylor, 2 Dec. 1908. BL, Balfour papers, Add.49860, f. 40.

[60] See Asquith in *Parl. Deb.,* 4th ser., CXXXIV, 11 May 1904, cols. 1072-82.

[61] *Parl. Deb.,* 4th ser., CXXXIII, 20 April 1904, cols 732 and 745-7.

[62] See the NTDA pamphlet, *Time Limit and Compensation* (NTDA, 1904).

[63] For the number of public houses suppressed with compensation, see the statistics given annually in the *Brewers' Almanack.*

[64] Grey to H.J. Crauford, 26 April 1904. University of Durham, Department of Palaeography, 4th Earl Grey papers, uncatalogued when consulted.

[65] Balfour in *Parl. Deb.,* 4th ser., CXXXV, 6 June 1904, cols. 832-33.

[66] Acland-Hood's conversation with Fitzroy, 5 June 1904. Quoted in Sir Almeric Fitzroy, *Memoirs* (Hutchinson, 1925) 1: 206.

[67] Lloyd George had welcomed this concession. Herbert Du Parcq, *Life of David Lloyd George* (Caxton, 1912) 3: 443-44.

[68] For instance, Edward Johnson at the Central Board. Central Board minutes, 5 May 1904.

[69] *Liberal Magazine,* July 1904, p. 408.

[70] *Licensed Trade News,* 11 June 1904, p. 5. For the estimate that the trade contributed about a quarter million pounds each year to religion, see *Licensing World,* 6 May 1905, pp. 308-09.

[71] Much earlier (17 Jan. 1904) Balfour reminded Kennaway that nearly the entire Unionist Party had supported his pledge to a trade deputation (or argued that Balfour had not gone far enough). BL, Balfour papers, Add. 49856, ff. 47-49.

[72] Some Conservatives agreed with Liberals that the local elected authority should have a voice on the creation of new licenses. On 12 July the former Home Secretary, Ritchie, called Lloyd George's amendment to that effect "eminently reasonable."

[73] *Licensed Trade News,* 23 July 1904, p. 1; NTDA, executive committee minutes, 15 July 1904 f. 125. See also the letter of John Brickwood, chairman of the National Trade Defence Association to Balfour, 18 July 1904. National Trade Defence Association, M.B. 2, ff. 128-30. Courtesy of David W. Gutzke. On 2 August, Buxton and several other brewers declared that they "preferred no bill at all to one containing Clause 4 (4)," as it encouraged the Gothenburg principle of municipalization of the drink trade. National Trade Defence Association, M.B. 2, ff.138-139. Courtesy of David W. Gutzke. See letter to *Times* by Buxton, reprinted in *Licensing World,* 6 Aug. 1894, p. 93.

[74] *Licensed Trade News,* 30 April 1904, p. 10.

[75] Whittaker was a vehement critic of the bill and of Balfour. In his diary (1 July) John Edward Ellis mentioned "Whittaker's pitiless and scathing reference to the dependence of the Government on the 'Trade' plainly had its effect on the Prime Minister." Arthur Tilney Bassett, *The Life of the Rt. Hon. John Edward Ellis, M.P.* (Macmillan, 1914), p. 210.

[76] Campbell-Bannerman in *Parl. Deb.,* 4th ser., CXXXIV, 10 May 1904, cols. 915-26.

[77] On obstruction and the consequent need for frequent use of closure, see Akers-Douglas to Edward VII, 14 June 1904. Royal Archives, Windsor Castle, RA R33/29.

[78] Gorst in *Parl. Deb.,* 4th ser., CXXXVII, 1 July 1904, cols. 361-62, 363.

[79] John P. Mackintosh, *The British Cabinet* (2nd ed., London, 1968), pp. 204-05, 210-11.

[80] J.E. Ellis, diary, 6 July 1904. Quoted in Bassett, *John Edward Ellis*, pp. 210-11.

[81] Davidson in *Parl. Deb.*, 4th ser., CXXXIX, 1 Aug. 1904, col. 188.

[82] See Grey to Sherwell, 9 Aug. 1904 (228/1); Whittaker to Grey, 22 and 31 May 1904. University of Durham, Department of Paleography, 4th Earl Grey papers, uncatalogued when consulted. Whittaker would not cooperate in seeking special facilities to aid the trusts in obtaining licenses, although he did not object to the justices granting existing licenses to the trusts. Whittaker complained that the trust companies pressed for the creation of more licenses and that the use of profits for local purposes was a form of bribery. For him any valuable experiments in disinterested management would have to include a local monopoly. Whittaker in *Parl. Deb.*, 4th ser., CXXXVIII, 12 July 1904, cols. 1394-95. In 1904 Grey was appointed Governor General of Canada and consequently no longer could take an active role in the trust house movement.

[83] *Parl. Deb.*, 4th ser., CXXXIX, 9 Aug. 1904, col. 1510.

[84] *Parl. Deb.*, 4th ser., CXCVII, 27 Nov. 1908, col. 832.

[85] Ray Anderson, "The Trade in 1905," *Brewery History* 111 (2005): 2-20.

[86] Ibid.

[87] For details on the Kennedy judgment, see (Amulee) Royal Commission on Licensing (England and Wales), 1929-31, Report. Cmd. 3988, 1932 [vol. XI], paragraph 120 (pp. 26-27). Sir William Rann Kennedy was a Liberal.

[88] See Paul Jennings "Liquor Licensing and the Local Historian: the 1904 Licensing Act and its Administration," *Local Historian* 39 no. 1 (Feb. 2009): 24-37, as well as local studies that include David J. Butler, "Defeating the Demon Drink: The 1904 Licensing Act and its Implementation in Durham City, 1906-1939," *Durham County Local History Society Bulletin* 54 (May 1995): 57-60; Ed [Edwin M.] Garman, "The Licensing Acts of 1904 and 1910 in Salisbury," Pub History Society. "What can one say about the effects of the 1904 and 1910 Acts? There were some pubs closed that were clearly not up to standard and with very poor trade. But one is left with the feeling that the closure of pubs by a process that purported to be rational and fair was in fact an arbitrary and biased system. Pubs were chosen to be closed by licensing Magistrates who would never have been seen in such premises. Having chosen a pub for closure, evidence was prepared that supported the closure. But even then, some evidence clearly showed, particularly in the case of the Goat, that successful and profitable pubs were chosen for closure for no apparent reason. Only eight pubs appear to have been closed under the compensation scheme in Salisbury but this represented 10% of the public houses and beer houses in the City." This undated article was published around 2017 which was the date for the publication of Garman's general history of Salisbury's public houses and inns.

[89] Gutzke, *Protecting the Pub*, p. 157.

[90] Geoffrey Block, *Free and Sober* (London: Conservative Political Centre, 1960), p. 8.

[91] "The 'Trade' and Parliament," *Daily News*, 20 April 1904, p. 6.

[92] George L. Bernstein, *Liberalism and Liberal Politics in Edwardian England* (Allen & Unwin, 1986), p. 62. Bernstein cites the *Methodist Recorder*, 28 April 1904, pp. 14-15; 12 May 1904, p. 3; 28 July 1904, pp. 4-5 (annual conference).

[93] Williams and Brake, *Drink in Great Britain*, p. 23.

---

[94] *Temperance Witness*, Dec. 1907, p. 56.

[95] *Temperance Chronicle*, 3 July 1904, p. 336.

[96] See also the presidential address of Lady Carlisle at the British Women's Temperance Association. *White Ribbon*, Aug. 1904, pp. 148-49.

[97] Alliance minutes, 13 July 1904.

[98] Lawson to Whyte, 1 May 1903; Leif Jones to Whyte, 3 May 1903; Lawson to Whyte, 5 May 1903, in Alliance minutes, 6 May 1903.

[99] *Licensing Magistrates and the Liquor Trade* (1903), 13-18 (quotation); *Alliance News*, 21 May 1903, p. 338. See also Arthur Chamberlain to Joseph Malins, 21 July 1903. Quoted in Malins, *Life of Joseph Malins*, p, 101; *Manchester Guardian* interview with Arthur Chamberlain, reprinted in *Alliance News*, 10 Sept. 1903, p. 591.

[100] Asquith to Campbell-Bannerman, 6 Dec. 1904. BL, Campbell-Bannerman papers. Add. 41210, ff. 237-38.

[101] Quoted in Arthur Sherwell, "Twenty-One Years Ago: Sir Thomas Whittaker's Views and a Forecast," *Monthly Notes* 15 (March 1925), p. 39. Gist of Whittaker's speech also cited in the presidential address of Edward Johnson at the annual meeting of the London licensed victuallers' central board. *Licensing World*, 28 January 1905, p. 62.

CHAPTER NINE

ASQUITH'S LICENSING BILL OF 1908

The enactment of Balfour's licensing bill in 1904 left the temperance party frustrated and angry. It was determined to strike back after the next general election. Regardless of their other differences, all temperance reformers objected to the absence of a time limit that made permanent the payment of money compensation and the financial restraints on the local licensing authority. The newspaper of the moderate Church of England Temperance Society editorialized: "from a national point of view, and from a Church point of view we are convinced that the most important question before the electors at the present time is the Temperance question."[1] Provisions for a gradual, compensated reduction in the number of licensed premises did not assuage temperance frustrations.[2] In some parts of the country the drink question extended beyond the temperance movement as the Conservatives were identified with the drink trade, notably in Liverpool where the Tory boss Archibald Salvidge was the manager of Bent's brewery.[3]

In July 1906 the courts aggravated the sense of grievance by including the wholesale profits of the brewers in the market value of tied houses. By inflating the cost of compensation, the Kennedy Judgment slowed the rate of reduction that a fixed levy could support.[4]

The Liberal Party shared the reformers' dislike for Balfour's Licensing Act. Liberals resented the Unionists forcing a controversial bill through a dying Parliament with the aid of closure by compartments. In 1906 the Liberal Party issued an unprecedented quantity of campaign literature, 25 million leaflets and books, "or more than three items for every elector in the country." The campaign cost £100,000 (and chief whip Herbert Gladstone boasted that he had made a profit in the campaign, having raised, £275,000).[5]

When Balfour resigned, Sir Henry Campbell-Bannerman accepted office. At first, he headed a minority government, but in January 1906 the Liberal Party won a general election with a huge, unprecedented majority.[6] Although personally popular in the House of Commons, the elderly new prime minister had "neither charisma, nor outstanding administrative competence, nor even personal dedication to public business and the exercise of political power."[7]

The manifesto of the National Trade Defence Association sadly acknowledged that, in contrast with 1895, the public did not think much about the drink question in 1906. "Their corns are not trodden upon by the Licensing Acts like yours are."[8] Other issues--protective tariffs, the Education Act of 1902 which offended Nonconformists, the Taff Vale decision which undermined the right of trade unions to strike, and "Chinese slavery" in the South African mines–overshadowed temperance reform in the general election of 1906. The new Liberal Government committed itself to some undefined kind of licensing reform which would undo Balfour's scheme that provided the trade with security. The new House of Commons included 157 Nonconformists, almost all of them sympathetic to temperance legislation.[9]

On April 5, 1906, a deputation that included both Lawson and Whittaker presented the claims of temperance reform to the new Prime Minister. As Lawson put it: "everyone is a Temperance reformer now, [but we claim] to be rather keener than some." Sir Henry Campbell-Bannerman cheerfully promised "an efficient measure" in 1907.[10] The collapse of what had remained of drink trade Liberalism in England other than the licensed grocers made the Liberal commitment easy to give. In the election landslide of 1906 S.H. Whitbread was the only English brewer elected as a Liberal and his father probably was the only English brewer to subscribe to the chief whip's campaign fund.[11] Yet the end of drink trade connections with the Liberal Party should not be exaggerated. The chief whip from 1905 to 1908, George Whiteley (later Lord Marchamley), had married into a family that owned a brewery, and he had served as its manager and as one of its directors.[12]

Outside Parliament temperance reformers were nervously optimistic while the drink trade was frightened and angry. For instance, in February 1907 Bristol trade societies encouraged their supporters to arrive early at the annual meeting of the Central Sunday Closing Association. "Over three thousand people crowded the Colston Hall" where "more than thirty policemen were required to maintain order." Repeatedly interrupted, speakers could not be heard. Appeals for order by embarrassed licensed victualler leaders could not quiet their people.[13]

Two temperance factions competed to shape Liberal licensing policy. Although Balfour's statute made many of the old controversies obsolete, important disputes persisted, while a previously peripheral one became divisive. Money compensation and a lengthy postponement of Direct Local Veto had become inevitable. Balfour's statute could not be repealed without accepting the enhanced status of the trade. Although the Liberals for the time being had a large majority in the House of Commons, the Unionists retained an enormous permanent majority in the House of Lords, composed of hereditary peers and the lifetime appointments of Church of England bishops. Alliance and Good Templar militants had to accept principles that they had disliked in Lord Peel's report. The temperance party disagreed about the length of the time limit that they would accept for money compensation and whether Local Veto should be authorized for the period after it. Perhaps these issues could have been compromised except for the shibboleth of disinterested management that bitterly divided temperance reformers. Even the hatred for Balfour's statute failed to bring about unity.

Sir Wilfrid Lawson died on 1 July 1906, after twenty-seven years as president of the United Kingdom Alliance. In the autumn Leif Jones succeeded him in that office. He probably owed his selection to his prestige as an M.P. In the Liberal landslide of January 1906, he was re-elected to Parliament by a five-vote margin, after he had entered the House the previous year in a bye-election. In contrast with the jovial Lawson, "Tea Leaf" Jones was a somewhat aloof and unemotional intellectual. G.B. Wilson described him as a logical but not rapid speaker. He added that Jones "did not make friends easily." Perhaps because of his deafness in his later years, he was lonely in his old age.[14] Like his patroness, Lady Carlisle, this son of a Welsh Congregational minister was an agnostic or atheist who led a strongly religious movement.[15]

A new generation took charge of the UKA. Three years earlier William Williams (1855-1925) had succeeded the ailing James Whyte as general secretary, a post that Whyte had occupied for twenty years. Williams served until only 1909 when George Bailey Wilson succeeded him for a decade. In January 1906 John Newton had replaced the octogenarian John Hilton as parliamentary agent.[16] Like his predecessor, Newton had been friendly toward Lord Peel's report, and like Hilton he was hostile to disinterested management. In contrast to Hilton who had held his office for nearly thirty-five years, Newton served only until 1909. He left the employ of the Alliance because of a heart condition and was succeeded by Alexander Thomson. In 1917 Thomson resigned to take a position in the whips' office of the Lloyd George Liberals

The UKA faced a critical challenge. Although the new Liberal majority presented the prohibitionists with a unique opportunity, it also posed the danger that unfriendly Government ministers could ignore old Vetoist allies. Whittaker's Temperance Legislation League disputed the Alliance's right to speak for temperance reform. Whittaker had been knighted in 1906, almost simultaneously with Lawson's death, a convenient symbol for the rise of the League at the expense of the Alliance. On 10 April 1906, the House of Commons by a handsome majority of 271 to 44 voted its approval of a resolution affirming the principle of Local Veto. Leif Jones was its sponsor. Unfortunately for the UKA a resolution was not a Government bill.

The controversy over what kind of licensing legislation a Liberal Government should sponsor began while Balfour remained the tenant of 10 Downing Street and continued until the belated introduction of the Liberal bill in 1908. One of the earliest plans came from a Liberal Unionist, A. Cameron Corbett, MP for Glasgow and president of both the Scottish Permissive Bill Association and the National Temperance Federation. He presented his scheme in 1904 at the public session of the Alliance annual meeting over which he presided. He did not offer a program to which the Alliance leadership had agreed. The UKA disliked his emphasis on high license fees to exact monopoly value as they might confer legitimacy and public sympathy for the trade. In his speech Corbett argued that the Licensing Act of 1904 could not simply be repealed. Even if the House of Lords accepted a repeal bill, the licensing justices would refuse to exercise their restored discretionary powers unless license holders retained compensation. Corbett built his strategy around a seven-year time limit and heavy taxation. He wanted an immediate substantial increase in taxes to persuade the Lords to let the reforms other than taxes to become law. (He assumed that the House of Lords would accept the right of the House of Commons to decide taxation.) During the time limit Corbett wanted the permissive Quarter Sessions compensation levy made compulsory with the surplus in any districts transferred to others to accelerate reduction. After the expiration of the time limit, he wanted all licenses treated as the 1904 statute treated new licenses, that is, required to pay the monopoly value that licensed status afforded.[17] Corbett sent a copy of his speech to Campbell-Bannerman. He added in a letter that no temperance organization represented in the National Temperance Federation would support a time limit of more than seven years (some rejected even that many years) and that all member societies rejected disinterested management.[18]

Campbell-Bannerman considered Corbett's speech important enough to circulate it among his leading colleagues. Herbert Gladstone advised his chief that, although the monopoly tax plan was worth consideration, no Liberal Government could get the House of Lords to adopt a time limit as short as seven years. A longer period seemed fair since the Liberals most likely would enact many of the recommendations in Lord Peel's report which would add to the trade's financial loss.[19] Asquith also doubted that seven years would give the House of Commons leverage with the peers. He also said that he was pleased about the "sensible and practicable" approach "by those who have hitherto been the intransigents of the Temperance party." Asquith added that he had "had some talk with Sherwell, who (with Whittaker) represents a great body of the best and sanest opinion in the sane [temperance] camp."[20]

In the following year the prohibition organizations offered their recommendations to the Liberal leadership. Deputations from the UKA and the National Temperance Federation presented Campbell-Bannerman with a joint statement, "Future Legislation on the Liquor Traffic," on 21 March 1905. It urged as its highest priority Local Veto for the entire United Kingdom. It requested the end to any vested interest in licensing renewal and the restoration of the licensing authorities. It opposed disinterested management. It asked for statutory Sunday closing, earlier closing on weekdays, election day closing, a ban on the employment of barmaids, and prohibition of the sale of drink to children. It did not mention Corbett's controversial taxation proposals. Though labeled "private and confidential," the statement contained nothing surprising. It conformed to the conventions of the advanced temperance party in omitting details. For instance, the statement avoided the vital question of a time limit. The Alliance published the declaration in its annual report in October 1905. Campbell-Bannerman's published reply said only that the Liberals would reverse the 1904 statute as soon as possible and restore and extend the discretionary powers of the local licensing authorities.[21]

On 11 January 1906, a temperance deputation met Gladstone for nearly an hour at the Leeds and County Liberal Club. His answers to questions served as a warning that the new Liberal Government might be a lukewarm friend. He argued that haste could result in an inadequate bill and that limitations in parliamentary time might make the first licensing bill that the Government proposed the last one that Parliament could consider seriously. Gladstone professed to favor a comprehensive measure based on Lord Peel's report. He opposed the introduction of a Government bill limited to a time limit to compensation and the licensing authority. Such a bill unfortunately would block more ambitious licensing legislation in the first parliamentary session. "The subject was so big that he refused to be rushed." He argued that "the Liberal party was too hasty in introducing their [1893] Bill." He was not opposed in principle to the Veto and would support a Veto bill for Scotland or Wales but "could not vote for an English Veto Bill." He could see "no keenness in the House of Commons for the Veto, even amongst its friends." Gladstone denied the charge that as chief whip he had discouraged MPs from supporting the Veto. As for the accusation that he was influenced by brewer subscriptions, he pointed out that "the Liberal party have no subscriptions from Brewers."[22]

In mid-July 1906, a few weeks after Lawson's death, the Alliance and the Federation submitted a new joint statement to Campbell-Bannerman. Unlike the earlier one it accepted a five-year time limit. For the period afterwards, the statement urged a local poll every three years on the three-fold option of the status quo, the prohibitive Veto, and the reduction in the number of licensed premises. Sunday closing would be mandatory. The two organizations also supported many lesser consensus reforms that Lord Peel's report had recommended. It opposed adding elected members to the licensing authorities. A few days afterwards, on 24 July, Leif Jones told Herbert Gladstone that the memorandum expressed the opinion of the many organizations affiliated with the Federation. The Federation and the UKA would offer their "unanimous and enthusiastic support" to any bill embodying the points of the memorandum."[23]

In presenting the case for the anti-UKA section of the temperance party, Whittaker accepted the necessity of paying a large price for the suppression of Balfour's Licensing Act. As early as August 1904, he had told a friend that suggestions of a time limit to compensation of seven or ten years lacked realism. It would have to be double that.[24] During the last months of the Balfour ministry he advanced his outline of "A Temperance Policy for the Liberal Party," published in the *Liberal Magazine* in July 1905. Whittaker's plan was notable for its discreet omissions: no specific time limit, merely a preference for as short a one as possible, and neither Local Veto nor disinterested management, but the possibility of their being added provided that the Liberals won a large majority in the next House of Commons. He had designed his limited program to prepare the way for disinterested management. Other than the principle of a time limit Whittaker's minimum program included a revision of the method of calculating compensation to diminish it, the restoration of the discretionary powers of the local licensing authorities, their extension to permit the authorities to require shortened hours and Sunday closing, the licensing of clubs under their supervision, and the introduction of a representative element in the composition of the local licensing authorities and the appellate bodies. Whittaker rejected Corbett's proposal that taxes on the trade be increased immediately on the grounds that higher taxes would force a lengthy time limit. He agreed with Corbett on the importance of exacting the monopoly value from all licenses after the expiration of the time limit.[25] Privately he considered a lengthy time limit politically indispensable and Local Veto not worth the bother.

Whittaker claimed only to speak for himself, but his minimum program largely anticipated the programs that the Central Temperance Legislation Board and its successor the Temperance Legislation League published late in 1905. The Board's pamphlet, *A Temperance Policy for the Present Time*, called for much the same reforms as Whittaker's article, other than being undecided about introducing a popular element in the composition of the licensing authorities.[26] The League's *Present Policy* went further than Whittaker in a couple of respects. It asked for local options of the Veto and of disinterested management. The latter would receive a local monopoly of on-licenses but would not take the form of municipalization.[27]

The loophole which Whittaker had left to allow a large reform program opened wide when the Liberals obtained a huge majority in the House of Commons in the January 1906 general election, a majority that might force the House of Lords to accept Liberal bills repugnant to the Unionist Party. Whitaker raised his ambitions in his elaborate, confidential "Rough Draft of Suggested Amendments of the Licensing Act of England and Wales," offered to the Liberal Government in September 1906. He proposed that after a twenty-year time limit to compensation, all licenses be required to pay their full monopoly value. The "Rough Draft" recommended that local licensing authorities be empowered to grant all retail licenses in a locality to an authorized non-commercial company under statutory conditions. It offered no equivalent permissive legislation for Direct Local Veto. It merely allowed the licensing authorities to conduct advisory polls. Wales would receive wider but undefined powers of local option.[28] Later Whittaker returned to his old, more realistic priorities. He would postpone his ultimate objective of disinterested management provided that the bill exacted monopoly value from all licenses. He could campaign for statutory authorization of disinterested management during the long years of the time limit.

The Liberal Government had taken office in December 1905 and then won a one-sided victory in the next month in the general election. It showed no hurry in introducing a licensing bill. Later James Bryce argued that the Government had erred in not tackling the difficult licensing question in the first parliamentary session. "The horse ought to have been put at the high fence while he was still fresh."[29] Unfortunately, a narrow bill restricted to putting a time limit on compensation would have displeased all the temperance party, while a larger one would have forced decisions on issues which divided temperance reformers. Moreover, a comprehensive bill would have consumed much parliamentary time for which other legislation competed. Nor could the financial and administrative technicalities of licensing reform be resolved in a few weeks or even a few months. For instance, the civil service chilled the widespread expectation that large new revenues could be obtained from the liquor trade.[30]

Herbert Gladstone and Herbert Asquith, the Home Secretary and the Chancellor of the Exchequer, served as successive chairmen of the Cabinet's licensing committee. Asquith was the obvious heir too of the elderly and ailing Prime Minister, Sir Henry Campbell-Bannerman. From the standpoint of advanced reformers Gladstone was an old enemy and Asquith no friend. The situation could have been worse for the UKA: Gladstone had offered Whittaker an appointment in the Home Office that he declined because of business commitments. After asking for some other form of recognition, he accepted a knighthood.[31]

For more than two years, Government struggled to give birth to a licensing bill. The Cabinet committee circulated its first draft bill in July 1906. Slightly modified versions followed on 12 and 19 November. If the advanced temperance organizations had known what was in the July 1906 bill and what was not, they would have been outraged. The heart of the bill provided for the statutory suppression of about 15,000 small beer houses and public houses, including off-beer houses, and the transfer of monopoly value at the end of an unspecified time limit. The bill allowed local licensing authorities to set up disinterested management schemes. It also provided a form of Local Veto for Wales, with an option of reduction as well as of prohibition (and, in the July bill, of disinterested management). The bill encouraged discretionary reduction, made the compensation levy mandatory for all Quarter Sessions, created a central compensation fund, and provided an automatic formula for determining the amount of compensation which reduced the amount paid. The compensation levy and the right to compensation were extended to off-licenses at half the rate for on-licenses.[32]

Some sections of the drink trade still hoped for an accommodation with the Liberal Government. The National Trade Defence Association sent a deputation to Asquith on 13 March 1906. More important, E.N. Buxton wrote to Gladstone in September 1906 as he hoped for Government concessions that might let the trade live with the Liberal bill. Buxton's principal concern lay not with the length of the time limit that would end compensation or with statutory reduction or with disinterested management or even with the old menace of Local Veto. Instead, Buxton protested principally against the policy pressed by the Temperance Legislation League, the transfer of the monopoly value of old licenses to the State through high license renewal fees. Its effect would be statutory in contrast with that of the Veto that would be permissive. Buxton characterized the monopoly value proposal as confiscation of private property, the profits of the brewery shareholders. He pointed out that the Liberal endorsement of Lord Peel's report did not imply a commitment to the exaction of monopoly value since it had not been part of the minority report. Recalling his discussions with the minority members when he was a member of the Royal Commission in 1899, he doubted that it had occurred to them at that time.[33]

Gladstone took several weeks to reply, presumably so that he might consult his colleagues. When he answered, he denied that the Government was committed to the League's proposal and interpreted the State's assumption of the monopoly value as entailing merely the right of the licensing authorities to impose local conditions for the sale of drink. He also implied that the time limit would be one of twenty years and that the bill would not provide a scheme of disinterested management. Apparently, Buxton and Gladstone met during the week of 15 October to continue their negotiations.[34] Afterwards Gladstone's committee softened its proposals.

Earlier, while Buxton had waited for an answer, he feared that there would be no reply or it would be an entirely negative one, so he sent the substance of his letter to the press.[35] Buxton later clashed in the *National Review* with Whittaker. Whittaker argued that the breweries that had invested in tied houses in the 1890s had been guilty of risky speculation and that Parliament should not protect brewery companies from the consequences of their imprudence. In Buxton's rebuttal he defended the soundness of past trade finance and minimized current trade profits and the capacity to absorb heavy new financial burdens.[36]

A memorandum circulated by Gladstone on 26 November 1906, failed to mention the monopoly value and urged the substantial time limit of twenty-one years. It criticized Whittaker's proposed club clauses as too drastic. The memorandum continued to allow Wales the Veto and to extend Welsh Sunday closing to adjacent Monmouthshire. A few days earlier J. Herbert Roberts led the Welsh Liberal MPs in a demand for special treatment of the Principality.[37] Gladstone's memorandum proposed statutory reduction in the number of licensed houses. It abandoned disinterested management. This decision apparently was a matter of tactics and not principle since Gladstone personally favored the Gothenburg principle. He argued that it was impossible to legislate for the distant period at the end of the time limit.[38] He used this argument also to dispose of the transfer of monopoly value and Local Veto.

Whittaker and his friends would accept the postponement of disinterested management. In its final statement of policy before the Government introduced its bill, a *Memorandum* published on December 12, 1907, the League dropped its demand for disinterested management.[39] It had too many enemies: the advanced temperance party hated any form of it, while the drink trade opposed disinterested management companies receiving a local monopoly or any other preferential treatment. What the League insisted upon was the exaction of monopoly value to prepare the way for disinterested management.[40]

Despite Gladstone, new draft bills circulated in January and February 1907 retained the transfer of the monopoly value. Sometime after Buxton's appeal and prior to these draft bills, Gladstone had vigorously attacked the monopoly value in a letter to Asquith.[41] A memorandum by a subordinate, perhaps the able and active undersecretary Herbert Samuel, continued the fight on 15 February, the day before the Cabinet held a "prolonged discussion" of the bill. The Samuel memorandum reduced the transfer of monopoly value to the status of one of the plans for the period after the expiration of the time limit. The other more moderate possibility that he proposed for the period after the expiration of the time limit was complete discretion by the licensing authority to renew or not to renew without compensation. Late in February another draft bill posed their two alternatives for the Cabinet to choose from.[42] The home secretary grumbled to the prime minister that licensing was "a veritable hornets' nest."[43]

Rumors about the shape of Government plans reached Whittaker. He sent Gladstone an anxious letter late in February or early in March. Two of Whittaker's points coincided with the home secretary's own sentiments, insistence that the time limit be at least fourteen years and opposition to Local Veto for existing licenses. The two men disagreed over the transfer of the monopoly value of all licenses at the end of the time limit. Whittaker insisted that all re-grants be treated as new licenses which meant that they would be subject to the payment of monopoly value which the Licensing Act of 1904 demanded of new licenses.

> *This is absolutely vital. A time limit without this is futile and worthless.* It would be a mere imposture and a complete victory for the liquor trade. The sole object of a Time Limit is to secure full control and possession of all licenses. Without that effective reform is impossible . . . .[44]

News of two alternative bills had alarmed Whittaker. One of them emphasized statutory reduction in proportion to population. Although few houses would be closed in Wales where the proportion was already low, no special provision for Wales was provided, other than the extension of Welsh Sunday closing to Monmouthshire. Perhaps the authors of the bill hoped to appease Welsh reformers by a general provision allowing the licensing authorities to make additional compensated reduction beyond that which was mandated. The bill allowed neither the Veto nor disinterested management. The Cabinet was asked to decide the length of the time limit and whether the transfer of monopoly value or complete discretion vested in the local authorities would follow it. Although not labeled as such, this draft may be styled as Licensing Bill No. 1. After earlier drafts on 4 January and 4 February, it reached its final form on 7 March.[45]

Licensing Bill No. 2–which did officially bear this name–went through several drafts very similar to one another on 4 and 6 March and two on 7 March. In this measure Gladstone's committee offered little more than an unspecified time limit to compensation and the restoration of magisterial discretion at its end. The bill provided for no statutory reduction. It also allowed no Veto, no disinterested management, no special provision for Wales. Monopoly value disappeared even as an option for the Cabinet to consider. The bill did provide a few minor reforms such as the regulation of clubs that sold drink.[46] Presumably the Government believed that this minimal bill could be enacted with relatively little trouble and that it could worry about the contents of a larger bill later.

It was this Licensing Bill No. 2 to which the Liberal MP Charles Roberts alluded in the biography of his mother-in-law Lady Carlisle. Sometime in March the Prime Minister confided to the temperance reformers that he was willing to introduce in the 1907 session a licensing bill limited to a time limit and a few minor reforms with the prospect of a more comprehensive bill later. Hoping for Local Veto, Leif Jones, president of the UKA, preferred to wait for a complete bill in 1908, as did Lady Carlisle. Whittaker and his League, insisting on the transfer of the monopoly value, rejected the limited bill too. Roberts favored the limited licensing bill, particularly if the Government would have added Local Veto for Wales.[47]

In March Campbell-Bannerman told the Cabinet that he questioned whether both a licensing bill and an Irish local government bill could be passed in the current session.[48] When the hesitation of the Government became obvious a group of eighty MPs chaired by H.J. Wilson, adopted by an overwhelming vote a resolution on 15 April to inform the Prime Minister about their "growing feeling of anxiety."[49] Even the effort to organize this meeting of temperance MP's showed temperance disunity. Whittaker wanted to serve as chairman but Leif Jones rejected the idea. Indeed, he told Lady Carlisle that "I rather hope the Whittakerites may boycott us."[50] In fact, Whittaker and Sherwell attended and voted for the resolution.

On 17 April 1907, Leif Jones had a "very cordial" meeting with the Prime Minister who professed himself a strong supporter of the Veto. What was expected to have been a non-controversial army bill was taking much time. Campbell-Bannerman said that although there was not time enough for a bill for an English Veto this year, he hoped for a Scottish Veto bill in 1907. Herbert Gladstone was the obstacle to including the Veto in the licensing bill that the Prime Minister promised for 1908. Jones suggested to him that Gladstone be moved from the Home Office or that Asquith or Lewis Harcourt be put in charge of the licensing bill.[51]

A week later Austen Chamberlain told his wife that he believed that the Government had abandoned its licensing bill in favor of an increase in taxes on drink.[52] In fact, after Leif Jones and Whittaker had rejected a limited bill and the Cabinet decided on 22 April against an Autumn session, the Government decided to hold back a licensing bill until 1908. A month later the Cabinet authorized Cabinet-Bannerman to announce this postponement.[53] He did so in the House of Commons on 3 June.[54]

Sherwell was deflated, according to Leif Jones after having a "longish talk" with him. Jones told Lady Carlisle (17 June): "I thought him vain, and I do not trust him; but his approach to me rather points to his feeling somewhat beaten as to his political position."[55]

In the second half of 1907 a new chapter in the genesis of the Government bill began. Although the Home Office remained responsibility for details, Asquith replaced Gladstone as the minister in charge of the bill.[56] For Liberals, this was "good news."[57] In his prime, Asquith was "a formidable, resolute, and resourceful radical politician."[58] On 11 November, Asquith reported the current thinking of the licensing committee. The committee had made two controversial decisions. (1) After the time limit all licenses would be treated as new licenses and so would be required to pay for their monopoly value status. (2) All clubs registered for the sale of liquor would be subject to the discretion of the local licensing authorities for the renewal of their registration, and the police would have powers of inspection on their premises. Unsettled topics and omissions involved even greater controversy. The length of the time limit remained undefined, and there was no allusion to the Veto except for the ambiguous question, "Option–with what limits, and at whose expense?"[59]

Later in the month Asquith circulated a new memorandum, twelve propositions proposed as a basis for a bill. The committee had not decided on the length of the time limit (or the fixed term as it preferred to call the period for compensation). It adopted the method for determining compensation proposed by Herbert Samuel–namely, the sum by which the annual value of the licensed premises under Schedule (A) of the Income Tax exceeded the amount that the Inland Revenue determined would be the annual value unlicenced. This formula illustrates the complexity of the technical details of much licensing legislation. The committee had not decided whether to recommend additional compensation for the license holder's tenant when the license holder did not personally work as publican. In reaffirming the earlier recommendation to regulate clubs, the committee cautioned: "this requires very careful consideration." Workingmen's clubs, if angered, could be troublesome. Again, there was no recommendation about the Veto but under the heading of "Option," the question was asked: "Should there be a power of popular veto as to *new* licenses during, and after the fixed term?"[60]

Ten days later Gladstone attacked the recommendation that all licenses pay monopoly value after the fixed term expired. He urged that discretionary power for the local licensing authorities to grant or to refuse renewal without compensation be considered as an alternative. At bottom, he rejected as politically impracticable any attempt to specify what the status of licenses would be after the expiration of the time limit. He said that only Whittaker and his section of the temperance party insisted on the transfer of the monopoly value. Leif Jones and the UKA cared nothing about it, if they got the Direct Veto at the end of the time limit. Gladstone suspected that Whittaker advocated the transfer clause to persuade the licensing authorities to grant monopolies to disinterested management companies.[61] Gladstone hoped perhaps to turn opponents of disinterested management into opponents of the transfer of the monopoly value. Once happy to support Whittaker against diehard Vetoists, Gladstone now sought to use the UKA against the League to get a bill which E.N. Buxton might regard as tolerable.

The Alliance was aware the fact that the drink trade hated exaction of monopoly value more than it did the Veto which made it likely that the Government would put the Veto in the bill. Leif Jones told Lady Carlisle that he had always considered the monopoly value as "extremist." "Apparently the trade agree." Consequently, "I am in some hopes the Govt. may slide down on to the Veto as the easiest policy after all."[62]

During the struggle over the shape of the Government bill the *Daily News* began an editorial campaign on 19 November to justify the exclusion of the Veto. Prohibitionists feared that the newspaper was acting in cooperation with the Government. The head of the English Good Templars, Joseph Malins, claimed that his letter of protest, published on 27 November, started the reaction that saved the Veto.[63] In fact, its fate remained insecure for many weeks.

Other pressure groups became active at this critical juncture. On 26 November, Asquith received four different deputations: the National Council of Evangelical Free Churches, the club interest led by the Working Men's Club and Institute Union, the Central Public House Trust Association with its sister organization, the People's Refreshment House Association, and a committee representing brewery shareholders and debenture holders.[64] On 13 December, advocates of Sunday closing sent a deputation.

Informal lobbying probably had more importance than did deputations. Lord Blyth, a member of the group of intermarried families that controlled the Gilbey firm, pressed Asquith about the fate of the licensed grocers. Advising Asquith, Gladstone told the Chancellor that the licensed grocers had little to fear from the current draft bill, but that the best tactics might be to omit them altogether. Then the Government could mollify the temperance groups by telling them that it would accept amendments in committee.[65] After the grocers were spared, Blyth, who had obtained his peerage in 1907, was among the handful of peers who supported the Liberal bill in the House of Lords.

On 8 December, another of Asquith's confidential memorandums accompanied a new draft bill that carried the date of 10 December. The memorandum criticized the bill drafted by the Cabinet committee as too extreme. The draft bill (in a version which included certain optional words in brackets) subjected all licenses after the expiration of the time limit to both the transfer of monopoly value and the prohibitive Veto. Supposedly, the financial meaning of the former lacked clarity, while the latter was hamstrung by the requirement of a two-thirds majority. The draft said nothing about the length of the time limit. Asquith personally preferred to see the monopoly value and Local Veto as alternatives. Although never an enthusiast for prohibition, he seemed anxious to use the Veto (which would probably be a dead letter) to block the transfer of the monopoly value. He asked: "if [the Veto is to be applied to all licensed after the fixed term], is there any necessity for what will be denounced as sheer confiscation, viz., the automatic transfer of the monopoly value?" Apparently, Gladstone had persuaded Asquith.[66] Anti-monopoly value Liberals played the UKA against the League.

In his memorandum Asquith characterized fourteen years as a minimum length for the time limit, an opinion, he conceded, "not shared by all my colleagues on the Committee." He claimed that "the best clause in the Bill" would be that which allowed local licensing authorities to impose conditions for renewal. Asquith wanted to reform the drink trade, not destroy it.[67] As the year 1907 ended and 1908 began, the most important disputes over the licensing bill within the Government continued to be those over the length of the time limit and, at its termination, the monopoly value and Local Veto.

On 14 January, Herbert Samuel sent Gladstone a long letter vigorously attacking the inclusion of the Veto. Samuel denied that the value of the Veto as a measure of temperance reform was worth the political sacrifice. Most Liberal MPs did not want it. The Veto would make "their advocacy of the bill in their own constituencies . . . apologetic and not enthusiastic." After an initial disappointment prohibitionists would rally to a Veto-less bill because of other reforms such as statutory reduction and the time limit, especially after trade attacks began to threaten the bill.

According to Samuel, the Veto in combination with a time limit would "offer too broad a target to the opposition." Although the trade was mainly concerned with the time limit, the Opposition would emphasize the Veto as a favorable ground for attracting public sympathy. If the Government intended eventually to withdraw the Veto in the House of Commons to save the rest of the bill, the result would be to force the Liberal MPs to alienate their constituents unnecessarily and to weaken the support of the advanced temperance men when the bill came before the House of Lords and would be most needed. "You would be far better to have slackness first and energy later than the other way around." If the Government intended to force the clause through the House of Commons, the Veto would weaken the fight over the powers of the House of Lords which would undoubtedly follow the Lords rejecting the bill. "The Tories would then have, what they have hitherto completely lacked, a case, fresh in the minds of the electorate, in which the Lords had stopped an unpopular measure from becoming law." During the years of the time limit the Veto would become the subject of efforts at repeal and endanger the time limit itself.[68]

Gladstone's response does not appear in his papers. Although long known as a critic of the Veto, at this point he probably would have accepted it, like Asquith, if by doing so he could block the monopoly value transfer.

After the death of the elder Harcourt, the Lord Chancellor Lord Loreburn stood out as the champion of the old-fashioned Alliance point of view within the Liberal leadership. In a long memorandum, dated 15 January 1908, he argued for a Veto on all licenses and a time limit of no more than seven years. He said that among those who favored the Veto in principle Whittaker was almost alone in doubting its tactical expediency. The Liberal opposition to the Veto in the House of Commons had been grossly exaggerated, while the spasmodic press campaigns against it have been "obviously due to sedulous wire-pulling." The Cabinet, the churches, the temperance party, most Liberal and all Labour MPs were committed to the Veto. Indeed, the Government could prevent the adoption of a Local Veto amendment only with the assistance of the Unionists. The Liberal Party could never expect a larger majority than it had, so the refusal to include a Veto in the bill would in effect be the permanent abandonment of it. Dropping the Veto would not mitigate trade opposition to the rest of the bill, but many temperance workers would leave the Liberal Party for a Labour or socialist party.

Loreburn argued that the chief benefit to be derived from Local Veto legislation would be indirect, the better administration of the law. The owners of licensed houses would have a reason to favor proper management and public opinion would have a means of enforcing it. The proper method of reform was the extension of popular self-government and not bureaucratic control such as in the reduction scheme.

For the Veto to be safe from Unionist repeal the time notice must be short. Loreburn personally would have repealed the 1904 statute without any time notice at all, even if this required the repayment of the moneys collected for compensation. Since a time limit seemed politically inevitable it should be no more than seven years. One of twenty-one years or even of fourteen would be "a bitter disappointment." Loreburn objected that the 1908 draft bill accepted the philosophy of the 1904 Act. It relied for a temperance reform on a scheme of reduction that in some degree delayed the Veto. The statutory reduction scheme would bring the proportion of licenses in England to that already attained almost everywhere in Scotland where the conditions scarcely approximated the ideal. The reduction scheme would provide an excuse for extending the time limit even more.

> In truth the choice lies between Sir Thomas Whittaker's ideal and the Local Option ideal. The former rests on the theory that statutory reduction is the ideal remedy, and so long as it is a real reduction the longer it goes on perhaps the better, and it does not matter what else you bar. The latter ideal rests on the theory that reduction is right enough, but that far more important is the effective control of the trade, which would bring reduction also.

Loreburn misrepresented Whittaker who wanted reduction for the same reason as Loreburn wanted the Veto, that is, to reform the way public houses were run. Loreburn agreed with Whittaker that the bill could not simply restore the renewal system of magisterial discretion. The monopoly value must be exacted from all licenses. If not, said Loreburn, "far better to propose no Bill at all."[69]

Two days later the Cabinet with near unanimity tentatively decided on a fourteen-year time limit. Six days after the Cabinet made this definite at its 22 February meeting, a virtually complete bill was circulated. In either January or February, the Cabinet must have decided how to deal with licenses at the expiration of the time limit: adopt both the Veto and the exaction of monopoly value. The records say nothing. The Cabinet settled other details on 19 February. It was then presumably that Wales received a special local option allowing plebiscites for additional compensation reduction during the time limit. It had not been in any recent draft but appeared when it mattered, in the bill presented to Parliament.[70]

The licensing bill that Asquith introduced in the House of Commons on 27 February 1908 was a large and comprehensive measure. It took the Prime Minister an hour and three quarters to present his complex bill. It occupied twenty-five columns in Hansard.[71] Asquith's licensing bill provoked an opposition that the Clerk of the House of Commons described as "very formidable and very skillfully organized." It "will doubtless cause the loss of many votes and seats to the Government." Sir Courtenay P. Ilbert told his correspondent: "Already many Liberals are feeling very weak-kneed about it."[72] The *Licensing World* warned that if the Government by act of Parliament could take one kind of property from its owners it could take other kinds of property too such as railroads and gasworks.[73]

The bill was designed to reduce substantially the number of licensed premises in England and Wales in a proportion to the local population. In contrast with earlier Liberal emphasis on local autonomy, this was a centralized scheme. At the end of a fourteen-year time limit for this statutory reduction and the compensation which accompanied it, the surviving licenses would be subject both to the transfer of monopoly value and Direct Local Veto. Wales got the right to local prohibition immediately, as did new licenses in England. By the end of the time-limit, "the number of existing licenses would have been reduced by about a third, representing at least twice as many reductions likely to be secured under the provisions of the 1904 Licensing Act."[74]

The bill reduced pub openings on Sunday to four hours in London and three hours elsewhere. The definition of bona fide travelers for Sunday sales was increased from three miles to six.

Asquith and Gladstone had been forced to give way to both the Alliance and the League to produce this radical bill. Perhaps Asquith preferred to concede to all temperance factions whatever they wanted rather than create enemies when the Prime Minister was dying and Asquith had yet to succeed him. George Bernstein argues that Asquith included both the Veto and monopoly value in the bill because he took for granted that the House of Lords would reject it and because he needed to improve his credibility with the Nonconformists, especially as he planned to introduce a compromise education bill that they would resent.[75] The Vetoist leader Leif Jones believed that the joint deputation of the United Kingdom Alliance and the National Temperance Federation, which waited on Asquith on 31 January had last minute influence. Asquith flattered Leif Jones by saying that the deputation was more like a demonstration.[76] Likely the Government had already decided to include the Veto for all licenses after the time limit expired and, as in Balfour's legislation, immediately for new licenses.

Instead of complaining about the demands pressed upon him, Asquith left the meeting claiming to be delighted about the deputation's moderation and spirit of cooperation.[77] Although the critics of the bill exaggerated when they claimed that Whittaker had written the Government bill, he too had his way on a controversial issue, probably the most controversial issue of all. Despite strong opposition to the transfer of monopoly value in the Cabinet and (of course) in the drink trade, the Liberal Government accepted the principal demand of the powerful new Temperance Legislation League.

The time limit, or fixed term, provided the key to the licensing bill. As a Liberal MP and historian, G.P. Gooch later said in his memoirs, it was "the heart of the fight."[78] In the 1880s and 1890s a time limit meant that at the termination of a certain period of years the expectation of license renewal would end. Thereafter, Parliament and the local licensing authorities would exercise a full discretion unfettered by any sense of equitable obligation to the existing license holders. Thus, the time limit cleared the ground for reforms and experiments. After the Licensing Act of 1904 created a statutory right to compensation, buttressing the old expectation of renewal, the time limit acquired the additional meaning of the termination of compensation for non-renewal. The trade objected to a time limit in principle, as did some Unionist backbenchers.

The biographer of F.E. Smith (later Lord Birkenhead) explained the Tory critique of Asquith's bill: "it was unjust, amounting--since the compensation was quite unrealistic--to the confiscation of licensees' property" and "it would not work anyway, since the mere reduction of drinking places had never been shown to reduce drunkenness." The latter complaint was awkward since Balfour's 1904 legislation had been defended on temperance grounds because it reduced the number of licensed premises.

F.E. Smith pointed out that the Government bill did not touch clubs then growing in numbers and membership. They were open when public houses were closed. He pointed out that in contrast with Liberal clubs which sold drink the Conservative working men's clubs in Liverpool were teetotal.[79]

Balfour and most Unionist leaders regretted that the expectation of automatic renewal had been allowed to develop.[80] They accepted the principle of a time limit to end it, provided that the period was long enough to constitute compensation for the market value of the licenses and that renewal was guaranteed during the time limit other than for license holders who seriously violated the law. The Unionists objected to combining the time limit with the principle of their own Licensing Act of 1904, that the trade would provide the compensation funds for the immediate reduction in the number of licensed houses. As the Unionists saw the situation, the trade could not underwrite the compensation fund, build up a depreciation fund, and pay its debenture holders the interest on their loans and its preference and ordinary shareholders appropriate dividends on their investments. Therefore, the Unionists rejected the time limit in the Liberal licensing bill.

The quarrel over the length of the time limit and the related dispute over the amount of compensation could have been compromised. From the beginning it was obvious that the Government attached no special importance to fourteen years as the length of the time limit. Writing to the King upon the introduction of the bill, Gladstone unhesitatingly reported the possibility of an amended time limit of twenty or twenty-five years. He said that there was a national consensus for "something like finality in Licensing Legislation" and that the Government wanted "to reach that goal without harsh treatment of existing interests under the Law."[81] After 1904 the Liberals reluctantly accepted market value as the standard for the length of the time limit and the payment of money compensation, although they defined market value to minimize it. Yet the decision to combine the time limit with the compensation levy and the reduction of the number of licensed houses probably was beyond compromise for the Unionist leaders. As far as their trade allies saw it, the Liberal bill confiscated property.

The decision of the Liberal Government to exact the payment of monopoly value from all licensed houses at the end of the time limit could not have been compromised. Monopoly value was the most abhorrent part of the licensing bill in the eyes of the Unionists and the drink trade. It was unacceptable in any version. (The 1904 Licensing Act imposed transfer of monopoly value on new licenses only.). The Opposition complained that the transfer of monopoly value had nothing to do with temperance, that it was simply a heavy discriminatory tax, totally unfair in the case of old licenses that had been purchased by their present owners at high prices. Supposedly it was a vindictive attack on a trade identified with the Government's political enemies. Furthermore, a practical definition of monopoly value was highly elusive. Not until 3 November did the Government offer an explicit definition.

The time when the monopoly value would be exacted and the time when statutory reduction and compensation expired were not necessarily the same, although they were identical in the original bill. As the major Government concession to the Opposition, the two time periods were separated on 17 October. Fourteen years remained the period for compensated reduction. The transfer of monopoly value was delayed for an additional seven years.[82] In some respects these seven years resembled the kind of time limit acceptable to the Unionists, as the licensed houses would not be burdened by a compensation levy. Yet they would have been subjected to optional reduction by local authorities and to the prohibitive Veto, both without any compensation. The trade would have preferred to extend the period for reducing the number of public houses to the allowed ratio, even at the cost of more payments into the compensation fund.

Reduction in numbers constituted the core of the licensing bill as a measure of temperance reform. Although still indispensable for the hearty support of the UKA, Local Veto played a minor role in the debates of 1908. Nearly everyone expected that it would be a dead letter. In contrast the reduction clauses, with what the trade considered only partial compensation, were mandatory and immediate. As in the case of the transfer of the monopoly value, the Liberals borrowed heavily from the licensing Act of 1904 for the general principles of compensated reduction, but applied them with modifications which greatly increased their damaging impact on the drink trade. They claimed that they had restored the definition of market value to that intended by the Unionists in 1904 before the Kennedy Judgment of 1906 had inflated it. The Liberals also reduced compensation proportionately as the compensation period neared its end.

More important than the amount of compensation was the provision in the bill that set up a maximum proportion of licensed houses per population. The ratio of on-licenses per population could not exceed one per 400 where the population density was two persons or less per acre, one per 500 where the population density was two to 25 per acre, one per 600 for 25 to 50 per acre, one per 700 for 50 to 75 per acre, one per 800 for 75 to 100 per acre, one per 900 for 100 to 200 per acre, and one per 1000 for more than 200 per acre. A reduction to these ratios had to be completed within the fourteen-year fixed term for compensation. The compensation fund was centralized under a three-man licensing commission which would have the authority to allow local variations from the ratio of licensing houses to population, for instance, in resort towns with a large temporary population of holiday seekers and in business districts with a large daytime population.

The Unionists protested the rigidity and arbitrariness of any ratio and denied that reduction in numbers advanced the cause of temperance. Indeed, some Unionists questioned the value of any legislation in furthering temperance. Counties such as Oxfordshire with many licenses in proportion to population had fewer convictions for drunkenness than some counties with proportionately fewer licenses such as Durham. Most Liberals defended reduction in numbers on the grounds of decreasing temptation. Serious students of the drink problem such as Sir Thomas Whittaker and Charles Roberts emphasized an indirect advantage: an increase in public control would encourage public houses to improve themselves out of desire to avoid selection as the houses to be closed. The Liberals also pointed out that the Unionists had built their own licensing act of 1904 around reduction in numbers. The Opposition complained about the failure of the Government to make available its working figures on how many licenses would be suppressed in each licensing area. The Liberals merely offered a general estimate of 30,000 or 35,000 licenses to be suppressed out of 90,000. The Government argued that local estimates would be misleading as the bill allowed for circumstances in which, at the request of the licensing justices, the licensing commissioners could make modifications. The Unionists also protested the bureaucratic centralization of the bill, that what discretionary authority existed would rest in the hands of the "paid trio" in London. They pointed out that four years earlier the Liberals had bemoaned the loss of local knowledge in transferring the power to suppress licenses from the local licensing benches to the Quarter Sessions which could refuse to impose a compensation levy, yet the Liberals proposed an even more extreme centralization. In fact, the Liberal bill strengthened the licensing benches by eliminating the right of the license holder to appeal to Quarter Sessions against a refusal to renew a license.

Of the lesser parts of the bill the regulation of off-licenses and clubs turned out to be particularly controversial. Clearly it was no different to become intoxicated from liquor bought in an off-license and drunk at home or drunk in a club than that drunk in a public house. Virtually all temperance reformers wanted to reduce the privileges of the licensed grocers and the clubs, as did licensed victuallers.[83] As Liberal supporters controlled most grocers' licenses and working men's clubs, the Unionists accused the Liberal Party of partisan bias when it dealt more gently with these sources of drink than with public houses. F.E. Smith described it as hypocritical.[84] Despite these jibes the Government backed off an early interpretation of the bill that required off-licenses to pay monopoly value and to risk being closed by the Veto. It did modify the bill to make grocers' licenses subject to Local Veto.

The Government suffered even more embarrassment over the clubs. Campbell-Bannerman had been sympathetic toward them. In contrast, Asquith repeatedly refused to consult with the club interest prior to formulating the relevant clauses.[85] It was not until late November 1907 that Gladstone and Asquith received a joint deputation which included the Working Men's Club and Institute Union, a large and well-established organization, as well as a Liberal club union formed only a few weeks earlier, two regional Liberal club federations, and a Conservative club federation, representing in all 2,780 clubs with 964,000 members.[86] In mid-December Asquith received an anti-club deputation in which T.P. Whittaker was prominent. A club publication described him as "the arch enemy."[87]

The Club and Institute Union led the fight against the provisions for magisterial control, police entry of premises, and restricted hours. It raised a £10,000 fund for its expenses but had to spend only £600 or £700 in its campaign.[88] Although many Unionist backbenchers and the provincial retail trade favored restrictions, Balfour preferred an alliance with the clubs on behalf of personal liberty.[89] The clubs bitterly complained about "a modern Holy Alliance" in which temperance reformers, licensing magistrates, boards of guardians in London and elsewhere, the drink trade, the Established and Nonconformist churches, and the press united.[90] Liberal MPs came under heavy pressure. For instance, F.A. Channing, a temperance-minded MP in whose East Northants division no fewer than 7,000 club members were electors, first tried to persuade the clubs that the bill would not harm them, then attempted to get the Government to revise the club clauses, and in the end regretted that the Government concessions to the clubs went too far.[91] Gladstone and Benjamin Tom Hall, secretary of the Club and Institute Union, negotiated the terms of peace on 26 October.[92]

Most of the rest of the bill provided no great excitement, although the Unionists quibbled line by line to help build a case that the bill was ill-conceived and ill-drafted. The Welsh MPs indulged in florid rhetoric in praise of Local Veto for Wales and the extension of Welsh Sunday closing to Monmouthshire. The Government risked a minor revolt on the part of Labour and temperance MP's by dropping the clause that would have authorized the justices to prohibit the employment of barmaids other than the women already working.[93] Ordinarily the extension of new permissive powers to the justices met with general approval. Indeed, responding to Unionist arguments, the Government ended the exemption of London from the grant of the permissive powers for shorter Sunday hours.

The procedural debate over the use of closure by compartments provoked some of the sharpest exchanges. As in 1904, both parties seemed to relish debating the guillotine more than the substance of the bill. Asquith introduced his resolution to limit debate before the committee stage had begun, the first time that the guillotine had been proposed by a Government before there had been clear evidence of obstruction. Bonar Law (29 Oct.) complained about rudeness: "The Prime Minister set up the guillotine and then left." With the aid of the Standing Orders of 1902 which increased the Government's control over the parliamentary time and an autumn session, the huge Liberal majority simply waited out the Opposition from 27 February until 27 November.

The Prime Minister and other Cabinet ministers rarely attended the licensing debates. Sometimes a Cabinet member would direct the debate for a single clause and then depart. Usually, the treasury bench was occupied only by the Solicitor General, Sir Samuel Evans, and Herbert Samuel, the undersecretary at the Home Office, or just one of them. To no avail, the Opposition complained about the absence of Cabinet members. On 29 October, a Unionist MP regretted that the Prime Minister "was away attending bazaars."

As Balfour was ill during the second reading, a newcomer to the House, George Cave, acted as the principal Unionist spokesman.[94] Ironically, he had been the chairman of the Surrey Quarter Sessions that by upholding the Farnham justices in 1902 had helped create the licensing crisis of 1903. Unionist speech often followed Unionist speech unanswered. The Opposition complained that the Liberal whips discouraged their own backbenchers from speaking. The Opposition could rarely lead more than a hundred members into its lobby even with the aid of Liberal drink traders such as the brewer Whitbread, the maltster Barnard, and the solicitor Julius Bertram who had ties to the drink trade, libertarian Radicals as varied as Hilaire Belloc and Horatio Bottomley, and a fair number of the Irish.[95]

The impregnable Liberal majority in the Commons and the equally firm control of the Lords by the Unionists made it futile for pressure groups to concentrate on changing the votes of individual MPs and peers. Instead, both the temperance organizations and the drink trade tried to sway party leaders by creating an image of an aroused public. The temperance societies had two objectives: preventing any major Liberal compromises dictated by fear of the licensing bill's electoral unpopularity and convincing the Unionist Party and the House of Lords that responsible public opinion would be outraged by a rejection of the bill. The United Kingdom Alliance and the Temperance Legislation League dominated the temperance agitation. The temperance party and its penumbra of social, benevolent, and religious workers rallied enthusiastically behind a bill which imperfectly satisfied them, although the CETS remained largely inactive until the crucial weeks in November.

The *Alliance News* correctly said: "this is not an 'Alliance' Bill. It rather follows the lines of Lord Peel's report. But the spirit in which it is drafted is the main thing."[96] The UKA had no wish to fight a Liberal Government for an ideal bill. It was enough that the omnibus licensing bill acknowledged the principle of Direct Local Veto and kept out disinterested management. The Alliance temporarily moved its headquarters to London where it booked offices in Westminster for the period from January to October 1908. The Alliance supervised a campaign that strained its finances and staff. For instance, it authorized £300 for "press work," including replies to letters in newspapers.[97] The Alliance helped organize most of the temperance public meetings in 1908 ranging from small provincial rallies to massive demonstrations of strength in the metropolis where it cooperated with the London United Temperance Council, an organization left over from Arnold Hills's United Temperance Bill agitation. The two organizations created the London Campaign Committee. It was funded in part by £100 from Lady Carlisle, £50 from Cameron Corbett, a substantial sum from the Wesleyan Connexional Temperance Committee, and £150 from the United Kingdom Alliance.[98] David Lloyd George addressed the meeting at Queen's Hall on 26 March, the Bishop of London and Lord Crewe that at Albert Hall on 16 May.[99] After a major meeting at Leeds on 18 July, the temperance movement held its climactic demonstration at Hyde Park on 25 July that attracted 100,000 people and was addressed by that unlikely temperance reformer the young Winston Churchill.[100] When the Hyde Park meeting had been scheduled it was assumed by the Alliance that the bill would have reached the Lords by the end of the summer.

The UKA also took the lead in a petition movement. According to the House of Commons committee on petitions, the opponents of the bill gathered more signatures than the proponents, 1,585,900 to 1,209,098.[101] Without the efforts of the Alliance the deficit would have been much greater. By late October, the Alliance office had sent 11,000 petitions to the all-important House of Lords. It provided comprehensive coverage of the agitation on behalf of the licensing bill in its own newspaper. Finally, the Alliance circulated a huge quantity of miscellaneous literature: summaries and reprints of the bill, tracts, pamphlets, and books, eight million leaflets, and gratis copies of the *Alliance News* to anybody who might be in a position to aid the bill.[102] An Alliance official, George B. Wilson, wrote the most elaborate statement of the UKA case for the Liberal bill, *The Licensing Bill as a Measure of Temperance Reform*. The activity of the Alliance as an organization overlapped with that of its members. For instance, Charles Roberts, Lady Carlisle's son-in-law, published an outstanding book, *Time Limit and Local Option*.[103]

The Temperance Legislation League emphasized printed propaganda in its part in the agitation but also provided speakers for public meetings.[104] Thomas Whittaker was a host in himself in print and on the platform. He wrote a book that can be paired with Roberts' in merit and exceeded it in attracting attention. *The Licensing Bill: Some Facts and Arguments in Support* was intended as a handbook for speakers. The League sent copies to members of both House of Parliament, temperance activists, and other supporters of the bill. According to the League's annual report, "a first edition of 100,000 copies was exhausted in three or four days," after which another 100,000 copies of a second, enlarged edition of more than a hundred pages were published. The second edition included 65,000 copies used in free distribution to clergymen and Nonconformist ministers, justices of the peace, religious workers, and others. The handbook was sold at cost to other groups that distributed it without charge. Replies to Whittaker's handbook made it necessary for him to write another substantial booklet of nearly a hundred pages, *The Licensing Bill of 1908: A Rejoinder to Critics*, which emphasized the financial aspects of the bill.[105] 75,000 copies were published, including 65,000 circulated free of charge.

The League published twenty other pamphlets and leaflets. Their circulation under the League imprint amounted to five million copies, while several were also circulated under the name of other societies. The League also issued eleven posters. Anonymous supporters provided a special donation of nearly £2,000 for large posters displayed on hoardings in metropolitan London during what had been expected to be the crucial months of June, July, and August. Later some 65,000 posters were supplied free of charge or at cost in provincial cities.

The League also sent a stream of letters to the principal London and provincial newspapers. Local citizens' committees were established in the provinces. The League dispatched two lucky agents to propagandize the sea bathers at Blackpool. Six agents and many volunteers worked in bye-elections. In this active year the League had an income of nearly £8,500, including a subscription of £1,000 from Joseph Rowntree, co-author of *The Temperance Problem and Social Reform*. The League spent nearly £7,700.[106]

The trade had a simpler task as it wanted only one thing, to persuade the Unionist leadership to wield its veto power in the House of Lords. Believing that it faced ruin if the Liberal licensing bill passed in any conceivable form, the trade gambled at alienating moderate public opinion by demanding the total rejection of the bill.[107] A trade official told Balfour's secretary: "We are absolutely pledged to no compromise, and amendments moved by the opposition to extend the Time Limit or to modify this or that will be taken as a sign of weakening."[108]

The London publicans decided to spend up to £2,000 on posters and advertisements and another £1,000 for "making use of the columns of various papers."[109] (For a price some newspapers allowed the licensed trade to supply what purported to be news stories.) Although the trade proposed for its position the slogan, "Defence, not Defiance," trade leaders saw no point in seeking an accommodation with the Liberal Government [110] On 3 March, a special conference of the trade ratified this unyielding policy of no compromise.[111] On 9 March, five thousand trade supporters attended a protest meeting at Queen's Hall, with others at an overflow meeting at a smaller hall. Feeling was even stronger than it had been in the dark days of 1903.[112] The time limit that the bill added to the right of compensation threatened a return to the insecurity of 1903. Worst of all, the provision for the exaction of monopoly value from existing licenses–and not just new ones as in the 1904 Licensing Act–seemed to endanger the financial survival of the trade.[113] Supported by a £100,000 guarantee fund, the trade poured out petitions and posters, advertised extensively in the press, and sat or stood through innumerable protest meetings to convince the Unionists to refuse any compromise.[114] An Allied Brewery Traders' Association, organized in 1907, had about 1,700 firms as members by the following year such as maltsters, hops growers, and sugar brewers. In April the new organization flew a propaganda kite over the football cup tie final at the Crystal Palace.[115] Privately, the trade provided the Unionists with arguments and evidence. On 4 May, Balfour's secretary praised the "admirable material which [H.A.] Newton [employed by the National Trade Defence Association] and some leading Brewery accountants supplied."[116]

The trade helped the Unionist Party win an impressive succession of bye-elections. The too conspicuous role of the trade at Peckham in South London, where supposedly even the dogs were dressed in party colors, embarrassed many Unionists, including the editors of the *Morning Post*. Balfour's secretary advised the National Trade Defence Association to exercise more discretion at the Northwest Manchester bye-election.[117] Ironically at both these elections the Unionist candidates were teetotalers whereas the Liberal in the latter case (Winston Churchill) definitely was not. When Balfour addressed a mass meeting on the licensing bill at Albert Hall in June, the trade remained in the background, although it had asked him to speak and had paid a full-time organizer to provide the audience.[118]

The trade abandoned circumspection at the climax of its campaign, a massive demonstration at Hyde Park on the last Sunday in September. A huge crowd, variously estimated as a quarter million or a half million people, reportedly attended this monster meeting in an open display of trade power. The provinces sent 172 special trains full of demonstrators. The huge throng, wearing buttons of blue enamel that bore the motto, "Honesty and Liberty," surrounded twenty carts that served as platforms for the prominent speakers who denounced the bill. Platform sixteen ran out of speakers early. E. Lawrence Levy, editor of the (Birmingham) *Licensed Trade News*, had to talk to occupy the remainder of the time while worrying that his new false teeth might fall out.[119] At the signal of a bugle a resolution was put from each platform condemning the Government bill. Predictably Liberal and temperance critics complained about drunkenness at the demonstration, bribery and coercion in assembling the crowd and desecration of the

Sabbath.[120] Describing how the breweries got their people to the demonstration, the *Liberal Magazine* reported: "Some brewery companies sold [train tickets] to their tenants and employees at reduced rate, some distributed them free, while others chartered special trains of their own, charging nothing and supplying refreshments." [121]

The trade also tried to manipulate the press. "The series of articles appearing in the [London] Times in defence of the Trade had been authorised by the [Central] Board, who would pay for them."[122] This startling statement appeared casually in the minutes of the Central Board of London's licensed victuallers.

The trade had to contend with the temperance reformers and the Church of England for influence with the Unionist Party.[123] In May, Balfour's private secretary was shocked by an interview with Lord Landowne (1845-1927), the Unionist leader in the Lords, who "made no secret of his preference for an amended Bill," which would modify the Liberal proposal for a time limit. "I am afraid that [Hicks-] Beach, whom I know he has seen, has been inspiring him and that he fears possibly to move in opposition to the Bishops."[124] The CETS central committee endorsed the bill by a vote of 77 to 25.[125] Yet the CETS did little to help the temperance agitation.[126] The upper house of Convocation unanimously supported the idea of a time limit to compensation. Although the Church was by no means united on temperance legislation, indignant publicans and brewers retaliated by withdrawing subscriptions to ecclesiastical charities and by threatening to work for disestablishment.[127] Such blatant pressures probably hurt the trade more than it did the Church or the CETS. The trade also organized boycotts of tradesmen known to support the Liberal bill. For instance, in Northampton a license holder "declined to let a Good Templar tune his pianoforte."[128]

The major figure in the Unionist Party in favor of amending the licensing bill rather than rejecting it altogether was the former Chancellor of the Exchequer, Sir Michael Hicks-Beach, who had been ennobled as Earl St. Aldwyn. In August he sent Balfour a long letter arguing that the licensing law needed amendment. Reduction in numbers should be compulsory, and compensation as misinterpreted by the Kennedy judgment should be decreased. He accepted the principle of a time limit to compensation, provided at its expiration there was no requirement of payment of monopoly value and no Veto. "If the time limit were extended to 21 or 20 years, and at the end of it the holders of existing licenses were simply put back to the position which they held before the passing of the Act of 1904, I do not see that any harm would be done." He argued that there was no serious danger of a revolt by the brewers since they could gain nothing by supporting the

Liberals. A compromise bill would save future Unionist Governments from having to deal with the chronic licensing question and save the brewers from Liberal retaliation through high license duties if the House of Lords simply rejected the bill.[129] Balfour did not react favorably. He told Lord Lansdowne, the Unionist leader in the House of Lords: "I shall have to write you again of the subject of St. Aldwyn and Licensing, but, for the moment, I spare you." Balfour's personal secretary A.S. Sandars expressed the "hope that Beach is not very mischievous in any temporizing policy over the Licensing Bill." In contrast, Lansdowne later implored Balfour: "Don't forget Beach's letter." [130]

Late in September a correspondent of Balfour reported a second-hand story that David Lloyd George disliked the bill and hoped that it would be amended.[131] Whether that story was true or not, the Government certainly would have compromised particularly over the length of the time limit. Late in October the Liberal newspaper, the *Daily Chronicle*, argued that the bill was overloaded and that parts of it should be abandoned.[132] Liberals worried that the House of Lords might argue that it had no alternative to rejecting the entire bill because the time limit and monopoly value both touched on the financial privileges of the House of Commons and consequently could not be amended by the Lords. Herbert Samuel suggested to Asquith that to obviate this danger the time limit should be extended while the bill was in the Commons.[133]

Asquith asked the King to tell the Unionists that the Government was willing to lengthen the time limit. Edward VII was anxious that the House of Lords pass the licensing bill. He feared that the defeat of the bill might endanger the survival of the powers of the hereditary chamber. The royal engagements diary recorded interviews with Asquith on Sunday, 11 October, at 6:30, and with Lansdowne, the Unionist leader in the Lords, on Monday, 12 October, at 12:45.[134] Lansdowne summarized the interview in a memorandum. The King implied that the Prime Minister had authorized him to say that the Government would concede a time limit of twenty or twenty-one years. In reply, Lansdowne denied that the Unionists already had decided to throw out the bill, but cited arguments for them doing so, the danger of misunderstanding: that the Opposition accepted the principle of the bill and then had quarreled with the Government over its details only and the recent treatment of the amendments which the Lords had tried to make in the Old Age Pensions bill which the Commons had rejected as an infringement on their privileges in regards money bills.[135]

The day after this interview the UKA held its annual meeting in an atmosphere of anticipation and trepidation. The length of the House of Commons debates meant that the meeting could be neither celebration nor wake. The high point of the influence of the UKA had been passed during the mid-1890s, but this meeting (over which the non-abstemious Churchill presided) was a splendid Indian summer when prohibitionists could dream that the Veto might soon become the law of the land.

Later in the same week the Government made its major concession at report stage. Although the Government did not change the time limit, it delayed the exaction of monopoly value by another seven years. This disappointed the disinterested management people. In contrast, the Alliance was willing to sacrifice the monopoly value as along as bill provided for Local Veto. Asquith supposedly described Whittaker as being "like a bear with a sore head."[136] Whittaker's influence had faded. He rarely spoke in Parliament and attended debate less and less. Part of the explanation was the impact of the ad hominem attacks by the renegade anti-temperance Liberal, Horatio Bottomley. His newspaper *John Bull* (7 November 1908, p. 463) published an article "Sir Thomas Whittaker's Public-House" about an insurance company that Whittaker headed, the United Kingdom Temperance and General Assurance Society. When it built a new headquarters on the Strand, it acquired the property on which a public house was situated. Because of the license holder's long-term lease, expiring 1936, the insurance company could not close the pub. Bottomley also had attacked Whittaker in the *Daily News* and in the *Times* (2 November 1908) about a financial newspaper, the *Daily Oracle*, that Whittaker had edited as a young man. It had published stories about investing in the drink trade even after the conclusion of the Sharp v. Wakefield case.[137] Leif Jones privately sympathized with Whittaker. He characterized the Bottomley attacks as a "sickening business: for poor old T.P. is not a serpent like some his associates, but only a hot tempered blunderer."[138]

Jones believed that Sherwell as well as Whittaker had lost influence with the Government, Sherwell because his speeches criticized so many parts of the Government licensing bill. As a result, the influence of the United Kingdom Alliance had risen.[139]

Some observers hoped–or feared–that the amendment might persuade the Lords to accept the bill. A Wesleyan layman prominent in Unionist politics in the West of England typified the minority of Opposition supporters who urged compromise on behalf of temperance reform. He said that sentiment in favor of reduction was strong in Cornwall and Devon.[140] At the end of October, Carson speculated worriedly that "faddists or funks" might induce the upper house to give the bill a second reading.[141] Jesse Collings told Joseph Chamberlain that he hoped that "the Lords will throw the Bill out at second reading. It cannot be amended and by so treating it the Lords would do a most popular act."[142] Walter Long was anxious that

Balfour reject any compromise that the Lords might offer.[143] The Liberal peer Lord Crewe asked whether Balfour and the Unionists might accept a drastically amended bill: "saying we can increase license duties if we please, but avoiding the time-limit at all costs, and local veto?"[144]

After the bill carried in the Commons on the third reading by the huge majority of 350 to 113, the slow pace of the past several months quickened. It would take the Lords less than half as many days to defeat the bill than it had taken months for the Commons to pass it. There were those who still hoped for the bill's enactment. The executive of the Church of England Temperance Society voted unanimously to urge the Lords to pass the bill. A letter sent to all the members of the upper house described the Liberal bill as reasonable and necessary.[145] After a long period of "masterly inactivity" the CETS was satisfied with the bill as modified in the House of Commons.[146] The CETS did not speak for the Church. The Representative House of Laymen condemned the 1908 bill. In contrast, no bishop voted against the bill and two voted for it

The decision taken by the Unionist peers did not take place in the House of Lords. It came at a private caucus held at Lansdowne House on fashionable Berkeley Square, the town house of the Unionist leader, at midday on 24 November.

Different accounts of the meeting agree on essentials. More than 240 peers attended the short meeting; nearly twenty of them spoke, most of them very briefly. One of the noble lords later pointed out that a meeting held at luncheon time discouraged prolonged debate, particularly when many of those attending had breakfasted early before a long train journey.[147] The assembled peers voted overwhelmingly to throw the bill out rather than to amend it. The dissenters numbered from eight to thirty, depending on which source one believes. The dissenters included St. Aldwyn, Cromer, Milner, Balfour of Burleigh, Lytton, and Carlisle.[148] Many of the Unionist peers who opposed the rejection of the bill were Free Traders.[149]

Lord Willoughby de Broke was a so-called backwoodsman who had rarely attended the House of Lords. In his memoir he said that "the meeting was great fun," and that afterwards the assembled peers "adjourned for a good luncheon at the Carlton Club." He conceded that the meeting was "a tactical blunder." When the newspapers reported the meeting of the peers, "in the language of the theatre the affair 'looked rude from the front'."[150]

In his biography of Lansdowne, Lord Newton said that the majority had been influenced by two arguments: that any important amendments would be treated as a breach of the House of Commons' financial privileges and that an early collision between the two Houses was inevitable in any event so there was no need to be conciliatory. The well-informed Sir Almeric FitzRoy claimed that in deciding to refuse the bill a second reading Lansdowne had capitulated to a thinly veiled threat of a Tory revolt led by Lord Cawdor and Lord Halsbury which as a Liberal Unionist he would have had difficulty in containing.[151] The UKA saw the action of the Lords as the result of a "financial conspiracy" led by Lord Rothschild who headed a committee which represented brewery share and debenture holders. Allegedly, Rothschild was "up to the eyes in brewery shares, either personally or through the companies of which he is chairman."[152]

Following the decision of the Lansdowne House meeting, the House of Lords on 27 November 1908, defeated the bill by a vote of 276 to 96. Some of the dissenters at the caucus, notably St. Aldwyn, voted with the majority.[153] Twenty Unionist peers voted for the bill or in one instance paired in its favor. The Unionists casting affirmative votes for a second reading included Balfour of Burleigh, Carlisle, Esher, Knollys, Lytton, Milner, Peel, and Ritchie. No bishop voted against the bill, while fifteen voted for it including both Archbishops and the best known episcopal temperance reformers, the Bishops of London and Chester. Others paired in its favor.

In retrospect, it had been folly for the Lords to throw out a bill that a large segment of disinterested opinion favored. Such staunch Tory newspapers as the *Times*, the *Morning Post*, and the *Pall Mall Gazette*, as well as the King and the bishops, had called for a compromise. The Lansdowne House meeting displayed an image of oligarchy defying the elected representatives of the people. After the Lords threw out the bill, the Government decided against an immediate appeal to the electorate. The consensus held the bill was unpopular.[154] One Unionist leaflet, "To the British Working Man," warned in verse about Asquith: "He'll take away your special pub/ and make you join and keep a club/ where (note his little plan)/ He'll have you WATCHED BY PLAIN [clothes] police/, and thus destroy the honest peace/ of every working man!"[155] Although widespread, this distaste for the bill does not seem to have been deep or intense outside the drink trade. Reduction in numbers and the transfer of monopoly value would have hurt the trade financially without serious inconvenience for its customers. According to the Unionists the bill contained little reform and much injustice. If there was injustice, it was mainly borne by the shareholders and debenture holders. The second reading attack emphasized the rights of property, not the liberties of the subject. Local Veto was a moribund issue. The working-class clubs and the Tories made uncomfortable allies. What advantage the Unionists gained in fighting a vaguely unpopular bill was lost by the provocative way that the Unionist peers had thrown it out. The Unionists also erred by making their alliance with the drink trade so close. Balfour's private secretary described the manager of the National Trade Defence Association as *"our Licensing Bill Expert."*[156] Since the omnibus bill had given the principal temperance groups the reforms that they most wanted, the temperance party united in vehement condemnation of the House of Lords and the Unionist Party. In 1908 Winston Churchill was a member of the Liberal government. Although certainly not a teetotaler, he was a fighter who raged against the House of Lords: he imagined "the heart of every Band of Hope in this country sinking within them." "We shall send them up a budget in June as shall terrify them, they have started the class war, they had better be careful."[157]

The trade had not necessarily triumphed permanently. In the last days of 1908 amendments to the Children's Act salvaged the clauses of the late licensing bill that excluded children from licensed premises except during closed hours.[158] More important, the trade had scarcely time to congratulate itself than it began to worry about the prospects during the 1909 session of a Sunday closing bill which it expected but which never came. On 8 May 1909 Herbert Gladstone proposed to the Cabinet proposed a consolidation of the licensing laws that would also be a "Salvage Bill" that would enact the non-contentious parts of the Licensing Bill of 1908 (and also address the clubs question).[159] It never reached Parliament.

More important, the Government proposed higher taxation on the trade as part of the famous People's Budget.[160] Lloyd George had made no secret of his wish that the Lords would give him an excuse to enact high license duties.[161] In the second edition of *The Taxation of the Liquor Trade*, appearing in 1908, Joseph Rowntree and Arthur Sherwell argued that "high licensing" would eliminate more licensed premises than the 1908 bill, if it had been enacted. Higher taxes would make many licenses unprofitable.[162] When Lloyd George drafted his new taxes, he had to find a balance between obtaining revenue and reducing the number of licensed premises paying the new taxes.[163] Although the budget sharply increased excise duties on spirits, it left beer alone. Surprisingly, the temperance reformer Sir Thomas Whittaker helped lead a Liberal revolt against the budget. Writing to Gladstone, Samuel quoted Whittaker as saying that the Budget was "absurd, preposterous and fantastic" and that the Government should "burn it tomorrow morning and introduce another Budget on business-like lines."[164]

The Unionists had expected higher taxes on the drink trade, something popular among the Liberals and retaliation against the Lords for rejecting the licensing bill. It was the amount of the taxes that surprised and infuriated the Unionists and the drink trade. The Permanent Secretary of the Treasury described the proposed rise in license duties as a "murderous increase."[165] Irish Nationalists protested the increase in the duties on whiskey. Preparing for a squeeze on profits, the drink trade raised prices for beer and spirits. According to a Tory politician, "the Trade would rather have had the Licensing Bill of last year than this [Budget] Bill." The editor of the *Spectator*, John St. Loe Strachey, although a Conservative, was no friend of the drink trade, but he admitted that he was "beginning to think that the brewers honestly believe themselves to be on the brink of ruin."[166]

When a rash House of Lords threw out the budget, the trade fought for the Unionists in the general election that followed, and the temperance party again rallied to the Liberals.[167] According to Neal Blewett, "against the Budget the brewers organised an expensive but more subtle campaign than that against the 1908 Licensing Bill."[168] In the 1910 elections the drink trade spent more money on newspaper advertising than all the other pressure groups combined.[169] In Liverpool the Liberal-supporting Bartenders' Union "condemned brewers and publicans who intimidated their employees at elections."[170]

Unlike Blewett, historian David Gutzke argues that the trade was less active in the 1910 elections than in 1908. Trade organizations mostly lacked funds. Poor trade made brewers and publicans feel defeated. Some licensed victuallers feared that active support for the Unionists would antagonize customers who might boycott their businesses. About half of all license holders did not belong to a retail society. "The situation was worse in the home and southern counties, where two-thirds of the 15,400 retailers were unorganized.[171]

The complaint about the proposed new license duties merged into a general defense of property. A frustrated Liberal candidate complained: "Every little beershop was covered by my opponent's [campaign] bills, until you might have mistaken them for Tory committee rooms. Every inn was a recruiting ground for Toryism, with the publican as agent."[172]

The Liberals responded. The Liberal Publication Department sent out forty-one million publications in two months. "This material included 104 different leaflets, four booklets, five sets of campaign notes, draft posters and printed pictures and posters."[173]

In January 1910, the Liberals won the general election but only with the help of their Irish and Labour allies. After the death of the King, there were unsuccessful negotiations for a Coalition Government joining the major political parties. During the negotiations Lloyd George proposed that an undefined scheme of temperance reform constitute part of the program for a Coalition Government that would deal with the major problems confronting the country.[174] After the secret negotiations with the Unionists failed, the Liberals called for a second general election in December 1910.

It witnessed a decline in trade activism. The trade had been disillusioned by the willingness of the Unionists to accept the new taxes on drink imposed by Lloyd George's budget.[175] There briefly was hope of a deal between the licensed trade and the Liberal Government, Preliminary negotiations in 1911 quickly fizzled when the trade refused to accept a new licensing bill in exchange for repealing the new drink taxes.[176] Although the trade had been hurt by the new taxes, they eventually were offset by a rise in beer consumption.[177]

In a postscript to the fight over Asquith's licensing bill, Local Veto finally became law but not in England. In 1913 Parliament passed the Temperance (Scotland) Act. Introduced by a private member in 1911, the bill was reintroduced by the Government in 1912. It authorized, beginning in 1920, referendums for prohibition and reduction in numbers. Sherwell unsuccessfully sought an amendment for a public management option. The House of Lords attempted to add disinterested management to the bill, and, according to a Tory M.P., the Government looked for a time that it would accept the amendments. "McKinnon Wood [Secretary of State for Scotland] was heard to threaten to resign if that was done." In the end, the Liberal Government rejected disinterested management, despite many of its supporters speaking in its favor.[178]

By 1914 many Nonconformists were restless about the failure of the Liberal Government to introduce a new licensing bill. The Free Church Council heard a speech that "warned the Government that if they went back to the electors without having attempted to redeem their explicit pledge on this matter they would certainly lose the support of many who had not only voted, but worked for them enthusiastically in the past."[179] Leif Jones complained that the Speech from the Throne had not mentioned licensing. Asquith told him that there was no legislative time available and added to a confidant that Jones was a "prime ass."[180]

During the First World War new challenges would confront the drink trade and the temperance movement. Wartime Coalitions made old-style pressure group politics much less effective.

Notes

[1] *Temperance Chronicle*, 22 Dec. 1905. Implicitly the newspaper asked readers to vote Liberal although "the Liberal Party is declared by its own leaders to be the party which is set on the dismemberment of the Church and the dismemberment of the nation."

[2] Compensated reduction had begun before Balfour's legislation. When the London County Council acquired Old King's Head in August 1905 and abandoned its

license, it was the one hundred thirty-fourth license that the LCC had abandoned since 1889. £18,000 had been paid for the freeholds while the premium values had been £384,450. A trade publication pointed out that the cost to the rates had been £29,700. *Brewers' Almanack* (1906), p. 54. See also *Brewers' Almanack* (1937), pp. 161-67

[3] Waller, *Democracy and Sectarianism,* pp. 290-91.

[4] For details on the Kennedy judgment, see (Amulee) Royal Commission on Licensing (England and Wales), 1929-31, Report, Cmd. 3988, 1932 [vol. XI], paragraph 120 (pp. 26-27). Sir William Rann Kennedy was a Liberal. See also Paul Jennings, "Licensing and the Local Historian: the 1904 Licensing Act and its Administration," *Local Historian* 39/1 (Feb. 2009): 24-37; and "Liquor Licensing and the Local Historian: The Victorian Public House," *Local Historian* 41/2 (May 2011): 121-37.

[5] Pack points put that Gladstone boasted about his big profit. Mark Pack "Liberal Landslide: The 1906 Election" 14 April 2020. http://www.markpack.org.uk/1166/the-1906-election./

[6] As an example of the massive electoral swing, an anti-vaccination zealot Arnold Lupton managed to be elected for the Sleaford division of Lincolnshire. He defeated Henry Chaplin who had held this seat and its predecessor since 1868. The standard work on the 1906 general election is A.K. Russell, *Liberal Landslide: the General Election of 1906* (David & Charle, 1973).

[7] Jose Harris and Cameron Hazelhurst, "Campbell-Bannerman as Prime Minister," *History* 55 (Oct. 1970): 361.

[8] *Licensing World,* 30 Dec. 1895, p. 472. Temperance is barely mentioned in Michael Craton and H.W. McCready, *The Great Liberal Revival, 1903-6* (Hansard Society, 1966), p. 21.

[9] The Nonconformists included 65 Congregationalists and Baptists, 55 Methodists, 10 Unitarians, 6 Quakers, and 3 Presbyterians. Craton and McCready, *The Great Liberal Revival,* p. 36. See also D.W. Bebbington, "The Free Church M.P.s of the 1906 Parliament," *Parliamentary History* 24 no. 1 (February 2005): 136-50. There were contemporary estimates that ranged from 178 to 199 (in 1907). Bebbington, pp. 139-40. 179 free churchmen sat in 1906 Parliament at some time, another 29 on the fringe. If one adds non-establishment and non-Anglican Protestants from Scotland and Ireland, it is 205 definite and 42 fringe. Compare with 134 in combined categories in 1905 Parliament. Divided denominationally. (Bebbington. p. 141) 61 Congregationalists plus 14 on fringe; Wesleyans 36 and 5 fringe; Unitarians 23 and 3 fringe; Baptists 17 and 4 fringe; Quakers 12; Primitive Methodists 11 and 1; fringe, United Methodists 7; Welsh Calvinist Methodists also 7; English Presbyterians 4 and 2 fringe; Bible Christians 1.

[10] *Alliance News,* 12 April 1907, pp. 328-29. For monopoly value as the key to reform, see Whittaker, "Practical Temperance Reform," *National Review* 18 (Jan. 1907): 881-97. The Liberal brewer E.N. Buxton argued that monopoly value had not been part of the Royal Commission minority report. "Temperance Reform: A Reply," *National Review* 18 (Feb. 1907): 1048-61. Buxton cited the *Daily News,* 8 Oct. 1906, for the figure £150 millions as the value of English and Welsh drink licenses. For Whittaker "as the principal exponent of what is known as 'constructive

Temperance reform'" and a summary of his article in the *Twentieth Century Quarterly*, see *Temperance Chronicle*, 17 Aug. 1906, pp. 400-01.

[11] S.H. Whitbread's total holdings in Whitbreads brewery amounted to £400 vested in trustees. S.H. Whitbread to Gladstone, 26 Aug. 1905. BL, Herbert Gladstone papers, Add. Ms. 46063, f. 158-159. For his contribution, see Samuel Whitbread (the elder) to Gladstone, 11 Dec. 1905. BL, Herbert Gladstone papers, Add. Ms. 46063 f. 193. Compare the refusal of E.N. Buxton to contribute. Buxton to Gladstone, 20 April [1904]; W.M. Crook to Gladstone, 15 Nov. 1904. BL, Herbert Gladstone papers, Add. Ms. 46061 ff. 222-23, Add. Ms. 46024 ff. 167-68.

[12] Whiteley urged Campbell-Bannerman to separate licensing reform into two bills, the first to set a time-limit and a scale of compensation, as well as minor reforms such as for clubs. The other bill could deal with more controversial reforms such as Local Veto and disinterested management. Whiteley to Campbell-Bannerman, 1 March 1907. BL, Campbell-Bannerman papers Add. 41231, ff. 234-35.

[13] Williams and Brake, *Drink in Great Britain*, p. 32. It summarized the report in the *Alliance News*, 14 Feb. 1907, p. 108.

[14] George B. Wilson, "The Right Hon. Lord Rhayader: An Appreciation," in *Alliance Year Book* (1940), pp. 13-16 (quotation at p. 15).

[15] Roberts, *The Radical Countess*, 84. See also George B. Wilson, *Leif Jones, Lord Rhayader, Temperance Reformer and Statesman, 1862-1939, President of the United Kingdom Alliance, 1906-1932* (n.p.: United Kingdom Alliance, [1948]). David M. Fahey, entry for Leif Jones, Lord Rhayader, in *Oxford Dictionary of National Biography*; and *Biographical Dictionary of Modern British Radicals*, ed. Joseph O. Baylen and Norbert J. Gossman, vol. 3 (Harvester Wheatsheaf, 1988). A bachelor, Lord Rhayader left no papers, but Lady Carlisle's papers at Castle House include many of his letters. Not everybody was enthusiastic about the new role in the Alliance of Lady Carlisle and her circle. On 7 January 1918, Lee Hicks, the bishop of Lincoln, described his visit to the Alliance headquarters. "[George B. Wilson] complained of the dubious loyalty of Bingham and others, who were ready at any moment to baffle the President [Leif Jones] in any place because of their utter dislike of Lady Carlisle and her circle."[15] William Bingham, JP, was managing director the Sceptre temperance life insurance company. Item #1169 in *The Diaries of Edward Lee Hicks, Bishop of Lincoln, 1910-1919*, ed. Graham Neville [Lincoln Record Society Publications] (Boydell Press, 1963).

[16] Newton (1864-1916), a former schoolmaster, had served the Alliance as a district agent from about 1887 to 1906 when he became parliamentary agent. He resigned in 1909 to take the less arduous job, secretary of the Native Races and the Liquor Traffic United Committee. He is best known for his biography of W.S. Caine. *Alliance News*, Oct. 1916, p. 172. *Who Was Who.*

[17] UKA annual report in *Alliance News*, 20 Oct. 1904, pp. 712-13. Corbett emphasized that the Alliance was not responsible for the contents of his speech.

[18] Corbett to Campbell-Bannerman, 3 Nov. 1904. BL, Campbell-Bannerman papers, Add. Ms. 41237 ff. 300-02 (text of speech, ff. 303-11). Corbett rejoined the Liberal Party in 1908 and was rewarded with a peerage in 1911.

[19] Campbell-Bannerman to Gladstone, 23 Nov., 5, 30 Dec. 1904, 3 Jan. 1905. BL, Herbert Gladstone papers, Add. Ms. 45988 ff. 129, 132, 137, 142. BL, Gladstone to

Campbell-Bannerman, 1 Jan. 1905. Campbell-Bannerman papers, Add. Ms. 41217 ff. 160-61.

[20] Unsigned memorandum, ca. Dec. 1904. BL, Campbell-Bannerman, Add. Ms. 41217 f. 145. Asquith to Campbell-Bannerman, 6 Dec. 1904. Campbell-Bannerman papers, Add Ms 41210, ff. 217-218. For what Sherwell hoped a Liberal government would do, see W.T. Stead's interview with Sherwell in *Review of Reviews* 33 (Jan.-June 1906): 42-43. A recent biography of Asquith is V. Markham Lester, *H.H. Asquith: Last of the Romans* (Rowman & Littlefield, 2019). Sherwell has been little studied by historians. A good contemporary biographical sketch appears in *Leeds Mercury*, 30 Nov. 1910, p. 6.

[21] BL, Herbert Gladstone papers, Add. Ms. 46092 ff. 36-40. The joint statement, together with Campbell-Bannerman's noncommittal reply was published in the annual report in *Alliance News*, 12 Oct. 1905, pp. 642-43. See also Alliance minutes, 18 Jan., 22 March 1905.

[22] Summary by J.J. Hatch, Alliance district agent. Alliance minutes, 16 Jan. 1906. A censured version was published in *Alliance News*, 18 Jan. 1906, p. 40.

[23] Leif Jones to Gladstone, 24 July 1906. PRO, H.O., 45/10346/143163/3. A typed copy of the memorandum is filed with the letter.

[24] Whittaker (?) to [Sherwell], [no day] Aug. 1904. Cited in *Monthly Notes*, March 1925, p. 39.

[25] Whittaker, "A Temperance Policy for the Liberal Party," *Liberal Magazine*, July 1905, pp. 350-57.

[26] Central Temperance Legislation Board, *A Temperance Policy for the Present Time* (London, 1905).

[27] Temperance Legislation League, *Present Policy*, Leaflets, No. 1 (London, [1905]).

[28] BL, Herbert Gladstone papers, Add. Ms. 46092 ff. 76-107 (misdated by cataloger, ca. March 1907). See also "Notes on Sir T.P. Whitaker's Scheme for Licensing Bill," ff. 108-33; and Sir H.W. Primrose, Cabinet Memorandum, "Sir T.P.Whittaker's Suggested Amendments of the Licensing for England and Wales," 3 Oct. 1906; N.J. Highmore, Cabinet Memorandum, 21 Nov. 1906. PRO, Cab. 37/84/79 ff. 463-52; Cab. 37/85/88 ff. 60-84.

[29] Bryce to J.A. Spender, 29 May 1908. BL, Spender papers, Add. Ms. 46391 f. 247.

[30] Sir H.R. Primrose, Cabinet memorandum, 29 Jan. 1906. PRO, Cab. 37/83/13 ff. 65-81. (?)

[31] Whittaker to Gladstone, 9 Dec. 1905. BL, Herbert Gladstone papers, Add. Ms. 46063 ff. 185-86.

[32] *Rough Draft of Suggested Amendments of the Licensing Acts for England and Wales (Rough Draft of Suggested Amendments of the Act of 1904)* [series of drafts] *Ms. Notes* [by Viscount Gladstone] ([1906]), hereafter cited as *Rough Draft*. BL, Gen. Cat., B.S. 91/61.

[33] Buxton to Gladstone, 12 Sept. 1906. BL, Herbert Gladstone papers, Add. Ms. 46064 ff. 77-83. By this time, Buxton's affiliation with the Liberal Party was nominal. See a summary of a conversation with his nephew Noel Buxton by a Liberal constituency worker. W.P. Crook to Herbert Gladstone. BL, Herbert Gladstone papers. Add. Ms. 46024, ff. 167-168. Noel Buxton himself remained a Liberal until after the First World War when he joined the Labour Party.

---

[34] Gladstone to Buxton, 4 Oct. 1906; Buxton to Gladstone, 6 Oct. 1906. BL, Herbert Gladstone papers, Add. Ms. 46064 ff. 88-90, 92-93.

[35] Buxton, 6 Oct. 1906, in *Morning Advertiser*, 8 Oct. 1906, p. 4. See also Buxton in *Times*, 3 Nov. 1906, p. 12.

[36] Whittaker, "Practical Temperance Reform," *National Review*, Jan. 1907, pp. 881-97; Buxton, "Temperance Reform: A Reply to Sir Thomas Whittaker," *National Review*, Feb. 1907, pp. 1048-61; Whittaker, *The Nation and Its Liquor Licenses, including a Reply to Mr. E.N. Buxton*, Temperance Legislation League, Pamphlets, No. 8 (London, [1907]).

[37] Roberts to Gladstone, 21 Nov. 1906. BL, Herbert Gladstone papers, Add. Ms. 46064 f. 105.

[38] Gladstone, "Further Notes on the Licensing Bill," 26 Nov. 1906. BL, Herbert Gladstone papers, Add. Ms. 46092 ff. 1-2. For Gladstone's personal preference for disinterested management, see Gladstone to Buxton, 4 Oct. 1906. BL, Herbert Gladstone papers, Add. Ms. 46064 f. 89. Supposedly Asquith also privately favored disinterested management. Arthur Sherwell on 9 July 1930 in *Minutes of Evidence taken before the Royal Commission on Licensing (England and Wales)*, ques. 30,125 (p. 1718).

[39] Temperance Legislation League, *Memorandum on the Parliamentary Situation*, Temperance Legislation League, Pamphlets, No. 9 (1907).

[40] See also *Tribune*, 10 Dec. 1907, and Sherwell's speech at the National Liberal Club, 2 Dec. 1907, in *Times*, day? Dec. 1907. (Reprinted as pamphlet)

[41] Gladstone to Asquith, n.d. BL, Herbert Gladstone papers, Add. Ms. 46064 ff. 149-50. See also undated memorandum from Home Secretary to Chancellor of the Exchequer which the British Library cataloguer places soon after March 1907. BL, Herbert Gladstone papers, Add. Ms. 45989, ff. 161-62.

[42] Memorandum, 15 Feb. 1907; draft bill, 27 Feb. 1907, in [1907. March 9] *Drafts of the Licensing Bill of 1909] Ms. Notes and_[By Viscount Gladstone]* (1907-09). Hereafter cited as *Drafts*. BL, Gen. Cat., B.S. 91/60. The date implied by the title provided in the British Library general catalog is misleading.

[43] George Whiteley to Campbell-Bannerman, 1 March 1907. BL, Campbell-Bannerman papers, Add. Ms. 41231 f. 233.

[44] Whittaker to Gladstone, n.d. BL, Herbert Gladstone papers, Add. Ms. 46064 ff. 149-50. Emphasis is Whittaker's.

[45] *Drafts*. BL, Gen. Cat., B.S. 91/60.

[46] Ibid.

[47] Leif Jones to Lady Carlisle, 4 March 1907 (two letters) and 17 April 1907. Castle Howard, Ninth Countess of Carlisle papers, J23/100. See also Roberts, *Radical Countess*, p. 94, based in part on Leif Jones to [Lady Carlisle], [4] March 1907. On March 13, 1907, Roberts met with the Archbishop of Canterbury to ask that the bishops speak out in favor of temperance legislation. There were fears that the Government might drop its planned bill as a waste of time because of the hostility of the House of Lords. Roberts believed that the Lords would pass a reasonable bill. Memorandum, summarizing the interview, 13 March 1907, and related correspondence, A. Cameron Corbett to Davidson, 14, 16 March 1907. Lambeth Palace Library, Davidson papers, "Temperance and Licensing, 1907-08."

48 Campbell-Bannerman to Edward VII, 13 March 1907. Royal Archives, Windsor Castle, RA R28/28.

49 UKA annual report in *Alliance News*, 10 Oct. 1907, p. ? For speculation about the reasons for the postponement, see J[ohn] N[ewton], "Our Parliamentary Letter," *Alliance News*, 30 May 1907, p. 344.

50 Leif Jones to Lady Carlisle, 11 April 1907. Castle Howard, Ninth Countess of Carlisle papers, J23/100.

51 Leif Jones to Lady Carlisle, 17 April 1908. Castle Howard, Ninth Countess of Carlisle papers, J23/100.

52 Austen Chamberlain to his wife, 16 April 1907, quoted in Chamberlain, *Politics from the Inside* (Cassell, 1936), p. 67.

53 Campbell-Bannerman to Edward VII, 22 April 1907, 31 May 1907. BL, Campbell-Bannerman papers, Add. Ms. 52512, unfoliated when consulted.

54 *Times*, 4 June 1907, p. 6.

55 Castle Howard, Ninth Countess of Carlisle papers, J23/100.

56 Sir Courtney Peregrine Ilbert to James Bryce, 22 July 1907. Bodleian, Bryce papers, MS Bryce 13 fol. 126.

57 Ilbert to Bryce, 22 July 1907. Bodleian, Bryce papers, MS Bryce 13, fol. 126.

58 H. C. G. Matthew in *Oxford Dictionary of National Biography*.

59 Asquith, Cabinet memorandum, 11 Nov. 1907. PRO, Cab. 37/89.

60 Asquith, Cabinet memorandum, 21 Nov. 1907. PRO, Cab. 37/90. Asquith's emphasis.

61 Gladstone, Cabinet memorandum, [23] Nov. 1907. PRO, Cab. 37/90. Also see undated manuscript. BL, Herbert Gladstone papers, Add. Ms. 46092 ff. 12-20. Earlier the Alliance had noted that Gladstone had told his constituents that he opposed "drastic steps" in transferring the monopoly value to the State. *Alliance News*, 13 June 1897, p. 376.

62 Leif Jones to Lady Carlisle, 26 Feb. 1907. Castle Howard, Ninth Countess of Carlisle Papers, J23/100.

63 Malins, *The Life of Joseph Malins*, p. 103.

64 PRO, H.O. 45/10346/143163/70; *Alliance News*, 28 Nov. 1907, p. 780. The progressive Liberal, C.F.G. Masterman said that working-class Liberal electors disliked temperance legislation. "Politics in Transition," *Nineteenth Century*, Jan. 1908.

65 Gladstone to Asquith, 15 Dec. 1907. Bodleian, Asquith papers, vol. 10, ff. 235-36. Earlier the Liberals heard that Walter Gilbey was leaving the Liberal Party whether out of a family quarrel with Blyth when he obtained a peerage or over grocers' licenses. Carrington to Ponsonby, 27 July 1907; Carrington to Alfred Gilbey, 27 July 1907. BL, Campbell-Bannerman papers, Add. Ms. 52519 (unbound when consulted).

66 See Gladstone's long undated memorandum (perhaps Nov. 1907). BL, Herbert Gladstone papers, Add. Ms. 46092, ff. 12-20. Gladstone also attacked the monopoly value in an undated letter to Asquith and in a Cabinet memorandum, 23 Nov. 1907. BL, Herbert Gladstone papers, Add. Ms. 45989 fols. 161-162; PRO, Cab. 27/90.

67 Asquith, Cabinet memorandum, 8 Dec. 1907. PRO, Cab. 37/90. See also Gladstone, *Drafts*, 10 Dec. 1907. BL, Gen. Cat., B.S. 91/60.

[68] Samuel to Gladstone, 8 Dec. 1907. BL, Herbert Gladstone papers, Add. Ms. 45992 ff. 194-98.

[69] Loreburn, Cabinet memorandum, 15 Jan. 1908. PRO, Cab. 37/91.

[70] Ripon to Edward VII, Jan. 1908; Campbell-Bannerman to Edward VII. Royal Archives, Windsor Castle, RA R28/102, 107. See also *Drafts.* BL, Gen. Cat. 91/60.

[71] Gladstone to Edward VII, 27 Feb. 1908. Royal Archives, Windsor Castle, RA R 37/99. Asquith managed the bill personally with the aid of Herbert Samuel, the undersecretary at the Home Office.

[72] Ilbert to Bryce, 12 March 1908, quoted by Neal Blewett, *The Peers, the Parties and the People: The British General Elections of 1910* (University of Toronto Press), p. 50. Blewett later was prominent in the Australian Labour Party.

[73] *Licensing World*, 7 March 1908, pp. 160-61. The title of this editorial was "Spite and Spoliation.".

[74] Bruce K. Murray, *The People's Budget 1909/10: Lloyd George and Liberal Politics* (Clarendon Press, 1980), p. 107. Murray was a South African whose Ph.D. had been awarded by the University of Kansas.

[75] George L. Bernstein, *Liberalism and Liberal Politics in Edwardian England*, pp. 93-94.

[76] Wilson, *Leif Jones*, p. 40.

[77] Bassett, *Life of Ellis*, p. 241.

[78] Gooch, *Under Six Reigns* (Longmans, Green, 1958), p. 144.

[79] Campbell, *F.E. Smith*, p. 182.

[80] Balfour's biographer said that he was "furious" that Asquith's bill would drive self-respecting men from the trade because it removed the security of their property. Blanche E.C. Dugdale, *Arthur James Balfour* (G.P. Putnam's Sons, 1937) 2: 23.

[81] Gladstone to Edward VII, 27 Feb. 1908. Royal Archives, Windsor Castle, RA R37/99.

[82] Whittaker had not been happy about the change. John Ellis told Leif Jones that Asquith described Whittaker "like a bear with a sore head." Leif Jones to Lady Carlisle, 21 October 1908. Castle Howard, Ninth Countess of Carlisle papers, J23/100. In the end, Whittaker voted for the change, while Sherwell did not vote. Leif Jones (17 Nov. 1908) believed that Bottomley's attacks in the *Times*, 2 Nov. 1908, and in *John Bull* (7 Nov. 1908, "Sir Thomas Whittaker's Public-House") weakened Whittaker's reputation. The company that Whittaker chaired, UK Temperance and General Assurance Society, owned the freehold for a public house whose lease did not end until 1936. Whittaker spoke little in the latter stage of the bill and did not attend the debate regularly. Sherwell's influence also had declined because of his criticism of many of the main features of the bill. As a result, argued Jones, the Alliance has gained in influence. Jones to Lady Carlisle, 17 Nov. 1908. Castle Howard, Ninth Countess of Carlisle papers, J23/100.

[83] The clubs feared that the Liberal government would introduce a bill similar to that of the Scottish act of 1903 and the Irish act of 1904. For the figures, see *Club and Institute Journal*, Dec. 1908, p. 13. In his memoir Hall said that the Union spent over £1000. B.T. Hall, *Over Sixty Years* (Working Men's Club and Institute Union, 1922), p. 239.

84 Campbell, *F.E. Smith*, 182-84. Smith enjoyed telling the House of Commons that a radical club in a Liberal minister's constituency has put on musical comedy called "The Hypocrites."

85 Hall to Asquith, 15 March 1906; Bradford to Hall, 17 March 1906. Working Men's Club and Institute Union, *Annual_Report* (1906), pp. 21-22. Hall to Asquith, 26 March 1907; Bradford to Hall, 27 March 1907. Working Men's Club and Institute Union, *Annual Report* (1907), pp. 39-40. Hall, *Over Sixty Years*, pp. 239-41.

86 Working Men's Club and Institute Union, *Annual Report* (1907), pp. 42-52. For the Cabinet discussion later that day, see Campbell-Bannerman to Edward VII, 26 Nov. 1907. BL, Campbell-Bannerman papers, Add. Ms. 52513, unfoliated when consulted.

87 *Club and Institute Journal* (Jan. 1908), p. 15.

88 For the figures, see *Club and Institute Journal*, Dec. 1908, p. 13. For the fullest expression of the Union's views, see the sixteen-page supplement to the March 1908 *Journal*. 100,000 copies were distributed. The fifty-nine-page pamphlet, *The Licensing Law and the Clubs*, was published in August 1908. See also the organizational history, George Temblett, *The First Century* (Working Men's Club and Institute Union, 1962), revised as *Clubmen: History of the Working-men's Club and Institute Union* (Martin Secker and Warburg, 1987). See also Ruth Cherrington, *Not Just Beer and Bingo! A Social History of Working Men's Clubs* (self-published, 2012).

89 Hall in *Club and Institute Journal*, April 1908, p. 10; Dec. 1907, p. 13. On May 23, 1906, the National Trade Defence League had called for a club regulation bill. For a copy of the League's supposedly strictly private and confidential draft bill, see Club and Institute Union, *Annual Report* (1906), pp. 21-25.

90 *Club and Institute Journal* (Dec. 1908), p. 13.

91 F.A. Channing, *Memories of Midland Politics, 1885-1910* (Constable, 1918), 358-62; Channing, "Licensing Bill, 1908. The Clauses. A Reply to Misunderstand (?) and an Appeal to Common Sense," 19 March 1908. BL, Herbert Gladstone papers, Add. Ms. 46018 ff. 209-10. Channing, "Notes on the Memorandum of the C.U. Executive, August 8, 1908." BL, Herbert Gladstone papers, Add. Ms. 45988 ff. 202-09. The last paper bears Asquith's annotations. Elsewhere Channing expressed optimism about public support for the bill. Channing to Gladstone, 10 and 13 April 1908. BL, Herbert Gladstone papers, Add. Ms. 46019, ff. 205, 207. Channing estimated that 7,000 club members were voters in his parliamentary district. Channing, *Memories*, p. 362.

92 Vaughan Nash (for Asquith) to Waller (for Gladstone), 24 Oct. 1908, "Recommendations and Notes on the Club Clauses of the Licensing Bill, following Interview [by Herbert Gladstone] with Mr. B.T. Hall, on October 26, 1908." BL, Herbert Gladstone papers, Add. Ms. 45988 ff. 201, 202-09, Add. Ms. 46092 ff. 138-40. Earlier the clubs, including Liberal ones, had appealed to the Unionists for support. See F. Rubie to A. Bonar Law, 25 May 1908; B.T. Hall to Bonar Law, 30 Sept. 1908; H. Culver to Bonar Law, 24 Oct. 1908. Beaverbook Library (now at the House of Lords Record Office), Bonar Law papers, 21/2/5, 18/4/76/ 18/4/79. Rubie and Culver represented "Liberal and Radical" clubs.

---

[93] For the barmaid controversy, see J. Ramsay Macdonald to Gladstone, 8 April 1908. BL, Herbert Gladstone papers, Add. Ms. 45986 ff. 102-03. Joint Committee on the Employment of Barmaids, *Women as Barmaids*, preface by Bishop of Southwark (London, 1905); Barmaids' Political Defence League deputation to Gladstone, 28 Nov. 1907(?); bishop of Southwark's deputation to Gladstone, 27 March 1907; Central Board, *Women as Barmaids: A Defence* (Central Board, 1906). See also Padma Manian (formerly V. Padmavathy), "The English Barmaid, 1874-1914: A Case Study of Unskilled and Non-Unionized Women Workers" (Ph.D. dissertation, Miami University, 1989); Sonja Tiernan, "In Defence of Barmaids: The Gore-Booth Sisters Take on Winston Churchill," *History Ireland* 20 no.3 (June 2012): 34-36. In the House of Commons debate, 2 Nov. 1908, Macdonald noted that of the 350 ads for barmaids in the *Morning Advertiser*, 220 asked for attractive women under the age of 20. He said that typically barmaids were dismissed after the age of 25.

[94] Alexander Acland-Hood (full surname Fuller-Acland-Hood) to Cave, 1 April 1908, quoted in Sir George Mallet, *Lord Cave: A Memoir* (John Murray, 1921), p. 131; Sandars to Balfour, 28 April 1908. BL, Balfour Papers, Add. Ms. 49765, f. 110.

[95] Belloc sometimes tried to place himself on the side of reformers: "the vast majority of publicans throughout England are the servants, and probably the debtors also, of a small and very wealthy clique whose power it is our business to destroy." Quoted in Joseph Pearce, *Old Thunder: A Life of Hilaire Belloc* (HarperCollins, 2002). S.H. Whitbread has promised to vote for the bill on its second reading. When he changed his mind, he offered his resignation to the local Liberal Party executive. By a vote of nineteen to three, it asked him to retain his seat. *Licensed Trade News*, 23 May 1908, p. 2.

[96] *Alliance News*, 5 March 1908, p. 158.

[97] Alliance minutes, 29 Feb. 1908. It hoped "to make some arrangement with Dr. Burns to undertake the work of replying to the opposition in the press."

[98] Alliance minutes, 12 March 1908. Corbett left the Unionist Party in August 1908.

[99] For Lloyd George in the early 1890s, including his maiden speech in the House of Commons, see William George, *My Brother and I* (Eyre & Spottiswoode, 1958), pp. 156-57. Bebbington points out that the 1908 demonstrations included both Nonconformist and Anglican speakers despite the intensity of the education controversy that otherwise divided them. *Nonconformist Conscience*, p. 51.

[100] About this time there was an exchange of letters between Churchill and Bonar Law. Was the Liberal Party against the licensed trade for partisan reasons? Churchill complained that Bonar Law had misquoted him as saying, "The publicans are all Tories; we will have no mercy on them." Bonar Law denied using this precise language but said it was a fair summary of the Liberal attitude. Considering the Liberal softness toward licensed grocers, it might be improved by saying: "Death to the publicans; they are all Tories; bless the licensed grocers, they are mostly Liberals." Churchill to Bonar Law, 27 and 29 July 1908; Bonar Law to Churchill, 29 July 1908. Beaverbrook Library, Bonar Law papers 18/4/69, 18/4/27, 18/8/8. Now at House of Lords Record Office.

[101] *Licensed Trade News*, 14 Nov. 1908, p. 3.

[102] See Alliance minutes, 29 Feb., 12, 20 March, 23 Oct. 1908; *Alliance News*, 26

Nov. 1908, p. ?

[103] Whenever an angry brewer criticized the bishop of Birmingham for his support of the bill, Dr. Gore sent the brewer a copy of Roberts' book, *Time Limit and Local Option*. Wilson, *Leif Jones*, p. 38.

[104] On propaganda work, see Temperance Legislation League, *Report* (1908), 9-13. The publication and other propaganda work had begun earlier. In 1906, for instance, the League distributed nearly a million pamphlets and leaflets, supplied speakers to 700 meetings, held ten great demonstrations late in the year, and maintained ten agents in England and Wales. *Temperance Chronicle*, 8 Feb. 1907, p. 61. One of its ablest propagandists was Alexander MacCullum Scott (1874-1928), author of *Licensing in Scandinavia* (Temperance Legislation League, 1908) and subsequently a Liberal MP. The Central Board castigated him as a "London Scot, with a ready pen." *Licensed Victuallers' Official Annual* (1907), 108.

[105] Among the answers to Whittaker's book were F.E. Smith (later Lord Birkenhead), *The "Facts" and "Arguments" of Sir Thomas Whittaker, M.P., An Examination* (P.S. King and Son, 1908); David Price Davies, *Facts, not Fiction: A Short Reply to the Miscalled "Facts" and "Arguments" of the Rt. Hon. Thomas Whittaker, P.C., M.P.* (E. Hulton, 1908); Cecil Holden and H. Hume Barne, *License and Compensation: A Reply to Sir Thomas Whittaker, M.P.* (Birkenhead, 1908).

[106] Temperance Legislation League, *Report* (1908), 20-21. The next largest contributors: Sir W.P. Hartley and Joseph Rank, £500; Dr. G.B. Hunter, £300; Sir John Brunner, £250; G.W. Brown, Lord Kinnaird, the Rt. Hon. G.W. Palmer, and Alexander Guthrie, £150; Sir Thomas Glen-Coats, £110; Lord Aredale, Lord Ashton, and Henry Holloway, £100. Other substantial contributors included such well-known names as George Cadbury, W.H. Lever, MP, B. Seebohm Rowntree, and H.J. Wilson, MP. Smaller donors included such reformers as Canon Samuel Barnett, Lord Courtney, F.W. Fox, G.P. Gooch, Theodore Neild, John Turner Rae, and the Rev. P.H. Wickstead.

[107] On March 18, brewery debenture holders met at the Cannon Street hotel to protest the bill. They were addressed by Lord Rothschild and others. On March 23, Cosmo Bonsor, managing director of Watney, Combe, Reid addressed a thousand employees at the Stag brewery, Pimlico. *Liberal Magazine*, 25 June 1908, p. 175. See also *Facts for Brewery Shareholders* (National Trade Defence Association, 1908), a twenty-page pamphlet.

[108] H.A. Newton to Sandars, 21 May 1908. Bodleian, Sandars papers, Mss English Hist. c. 756, ff. 147-148.

[109] London licensed victuallers, executive committee minute book, 2 March 1908.

[110] *Licensed Trade News*, 7 April 1908, p. 2.

[111] *Brewers' Almanack* (1909), 58; *Brewing Trade Review*, April 1908, pp. 174, 232-33.

[112] *Licensing World*, 14 March 1908, pp. 172-174.

[113] On July 18, 1908, E.N. Buxton (a Liberal during most of his career) complained that the monopoly value provision "represented on a low valuation a hundred million of pounds." *Morning Advertiser*, 20 July 1908, quoted in *National Union Gleanings* 31 (Sept. 1908): 236.

[114] A meeting of 400 to 500 brewers held at the Westminster Palace Hotel, on March 3, 1908, proposed the £100,000 guarantee fund and the method of assessment. *Brewing Trade Review*, April 1908, pp. 232-33. Trade organization was imperfect. John Gretton grumbled that in Newcastle it was "not well organized." Gretton to "Pinkie," 23 Sept. 1908. Bodleian, Sandars papers, Mss Eng Hist c. 757, f. 145.

[115] *Brewers' Journal Centenary Number* (1965), pp. 251-252.

[116] Sandars to Balfour, 4 May 1908. BL, Balfour papers, Add. Ms. 49765, f 141.

[117] *Morning Post*, 23 March 1908, p. 7; Sandars to Balfour, 1 May 1908. BL, Balfour papers, Add. Ms. 49765 ff. 134-35.

[118] Sandars to Wilfrid M. Short, 30 April 1908; Sandars to Balfour, 1, 8 May 1908. BL, Balfour papers, Add. Ms. 49765 ff. 125-29, 134-35, 162. The brewers avoided offensive demands. After an interview with Newton, the secretary of the National Trade Defence Association, and Whitbread, its chairman, Sandars characterized them as "most reasonable." Sandars to Balfour, 15 May 1908. BL, Balfour papers, Add. Ms. 49765, f. 170.

[119] David M. Fahey, ed., E. *Lawrence Levy and Muscular Judaism, 1851-1932* (Edwin Mellen Press, 2014), pp. 430-31. The pages cited are part of an edited version of Levy's 1913 autobiography.

[120] *Licensed Trade News*, 3 Oct. 1908, pp. 2-13; *Brewing Trade Review*, Oct. 1908, p. 556; *Liberal Magazine*, Oct. 1908, pp. 546-49; *National Union Gleanings*, June-Dec. 1908, p. 407. See Tim Holt, "Demanding the Right to Drink: Two Hyde Park Demonstrations," *Brewery History* 118 (2005): 26-40. Holt's article includes images of many trade posters. There also were local demonstrations. David Russell reports: "In Hastings a nine day open air campaign against the bill was conducted by Harry Johnson, landlord of the Angel on West Hill and for the bill by the Salvation Army, Methodists and others on the beach at Denmark Place." "The Temperance Lobby in Hastings 1840-1940." http://www.hastingspubhistory.com/page12.html

[121] *Liberal Magazine*, April 1908, p. 547.

[122] Central Board, minute books, 22 Oct. 1908 (p. 259).

[123] Temperance reform was strong enough in the North of Ireland to persuade its MPs to violate Unionist party discipline. "It would have been regrettable that they should *abstain* on a matter of such interest to the Party as the Licensing Bill, but that they should deliberately vote against their Party in respect of a bill which applies to England but does *not* apply to Ireland is outrageous." Sandars to W. Short (for Balfour), 5 May 1908. BL, Balfour papers. Add. 49765, f. 150.

[124] Sandars to Balfour, 8 May 1908. BL, Balfour papers, Add. Ms. 49765 ff. 163-66. See also Curzon's admission that he hoped that the House of Lords would not throw out the bill, "whisper this not in Askalon." Curzon to Selborne, 8 May 1908. Earl of Ronaldshay, *Life of Lord Curzon* (E. Benn, 1908) 3: 54. Curzon was Sir Wilfrid Lawson's nephew.

[125] Lambeth Palace Library, Church of England Temperance Society, minutes, 17 March 1908. MS 2031, f. 115. There is much related correspondence in the Davidson papers, "Temperance and Licensing, 1907-08." I am grateful to the Librarian for permission to consult the papers of the CETS and those of Archbishop Davidson.

[126] A.F. Harvey (secretary, Temperance Legislation League) to A. Holland-Hibbert, 2 April 1908. Lambeth Palace Library, Davidson papers, "Temperance and

Licensing, 1907-08." The Archbishop pointed out that public demonstrations were not part of the CETS tradition. Davidson to Holland-Hibbert, 4 April 1908. Lambeth Palace Library, Davidson papers, "Temperance and Licensing 1907-08." See also *Temperance Chronicle*, 6 Nov. 1908, p. 551; 16 Oct. 1908, p. 510.

[127] *Licensing World*, 6 May 1905, pp. 308-09; 13 May 1905, p. 321; 23 March 1907, pp. 204-05; *Liberal Magazine*, April 1908, pp. 171-73; Archbishop Davidson to the Rev. G.M. Scott, 24 March 1908, in *Temperance Chronicle*, 27 March 1908, p. 157; *Licensed Victuallers' Official Annual* (1909), 143.

[128] *Northampton Daily Report*, 10 March 1908, quoted *in Liberal Magazine*, April 1908, p. 174.

[129] St. Aldwyn to Balfour, [no day] Aug. 1908. BL, Balfour papers, Add. Ms. 49695 ff. 167-70. Another copy is in the Gloucestershire Records Office, Earl St. Aldwyn papers, D 2455/PCC/12.

[130] Balfour to Lansdowne, 10 Sept. 1908. BL, Balfour papers. Add. Ms. 49729 ff. 318-319. Sandars to Balfour, 20 Sept. 1908. BL, Balfour papers. Add. Ms. 49765 ff. 177-178. Lansdowne to Balfour, 15 Oct. 1908. BL, Balfour papers. Add. Ms. 49729 f. 321.

[131] Walter Taber (?) to Balfour, 28 Sept. 1908. Bodleian, Sandars papers, Mss. Eng. Hist. C. 757, ff. 47-48.

[132] *Daily Chronicle*, 29 Oct. 1908, p. 4.

[133] Samuel to Asquith, 10 Sept. 1908. House of Lords Records Office, Lord Samuel papers, A/24/15. Ian Packer argues that the Liberal Government would have accepted any compromise that included radical reduction in the number of licensed premises. Packer, *Liberal Government and Politics, 1905-15*, p. 113.

[134] Royal Archives, Windsor Castle, King Edward VII's engagements diary. I am grateful to Miss Gander, then a member of the Royal Archives staff, for bringing the engagements diary to my attention. The King warned Lansdowne: "if the attitude of the Peers was such as to suggest the idea that they were obstructing an attempt to deal with the evils of intemperance, the House of Lords would suffer seriously in popularity." Lansdowne agreed: "for the sake of the House of Lords, it was not desirable that the peers and the brewers should be represented as in too close alliance." Quoted in Lord Newton, *Lord Lansdowne: A Biography* (Macmillan, 1929), pp. 368-69.

[135] Lord Newton, *Lord Lansdowne*, pp. 368-69.

[136] John Ellis reporting Asquith. Castle Howard, Ninth Countess of Carlisle papers, J23/100, Jones to Lady Carlisle, 21 Oct. 1908. Ellis told Asquith that the entire Whittaker family "let their temper run away with them." T.P. Whittaker's father Thomas Whittaker (1813-1899) had been an early working-class teetotal organizer.

[137] Castle Howard, Ninth Countess of Carlisle papers, J23/100, Jones to Lady Carlisle, 10 November 1908.

[138] Castle Howard, Ninth Countess of Carlisle papers, J23/100, Jones to Lady Carlisle, 4 November 1908.

[139] Castle Howard, Ninth Countess of Carlisle papers, J23/100, Jones to Lady Carlisle 17 November 1908.

[140] Sir George Smith to Imbert Terry, 13 Oct. 1908. Bodleian, Sandars papers, Mss. Eng. Hist., c. 757, ff. 147-50.

[141] *Licensed Trade News*, 14 Nov. 1908, pp. 1-2; *Birmingham Daily Post*, 10 Nov. 1908, quoted ibid., p. 7; Carlson to Lady Londonderry, 29 Oct. 1908. Quoted in H. Montgomery Hyde, *Carson* (Heinemann, 1953), p. 244. For earlier predictions that the House of Lords would accept the bill, see Gladstone to Edward VII, 27 Feb. 1908; Lord Esher to Lord Knolls, 10 March 1908. Royal Archives, Windsor Castle, RA R 37/99, RA W41/35.

[142] Collings to Chamberlain, 27 Oct. 1908. University of Birmingham, Joseph Chamberlain papers. JC 22/43.

[143] Long to Balfour, 18 Nov. 1908; Long to Sandars, 18 Nov. 1909. Bodleian, Sandars papers, Mss Eng Hist c 757, ff. 161-164.

[144] Crewe to Ripon, 12 Nov. 1908. BL, Ripon papers. Add. Ms. 43552 f. 231-32.

[145] *Temperance Chronicle*, 20 Nov. 1908, pp. 477-78.

[146] *Temperance Chronicle*, 6 Nov. 1908, pp. 550-51.

[147] Lord Willoughby de Broke, *The Passing Years* (Constable, 1924), p. 247.

[148] *Annual Register* (1908), p. 232. Lord Newton (who was present) said that no more than ten voted in the minority. Newton, *Lord Lansdowne*, p. 370. For the arguments of one of this minority, see Milner to Lansdowne, 22 Nov. 1908. Quoted in A.M. Gollin, *Proconsul in Politics* (Macmillan, 1964), p. 155. Compare Walter Long to Balfour, 10 Oct. 1908. Bodleian, Sandars papers, Mss. Eng. Hist., c. 757, f. 139.

[149] See H.W. McCready, "The Revolt of the Unionist Free Traders," *Parliamentary Affairs* 16 (1963): 188-206.

[150] Willoughby de Broke, *The Passing Years*, pp. 246-47. See the revisionist study by Gregory D. Phillips. *The Diehards - Aristocratic Society and Politics in Edwardian England* (Harvard University Press, 1979).

[151] Fitzroy, *Memoirs* 1:368. Fitzroy noted: "Cawdor's denunciation of the tyranny of the Local Option clauses came with particular irony from a man who, on his Welsh property of five or six parishes, does not permit a single public-house."

[152] UKA, annual report, in *Alliance News*, 8 Oct. 1908, p. 882.

[153] Lady Victoria Hicks, *Life of Sir Michael Hicks Beach (Earl St. Aldwyn)* (Macmillan, 1932) 2: 251-52.

[154] Asquith to Edward VII, 9 Dec. 1908. Royal Archives, Windsor Castle, RA R29/69. Gladstone's constituency agent was anxious for a general election over the Lords having killed the licensing bill. Henry to Gladstone, 28 Nov. 1908. BL, Herbert Gladstone papers, Add. Ms. 46037 f. 107.

[155] National Union of Conservative and Constitutional Associations (N.U. No. 706), *"To the British Working Man. The Licensing Bill 1908. What It Means to You."*

[156] Sandars to Lansdowne, undated annotation on letter, Newton to Sandars, 7 Dec. 1908. Bodleian, Sandars papers, Mss. Eng. Hist., c. 757, f. 196.

[157] Lucy Masterman's diary, 26 Nov. 1908, quoted in Randolph S. Churchill, *Winston S. Churchill* (Houghton Mifflin, 1967): 2: 311. Several months earlier Sir C.P. Ilbert, Clerk of the House of Commons, had speculated about the fate of the licensing bill in the House of Lords. He argued that Balfour "hates any meddling with either of his pet measures, the Licensing Act or the Education Act." On the other hand, he saw three things that made the Government "pretty hopeful." The archbishops supported the bill, the "shyness" of the Lords when Labour united with

the Liberals, and "the second string to Asquith's bow," heavy taxation of the trade if the Lords rejected the licensing bill. Ilbert to Bryce, 7 May 1908. Bodleian, Bryce papers, MS Bryce 13, f. 151.

[158] Lansdowne to Sandars, 8 Dec. 1908. Bodleian, Sandars papers, Mss. Eng. Hist., c. 757, f. 198.

[159] British Library, Home Office Papers and Memoranda, B.P. 2/4 (3). Prohibitionists were divided on whether it was best to get minor reforms enacted or wait for another comprehensive bill. Charles Roberts favored the first strategy, Leif Jones the other. Castle Howard, Ninth Countess of Carlisle papers, J23/100, Leif Jones to Lady Carlisle, 13 December 1908.

[160] London brewers argued that they were treated more harshly than country brewers, while English brewers in general were treated more harshly than Irish and Scottish brewers.

[161] Castle Howard, Ninth Countess of Carlisle papers, L23/100, 19 Nov. 1908 (Jones to Lady Carlisle). See also Lord Riddell, *More Pages from My Diary, 1908-1914* (Country Life, 1934), p. 10. Riddell summarized a breakfast conversation with Lloyd George, 24 Nov. 1908. Lloyd George "did not seem at all disturbed by the fate of the Licensing Bill. He said that a thanksgiving service would take place in the Treasury at 10:30, as he was looking forward to taxing the trade."

[162] Murray, *The People's Budget*, p. 108. The first edition of this Rowntree and Sherwell book had appeared in 1906.

[163] For details about Lloyd George's proposals, see Murray, *The People's Budget*, pp. 138-43.

[164] Samuel to Gladstone, 29 April 1909, quoted in Murray, *People's Budget*, p. 174. Whittaker published a major book in 1914, *The Ownership, Tenure and Taxation of Land, Some Facts, Fallacies and Proposals Relating Thereto*, a conservative attack on Lloyd George's land taxes.

[165] Sir George Murray to Asquith, 7 April 1909, quoted Blewett, *The Peers, the Parties and the People*, p. 69.

[166] Sandars to Balfour, 15 Sept. 1909; and Strachey to Cromer, 3 Sept. 1909, quoted Blewett, *The Peers, the Parties and the People*, p. 77. For the arguments of the drink trade, see pamphlet by the National Trade Defence Association, *The Budget Proposals and the Licensed Trade* (1909).

[167] The Alliance blamed the defeat of the bill in the House of Lords on "Lord Rothschild, who is up to the eyes in brewery shares, either personally or through the companies of which he is chairman." *Alliance News*, 26 Nov. 1908, p. 882.

[168] Blewett, *The Peers, the Parties and the People*, p. 330. This is as good a time as any to note the absence of the drink question in a very good book, Stephen Koss, *The Rise and Fall of the Political Press in Britain*, vol. 2, *The Twentieth Century* (University of North Carolina Press, 1984).

[169] Blewett, *The Peers, the Parties and the People*, p. 333. I have not seen the small collection of Arthur Sherwell's papers at the British Library of Political and Economic Science dealing with the role of the drink trade in the 1910 elections.

[170] Waller, *Democracy and Sectarianism*, p. 212.

[171] Gutzke, *Protecting the Pub*, pp. 175-79 (quotation, p. 178).

[172] *Westminster Gazette*, 28 Jan. 1910, quoted in Blewett, *The Peers, the Parties, and the People*, p. 333. Another Liberal candidate, Silas Hocking, reported that he had been defeated by the votes of drunks, "happy and no doubt grateful for an abundant supply of cheap beer." Hocking's interview published in the *Birmingham Daily Post*, 22 Jan. 1910, quoted in Blewett, *The Peers, the Parties and the People*, p. 372.

[173] Mark Pack, "The 1910 and 2010 Elections," online.

[174] Lloyd George, memorandum, 17 Aug. 1908. It would have included State Purchase. Quoted in Charles Petrie, *Life and Letters of Austen Chamberlain* (London, 1940) 2: 381-88.

[175] Blewett, *The Peers, the Parties, and the People*, p. 331.

[176] Report of a meeting with Arthur Sherwell on 26 April 1911. Ms. Truman, Hanbury, Buxton and Co. Ltd., ff. 2-3. Courtesy of David W. Gutzke.

[177] Murray, *The People's Budget*, pp. 300-302. London brewers had paid too much for licensed premises in 1896-1902 boom. Prices fell drastically beginning in 1903, but brewers were helped by improved sales in 1910, the first year since 1899 that beer consumption and production rose.

[178] *Real Old Tory Politics: The Political Diaries of Sir Robert Sanders, Lord Bayford, 1910-35*, ed. John Ramsden (Historians' Press, 1984), p. 61 (16 Feb. 1913). Supporters of disinterested management included Eliot Crawshay-Williams, "in order to break the power of 'the trade' by removing the profit motive." Bernstein, *Liberalism and Liberal Politics in Edwardian England*, p. 140.

[179] Rev. J. Tolefree Parr, a Primitive Methodist minister, quoted in Bernstein, *Liberalism and Liberal Politics in Edwardian England*, p. 140.

[180] Asquith to Venetia Stanley, 15 Feb. 1914, in H.H. Asquith, *Letters to Venetia Stanley*, ed. Michael and Eleanor Brock (Oxford University Press, 1982), #36.

CHAPTER TEN

FROM THE FIRST WORLD WAR
TO THE LICENSING ACT OF 1921

War transformed the dormant politics of drink and provoked an animated debate about alcohol.[1] Several of the other countries fighting in the war quickly made changes in the sale of alcoholic beverages. In Britain the struggle between the old anti-drink organizations and the licensed drink trade did not disappear, but what now mattered was the war. On 12 October 1914, the temperance reformer Robert B. Batty argued in a letter published in the *Manchester Guardian* that "the greatest enemy to military efficiency is insobriety."[2]

The historian John Greenaway described the wartime near hysteria over drink "as a classic example of a 'moral panic' in which the media played a role."[3] As in the past, the drink problem was construed in class and gendered terms. Middle-class opinion worried that workingmen who missed work or worked poorly because of their drinking posed a threat to victory over Germany. National efficiency became a watchword. The war also brought changes in the gendering of drink as more women ventured into the pub. The Government warned about drinking by female munitions workers and by the wives of servicemen who spent their dependents' allotments on drink.[4] The Archbishop of Canterbury worried that the allotments were too generous for wives to manage prudently.[5] Women did drink. "A survey of four pubs in London revealed that in one hour on a Saturday night alcohol was consumed by 1,483 men and 1,946 women."[6]

During the war the drink question evoked a variety of answers both by individuals and the State. For the State, we should look at DORA (Defence of the Realm Act, August 1914, and later amendments), the Central Control Board (May 1915), proposals for State Purchase (1915 and later), and the postwar settlement which produced the Licensing Act of 1921.

A brief glance at wartime voluntary anti-drink activity follows. There were many attempts to encourage civilians to give up drink voluntarily. "In late 1914, a League of Honour was established to promote 'prayer, purity and temperance' as a means to combat the 'abnormal excitement' which had apparently gripped women." Members of the League pledged themselves to total abstinence during the war.[7] A sociologist has drawn attention to a forgotten wartime religious pledge campaign. Rooted in an evangelical belief in human depravity, it sought to win God's blessings on British soldiers by purifying a "drunkard nation."[8]

At the first wartime conference of bishops Edward Lee Hicks, president of the Church of England Temperance Society, was met with "a general silence" when he asked his fellow bishops to address the problem of drink."[9] The mood of the bishops quickly changed. In November 1914 an episcopal conference chaired by the Archbishop of Canterbury called for voluntary wartime teetotalism.

In March 1915 Lloyd George persuaded George V to make a private promise that he and the royal household would abstain from drink for the duration of the war. In April, news leaked to the press about what was called the King's Pledge. Lord Kitchener, the secretary of state for war, made a similar pledge, as did Richard Haldane, the lord chancellor, although he abandoned the pledge when he left the Cabinet. No other prominent politician, not Lloyd George and certainly not the hard-drinking prime minister Asquith, followed the King in his pledge.[10] The King complained that Lloyd George had "made a fool of him."[11] On the advice of his physician, the King continued to drink in private. The former prime minister A.J. Balfour ridiculed the King's Pledge in a private letter.

> I am looking forward with amusement to seeing whether I shall be served ginger beer at the Royal table:-- or whether 'total prohibition' is to be deferred. I understand Rosebery is to be of the party -- he will not like his champagne being cut off. Squish [Asquith], who would like it still less, is not to be there.[12]

Old time temperance societies such as the United Kingdom Alliance took the opportunity to call for State prohibition.[13] They were joined by new organizations that lobbied for wartime national prohibition to promote national efficiency. The National Efficiency Committee of 1915 was succeeded by the Strength of Britain Movement, organized in April 1916, which advocated wartime prohibition. It won the support of wealthy businessmen who had not belonged to the old temperance societies. It boasted that nearly a hundred generals and admirals had endorsed its program. Dr. Caleb Saleeby (1878-1940), a medical doctor and eugenicist, chaired the executive committee.

The best-known figure in the Strength of Britain Movement was Arthur Mee (1875-1943), a Baptist teetotaler who had not been active in the prewar temperance movement.[14] Mee was a journalist who wrote or edited many books such as the *Children's Encyclopedia* which sold 1.5 million sets in Britain and the British Empire.[15] He argued that the wartime choice that he proposed between empty cupboards and empty glasses was an easy one. Mee wrote twenty controversial pamphlets such as *The Fiddlers, The Parasite*, and *Defeat or Victory?* They sold 1.5 million copies. Accused of undermining the war effort, he defended himself in *Who Giveth Us the Victory* (1917).

Mee complained that leaders in the Strength of Britain Movement used money raised for the cause to pay themselves fees for their work. In turn, they claimed that Mee rarely attended meetings of the executive committee. By August 1917, believing that he had been misused and exploited, Mee left for the more religious National Prohibition Crusade. Mee became honorary secretary, while his sometime collaborator in writing Dr. (John) Stuart Holden (1870-1934) chaired the new organization.[16] Wealthy capitalists were prominent in the Strength of Britain. Mee hoped that workingmen would be the backbone of the Crusade.[17]

Mee opposed State Purchase of the drink trade unless there was a guarantee that it would be followed by wartime prohibition.[18] He threatened to organize "a Covenant by which we hope to bind at least a million votes for Prohibition at the Demobilsation Election. The government will listen then, & not before."[19]

There were bitter disputes in the organization between those who demanded no compromise on wartime prohibition and those who considered other ways of dealing with the drink problem such as State Purchase. In September 1917, Sir Alfred Booth (1872-1948) a director of the Cunard Steamship company who was the first president of the Strength of Britain Movement, left to support State Purchase. He was joined in his resignation by St. Loe Strachey (1860-1927), the editor of the *Spectator*.[20]

It was Government and not private organizations that did the most to reduce drinking. Upon the outbreak of the war, Parliament passed the Defence of the Realm Act, and a year later it created the Liquor Traffic Central Control Board. The statute and the Central Control Board are treated together here. They regulated and restricted the sale of drink, first in places important to the war effort such as naval bases and districts that manufactured munitions, but eventually almost everywhere. The sale of drink on trains was banned. In October 1915 the British government announced a "No Treating Order."[21] Any drink ordered had to be consumed by the person who paid for it, to avoid patriotic civilians from buying drinks for soldiers and sailors. Ironically, on duty the military was served a rum ration, about 2.5 fluid ounces of thick, dark rum every two days when not on the front line or daily when on the front line, and sometimes more during heavy fighting.[22]

The war made relevant many long debated proposals for the retail drink trade: reducing the number of pubs, much more than already occurring through the Licensing Act of 1904, disinterested management, and changes in the conduct of the surviving public houses, for instance, by reducing the hours that drink was sold. The last of these strategies saw the greatest progress during the war.

The hours for the sale of drink in pubs were drastically curtailed. Before the war, London pubs had been open from 5 am until 12:30 am, a total of 19.5 hours. Pub operating hours were slashed to just 5.5 hours, that is, noon to 2:30 pm and 6 pm to 9 pm. Redefined as 3 to 5:30 pm, afternoon closing lasted until 1988. It was not only London where pub hours were reduced. By the beginning of 1916 half the country saw the opening hours of licensed premises go from 16 or 19 hours a day to 5.5, with evening closing times at 9:00 or 9:30 pm. Within two years these restrictions expanded to almost the entire country other than a few rural districts.

Taxes on alcohol were progressively increased, eventually tripled. As early as November 1914, the beer duty was sharply increased. Even more than beer, new taxes on spirits increased retail prices. In 1918, a bottle of whiskey cost £1, five times what it had cost before the outbreak of war.

The strength of beer did not change until early 1917, when the unrestricted German U-Boat campaign started to impact transatlantic trade. With grain from North America running low, the government imposed a series of restrictions on brewers. In April 1917 the Food Controller limited annual beer production by a third. A couple of months later, breweries were forced to brew half of their beer at a much lower gravity. Weak beer was sometimes ridiculed as "Lloyd George's beer."[23]

Higher prices, weaker beers and fewer pub hours reduced drunkenness. Per capita beer consumption already had been plummeting before the war. Convictions for drunkenness fell dramatically during the war. In London in 1914, 67,103 people were found guilty of being drunk. In 1917 the number had fallen to 16,567. Of course, large numbers of young men were in France in the military and so were not drinking in the UK.

Central Control Board

The formation of the Central Control Board received general approval. For instance, the *Brewers' Gazette* (13 May 1915) greeted it "with satisfaction."[24] Criticism began when the Board began to act.

The Control Board wanted less drinking and much less drunkenness. Increasingly, it saw its role as more than the war emergency. Instead, it wanted "a solution to the underlying problem of intemperance."[25] It sought to create a new environment for public houses that emphasized food as much as drink. It anticipated the new philosophy of drinking, encapsulated in progressive brewers' promotion of the interwar improved public house. Sobriety was demanded and, with less success, pub appeal to women

The Central Control Board was chaired by the Lord D'Abernon (1857-1941), a respected diplomat, banker, and former MP.[26] As Sir Edgar Vincent, he had been a council member at two public house trust companies.[27] In the Spring of 1915 the membership of the Central Control Board included nobody identified with temperance organizations or the licensed drink trade. In 1916 it added Henry Carter, the temperance secretary of the Wesleyan Methodists, and the Birmingham brewer, W. Waters Butler. They joined as individuals and not as representatives of their organization or business. Another brewer Sydney Nevile later joined the Board.[28] Butler and Nevile were progressives who persuaded other big brewers to embrace State Purchase and, after the war, the reformed public house.

In his history of the Central Control Board, Robert Duncan sees it as influenced by traditional temperance views, but other historians regard the Board as independent of old drink quarrels and as following a scientific approach toward alcohol.[29] It favored moderate drinking and not total abstinence.

In her article, "The Medical Cromwell," Joanne Woiak entitled a section "The New Moderationist Paradigm, 1914-1920." It began as follows:

> A clean break with the ideology of the temperance movement was not made until the First World War, by the Scientific Advisory Committee to the Central Control Board, appointed in 1916 and headed by Lord D'Abernon. This was the first organized group of medical scientists to offer a science-based alternative to the temperance and prohibitionist solutions to the drink problem.[30]

Scientific reformers sought to change the environment for drinkers and prospective drinkers. For instance, it encouraged installing canteens in factories for the convenience of workers and to make eating at pubs unnecessary.

Although the Central Control Board imposed restrictions on drink throughout nearly all of Britain, its most dramatic innovation was the so-called Carlisle experiment (1916-73).[31] Lord D'Abernon called it his "model farm."[32] Launched in June 1916, it centered on Carlisle in northeastern England and nearby Gretna across the Scottish border. Carlisle and the surrounding district had 339 pubs and five breweries. Carlisle alone had 119 public houses and seven clubs.[33]

The experiment included two districts far from Carlisle and Gretna: Middlesex Enfield Lock, the site of a small arms factory and, at the request of the Admiralty, Cromarty Firth in northern Scotland, the home of a major Royal Navy base. The Carlisle experiment took over four pubs at Enfield and thirteen at Cromarty Firth. At Enfield, the local pubs had been overwhelmed by the wartime increase in hungry workingmen. As "many workers [were] unable to find places to sit down," "dimly lit passages were lined with tired men seeking what rest they could by leaning against walls."[34]

Gretna was by far the most important for the war effort. To build the factory and associated housing, thousands of mostly Irish navvies were employed in 1915. In November 1916 there were still 5,000 Irish construction workers. They threatened to leave for their homeland to avoid military conscription. To prevent their return to Ireland, they were promised an exemption from military service.

At its peak Gretna produced 800 tons of cordite a week, more than all the other cordite producers combined. In late 1917 Gretna employed 11,576 women and 5,066 men. Over 60% of all workers were under age 18. Two model towns were built for married employees. The young female workers lived mostly in wooden huts, so they were "Timbertown Girls."

The Carlisle experiment began before the women arrived. Instead, there were thousands of construction laborers. For recreation they could travel by train the twelve miles to Carlisle, a city of 50,000 which had many public houses. "To the quiet cathedral city this seemed like an invasion of Goths and Vandals."[35] A pub near the train station lined up 500 whiskies on the bar for the convenience of thirsty train passengers. Convictions for drunkenness exploded, nearly an eight-fold increase "since the arrival of the navvies."[36]

Carlisle encouraged sobriety among war workers. There was a second motive: "to placate the Temperance Movement and also the United States which was turning towards prohibition and saw precious cereal exports being wasted in Britain on beer production."[37]

The Carlisle scheme sought to fight the drink problem by changing the public house environment in which drink was consumed.[38] The old pubs that it replaced had multiple front and back entrances, partitions and snugs, no seats in the public bar, no food, and poor hygiene. Some public houses lacked even outdoor toilets. The Carlisle experiment drastically reduced the number of pubs (closing 53 in Carlisle itself) and created seven very large public houses which provided food, entertainment, and comfortable seating. Their décor was meant to attract women as well as men.[39] The Carlisle experiment left alone pubs and hotels with middle-class clienteles. Pub managers were paid a salary and had no financial interest in selling alcoholic drink. To encourage other sales, managers received a commission on sales of food and non-alcoholic drink.

The beer was brewed at a reduced alcoholic content at nationalized breweries.[40] Advertising was prohibited. Most off-licenses were closed. Unlike other English pubs, Carlisle's observed Sunday closing as nearby Scotland did. It also prohibited the sale of spirits on Saturdays. The old Carlisle favorite, a heater and cooler, or a whiskey and a pint of beer, was no more.

Some of the new pubs were enormous. The Gretna Tavern despite its name was located in Carlisle. Opened in July 1916, it was a former post office with a long bar, a dining room that could serve 180 persons, and a stage where a piano or gramophone played music. There also was a small stand-up bar room. In the dining room, in addition to waitress service at tables, there was a buffet that offered soup, meat pies, sandwiches, scones, teacakes, and non-alcoholic drinks. The Gretna opened for breakfast and served lunch. Its hours were from 7:30 am to 9 pm.[41] Another large tavern, Gracie's Banking, located in Scotland, "boasted a cinema."[42] Outside were a bowling green and quoit pitches. On Fridays and Saturdays, a post office provided banking services.

"Timbertown girls" were not big drinkers. In the month of April 1917, 75% of the Gretna takings were for food.[43] Food was also the attraction for local mill girls at a pub located near a biscuit factory. Its first floor Working Girls' Café sold cheap hot meals at lunchtime.[44]

Although the Board hoped that the presence of women would modify the rough behavior of workingmen, it added women's bars (or sections of bars) at some pubs that catered to workingmen.

Carlisle was Britain's largest experiment in disinterested management.[45] Its importance should not be exaggerated. The Central Control Board regarded "the quality of state control" more important than disinterested management.[46] Its restrictions on drinking hours throughout most of the country affected more drinkers that did the Carlisle experiment.

Unlike earlier proposals, the Carlisle experiment included breweries as well as pubs. More important, unlike most prewar proposals for disinterested management, it provided entertainment in public houses. In contrast, the Temperance Legislative League had feared tempting people to frequent barrooms who otherwise would avoid them.

Lloyd George

David Lloyd George played a prominent role in the wartime drink question.[47] Early in 1915 he told an acquaintance "Ï wish I could do something to settle the drink question. I should die happy."[48] He played a leading role in the government's approach to wartime drinking as chancellor of the exchequer, minister for munitions, and prime minister.

On 28 February 1915, Lloyd George met at Bangor with the Shipbuilding Employers' Federation which had asked for national prohibition during the war. Although he did not endorse prohibition, he acknowledged: "Drink is doing us more damage in the war than all the German submarines put together." On 15 March, he famously added: "we are fighting Germany, Austria and Drink, and, as far as I can see, the greatest of these three deadly foes is Drink." As a result, "for nearly three months, the drink question was the main subject of debate in the press and in private circles."[49] Yet there was "little [evidence] to convince a disinterested observer that drinking had a serious effect on munitions production or shipping."[50]

On 4 April 1915, Lloyd George's secretary (and mistress) Frances Stevenson wrote in her diary: "C[hancellor of the Exchequer] is steeped in drink …. He has been drink mad this last week—can talk and think of nothing else." She added that Asquith was appalled at the prospect of national prohibition, but he felt better about it personally when reminded that people could drink with a doctor's certificate.[51]

A biographer of Lloyd George, Bentley Gilbert, argues that drink had not obstructed the war effort in Britain as a whole. Drink was a Scottish problem, specifically at Clydeside dockyards. Gilbert points out that drink was not a problem at the royal dockyards at Plymouth.[52]

Lloyd George argued for State Purchase of the drink trade on two occasions, once in the 1915 and again in 1916 and 1917.[53] "The historiography of temperance reform has represented State Purchase during the war as a temperance measure, which it was not."[54] On the first occasion, it was about producing military supplies. In the second, it was about allocating scarce North American grain.

When Lloyd George endorsed State Purchase of the licensed drink trade in 1915, it was aimed at reducing drunkenness among munitions workers and increasing production of ships and ammunition. Shortly after he had made his proposal, the shell crisis (a shortage of ammunition for British artillery at the Battle of Aubers) led to Lloyd George becoming minister for munitions in May.

The Tory leader Bonar Law "rather liked" State Purchase from a party perspective. Writing to a senior member of his party on 2 April 1915, he said "if it can be carried, which I doubt, it would free us of the Trade incubus and it would mean the universal adoption of disinterested management in regard to which I have always taken a favourable view."[55]

Some big brewers favored State Purchase while most prohibitionists opposed it.[56] "The dire financial position of many of the larger brewers" made State Purchase appealing if the price was right.[57] Brewers struggled under declining beer consumption. To reduce competition, they wanted to eliminate small, inefficient breweries. They wanted to free themselves from the debts they had incurred when they had bought Edwardian tied houses at inflated prices. To make matters worse, Government restrictions without compensation multiplied endlessly. Big brewers supported State Purchase only if it included the entire licensed trade, public houses as well as breweries. In April 1915, it was estimated that this would cost £225 millions.

In 1915 Lloyd George got the support of such diverse people as St. Loe Strachey, Joseph Rowntree, and George Lansbury.[58] In contrast, he got little support in Cabinet. The cost of purchasing the entire drink trade, notably the thousands of tied houses, would have been enormous and, what the government wanted, it thought, could be achieved through regulation and negotiation with the brewers such as a reduction in beer production and alcoholic content. Asquith was strongly opposed to State Purchase. He said:

> On the question of drink ... [Lloyd George] has completely lost his head. His mind apparently oscillates from hour to hour between the two poles of absurdity: cutting off all drink from the working man, wh. wd. lead to something like a universal strike; and buying out (at this moment of all others) the whole liquor traffic of the country, and replacing it by a huge State monopoly, wh. wd ruin our finances and create a vast engine of possible corruption. (Asquith to Venetia Stanley, 31 March 1915).[59]

Asquith was pleased when Lloyd George abandoned State Purchase in favor of another scheme, with higher drink taxes and restrictions on sales.[60] Only in districts important for the war would the Government take over the drink trade. A committee on Scotland proposed that the Government take over the pubs but not the breweries. Asquith told Venetia Stanley:

> Lloyd George] has produced an ingenious substitute of much more modest dimensions, which we are now discussing. .... The whole thing bristles with the most contentious points, but it is a gain to have got it down from the Alpine (or Cambrian [Welsh mountains]) altitudes to the sober level

of business & common-sense. … The result is that Ll. G. is going to open a new series of pour parlers with brewers, teetotallers & the whole motley crowd of interests. (Asquith to Venetia Stanley, 15 April 1915).

Lloyd George's new scheme depended on steep drink taxes. This proved to be politically impossible. Asquith reported the interview of Lloyd George with Bonar Law. He told Lloyd George that "the Tory party was so much in the hands of the trade that they must oppose them root & branch."[61] The Irish MPs also were vehemently opposed.

The brewer and Unionist whip for Scotland, Sir George Younger, had already dismissed the plan of partial nationalization. On 19 April, he told Lloyd George: "This is a case of taking the whole or none. You must have a complete monopoly both of the means of production and of the provision for the sale if the scheme is to bear good fruit, and you must pay honestly."[62]

Lloyd George revived State Purchase in 1916 and 1917.[63] The German submarine offensive had reduced the amount of grain shipped from North America. State Purchase was meant to conserve scarce foodstuffs and shipping. The arguments for and against State Purchase were much the same as in 1915. The trade feared a proposal for wartime Government control of the drink trade without purchase. The historian Turner argues that the brewer John Gretton worried about temporary government control and restriction if followed, after the war ended, with the return of a crippled trade to the brewers. The unsatisfactory status quo was better than that.

D'Abernon wanted State Purchase only if it meant improvement in the behavior of the retail trade. He wanted social reform by regulation and did not give priority to state ownership of the trade or disinterested management as a strategy.

Lloyd George waffled. In May 1917 Lloyd George reluctantly supported State Purchase instead of temporary State control without compensation. In June he changed his mind and, as an alternative, proposed a drastic reduction in beer production.

The call for State Purchase did not end with the Armistice. For instance, Rowntree and Sherwell argued in 1919 that "public sobriety and private profit cannot be combined."[64] After the end of the war a few members of the Coalition government still favored State Purchase.[65] More of them favored continued government control without Purchase.

The trade soon got much of what it wanted but not everything. By July 1921 the Government had removed controls on the amount and strength of beer that could be brewed.[66]

It was not until later that year that the drink trade got rid of the Central Control Board which had exercised almost dictatorial powers.[67] The

Central Control Board held its last meeting in September 1921. Its powers already had been transferred to the Home Office.

The big brewers drafted a bill that, among other things, would have made it difficult for tradition-minded licensing justices from blocking reformed public houses. The Government considered that the trade bill was one-sided and sought a compromise.

The Cabinet assigned the writing of a compromise bill to the brewer Gretton and a Coalition Liberal, Thomas Broad, a Congregational minister who supported temperance. The Licensing Act continued a few wartime reforms, shorter hours for pubs, notably the midafternoon break. This lasted in England and Wales until 1988. There were other restrictions on pub and club hours. Buying on credit remained illegal as were the long pull and beer hawking. The Licensing Act scrapped the bona fide traveler privilege that had been created in 1872. As during wartime, Welsh Sunday closing was extended to Monmouthshire although it was controversial there.[68] It was hoped that shorter hours when pubs could sell alcoholic drink would encourage them to focus on selling food and non-alcoholic beverages during the rest of the day.

Reform-minded brewers did not get the checks on the power of the licensing justices to obstruct refurbishing pubs and building new or rebuilding improved public houses. Nor did progressive brewers such as Butler and Nevile get a reduction of redundant pubs. Without a reduction in the number of pubs, licensing justices saw applications to build reformed public houses as a pretext to sell more beer. Progressive brewers argued that the drink trade needed reform in collaboration with the Government. "Too many pubs with too much drinking by too few people" was the deplorable status quo.[69] Some leading brewers began formulating broad coalitions to influence public opinion and magistrates.[70] In Birmingham, progressive brewers co-operated with magistrates in a new stage of "fewer and better" producing the most dynamic, extensive, and costly improved pubs in the provinces.[71]

Although the Carlisle experiment quickly abandoned its remote Enfield enclave, it was surprisingly ambitious during the postwar years. Between 1927 and 1940 its chief architect Harry Redfern (1861-1950) demolished and rebuilt 15 public houses and radically redesigned another 87, some as late as in the 1960s. His style was inspired by William Morris' arts and crafts movement.[72] The Carlisle experiment made a profit every year of its existence.

In 1971, Parliament voted to end the Carlisle scheme as of 1973.[73] The afternoon break for serving drink ended in 1988 for England and Wales. Belatedly, the First World War ended for the drink trade and drinkers.

Notes

[1] See two chapters in Greenaway, *Drink and British Politics since 1830,* ch. 6, "The First World War: Drink and National Efficiency," ch. 7, "The Postwar Settlement, 1919-21," and the more detailed account by Robert Duncan, *Pubs and Patriots: The Drink Crisis in Britain during World War One* (Liverpool University Press, 2013). Although Duncan's book has generally been praised, it was sharply criticized by William Haydock, in *Reviews in History* (Sept. 2014), who disliked what he saw as a polemical approach. In contrast, Ryosuke Yokoe, "Alcohol and Politics in Twentieth-Century Britain," *Historical Journal* 62 no. 1 (March 2019): 275-77, regards Duncan's work as an important contribution. An old article by Michael E. Rose remains helpful. "'The Success of Social Reform?' The Central Control Board (Liquor Traffic) 1915-1921," M.R.D. Foot, ed., *War and Society: Historical Essays in Honour and Memory of J.R. Western, 1928-1971* (Elek, 1973). Rose argues that the Central Control Board saw its role as social reform and not only wartime efficiency. See also James Nicholls, *The Politics of Alcohol: A History of the Drink Question in England*, ch. 11, "Central Control: War and Nationalisation," Gourvish and Wilson, *The British Brewing Industry*, pp. 317-35, and for Scottish distillers, R.B. Weir, "Obsessed with Moderation: The Drink Trades and the Drink Question (1870-1930)." *British Journal of Addiction* 20 (1984): 101-05.

[2] Robert Bradshaw Batty (1863-1927), a solicitor, was United Kingdom Alliance honorary secretary, 1909-14. Later he broke with the Alliance by supporting State Purchase

[3] Greenaway, *Drink in British Politics*, p. 97. See also Stella Moss, "'Wartime Hysterics': Alcohol, Women and the Politics of Wartime Social Purity in England," in Jessica Meyer, ed., *British Popular Culture and the First World War* (Leiden and Boston: Brill, 2008).

[4] David W. Gutzke, "Gender, Class and Public Drinking in Britain during the First World War," *Histoire sociale* 27 (1994): 367-91; Gutzke, *Women Drinking Out in Britain since the Early Twentieth Century* (Manchester University Press, 2016), ch. 1; Richard Brown, "The Thirsty Sex," *Looking at History*, 7 July 2014.

[5] Stuart Mews, "Urban Problems and Rural Solutions: Drink and Disestablishment in the First World War," in *The Church in Town and Countryside*, ed. Derek Baker (Basil Blackwell, 1979), p. 453.

[6] John Simkin, "Alcohol and the First World War," *Spartacus Educational.*

[7] Henry Yeomans, "Another Round? Teetotal Pledges and World War One," *Points,* 3 April 2012.

[8] Henry Yeomans, *Alcohol and Moral Regulation: Public Attitudes, Spirited Measures and Victorian Hangovers* (Policy Press, 2014), p. 245. Yeomans also discussed the pledge movement in "Providentialism, the Pledge and Victorian Hangovers: Investigating 'Moderate Alcohol Policy in Britain, 1914-1918'," *Solon* 1 (2011).

[9] Mews, "Urban Problems," p. 452.

[10] About Asquith's drinking, see Marvin Rintala, "Taking the Pledge: H. H. Asquith and Drink," *Biography* 16 no. 2 (Spring

1993).

[11] Quoted in Bentley Brinkerhoff Gilbert, *David Lloyd George: A Political Life*, vo. 2, *The Organizer of Victory, 1912-16* (B.T. Batsford, 1992), p. 163.

[12] *The Letters of Arthur Balfour and Lady Elcho, 1875-1917*, ed. Jane Ridley and Clayre Percy (Hamish Hamilton, 1992), p. 320.

[13] The United Kingdom Alliance was weakened in 1914 by a lawsuit. Bendle's Meat Port Nutrient wine had sued it for defamation after the Alliance published pamphlets attacking what it called the medicated wines fraud. The Alliance had to pay damages and costs for more than £7,700 at a time when the Alliance's average yearly income was less than £5,000. John Turner, "State Purchase of the Liquor Trade in the First World War," *Historical Journal* 23 no. 3 (Sept. 1980): 592; *Alliance News*, Sept. 1915, p. 175. See also Lori Loeb, "Desperate Housewives: The Rise and Fall of the Campaign against Medicated Wines in Twentieth-Century Britain," *Phamaceutical Historian* 50 no. 1 (March 2020). In another sign of weakness, the Alliance lamented in early 1917 that its former general secretary Alexander Thomson had joined the Government at the handsome salary of £700 as political secretary to Neil Primrose, Lloyd George's chief whip. Primrose was the second son of Lord Rosebery. The Alliance expected that Thomson would work against it for drink nationalization. G.W. Wilson to Leif Jones, 27 January 1917. Castle Howard, Ninth Countess of Carlisle, J23/242; *Alliance News*, Jan. 1917, p. 25.

[14] The most recent biography is Keith Crawford, *Arthur Mee: a Biography* (Lutterworth, 2016), which has a section "Temperance and the Evils of Drink." The best sketch of the Strength of Britain Movement is Kenneth Pearl in Blocker, *Alcohol and Temperance in Modern History*, pp. 597-98.

[15] Revised as *The Book of Knowledge*, it sold 3.5 million sets in the United States.

[16] For an undated fragment of Mee's angry letter, see Castle Howard, Ninth Countess of Carlisle, J23/242. For the formation of the Crusade, see *National Advocate*, Oct. 1917, p. 164; *Newcastle Journal*, 10 Aug. 1917, p. 7; and a hostile report, "Dreamers and Schemers," in *Globe*, 10 Aug. 1917, p. 4.

[17] Strength of Britain merged with the National Commercial Temperance League in 1923.

[18] In contrast, (later Sir) Angus Watson, who helped finance Mee's work, was willing to accept State Purchase without prohibition.

[19] Mee to Nicoll, 2 July 1917. [Misplaced source for quotation] Sir William Robertson Nicoll was the editor of the *British Weekly*, a Nonconformist newspaper.

[20] St. Loe Strachey to Lord Channing, 26 Sept. 1917, St. Loe Strachey papers. Beaverbrook Library (now at House of Lord Record Office).

[21] Jim Grundy, "'Lloyd George's Beer' or When It Was Illegal to Buy Your Round," *Western Front Association*, 11 December 2010.

[22] Nicholas K. Johnson, "World War I, Part 2, The British Rum Ration," *Points*, 29 May 2014; Theodore Sutcliffe, "Booze in World War I," online. In 1902, when the Army Temperance Association acquired the prefix Royal, the organization claimed as members 25% of the troops in the British Isles and 40% of those in India. It was not popular among World War I troops. The organization was dissolved in 1958. The rum ration ended in 1970.

---

[23] Ron Pattinson, "How World War I Changed Pub Culture, and Beer Itself" [History by the Glass], *Beer Advocate* (August 2019).

[24] Duncan, *Pubs and Patriots*, p. 100.

[25] Greenaway, *Drink and British Politics*, p. 102.

[26] Lord D'Abernon was briefly a Conservative MP. As he was opposed to Joseph Chamberlain's tariff reform, he later joined the Liberal Party. He owed his peerage to Asquith. He was a career diplomat who became ambassador to Germany after the war. He was active in philanthropies such as the YMCA and an art collector. He also was a womanizer nicknamed the Piccadilly Stallion. Duncan, *Pubs and Patriots*, p. 96.

[27] David W. Gutzke, *Pubs and Progressives: Reinventing the Public House in England 1896-1980* (Northern Illinois University Press, 2006), ch. 3, "The Carlisle Experiment."

[28] For the composition of the Board, see Gutzke, *Pubs and Progressives*, pp. 49-50.

[29] Lord D'Abernon, "Scientific Basis of Drink Control," *British Journal of Inebriety* 17(1920).

[30] Joanne Woiak, "A Medical Cromwell to Depose King Alcohol": Medical Scientists, Temperance Reformers, and the Alcohol Problem in Britain," *Sociale histoire* 27 (November 1994): 35.

[31] For Carlisle, see Justin Willis in the Blocker encyclopedia and Olive Seabury, *The Carlisle State Management Scheme: Its Ethos and Architecture* (Bookcase Carlisle, 2007), which I have not seen, as well as Phil Mellows, "The People's Pubs," *Publican* (22 June 2009); Phil Mellows, "Nationalize the Pub," *Jacobin*, 21 Nov. 2017; R.M. Punnett, "State Management of the Liquor Trade," *Public Administration* 44 (Summer 1966). Available online is H.B. Wilson, "History of the Carlisle State Management Scheme 1916-1974" (apparently completed by early 1977), a typescript with handwritten corrections.

[32] Robert Duncan, "Lord D'Abernon's 'Model Farm': The Central Control Board's Carlisle Experiment," *Social History of Alcohol and Drugs* 24 no. 2 (Summer 2010): 119-40.

[33] Christopher Brader, "Timbertown Girls: Gretna Female Munitions Workers in World War I (Ph.D. thesis, University of Warwick, 2001), ch. 4, "Munition Workers and Drink." More briefly, see Emily Cole, *The Urban and Suburban Public House in Inter-War England, 1918-1939* (Historic England, 2015).

[34] Quoted in Ian Donnachie, "World War I and the Drink Question: State Control of the Drink Trade," *Scottish Labour History Society Journal* 17 (1982): 24.

[35] Rose, "The Success of Social Reform," p. 78.

[36] Ian Spencer Hornsey, *A History of Beer and Brewing* (Royal Society of Chemistry, 2003), p. 582.

[37] Quoted in Neil Robinson, "Lloyd George's Quest to Quench," *History Today* 44 no. 4 (June 1994): 4.

[38] Steve Matthews, "Changing the Culture of Drinking: The Public Houses in Carlisle before and after the Introduction of The State Management Scheme in 1916," *Folk Life* 59 no. 1 (2021). Matthews is a Carlisle local historian.

[39] In 1925 the Carlisle Experiment added women's bars.

[40] Carlisle bottled its own blended Border whiskey, brandy and rum.

[41] Duncan, *Pubs and Patriots*, p. 13.

[42] Rose, "The Success of Social Reform," p. 79.

[43] Brader, "Timbertown Girls," p. 117.

[44] *Mirror*, 19 May 2021.

[45] Today Scotland still has a few Goths, disinterested management pubs named after the Gothenburg Scheme.

[46] Greenaway, *Drink and British Politics*, p. 106.

[47] Turner, "State Purchase;" Greenaway, *Drink and British Politics*, pp. 107-13. Turner's impressive article occasionally stumbles re the temperance movement. For instance, he says (pp. 599-600) that T.P. Whittaker favored municipalization. He did not.

[48] J. Herbert Lewis' diary, 2 March 1915, in J. Herbert Lewis (later Lord Clwyd) papers. National Library of Wales, quoted in Chris Wrigley, *David Lloyd George and the British Labour Movement* (Harvester Press, 1976) p. 264.

[49] These were the words of a teetotal (but not prohibitionist) activist, Henry Carter, *The Control of the Drink Trade* (Longmans, Green, 1919), p. 48.

[50] Turner, "State Purchase," p. 597.

[51] Frances Stevenson, *Lloyd George: A Diary*. Edited by A.J.P. Taylor (Harper & Row,1971), p. 39.

[52] Gilbert, *David Lloyd George* 2: 170. See also pp. 157, 167-69, 171.

[53] For State Purchase during the war, see Turner, "State Purchase;" Greenaway, *Drink and British Politics*, pp. 107-13.

[54] Turner, "State Purchase," p. 614.

[54] Writing to Austen Chamberlain, quoted in Turner, "State Purchase," p. 600.

[56] Edward Lee Hicks, *The Diaries of Edward Lee Hicks, Bishop of Lincoln, 1910-1919,* ed. Graham Neville [Lincoln Record Society Publications] (Boydell Press, 1963), pp. 144-45 (12 April 1915). Hicks was part of a temperance deputation to Lloyd George. "He wants to suppress all sales of spirits, & to buy up the Beer trade: this the Brewers themselves had suggested to him in their interview last week." Hicks said that he would not criticize emergency war measures, but as a temperance reformer he saw national purchase as facilitating Local Veto.

[57] Greenaway, *Drink and British Politics*, p. 96. Unlike the brewers, the distillers opposed State Purchase. In 1917 the Whisky Association organized the Freedom of Britain Movement, a name presumably meant as a slap at the Strength of Britain Movement.

[58] Cameron Hazlehurst, *Politicians at War, July 1914 to May 1915: A Prologue to the Triumph of Lloyd George* (Jonathan Cape, 1971), ch. 12 "Another Little Drink," p. 212.

[59] H.H. Asquith, *Letters to Venetia Stanley*, ed. Michael and Eleanor Brock (Oxford University Press, 1982), 31 March 1915. #380.

[60] In his war memoirs, Lloyd George explained his dropping State Purchase as not because of Nonconformist opposition but because of "widespread discontent" among drinkers in munitions cities. Lloyd George, *War Memoirs* 1 (Odhams, 1933): 791-92. Nika Lee Sims, "David Lloyd George and the British Temperance Movement, 1890-1922" (M.A. thesis University of Alabama in Huntsville, 1988), p. 108, argues "The major obstacles to state purchase in 1917 were the staggering

cost and the opposition of the Labour Party." In fact, the Labour Party favored State Purchase.

[61] Asquith, *Memories and Reflections, 1852-1927* (Cassell, 1928), p. 75. See also Asquith to Venetia Stanley, 3 May 1915).

[62] Turner, "State Purchase," p. 603.

[63] On 17 March 1917, Lady Carlisle was unhappy. "The latest news about State purchase of the Trade crowns all Lloyd George's infamies." Quoted in Roberts, *Radical Countess*, p. 96.

[64] Rowntree and Sherwell, *State Purchase of the Liquor Trade* (Allen and Unwin, 1919), p. 26, quoted in Nicholls. *The Politics of Alcohol*, p. 158.

[65] Duncan (*Pubs and Patriots*, p. 213) mentions H.A.L. Fisher, Waldorf Astor, and Lord Milner.

[66] For details, see Greenaway, *Drink and British Politics*, ch. 7, "The Postwar Settlement, 1919-21.

[67] Lord Askwith, *British Taverns: Their History and Laws* (Routledge, 1928), ch 12, "The Act of 1921." The whiskey trade was badly hit by prohibition in the United States.

[68] Terence R. Gourvish, "The Business of Alcohol in the US and the UK: UK Regulation and Drinking Habits, 1914-39," *Business and Economic History* 26 no.2 (Winter 1987).

[69] Gutzke, *Pubs and Progressives*, p.108.

[70] See Gutzke, *Pubs and Progressives*, ch. 6, "Building Coalitions."

[71] See Gutzke, "W. Waters Butler and the Making of a Progressive Brewer in Britain, 1890-1922," *Histoire sociale* 48 (May 2016). See also Gutzke, "Progressivism and the History of the Public House, 1850–1950," *Cultural and Social History* 4 no.2 (2007).

[72] The Labour Party did not give up on the Carlisle model as shown by the New Towns Act (1946).

[73] Stephen G. Jones, "Labour, Society and the Drink Question in Britain, 1918-39," *Historical Journal* 30 (1987); Ian S. Wood, "Drink, Temperance and the Labour Movement," *Scottish Labour History Society Journal* 5 (1972); Peter Catterell, *Labour and the Politics of Alcohol: The Decline of a Cause* (Institute of Alcohol Studies, 2014).

COMPARISONS

A new book by Mark Lawrence Schrad, with the subtitle *A Global History of Prohibition*, offers a new interpretation of the British Isles. England is the anomaly and not its Welsh, Scottish and Irish neighbors.[1] In England the temperance movement was noticeably weaker and the licensed drink trade stronger.

The English temperance movement (and drink trade) need to be put in international context. Scotland and Ireland were different, as was Wales.[2] So were the British settler colonies, Canada, Australia, and New Zealand.[3] Temperance movements flourished in Sweden and elsewhere in Europe, as well as in distant Mexico and India. The most important comparison for England is with America.[4]

Temperance publications, speakers, and ideas crossed the oceans freely in the English-speaking world.[5] The United States pioneered organizations dedicated to fight drink, first against "hard liquor," next for total abstinence from alcohol as a beverage, and finally for prohibitory laws. England coined the term teetotal and probably created "taking the pledge" as a written baptism into the total abstinence community. The call for prohibition in Britain evoked America's Maine law of the 1850s. Originating in the United States, the Good Templar fraternal temperance society became powerful in England and Scotland. Gospel Temperance imported from the United States, flourished in Britain in the late 1870s and the 1880s. Blurring the distinction between religion and total abstinence, Gospel Temperance enlisted working-class and lower middle-class drinkers into a moral suasion Blue Ribbon Army.[6]

For all the similarities, there were major differences between the American and the English temperance movements.[7] Organized teetotalism in England began among working class militants in the north of England, but nothing followed in England comparable to the Washingtonian movement of reformed drunkards that occurred in America in the 1840s. The Woman's Christian Temperance Union, powerful in the United States under the charismatic Frances Willard, had only a limited parallel in England. The English women's temperance societies lacked the influence of America's WCTU. Willard, who had been reared in a middle-class Methodist family, had a natural relationship with her members not easily matched by the titled aristocrats who led the major Englishwomen's temperance organization, one of them separated from her homosexual husband (Lady Henry Somerset) and the other an agnostic or atheist (Lady Carlisle). The mostly German brewers in the United States lacked the social status and political influence that English brewers enjoyed and so were easier for temperance reformers to attack. Temperance-minded evangelical Protestants dominated public life in the United States much more than in England. Prohibition sentiment was stronger in American farm states than in big cities, while in England prohibitionists often lived in industrial towns such as Manchester.

The American constitutional structure facilitated experimentation with local option and statewide prohibition.[8] The opportunities were similar in Canada and Australia. Although constitutionally a unitary country, New Zealand authorized local option. Parliament allowed Scotland and Ireland to have separate licensing laws and enacted Sunday closing for Wales, but such concessions happened only to the extent that the parliamentary majority consisting of Englishmen was willing.

It is easy to dismiss the English temperance movement as a failure because it lacked the dramatic success of its American cousin, a constitutional amendment for National Prohibition. A closer look shows the influence of the English temperance movement on society at large. The number of pubs declined as did per capita consumption of alcoholic drink. The temperance movement does not explain such changes by itself, but it contributed to creating a more sober England on the eve of the First World War than what had existed in the mid-nineteenth century when per capita consumption of alcoholic drink peaked.

Notes

[1] *Smashing the Liquor Machine* (Oxford University Press, 2021), p. 592 n. 21. Schrad sees northern England as more like Scotland than like London and the Home counties.

[2] For Scotland, see D.C. Paton, "Drink and the Temperance Movement in Nineteenth-Century Scotland" (Ph.D. dissertation, University of Edinburgh, 1977); Norma Davies Logan (later Denny), "Drink and Society: Scotland, 1870-1914" (Ph.D. dissertation, Glasgow University, 1983). These two doctoral dissertations are available online. See also Ian Donnachie, *A History of the Brewing Industry in Scotland* (John Donald, 1979); Ronald B. Weir, *The History of the Distilling Company, 1887-1939* (Clarendon, 1996); Anthony Cooke, *A History of Drinking: The Scottish Pub since 1700* (Edinburgh University Press, 2015); and Megan Smitley, *The Feminine Public Sphere: Middle Class Women in Civic Life in Scotland, c. 1820-1914* (Manchester University Press, 2009), for the women's temperance movement. For Ireland, see Elizabeth Malcolm, *"Ireland Sober, Ireland*

Free": Drink and Temperance in Nineteenth-Century Ireland (Syracuse University Press, 1986); and Bradley Kadel, *Drink and Culture in Nineteenth-Century Ireland: The Alcohol Trade and the Politics of the Irish Public House* (Tauris, 2015). For Wales, see W.R. Lambert, *Drink and Sobriety in Victorian Wales, c. 1820-c. 1895* (University of Wales Press, 1983).

[3] For Canada, see Craig Heron, *Booze: A Distilled History* (Between the Lines, 2003); for Australia, Trevor L. Jordan, *Under the Influence: A History of Alcohol in Australia* (ABC Books, 2009); for New Zealand, Greg Ryan, "Drink and the Historians: Sober Reflections on Alcohol in New Zealand, 1840-1914," *New Zealand Journal of History* 44 no. 1 (April 2010). For Sweden, there is little in English, but see Madeleine Hurd, "Liberals, Socialists, and Sobriety: The Rhetoric of Citizenship in Turn-of-the-Century Sweden," *International Labor and Working-Class History* 45 (Spring 1993); for Germany, James S. Roberts, *Drink, Temperance, and the Working Class in Nineteenth Century Germany* (Allen and Unwin, 1984); for Russia a large English-language literature such as Patricia Herlihy, T*he Alcoholic Empire: Vodka and Politics in Later Imperial Russia* (Oxford University Press, 2002); for Mexico, Gretchen Pierce, "Parades, Epistles and Prohibitive Legislation: Mexico's National Anti-Alcohol Campaign and the Process of State-Building, 1934-1940," *Social History of Alcohol and Drugs* 23 no. 2 (Spring 2009); for India, David M. Fahey and Padma Manian, "Poverty and Purification: The Politics of Gandhi's Campaign for Prohibition*" Historian* 67 no. 3 (Fall 2005); Robert Eric Colvard, "A World Without Drink: Temperance in Modern India, 1880-1940" (Ph.D. dissertation, Iowa, 2013).

[4] The best modern survey remains Jack S. Blocker, Jr., *American Temperance Movements: Cycles of Reform* (Twayne, 1989). Note his use of the plural. There are innumerable specialized studies.

[5] For a pioneering international study, see Bernard Aspinwall, *Portable Utopia: Glasgow and the United States, 1820-1920* (Aberdeen University Press, 1984), ch. 4, "The Demon Drink: The Drift to Prohibition." For a comparative study of the USA, Sweden, and Russia, there is Mark Lawrence Schrad, *The Power of a Bad Idea: Networks, Institutions, and the Global Prohibition Wave* (Oxford University Press, 2010); and for the English-speaking world see Ian R. Tyrrell, *Women's World/Women's Empire: The Woman's Christian Temperance Union in International Perspective, 1880-1930* (University of North Carolina Press, 1991). See also Xi Chen, "The Making of John B. Gough (1817-1886): Temperance Celebrity, Evangelical Pageantry, and the Conservatism of Popular Reform in Victorian Society" (Ph.D. dissertation, University of Washington, 2013); Lilian Lewis Shiman, "John B. Gough: Trans-Atlantic Temperance Orator." *Social History of Alcohol Review*, 15 no. 3-4 (Spring/Summer 2001).

[6] Shiman, *Crusade against Drink*, pp. 109-21.

[7] K. Austin Kerr, the author of the major study of the Anti-Saloon League, said (26 October 1998): "I never have met a British scholar who seemed to understand that American prohibition fits in with a long tradition of seeking to control business corporations." ATHG@miamiu.acs.muohio.edu.

[8] David M. Fahey, "The Politics of Drink in Britain: Anglo-American Perspectives," in *Proceedings of the Ohio Academy of History* (2000). See also Jessica Warner,

---

"On Wit, Irony, and Living with Imperfection: How Britain Said No to Abstinence," *American Journal of Public Health* 98 no. 7 (July 2008).

MANUSCRIPTS

Bodleian

*Sir William Harcourt (cataloged)
*H.H. Asquith
*J.S. Sandars
*James Bryce

British Library (formerly British Museum)

*W.E. Gladstone
*Herbert Gladstone (Viscount Gladstone)
*Sir Henry Campbell-Bannerman
*A.J. Balfour
*Lord Ripon
*Sir Edward Hamilton
*J.A. Spender
*John Bright

Castle Howard

*Ninth Countess of Carlisle (includes many letters from Leif Jones)

Churchill College, Cambridge

*Lord Randolph Churchill

Guildhall Library

*Brewers' Company (Brewers' Hall), now at London Metropolitan Archives

Hatfield House

*Salisbury (including papers of Sir S. K. McDonnell), read at Christ Church

House of Lords Record Office (read at Beaverbrook Library)

*Andrew Bonar Law
*David Lloyd George
*Lord Samuel
*St. Loe Strachey

Institute of Alcohol Studies

*Alliance minutes, read at Alliance House, United Kingdom Temperance Alliance, formerly United Kingdom Alliance

Kent Record Office

*Lord Chilston (A. Akers-Douglas)

Lambeth Palace Library

*Church of England Temperance Society
*Archbishop E.W. Benson
*Archbishop Randall Davidson

London Metropolitan Archives

*Licensed Victuallers of London, Central Board, read at Bedford Square and Kilburn High Road offices of Central Board and at Farnham in Surrey after Londoners merged with provincial league
*National Defence League, read at Farnham after a merger with the Londoners

Modern Records Centre, University of Warwick

*Brewers' Society
*Country Brewers' Society
*National Trade Defence Association (earlier Fund), all of these read at Brewers' Society offices

National Library of Scotland

*Lord Rosebery

Public Record Office

*Home Office and Cabinet

Royal Archives, Windsor Castle

*Edward VII
*Victoria

Staffordshire Record Office

*Birmingham-based records of the National Trade Defence Association

Stanton Harcourt

*Sir William Harcourt (uncataloged)

University of Birmingham

*Joseph Chamberlain

University of Central Lancashire

*National British Temperance League and predecessor organizations, read
   at Livesey-Clegg House in Sheffield

University of Durham, Department of Paleography
and Diplomatic

*Earl Grey (4th Earl)

W.H. Smith archive, Swinden

*Hambleden papers, read at London offices

Worcestershire Record Office

*St. Aldwyn (Sir Michael Hicks-Beach)

Other manuscripts read as cited in publications.

BIBLIOGRAPHY

Government

Parl. Deb.> Parliamentary Debates
Parl. Pap.> Parliamentary Papers
  *Royal Commission on the Liquor Licensing Laws, *Minutes of Evidence* and *Reports* (1897-99).
PRO. > Public Record Office

Books

Anderson, Moa. *Noel Buxton: A Life* (George Allen & Unwin, 1951).

Andrews, Sir Linton, and H.A. Taylor. *Lords and Laborers of the Press* (Southern Illinois University Press, 1970).

Archer, John E. *The Monster Evil: Policing and Violence in Victorian Liverpool* (Liverpool University Press, 2011).

Askwith, Lord (G.R.). *British Taverns: Their History and Laws* (Routledge, 1928).

Askwith, Lord (G.R.). *Lord James of Hereford* (Ernest Benn, 1930).

Aspinwall, Bernard. *Portable Utopia: Glasgow and the United States 1820-1920* (Aberdeen University Press, 1984).

Asquith, H.H. *Letters to Venetia Stanley*, ed. Michael and Eleanor Brock (Oxford University Press, 1982).

Asquith, H.H. *Memories and Reflections, 1852-1927* (Cassell, 1928).

Bahlman, Dudley W.R., ed. *The Diary of Sir Edward Walter Hamilton, 1885-1906* (University of Hull Press, 1993).

Balfour, Arthur, and Lady Elcho. *The Letters of Arthur Balfour and Lady Elcho, 1875-1917*, ed. Jane Ridley and Clayre Percy (Hamish Hamilton, 1992).

Barker, Michael K. *Gladstone and Radicalism: The Reconstruction of Liberal Policy, 1885-94* (Harvester, 1975).

Barnett, Richard. *The Book of Gin* (Grove Press, 2012).

Barr, Andrew. *Drink: A Social History* (Pimlico, 1998).

Bassett, Arthur Tilney. *The Life of the Rt. Hon. John Edward Ellis, M.P.* (Macmillan, 1914).

Baylen, Joseph O., and Norbert J. Gossman, eds. *Biographical Dictionary of Modern British Radicals*, vol. 3 (Harvester Press, 1988).

Beaverbrook, Lord. *Politicians and the War 1914-16* (Collins, 1960).

Bebbington, David W. *Evangelicalism in Modern Britain* (Unwin Hyman, 1989).

Bebbington, David W. *The Nonconformist Conscience: Chapel and Politics, 1870-1914* (G. Allen & Unwin, 1982).

Beckingham, David. *The Licensed City: Regulating Drink in Liverpool, 1830-1920* (Liverpool University Press, 2017).

Bentley, Gilbert B. *David Lloyd George: Organizer of Victory, 1912-1916* (Ohio State University Press, 1987).

Bernstein, George L. *Liberalism and Liberal Politics in Edwardian England* (Allen & Unwin, 1986).

Blewett, Neal. *The Peers, the Parties and the People: The British General Elections of 1910* (University of Toronto Press, 1972).

Block, Geoffrey. *Free and Sober* (London: Conservative Political Centre, 1960).

Blocker, Jack S., Jr. *American Temperance Movements: Cycles of Reform* (Twayne, 1989).

Blocker, Jack S., Jr., David M. Fahey, and Ian R. Tyrrell, eds. *Alcohol and Temperance in Modern History* (ABC-CLIO, 2003).

Bridgeman, William. *The Modernisation of Conservative Politics: The Diaries and Letters of William Bridgeman, 1904-1935*, ed. Philip Williamson (Historians' Press, 1988).

Bridges, Jack A. *Reminiscences of a Country Politician* (T. Werner Laurie, 1906).

Bright, John. *Diaries of John Bright*, ed. R.A.J. Walling (Cassell, 1930).

Broadhurst, Henry. *The Story of His Life* (Hutchinson, 1901).

Brown, Stewart J., and others, eds. *Religion, Identity and Conflict in Britain* (Routledge, 2016).

Bruce, Henry. *Letters of the Rt. Hon. Henry Austen Bruce, G.C.B., Lord Aberdare of Duffyrn* (printed for private circulation, 1902).

Burnett, John. *Liquid Pleasures: A Social History of Drinks in Modern Britain* (Routledge, 1999).

Campbell, John. *F.E. Smith, First Earl of Birkenhead* (Jonathan Cape, 1983).

Carter, Henry. *The Control of the Drink Trade* (Longmans, Green, 1919).

Carter, Henry. *The English Temperance Movement: A Study in Objectives)*, Volume One: *The Formative Period, 1830-1899* (Epworth Press, 1933). The second volume never was published.

Catterell, Peter. *Labour and the Politics of Alcohol: The Decline of a Cause* (Institute of Alcohol Studies, 2014).

Chamberlain, Austen. *Down the Years* (Cassell, 1935).

Chamberlain, Austen. *Politics from the Inside (*Cassell, 1936).

Chamberlain, Joseph. *A Political Memoir, 1880-92*, ed. C.H.D. Howard (Batchworth, 1953).

Channing, F.A. *Memories of Midland Politics, 1885-1910* (Constable, 1918).

Cherrington, Ruth. *Not Just Beer and Bingo! A Social History of Working Men's Clubs* (self-published, 2012).

Chilston, Lord. *W.H. Smith* (Routledge and Kegan Paul, 1965).

Collins, Tony, and Wray Vamplew. *Mud, Sweat and Beers: A Cultural History of Sport and Alcohol* (Berg, 2002).

Cole, Emily. *The Urban and Suburban Public House in Inter-War England, 1918-1939* (Historic England, 2015).

Cooke, Anthony. *A History of Drinking: The Scottish Pub since 1700* (Edinburgh University Press, 2015).

Corder, Percy. *The Life of Robert Spence Watson* (Headley, 1914).

Craton, Michael, and H.W. McCready. *The Great Liberal Revival, 1903-6* (Hansard Society, 1966).

Cripps, Reginald. *Public House Reform, with a Brief Account of the Public-House Trust Movement* (Church of England Temperance Society Depot, [1901]).

Crosby, Travis L. *The Unknown Lloyd George* (I.B. Tauris, 2014).

Davies, Alfred T. *The Licensing Problem and Magisterial Discretion* (3rd ed., Licensing Laws Information Bureau, 1902).

DeMontmorency, James E.G. *Francis William Fox* (Oxford University Press, 1923).

Dingle, A.E. *The Campaign for Prohibition in Victorian England: The United Kingdom Alliance, 1872-1895* (Croom Helm, 1980).

Donnachie, Ian. *A History of the Brewing Industry in Scotland* (John Donald, 1979).

Doyle, Robert, and Joseph Nowinski. *Almost Alcoholic* (Hazelden Books, 2012).

Drus, Ethel, ed. *A Journal of Events during the Gladstone Ministry, 1868-74, by John, first Earl of Kimberley* (Camden Miscellany, 21 (1958).

Dugdale, Blanche E.C. *Arthur James Balfour* (G.P. Putnam's Sons, 1937).

Duncan, Robert. *Pubs and Patriots: The Drink Crisis in Britain during World War One* (Liverpool University Press, 2013).

Elliott, Arthur. *The Life of George Joachim Goschen* (Longmans, 1911).

Emy, H.V. *Liberals, Radicals and Social Politics, 1892-1914* (Cambridge University Press, 1973).

Fahey, David M., ed. *E. Lawrence Levy and Muscular Judaism, 1851-1932* (Edwin Mellen Press, 2014).

Fahey, David M. *Temperance and Racism: John Bull, Johnny Reb, and the Good Templars* (University Press of Kentucky, 1996).

Fahey, David M. *Temperance Societies in Late Victorian and Edwardian England* (Cambridge Scholars Publishing, 2020).

Fanshawe, E.L. *Liquor Legislation in the United States and Canada: Report of a Non-Partisan Inquiry* (Cassell, 1893).

Fitzroy, Sir Almeric. *Memoirs* (Hutchinson, 1925).

Forwood, Sir William B. *Recollections of a Busy Life* (Lee and Nightingale, 1910).

Foster, John. *Class Struggle and the Industrial Revolution* (Routledge, 1974).

Fowler, J.H. *Life and Letters of Edward Lee Hicks (Bishop of Lincoln, 1910-1919)* (Christophers, 1922).

Fraser, Mary. *Policing the Home Front 1914-1918: The Control of the British Population at War* (Routledge, 2018).

French, Michael, and Jim Phillips, *Cheated not Poisoned? Food Regulation in the United Kingdom, 1875-1938* (Manchester University Press, 2000).

Gardiner, A.G. *Life of Sir William Harcourt* (Constable, 1923).

Garvin, J.L., and Julian Amery. *Life of Joseph Chamberlain* (Macmillan, 1931-69).

George, William. *My Brother and I* (Eyre & Spottiswoode, 1958).

George, W.R.P. *The Making of Lloyd George* (Faber and Faber, 1976).

George, W.R.P. *Lloyd George: Backbencher* (Gomer Press, 1983).

Gibson-Brydon, Thomas R.C. *Moral Mapping of Victorian and Edwardian London: Charles Booth, Christian Charity, and the Poor-but-Respectable* (McGill-Queen's, 2016).

Gibson, William, Peter Forsaith, and Martin Wellings. *Ashgate Research Companion to World Methodism* (Ashgate, 2013).

Gilbert, Bentley B. *David Lloyd George: Organizer of Victory, 1912-1916* (B.T. Batsford, 1992).

Girouard, Mark. *Victorian Pubs* (Yale University Press, 1984).

Gollin, A.M. *Proconsul in Politics: A Study of Lord Milner in Opposition and in Power* (Macmillan, 1964).

Gooch, G.P. *Under Six Reigns* (Longmans, Green, 1958).

Gourvish, T.R., and R.G. Wilson, *The British Brewing Industry, 1830-1980* (Cambridge University Press, 1994).

Greenaway, John R. *Drink and British Politics since 1830* (Palgrave Macmillan, 2003).

Gutzke, David W. *Protecting the Pub: Brewers and Publicans against Temperance* (Royal Historical Society, 1989).

Gutzke, David W. *Pubs and Progressives: Reinventing the Public House in England 1896-1980* (Northern Illinois University Press, 2006).

Gutzke, David W. *Women Drinking Out in Britain since the Early Twentieth Century* (Manchester University Press, 2014).

Gwyn, Stephen, and Gertrude W. Tuckwell. *Life of Sir Charles W. Dilke* (John Murray, 1918}.

Gwyn, William B. *Democracy and the Cost of Politics in Britain* (Greenwood Press, 1962).

Hall, Benjamin Tom. *Over Sixty Years: The Story of the Working Men's Clubs and Institute Union* (Club and Institute Union, 1912).

Hamer, D.A. *John Morley: Liberal intellectual in Politics* (Clarendon Press, 1968).

Hamer, D.A. *Liberal Politics in the Age of Gladstone and Rosebery* (Clarendon Press, 1973).

Hamer, D.A. *The Politics of Electoral Pressure: A Study in the History of Victorian Reform Agitations* (Harvester, 1977).

Hamilton, Sir Edward. *The Destruction of Lord Rosebery: From the Diary of Sir Edward Hamilton, 1894-1895.* Ed. David Brooks (Historians' Press, 1986).

Hammerton, Sir John. *Child of Wonder: An Intimate Biography of Arthur Mee* (Hodder and Stoughton, 1946).

Hammond, J.L. *C.P. Scott of the Manchester Guardian* (G. Bell & Sons, 1934).

Hands, Thora. *Drinking in Victorian and Edwardian Britain: Beyond the Spectre of the Drunkard* (Palgrave Macmillan, 2018).

Harding, Graham. *Champagne in Britain, 1800-1914: How the British Transformed a French Luxury* (Bloomsbury Academic 2021).

Hanham, H.J. *Elections and Party Management: Politics in the Time of Disraeli and Gladstone* (Longmans,1959).

Hardy, Gathorne. *The Diary of Gathorne Hardy, Later Lord Cranbrook, 1866-1892*, ed. Nancy E. Johnson (Clarendon Press, 1981).

Harrison, Brian. *Dictionary of British Temperance Biography* (Society for the Study of Labour History, 1973).

Harrison, Brian. *Drink and the Victorians: The Temperance Question in England, 1815-1872* (1971; 2nd ed., Keele University Press. 1994).

Harrison, Brian. *Peaceable Kingdom* (Oxford University Press, 1982).

Hayler, Guy. *Temperance Tracts* [University of Wisconsin] (Brookhaven Press, 1982).

Hayler, Mark H.C. *The Vision of a Century, 1853-1953: The United Kingdom Alliance in Historical Retrospect* (United Kingdom Alliance, 1953).

Hazlehurst, Cameron. *Politicians at War, July 1914 to May 1915: A Prologue to the Triumph of Lloyd George* (Jonathan Cape, 1971).

Healy, T.M. *Letters and Leaders of My Day* (Frederick A. Stokes, 1928).

Hennock, E.P. *Fit and Proper Persons: Ideal and Reality in Nineteenth-Century Urban Government* (Edward Arnold, 1973).

Henley, Lady Dorothy. *Rosalind Howard, Countess of Carlisle* (Hogarth Pres, 1958).

Herlihy, Patricia. T*he Alcoholic Empire: Vodka and Politics in Later Imperial Russia* (Oxford University Press, 2002).

Heron, Craig. *Booze: A Distilled History* (Between the Lines, 2003).

Hicks, Edward Lee. *The Diaries of Edward Lee Hicks, Bishop of Lincoln, 1910-1919,* ed. Graham Neville [Lincoln Record Society Publications] (Boydell Press, 1963).

Hicks, Lady Victoria. *Life of Sir Michael Hicks Beach (Earl St. Aldwyn)* (Macmillan, 1932).

Hilton, J. Deane. *A Brief Memoir of James Hayes Raper* (Ideal Publishing Union, 1898).

Horsey, Ian Spencer. *A History of Beer and Brewing* (Royal Society of Chemistry, 2003).

Hughes, Thomas. *My Life-Work* (Hodder and Stoughton, 1902).

Hyde, H. Montgomery. *Carson* (Heinemann, 1953).

Hyslop, Sir R. Murray. *The Centenary of the Temperance Movement, 1832-1932* (Independent Press, 1932).

Jackson, Patrick. *Harcourt and Son: A Political Biography of Sir William Harcourt, 1827-1904* (Fairleigh Dickinson University Press, 2004).

Jackson, Patrick. *The Last of the Whigs: A Political Biography of Lord Hartington Later Eighth Duke of Devonshire (1833-1908)* (Farleigh Dickinson Press, 1994).

Jackson, Patrick, ed. *Loulou: Selected Extracts from the Journals of Lewis Harcourt (1880-1895)* (Fairleigh Dickinson University Press, 2006).

James, R.R. *Lord Randolph Churchill* (Phoenix, 1959).

Jennings, Paul. *A History of Drink and the English, 1500-2000* (Routledge, 2016).

Jennings, Paul. *The Local: The History of the English Pub* (Tempus, 2007).

Jeremy, David J., ed. *Dictionary of Business Biography* (Butterworths, 1984-86).

Jordan, Trevor L. *Under the Influence: A History of Alcohol in Australia* (ABC Books, 2009).

Kadel, Bradley. *Drink and Culture in Nineteenth-Century Ireland: The Alcohol Trade and the Politics of the Irish Public House* (Tauris, 2015).

Kimberley, Lord. *The Journal of John Wodehouse First Earl of Kimberley, 1862-1902* (Camden Fifth Series), edited by Angus Hawkins and John Powell (Cambridge University Press, for the Royal Historical Society, 1998).

Koss, Stephen. *Fleet Street Radical: A.G. Gardiner and the Daily News* (Archon Books,1973).

Koss, Stephen. *Nonconformity in Modern British Politics* (Archon Books, 1975)

Koss, Stephen. *The Rise and Fall of the Political Press in Britain: The Nineteenth Century* (University of North Carolina Press, 1981).

Lambert, W.R. *Drink and Sobriety in Victorian Wales, c. 1820-c. 1895* (University of Wales Press, 1983).

Lawrence, Jon. *Speaking for the People: Party, Language and Popular Politics in England, 1867-1914* (Cambridge University Press, 1998).

Lawson, Sir Wilfrid. *Sir Wilfrid Lawson: A Memoir*, ed. George W.E. Russell (Smith Elder, 1909).

Lawson, Sir Wilfrid. *Wisdom, Grave and Gay, Being Select Speeches of Sir Wilfrid Lawson, Bart., M.P., Chiefly on Temperance and Prohibition.* Ed. R.A. Jameson (S.W. Partridge, 1889).

Lawson, Sir Wilfrid, and F. Carruthers Gould. *Cartoons in Rhyme and Line* (T. Fisher Unwin, 1905).

Lawson, Sir Wilfrid, and Alexander Guthrie. *Disinterested Company Management: Correspondence between Sir Wilfrid Lawson, Bart., M.P., and Mr. Alexander Guthrie* (1905]).

Leigh, J.W., *Other Days* (Macmillan, 1921).

Leighton, Denys P. *The Greenian Moment: T.H. Green, Religion and Political Argument in Victorian Britain* (Imprint Academic, 2004).

Lester, V. Markham. *H.H. Asquith: Last of the Romans* (Rowman & Littlefield, 2019).

Licensing Struggles of a Generation: A History of the Brewers' Central Association (Manchester) from its Foundation in 1860 to the Present Day (Manchester, 1897).

Liverpool Vigilance Committee. *Licensing Administration in Liverpool: Summary of Reforms (1889-1898)* (Licensing Laws Information Bureau, 1899).

Longmate, Norman. *The Waterdrinkers: A History of Temperance* (Hamish Hamilton, 1968).

Lough, David. *No More Champagne: Churchill and His Money* (Picador, 2015).

Luddington, Charles, *The Politics of Wine in Britain* (Palgrave Macmillan, 2013).

Lyttelton, Edith. *Alfred Lyttelton: An Account of His Life* (Longmans, 1917).

McAllister, Annemarie. *Demon Drink? Temperance and the Working Class* (self-published, 2014).

McEwen, John M., ed. *The Riddell Diaries 1908-1923* (Athlone Press, 1986).

McKie, David. *Jabez: The Rise and Fall of a Victorian Scoundrel* (Atlantic Books, 2004).

Mackintosh, John P. *The British Cabi*net (2nd ed., University of Toronto Press, 1968).

Malcolm, Elizabeth. *"Ireland Sober, Ireland Free": Drink and Temperance in Nineteenth-Century Ireland* (Syracuse University Press, 1986).

Malins, Joseph (the younger). *The Life of Joseph Malins: Patriarch Templar, Citizen and Temperance Reformer* (Templar Press, 1932).

Malleck, Dan, ed. *Drugs, Alcohol and Addiction in the Long Nineteenth Century* (Routledge, 2020).

Mallet, Sir Charles E. *Herbert Gladstone: A Memoir* (Hutchinson, 1932).

Mallet, Sir George. *Lord Cave: A Memoir* (John Murray, 1921).

Martin, Scott C., ed. *The Sage Encyclopedia of Alcohol* (Sage, 2015).

Marsh, Peter. *The Discipline of Popular Government: Lord Salisbury's Domestic Statecraft, 1881-1902* (Harvester Press, 1978).

Marsh, Peter T. *Joseph Chamberlain: Entrepreneur in Politics* (Yale University Press, 1994).

Matthew, H.C.G. *Gladstone, 1875-1898* (Clarendon Press, 1995).

Maxwell, Sir Herbert, Bt. *Half-a Century of Successful Trade: Being a Sketch of the Rise and Development of the Business of W & A. Gilbey, 1857-1907* (W. & A. Gilbey, Ltd., 1907).

Mills, J. Saxon. *Sir Edward Cook, K.B.E., A Biography* (Constable, 1921).

Morley, John, *Life of William Ewart Gladstone* (Macmillan, 1903).

Murray, Bruce K. *The People's Budget 1909/10: Lloyd George and Liberal Politics* (Clarendon Press, 1980).

Nevile, Sir Sydney. *Seventy Rolling Years* (Faber and Faber, 1958).

Neville, Graham. *Radical Churchman: Edward Lee Hicks and the New Liberalism* (Clarendon Press, 1998).

Newton, John. *W.S. Caine, M.P., A Biography* (James Nisbet, 1907).

Newton, Lord. *Lord Lansdowne: A Biography* (Macmillan, 1929).

Nicholls, James. *The Politics of Alcohol: A History of the Drink Question in England* (Manchester University, 2009).

Oldstone-Moore, Christopher. *Hugh Price Hughes* (University of Wales Press, 1999).

Our Position and Our Policy: A Reply to Charges Made against a Minority of the Executive Committee of the British Women's Temperance Association, by its President, Lady Henry Somerset, at Our Annual Council Meeting, 1893.

Oxford Dictionary of National Biography.

Packer, Ian. *Liberal Government and Politics, 1905-15* (Palgrave Macmillan, 2006).

Paton, J. L. *John Brown Paton: A Biography* (Hodder and Stoughton, 1914).

Paul, Herbert, ed. *Famous Speeches* (Pittman and Sons, 1912).

Pearce, Joseph. *Old Thunder: A Life of Hilaire Belloc* (HarperCollins, 2002).

Petrie, Charles. *Life and Letters of Austen Chamberlain* (London, 1940).

Petrow, Stefan. *Policing Morals: The Metropolitan Police and the Home Office, 1870-1914* (Clarendon Press, 1994).

Phillips, Gregory D. *The Diehards - Aristocratic Society and Politics in Edwardian England* (Harvard University Press, 1979).

Power, J. Danvers. *Sharpe [sic] v. Wakefield: A Full & Revised Report of the Judgments in the Queen's Bench Division, Court of Appeal, and the Arguments and Judgments in the House of Lords* (J.S. Phillips, 1891)

Price, Seymour J. *From Queen to Queen: The Centenary Story of the Temperance Permanent Building Society, 1854-1954* (Franey & Co., [1954]).

Pugh, Martin. *State and Society: A Social and Political History of Britain since 1870* (4th ed,, Bloomsbury Academic, 2012).

Rae, John Turner. *World's Temperance Congress 1900* (Ideal Publishing Union, 1901)

Rainy, Mrs. A. [Annabella Matheson]. *Life of Adam Rainy, M.P.* (James Maclehose & Sons, 1915.

Reade, Alfred Arthur. *Study and Stimulants: Or the Use of Intoxicants and Narcotics in Relation to Intellectual Life, as Illustrated by Personal Communications on the Subject, from Men of Letters and of Science* (A. Heywood, 1883).

Roberts, Andrew. *Salisbury, Victorian Titan* (Weidenfeld and Nicholson, 1999).

Roberts, Charles H. *The Radical Countess: The History of the Life of Rosalind, Countess of* Carlisle (Steel Brothers, 1962).

Roberts, James S. *Drink, Temperance, and the Working Class in Nineteenth Century Germany* (Allen and Unwin, 1984).

Roberts, M.J.D., *Making English Morals: Voluntary Association and Moral Reform in England, 1787-1886* (Cambridge University Press, 2009).

Roberts, Robert. *The Classic Slum: Salford Life in the First Quarter of the Century* (Penguin, 1971).

Rowntree, Arnold Stephenson. *The Letters of Arnold Stephenson Rowntree to Mary Katherine Rowntree, 1910-1918*, ed. Ian Packer (Cambridge University Press for the Royal Historical Society, 2002).

Rowntree, Joseph. *A Paper on Temperance Legislation Read at a Conference of the Friends' Temperance Union of London, February 3rd, 1892.*

Rowntree, Joseph. *Joseph Rowntree (1836-1925), A Typescript Memoir, Probably by Luther Worstenholm (Editor Northern Echo 1908-1926) and Related Papers* ([Joseph Rowntree Charitable Trust, ca. 1986).

Rowntree, Joseph, and Arthur Sherwell. *British "Gothenburg" Experiments and Public-House Trusts* (Hodder and Stoughton, 1901).

Rowntree, Joseph, and Arthur Sherwell. *State Purchase of the Liquor Trade* (Allen and Unwin, 1919).

Rowntree, Joseph, and Arthur Sherwell. *The Temperance Problem and Social Reform* (1899).

Russell, George W.E. *Portraits of the Seventies* (T.F. Unwin, 1909).

Salisbury, Lord, and Arthur James Balfour. *Salisbury-Balfour Correspondence: Letters Exchanged between the Third Marquess of Salisbury and his Nephew Arthur James Balfour, 1869-1892*, ed. Robin Harcourt Williams (Hereford Record Society, 1988).

Sanders, Sir Robert. *Real Old Tory Politics: The Political Diaries of Sir Robert Sanders, Lord Bayford, 1910-35*, ed. John Ramsden (Historians' Press, 1984).

Schrad, Mark Lawrence. *The Power of a Bad Idea: Networks, Institutions, and the Global Prohibition Wave* (Oxford University Press, 2010).

Schrad, Mark Lawrence. *Smashing the Liquor Machine: A Global History of Prohibition* (Oxford University Press, 2021).

Scott, Wendy Bell. *A Pub on Every Corner? Drink and the Licensed Trade in Nineteenth-Century Berwick upon Tweed* (Blue Ribbon Publications, 2009).

Searle, G.R. *The Quest for National Efficiency: A Study in British Politics and Political Thought, 1899-1914* (University of California Press, 1971).

Shadwell, Arthur. *Drink, Temperance and Legislation* (Longmans, Green, 1903; revised in 1915).

Shannon, Richard. *Gladstone: Heroic Minister, 1865-1898* (Allen Lane/Penguin Press, 1999).

Shaw, Thomas. *The Bible Christians, 1815-1907* (Epworth Press, 1965).

Sherwell, Arthur. *The Drink Peril in Scotland* (Oliphant, Anderson, and Ferrier, 1903).

Sherwell, Arthur. *Life in West London: A Study and a* Contrast (1897; 3rd ed., Methuen: 1903).

Shiman, Lilian Lewis. *Crusade against Drink in Victorian England* (Macmillan, 1988).

Shiman, Lilian Lewis. *Women and Leadership in Nineteenth-Century England* (St. Martin's Press, 1992).

Smith, E. Tennyson. *From Memory's Storehouse* (S.W. Partridge, 1914).

Smith, Paul. *Disraelian Conservatism and Social Reform* (Routledge and Kegan Paul, 1967).

Smitley, Megan. *The Feminine Public Sphere: Middle Class Women in Civic Life in Scotland, c. 1820-1914* (Manchester University Press, 2009).

Soper, J. Christopher. *Evangelical Christianity in the United States and Great Britain: Religious Beliefs, Political Choices* (New York University Press, 1994).

Spartacus Educational.

Spencer, Earl. *The Red Earl: The Papers of the Fifth Earl Spencer, 1835-1910,* ed. Peter Gordon, 2 vols.; Publications of the Northamptonshire Record Society, vol. 34 (1986).

Spender, J.A., and Cyril Asquith. *Life of Herbert Henry Asquith* (Hutchinson, 1932).

Stevenson, Frances. *Lloyd George: A Diary.* Edited by A.J.P. Taylor (Harper & Row, 1971).

Spinner, Thomas J. *George Joachim Goschen* (Cambridge University Press, 1973).

Standard Encyclopedia of the Alcohol Problem, ed. Ernest Hurst Cherrington (American Issue, 1926-30).

Stansky, Peter. *Ambitions and Strategies: The Struggle for the Leadership of the Liberal Party in the 1890s* (Oxford University Press, 1964).

Temlett, George. *Clubmen: History of the Working Men's Club and Institute Union* (Secker & Warburg, 1987).

Toner, Deborah, ed. *Alcohol in the Age of Industry, Empire, and War* (Bloomsbury Academic, 2021).

Tyrrell, Ian. *Woman's World, Woman's Empire: The Woman's Christian Temperance Union in International Perspective, 1880-1930* (University of North Carolina Press, 1991).

Urwin, E.C. *Methodism and Sobriety* (Epworth Press, 1945).

Vaizey, John. *The Brewing Industry, 1886-1951* (Pitman, 1960).

Vernon, Anne. *A Quaker Business Man: The Life of Joseph Rowntree, 1836-1925* (Allen & Unwin, 1958).

Waller, Philip J. *Democracy and Sectarianism: A Political and Social History of Liverpool, 1868-1939* (Liverpool University Press, 1981).

Weir, Ronald B. *The History of the Distilling Company, 1887-1939* (Clarendon, 1996).

West, Sir Algernon. *Private Diaries of the Rt. Hon. Sir Algernon West*, ed. Horace G. Hutchinson (John Murray, 1922).

Whittaker, Sir Thomas. *Temperance Reform and State Purchase: Some Lessons of the Past* (Temperance Legislation League, 1919).

Williams, Gwylmor Prys, and George Thompson Brake, *Drink in Great Britain, 1900 to 1979* (Edsall, 1980).

Williams, J. Fischer, and others, *Memories of John Westlake* (Smith Elder, 1914).

Willoughby de Broke, Lord. *The Passing Years* (Constable, 1924).

Wilson, George B. *Alcohol and the Nation: A Contribution to the Study of the Liquor Problem in the United Kingdom from 1800 to 1935* (Nicholson & Watson, 1940).

Wilson, George B. *Leif Jones, Lord Rhayader, Temperance Reformer and Statesman, 1862-1939, President of the United Kingdom Alliance, 1906-1932* (United Kingdom Alliance, [1948].

Wilson, John. *CB, The Life of Sir Henry Campbell-Bannerman* (Constable, 1973).

Wrigley, Chris J. *David Lloyd George and the British Labour Movement: Peace and War* (1976; second ed., Edward Everett Root, 2019).

Articles

Aldcroft, D.H. "Control of the Liquor Trade in Great Britain, 1914-1921," in W.H. Chaloner and B.M. Ratcliffe, eds., *Trade and Transport: Essays in Economic History in Honour of T.S. Willan* (Manchester, 1977).

Anderson, Ray. "The Brewing Connection in the Oxford Dictionary of National Biography," *Brewery History* 119 (Summer 2005).

Auld, John W. "The Liberal Pro-Boers," *Journal of British Studies* 14 no. 2 (May 1975).

Bailey, Victor. "Salvation Army Riots, the 'Skeleton Army' and Legal Authority in the Provincial Town," in *Social Control in Nineteenth Century Britain,* ed. A.P. Donajgrodski (Croom Helm, 1977).

Bebbington, David W. "The Free Church M.P.s of the 1906 Parliament," *Parliamentary History* 24 no. 1 (February 2005):

Bebbington, David W. Review of Dominic Erdozain, *The Problem of Pleasure: Sport, Recreation and the Crisis of Victorian Religion*, in *Reviews in History*, 23 Sept. 2010 (online).

Beckingham, David. "Geographies of Drink Culture in Liverpool: Lessons from the Drink Capital of Nineteenth-Century England," *Drugs, Education, Prevention and Policy* 15 no. 3 (2008).

Beckingham, David. "Private Spirits, Public Lives: Sober Citizenship, Shame and Secret Drinking in Victorian Britain.' *Journal of Victorian Culture*, 22 April 2021.

Bell, Bethany. "Menace to Sobriety: When Salvationists fought Skeletons," *BBC News*, 17 Oct. 2020.

Bennison, Brian. "Lord Grey's Public House Reform," *Journal of the Northumberland Local History Society* 48 (1994): 68-73.

Berridge, Virginia. "History and Addiction Control: The Case of Alcohol," in John Maynard and others, ed., *Controlling Legal Addictions* (St. Martin's Press, 1989).

Binfield, Clyde. "Temperance and the Cause of God," *History* 57 (October 1972).

Brown, James B. "The Pig or the Stye: Drink and Poverty in Victorian England," *International Review of Social History* 18 (1973).

Brown, James B. "The Temperance Career of Joseph Chamberlain, 1870-1877: A Study in Political Frustration," *Albion* 4 (1972): 29-44.

Brown, Richard. "The Thirsty Sex," *Looking at History*, 7 July 2014.

Butler, David J. "Defeating the Demon Drink: The 1904 Licensing Act and its Implementation in Durham City, 1906-1939," *Durham County Local History Society Bulletin* 54 (May 1995).

Buxton, Noel, and Walter Hoare, "Temperance Reform," in C.F. G. Masterman, ed., *The Heart of the Empire: Discussions of Problems of Modern City Life in England* (1901), edited and introduced by Bentley B. Gilbert (Harvester Press, 1973).

Burns, Dawson. "Nonconformist Temperance Societies in England," in J.N. Stearns, ed., *Temperance in All Nations* (National Temperance Society and Publication House, 1893).

Burns, Dawson. "The Sunday Closing Movement--Historical and Statistical," in Arnold F. Hills and others, *The Case for Sunday Closing Compiled for the Service of the Sunday Closing Special Campaign* (Ideal Publishing Union, 1899).

Caine, W.S. "The Attitude of the Advanced Temperance Party," *Contemporary Review* 69 (January 1893).

Cornell, Martyn. Review of Ian Webster, *Ind Coope & Samuel Allsopp Breweries,* in *Brewery History* 164 (Winter 2015).

D'Abernon, Lord. "Scientific Basis of Drink Control," *British Journal of Inebriety* 17 (1920).

Davis, John W. "Working-Class Make-Believe: the South Lambeth Parliament, (1887-1890)," *Parliamentary History* 12 no. 3 (1993).

Dingle, A.E., "Drink and Working-Class Living Standards in Britain, 1870-1914," *Economic History Review* 25 no. 4 (Nov. 1972).

Donnachie, Ian. "Men of Brewing, Viscount Younger of Leckie," *Scottish Brewing Archive Newsletter,* no. 6 (Winter 1985).

Donnachie, Ian. "Men of Brewing: William McEwan," *Scottish Brewing Archive Newsletter* no. 5 (Summer 1985).

Donnachie, Ian. "World War I and the Drink Question: State Control of the Drink Trade," *Scottish Labour History Journal* 17 (1982).

Doyle, Barry M. "Modernity or Morality? George White, Liberalism and the Nonconformist Conscience in Edwardian England," *Historical Research* 71 (October 1998).

Doyle, Barry M. "'Through the Windows of a Baptist Meeting House': Religion, Politics and the Nonconformist Conscience in the Life of Sir George White, M.P.," *Baptist Quarterly* 36 no. 6 (1996).

Doyle, Barry M. "Temperance and Modernity: The Impact of Local Experience on Rank and File Liberal Attitudes to Alcohol," *Journal of Regional and Local Studies* 16 no. 2 (1996).

Duncan, Robert. "Lord D'Abernon's 'Model Farm': The Central Control Board's Carlisle Experiment," *Social History of Alcohol and Drugs* 24 no. 2 (Summer 2010).

Fahey, David M. "Brewers, Publicans, and Staff in Late Victorian and Edwardian Licensed Trade Societies," Part I *Brewery History* 179 (Summer 2019); Part II 181 (Winter 2019).

Fahey, David M. "Brewers, Publicans, and Working-Class Drinkers: Pressure Group Politics in Late Victorian and Edwardian England," *Histoire sociale* 13 (May 1980).

Fahey, David M. "Drink and the Meaning of Reform in Late Victorian and Edwardian England," *Cithara* 13 (May 1974).

Fahey, David M. "E.N Buxton (1840-1024): Liberal Brewer, Big Game Hunter and Conservationist," *Brewery History* 178 (Spring 2019).

Fahey, David M., "The Politics of Drink in Britain: Anglo-American Perspectives," in *Proceedings of the Ohio Academy of History* (2000).

Fahey, David M. "The Politics of Drink: Pressure Groups and the British Liberal Party, 1883-1908," *Social Science* 54 (Spring, 1979) [now *International Social Science Review*].

Fahey, David M. Review of A.E. Dingle, *The Campaign for Prohibition in Victorian England: The United Kingdom Alliance, 1872-1895*, in *Victorian Studies* 24 no. 4 (Summer 1981).

Fahey, David M. "Sir Sydney Oswald Nevile (1873-1969)," in *Dictionary of Business Biography*, ed. David Jeremy (Butterworths, 1984-86) vol. 4

Fahey, David M. "Temperance and the Liberal Party–Lord Peel's Report, 1899," *Journal of British Studies* 10 (May 1971).

Fahey, David M. "Worrying about Drink," *Brewery History* 166 (Summer 2016).

Fahey, David M., and Padma Manian. "Poverty and Purification: The Politics of Gandhi's Campaign for Prohibition*" Historian* 67 no. 3 (Fall 2005).

Franberg, Per. "The Social and Political Significance of Two Swedish Restrictive Systems," *Contemporary Drug Problems* (Spring 1985).

Franberg, Per. "The Swedish Snaps," in *Svenska Supen. En Historia om Brannvin, Bratt och Byrakrati* (Drink in Sweden. A History of Brandy, Bratt and Bureaucracy), ed. Kettil Bruun and Per Franberg (Stockholm, 1985). Snaps is sometimes spelled schnapps.

Garman, Ed [Edwin M.]. "The Licensing Acts of 1904 and 1910 in Salisbury," Pub History Society, *Historical Sources for Pub Research*: Part 4 [probably around 2017]

Goodlad, Graham D. "Gladstone and His Rivals: Popular Liberal Perceptions of the Party Leadership in the Political Crisis of 1885-1886," in Eugenio F. Biagini and Alastair J. Reid, eds., *Currents of Radicalism: Popular Radicalism, Organised Labour and Party Politics in Britain, 1850-1914* (Cambridge University Press, 1991).

Greenaway, John R. "Bishops, Brewers and the Liquor Question in England, 1890-1914," *Historical Magazine of the Protestant Episcopal Church* 53 no. 1 (1984).

Greenaway, John R. "Calling 'Time': The Rise and Fall of Public House Closing Hours in Britain," *Revue Française de Civilisation Brittanique* 14 (January 2007).

Greenaway, John R. "The 'Improved' Public House, 1870-1950: the Key to Civilized Drinking or the Primrose Path to Drunkenness?," *Addiction* 93 no. 2 (Feb. 1998).

Gutzke, David W. "'The Cry of the Children': The Edwardian Medical Campaign against Maternal Drinking," *British Journal of Addiction* 79 (1984).

Gutzke, David W. "Gender, Class and Public Drinking in Britain during the First World War," Histoire sociale 27 (November 1994).

Gutzke, David W. "Gentrifying the British Public House, 1896-1914," *International Labor and Working-Class History* 45 (Spring 1994).

Gutzke, David W. "Rhetoric and Reality: The Political Influence of British Brewers, 1832-1914," *Parliamentary History* 9 (May 1990).

Gutzke, David W. "W. Waters Butler and the Making of a Progressive Brewer in Britain, 1890-1922," *Histoire sociale* 48 (May 2015).

Hare, Chris. "The Skeleton Army and the Bonfire Boys, Worthing, 1884," *Folklore* 99 no. 2 (1988).

Harris, Jose, and Cameron Hazelhurst, "Campbell-Bannerman as Prime Minister," *History* 55 (Oct. 1970).

Harrison, Brian. "Sunday Closing Riots of 1855," *Historical Journal* 8 no. 2 (1965).

Haslam, Sara. "A Literary Intervention: Writing Alcohol in British Literature, 1915-1930," *First World War Studies* 4 no. 2 (Oct. 2013).

Haydock, William. "*Prohibition Review Article*," *Reviews in History,* Sept. 2014 (review no. 1647).

Holt, Tim. "Demanding the Right to Drink: Two Hyde Park Demonstrations," *Brewery History* 118 (Spring 2009).

Hurd, Madeleine. "Liberals, Socialists, and Sobriety: The Rhetoric of Citizenship in Turn-of-the-Century Sweden," *International Labor and Working-Class History* 45 (Spring 1993).

Jennings, Paul. "'Grasping a Nettle': The 1904 Licensing Act," in Mark Hailwood and Deborah Toner, eds., *Biographies of Drink: A Case Study Approach to Our Historical Relationship with Alcohol* (Cambridge Scholars Publishing, 2015).

Jennings, Paul. "Licensing and the Local Historian: the 1904 Licensing Act and its Administration," *Local Historian* 39 no. 1 (Feb. 2009).

Jennings, Paul. "Liquor Licensing and the Local Historian: The Victorian Public House," *Local Historian* 41 no. 2 (May 2011).

Jennings, Paul. "Policing Drunkenness in England and Wales from the Late Eighteenth Century to the First World War," *Social History of Alcohol and Drugs* 26 no. 1 (Winter 2012).

Jennings, Paul. "Policing Public Houses in Victorian England," *Law, Crime and History* 3 no. 1 (2013).

Johnson, Nicholas K. "World War I, Part 2, The British Rum Ration," *Points*, May 29, 2014.

Jones, Stephen G. "Labour, Society and the Drink Question in Britain, 1918-39," *Historical Journal* 30 (1987).

Kneale, James. "Good, Homely, Troublesome or Improving? Historical Geographies of Drinking Places, c. 1850–1950," *Geography Compass* (2021).

Kneale, James. "The Place of Drink: Temperance and the Public, 1856-1914," *Social & Cultural Geography* 2 no. 1 (January 2001).

Kneale, James. "'These Are the Cases Who Call Themselves Moderate Drinkers,' Because They Are Never Seen Embracing a Lamp-Post": The Problem of Moderate Drinking in Nineteenth- and Early Twentieth-Century Britain.' In Matthew Ingleby and Samuel Randalls, eds. *Just Enough. The History, Culture and Politics of Sufficiency* (Palgrave Macmillan, 2018).

Kneale, James. "Victorian England," in Scott C. Martin, ed., *The Sage Encyclopedia of Alcohol* (Sage, 2015).

Kneale, James, and Shaun French, "Moderate Drinking before the Unit: Medicine and Life Assurance in Britain and the US, c.1860–1930," *Drugs: Education, Prevention, and Policy* 22 no. 3 (2015).

Knight, Frances. "Recreation or Renunciation: Episcopal Interventions in the Drink Question in the 1890s," in Stewart J. Brown and others, ed., *Religion, Identity and Conflict in Britain* (Routledge, 2016).

Lambert, W.R. "The Welsh Sunday Closing Act, 1881," *Welsh History Review* 6 (1972).

Lea, John. "W.S. Caine and Irish Home Rule--A Study of the Radical Opposition of 1886," *Historical Studies* 1 no. 2 (Oct.1968).

Lees, Lynn Hollen. "Getting and Spending: The Family Budgets of English Industrial Workers in 1890," in John M. Merriman, ed., *Consciousness and Class Experience in Nineteenth Century Europe* (Holmes and Meier, 1979).

Loeb, Lori. "Desperate Housewives: The Rise and Fall of the Campaign against Medicated Wines in Twentieth-Century Britain," *Phamaceutical Historian* 50 no. 1 (March 2020).

Marlow, Laurence. "A Menace to Sobriety? The Drinking Question and the Working Men's Club, c. 1862-1906," in Lex Heerma van Voss and F.L. van Holthoon, eds., *Working Class and Popular Culture* (Stichting Beheer, 1988).

McCready, H.W. "Chief Whip and Party Funds: The Work of Herbert Gladstone in the Edwardian Liberal Party, 1899 to 1906," *Canadian Journal of History* 6 no. 3 (December 1971).

McCready, H.W. "The Revolt of the Unionist Free Traders," *Parliamentary Affairs* 16 (1963).

MacLeod, Roy M. "The Edge of Hope: Social Policy and Chronic Alcoholism, 1870-1900," *Journal of the History of Medicine* 22 no. 3 (July 1967).

McMaster, Charles. "The Brechin Bolag," *Scottish Brewing Archive Newsletter*, no. 6 (Winter 1985).

Mellows, Phil. "Nationalize the Pub," *Jacobin* (21 Nov. 2017).

Mellows, Phil. "The People's Pubs," *Publican* (22 June 2009).

Mews, Stuart. "Urban Problems and Rural Solutions: Drink and Disestablishment in the First World War," in *The Church in Town and Countryside*, ed. Derek Baker (Basil Blackwell, 1979).

Mutch, Alistair. "Public Houses as Multiple Retailing: Peter Walker & Son, 1846-1914," *Business History* 48 no. 1 (2006).

Moss, Stella. "'Wartime Hysterics': Alcohol, Women and the Politics of Wartime Social Purity in England," in Jessica Meyer, ed., *British Popular Culture and the First World War* (Leiden and Boston: Brill, 2008).

Neilson, Francis. "The Land Values Movement in Great Britain," *American Journal of Economics and Sociology* 18 (April 1959).

Nicholson, Peter P. "T.H. Green and State Action: Liquor Legislation," *History of Political Thought* 3 (Winter 1985).

Olsen, G.W. "'Physician Heal Thyself': Drink, Temperance and the Medical Question in the Victorian and Edwardian Church of England," *Addiction* 89 (1994).

Pack, Mark. "Liberal Landslide: The 1906 Election," 14 April 2020 http://www.markpack.org.uk/1166/the-1906-election.

Packer, Ian. "Religion and the New Liberalism: The Rowntree Family. Quakerism, and Social Reform," *Journal of British Studies* 42 no. 2 (April 2003).

Pattinson, Ron. "How World War I Changed Pub Culture, and Beer Itself," [History by the Glass], *Beer Advocate* (August 2019).

Pattinson, Ron. "The Rise and Fall of Beer Houses" [History by the Glass], *Beer Advocate* (Oct. 2016).

Payne, P.L. "The Emergence of the Large-Scale Company in Great Britain, 1870-1914," *Economic History Review*, 2nd ser., 20 (1967).

Pierce, Gretchen. "Parades, Epistles and Prohibitive Legislation: Mexico's National Anti-Alcohol Campaign and the Process of State-Building, 1934-1940," *Social History of Alcohol and Drugs* 23 no. 2 (Spring 2009).

Punnett, R.M. "State Management of the Liquor Trade," *Public Administration* 44 (Summer 1966).

Quinault, Roland. "Winston Churchill and the Drink Question," *Cercles* 37 (2020).

Readman, Paul. "The 1895 General Election and Political Change in Late Victorian Britain," *Historical Journal* 42 no. 2 (1999).

Reinarz, Jonathan. "Promoting the Pint: Ale and Advertising in Late Victorian and Edwardian England," *Social History of Alcohol and Drugs* 22 no. 1 (Fall 2007).

Rintala, Marvin. "Family Portrait: Churchills at Drink," *Biography* 21 no. 1 (Winter 1998).

Rintala, Marvin. "Taking the Pledge: H. H. Asquith and Drink," *Biography* 16 no. 2 (Spring 1993).

Roberts, Andrew. "Lord Salisbury (1830-1903): The Libertarian," *Libertarian Heritage*, no 20 (1999).

Roberts, David. "Thomas Howe, Bristol Missioner, by Love Serving One Another," *Baptist Quarterly* 38 no. 4 (October 1999).

Robinson, Neil. "Lloyd George's Quest to Quench," *History Today* 44 no. 4 (June 1994),

Robinson, Richard. "Off Beat and in Drink: Impropriety and Insobriety in Brighton's Police, 1880-1921," *Social History of Alcohol and Drugs* 30 (2016).

Rose, M.E. "'The Success of Social Reform?' The Central Control Board (Liquor Traffic) 1915-1921," M.R.D. Foot, ed., *War and Society: Historical Essays in Honour and Memory of J.R. Western, 1928-1971* (Elek, 1973).

Rubinstein, W.D. "British Millionaires, 1809-1947," *Bulletin of the Institute of Historical Research* 47 (1974).

Scarlett, Joshua. "Pitt and Port: A Study of a Prime Minister's Drinking" (Internet, 14 April 2015).

Sharpe, Iain. Review of Kenneth D. Brown, *The Unknown Gladstone: The Political Life of Herbert Gladstone, 1854-1930*, in *Reviews in History*, May 2018.

Shiman, Lilian Lewis. "The Blue Ribbon Army: Gospel Temperance in England," *Historical Magazine of the Protestant Episcopal Church* 50 (1981).

Shiman, Lilian Lewis. "John B. Gough: Trans-Atlantic Temperance Orator." *Social History of Alcohol Review* 15 no. 3-4 (Spring/Summer 2001).

Shiman, Lilian Lewis. "Reflections: 'Lilian Turns to Booze'," *Social History of Alcohol Review* (Spring/Fall 1998).

Simkin, John. "Alcohol and the First World War," *Spartacus Educational*.

Skelly, Julia, "When Seeing is Believing: Women, Alcohol and Photography in Victorian England," *Shift: Queen's Journal of Visual & Material Culture* 1 (2008).

Thorne, Robert. "The Movement for Public House Reform, 1892-1914," *Diet and Health in Modern Britain*, ed. Derek J. Oddy and Derek S. Miller (Croom Helm, 1985).

Turner, John. "State Purchase of the Liquor Trade in the First World War," *Historical Journal* 23 no. 3 (Sept. 1980).

Walker, W.M. "The Scottish Prohibition Party and the Millennium," *International Review of Social History* 13 (1973).

Warner, Jessica. "On Wit, Irony, and Living with Imperfection: How Britain Said No to Abstinence," *American Journal of Public Health* 98 no. 7 (July 2008).

Weir, R.B. "Obsessed with Moderation: The Drink Trades and the Drink Question (1870-1930)." *British Journal of Addiction* 20 (1984).

Whittaker, T.P. "The Lessons Taught by Legislation for the Promotion of Temperance," in John Turner Rae, ed., *The World's Temperance Congress of 1900* (Ideal Publishing Union, [1900]).

Williams, R.J., and J.R. Greenaway. "The Referendum in British Politics: A Dissenting View," *Parliamentary Affairs* 28 no. 3 (1974).

Wilson, George B. "Looking Back," *Alliance Year Book* (1947).

Wilson, George B. "The Right Hon. Lord Rhayader: An Appreciation," *Alliance Year Book* (1940).

Wilson, R.G. "The Changing Taste for Beer in Victorian England," in T.R. Gourvish and R. G. Wilson, eds., *The Dynamics of the International Brewing Industry* (Routledge, 1998).

Woiak, Joanne. "'A Medical Cromwell to Depose King Alcohol'": Medical Scientists, Temperance Reformers, and the Alcohol Problem in Britain," *Historie Sociale* 27 (November 1994).

Wood, Ian S. "Drink, Temperance and the Labour Movement," *Scottish Labour History Society Journal* 5 (1972).

Wright, David E. and Cathy Chorniawry, "Women and Drink in Edwardian England," *Historical Papers* 20, no. 1 (1985).

Yeomans, Henry, "Another Round? Teetotal Pledges and World War One," *Points,* 3 April 2012.

Yeomans, Henry. "Providentialism, the Pledge and Victorian Hangovers: Investigating 'Moderate Alcohol Policy in Britain, 1914-1918'," *Solon* 1 (2011)

Yeomans, Henry. "What Did the British Temperance Movement Accomplish? Attitudes to Alcohol, the Law and Moral Regulation," *Sociology* 45 no.1 (February 2011).

Yokoe, Ryosuke. "Alcohol and Politics in Twentieth-Century Britain," *Historical Journal* 62 no. 1 (March 2019).

Newspapers and Other Periodicals

Alliance News
Birmingham Daily Post
Brewers' Almanack
Brewers' Guardian
Brewing Trade Review
Cheltenham Chronicle
Daily Argus
Daily News
Globe
Good Templars' Watchword
Grand Lodge of England, Journal of Proceedings
Leeds Mercury
Liberal Magazine
Licensed Trade News
Licensed Victuallers' Year Book
Licensing World
Methodist Times
Mirror
Monthly Notes
Morning Advertiser
Morning Chronicle
National Advocate
National Temperance League, *Annual*
National Union Gleanings
Newcastle Journal
North British Daily Mail
Northern Brewers' and Victuallers' Journal,
Speaker
Temperance Chronicle
Temperance Witness
Times (London)
Weekly Reporter
Westminster Gazette
White Ribbon

Dissertations and Other Unpublished Work

Campbell, Orfhlaith, "A Platform upon which All Could Unite?: Temperance in Ulster and the Irish Temperance League, 1858-1914" (Ph.D. thesis, Open University, 2017).

Carrick, Terry. "Wilfrid Lawson: Attitudes and Opinions on Britain's Imperial and Foreign Policy (1868-1892)" (Ph.D. dissertation, Sheffield Hallam University, 2007).

Crapster, Basil L. "Our Trade, Our Politics: A Study of the Political Activity of the British Liquor Industry, 1868-1910" (Ph.D. dissertation, Harvard University, 1949).

Brader, Christopher. "Timbertown Girls: Gretna Female Munitions Workers in World War I (Ph.D. thesis, Warwick, 2001).

Bristow, Edward J. "The Defence of Liberty and Property in Britain, 1880-1914" (Ph.D. dissertation, Yale University, 1970).

Colvard, Robert Eric. "A World Without Drink: Temperance in Modern India, 1880-1940" (Ph.D. dissertation, Iowa, 2013).

Davis, Peter George. "The Role of the Liberal Unionist Party in British Politics, 1886-1895" (Ph.D. dissertation, University of London, 1974).

(later Denny) Logan, Norma Davies. "Drink and Society: Scotland, 1870-1914 (Ph.D. thesis, Glasgow University, 1984).

Dunn, James Clifford. "'A Force to be Reckoned With': The Temperance Movement and the 'Drink Question'" (M.A. thesis, University of Central Lancashire, 1999).

Ferris, Wesley. "The Liberal Unionist Party, 1886-1912" (Ph.D. dissertation, McMaster University, 2008).

Franberg, Per. "Drink and Drinking Culture in 19th Century Sweden--Some New Perspectives" (unpublished paper, 1987).

Greenaway, John R. "The Local Option Question in British Politics, 1864-1914" (University of Leeds, Ph.D. dissertation, 1974).

Heyck, Thomas William. "Studies in Late-Victorian Anti-Imperialism" (M.A. thesis, Rice University, 1962).

Krinsky, Philip A. "The Cause of Sobriety: David Lloyd George and Temperance Reform" (B.A. honors thesis, University of Richmond, 1980).

Legg, Douglas Reid. "The Fourth Cabinet of William E. Gladstone, 1892-1894" (M.A. thesis, University of Notre Dame, 1957).

Manian, Padma (formerly V. Padmavathy). "The English Barmaid, 1874-1914: A Case Study of Unskilled and Non-Unionized Women Workers" (Ph.D. dissertation, Miami University, 1989).

Martin, Charles C. "The British Liquor Licensing Act of 1904" (Ph.D. dissertation, University of North Carolina, 1953).

Martin, Janette Lisa. "Popular Political Oratory and Itinerant Lecturing in Yorkshire and the North East in the Age of Chartism, 1837-60" (Ph.D. thesis, University of York, 2010).

Morrison, Bronwyn Louise. "Ordering Disorderly Women: Female Drunkenness in England c.1870-1920" (Ph.D. dissertation, Keele University, 2005).

Olsen, Gerald W. "Drink and the British Establishment: The Church of England Temperance Society, 1873-1919" (unpublished typescript, 2003).

Olsen, Gerald W. "Pub and Parish--The Beginnings of the Temperance Reform in the Church of England, 1835-1875" (Ph.D. dissertation, Western Ontario, 1972).

Paton, D.C. "Drink and the Temperance Movement in Nineteenth-Century Scotland" (Ph.D. dissertation, University of Edinburgh, 1977).

Purinton, Malcolm F. "Empire in a Bottle: Commodities, Culture, and the Consumption of Pilsner Beer in the British Empire, c. 1870-1914" (Ph.D. dissertation, Northeastern University, 2016).

Sherwell, Arthur. "'Rough Notes' by Arthur Sherwell on an Ms of H. Carter re Origins of Gothenburg." Methodist Church Archives, Division of Social Responsibility. [summarized in Greenaway, *Drink and British Politics*]

Sims, Nika Lee. "David Lloyd George and the British Temperance Movement, 1890-1922" (M.A. thesis University of Alabama in Huntsville, 1988).

Wilson, H.B. "History of the Carlisle State Management Scheme 1916-1974" (apparently completed by early 1977, a typescript with handwritten corrections).

Wright, David Edwin. "The British Liberal Party and the Liquor Licensing Question, 1895-1905" (McMaster University, Ph.D. dissertation, 1972).

Xi Chen, "The Making of John B. Gough (1817-1886): Temperance Celebrity, Evangelical Pageantry, and the Conservatism of Popular Reform in Victorian Society" (Ph.D. dissertation, University of Washington, 2013);

Internet

Ancestry
British Newspaper Archive
Google Books
Victorian Web

Emails

Margaret Barrow to David M. Fahey, 11 December 1995.
Lori Loeb to David M. Fahey, 25 April 2020.
Annemarie McAllister to David M. Fahey, 24 August 2010.

INDEX